ANNA FREUD

A life dedicated to children

Uwe Henrik Peters

Schocken Books • New York

For my daughters, Eva and Caroline

First published by Schocken Books 1985
10 9 8 7 6 5 4 3 2 1   85 86 87 88

English translation copyright © 1985 by Schocken Books Inc.
Originally published in German as *Anna Freud: Ein Leben
für das Kind* by Kindler; © 1979 by Kindler Verlag GmbH, Munich
All rights reserved

Library of Congress Cataloging in Publication Data
Peters, Uwe Henrik, 1930–
    Anna Freud : a life dedicated to children.
    Translation of: Anna Freud.
    Includes bibliographical references and index.
    1. Freud, Anna, 1895–1982. 2. Psychoanalysts—
Austria—Biography. 3. Child analysis. 4. Psycho-
analysis—History. I. Title.
RC339.52.F73P4713 1984 618.92′89′00924 [B] 84–1278

Designed by Betty Palmer
Manufactured in the United States of America
ISBN 0–8052–3910–3

SOURCES OF PHOTOGRAPHS
Associated Press, Frankfurt: 44. Belser Verlag, Stuttgart (from Edmund Engelmann, *Berggasse 19.
Sigmund Freuds Wiener Domizil*): 13, 25. Bilderdienst Süddeutscher Verlag, Munich: 12. Case
Western Reserve University, Cleveland: 39, 40. Clark University, Worcester, Mass.: 41. Marianne
von Eckardt: 27. Foto-Zentrum am Schwarzenbergplatz, Vienna: 22. Phyllis Greenacre, New York:
37, 38. Keystone, Hamburg: 15. Heinz Kohut, Chicago: 30, 31, 32, 42, 44. Library of Congress,
Washington, D.C.: 21. Mobil Oil, Vienna: 35. Eta Neumann, Vienna: 22, 24. Österreichische
Nationalbibliothek, Vienna: 2, 29 *(left)*. Fred Prager, Vienna: 50. Leo Rangell, Los Angeles: 20, 47,
48. Robertson Centre, London: 33. Schikola, Vienna: 19, 49. Sigmund Freud Gesellschaft, Vienna:
10, 13, 16, 17, 26, 28, 29 *(right)*, 34, 46. Ullstein Bilderdienst, Berlin: 23. Samuel Weiss, Chicago:
42. Wide World Photo, New York: 36.
    The portraits following Plate 39 are from: Bildarchiv Preussischer Kulturbesitz (S. Bernfeld); In-
stitut für Geschichte der Medizin, Vienna (J. Wagner-Jauregg); Kindler Archiv, Munich: (M. Klein,
W. Reich, O. Rank, J. Bowlby); Klett Archiv, Stuttgart: (H. Hartmann, R. Waelder, R. Spitz);
Österreichische Nationalbibliothek, Vienna (P. Schilder, M. Mead); U. H. Peters, Cologne (H.
Deutsch); Ernst Pfeiffer, Göttingen (L. Andreas-Salomé); Suhrkamp Archiv, Frankfurt (M. Schur);
Ullstein Bilderdienst, Berlin (M. Eitingon, M. Montessori, M. Bonaparte).
    All other photographs are from the Mary Evans Picture Library, London, and the Sigmund Freud
Copyrights, Colchester, England.

Contents

Preface to the English-language Edition

When I met Anna Freud for the first time, she slowly looked me over from head to toe and said, "You look like an SS man." One sometimes finds oneself in such a situation, especially if one comes into contact with people who had to flee Nazi Germany. (It does not even help to belong to the younger generation that had nothing to do with the war.) Anna Freud's customary frankness is evident in these surprising words. Interestingly, what appeared to be an expression of distrust was at the same time the introduction to lengthy and candid talks. This small scene reveals how deep were the wounds that were inflicted on her by Nazi rule and her expulsion from her country.

I have often been asked how much Anna Freud actually contributed to this biography. She remained true to her resolve that psychoanalysis and not her person should be the focus of interest: that is why she never agreed to support anybody who wanted to write about her. Nevertheless, she helped with some information and even contributed some pictures over the years. She read the biography and made several notes with regard to facts and actual events, without intruding into the portrayal or giving the book the characteristics of an official biography. Diaries and letters, which are normally the core of every historical portrayal of a person, could not be consulted as a result. That would have been impossible anyway in this biography, written while she was still alive. In any case, the work of a psychologist unwillingly unveils major parts of his personality.

Since the first publication of this book, many things have changed. After a short illness, Anna Freud died on October 8, 1982. Shortly before that, on November 11, 1979, her friend and companion Dorothy Burlingham had died. This book had a happy consequence in the short time between its publication and Anna Freud's death. In 1981, Anna Freud was awarded an honorary doctorate by the University of Frankfurt. Actually, 1980 would have been the more fitting and symbolic year, because fifty years previously she had accepted the Goethe Prize in Frankfurt on behalf of her father, who was prevented from attending because of his illness. The Peace Prize of the German book trade, which is awarded at the Frankfurt Book Fair each year, is the honor she actually deserved for her active contributions toward peace through her wartime care of children during the blitz and her care and education of children who survived the concentration camps. However, various attempts from different quarters to obtain this prize for her failed, and 1980 passed unobserved.

Since her death, people have continued to show an avid interest in Anna Freud's person and in her work. Four years after the publication of this book, Raymond Dyer's biography, *Her Father's Daughter: The Work of Anna Freud,*[1] appeared. Dyer's work was not based on letters and diaries either, but concentrated very much on those of her writings that have been published in English. This is quite typical of Anna Freud's fate as an emigrant: the emigration divided her life into two nearly equal parts. The first half is almost inaccessible to English-speaking readers and therefore tends to remain undiscovered.

To me, one surprising result of the first publication of my biography was becoming acquainted with Anna Freud's letters to Lou Andreas-Salomé. After Ernst Pfeiffer, the administrator of Lou Andreas-Salomé's literary estate, had read this book, he placed the estate in a most generous way at my disposal, so it is possible to refer to the letters here.

The extensive correspondence between these two women could fill a whole volume. Despite their openness and intimacy, however, they do not offer any sensations or even surprises. In these letters, we can see Anna Freud as she is known otherwise: precise, warmhearted, and always capable of summing up complicated matters in a few words. In the personal language of her letters, an important aspect of the history of psychoanalysis comes alive. Sigmund Freud's cancer is depicted, sometimes daily, from the direct experience of his daughter. But some personal aspects of Anna Freud are clarified as well.

The correspondence started in December 1921, a few days after Andreas-Salomé's lengthy visit to Vienna, where the two women—despite their age and temperamental differences—became good friends (see pp. 41–47). It ended with the death of Andreas-Salomé in 1937. In another file of letters to Ernst Pfeiffer, which cover almost the whole span of time between Andreas-Salomé's death and that of Anna Freud, she writes about her friend from the perspective of her own past life and with the distance of time, but with unchanged devotion and love.

The letters confirm what we concluded from indirect sources: that Andreas-Salomé never was Anna Freud's training analyst. She was rather a mentor, thirty-four years her senior, who accompanied and supported Anna Freud's psychoanalytical and personal maturing from a distance. Perhaps these letters and the occasional intense meetings were more effective than daily personal contacts would have been. One is reminded somewhat of the relationship between Freud and Wilhelm Fliess. However, these relationships are not really comparable. According to Anna Freud's letters, the training analysis with her father was much more extensive than has been assumed and technically showed no difference from any normal analysis. In 1924 and 1925 she remarked that the training analysis had been taken up again and that her resistance was less intense than "all those years before." She was also aware of the difficulties that resulted from being close to the father–analyst outside the analysis.

What is surprising is the fact that Anna Freud frequently portrays herself as a daydreamer. She does not even leave out beating fantasies and thus relates her first psychoanalytical work to her own experience. She has left a novel, *Heinrich Mühsam* ["Henry Laborious"], in which her imagination takes the form of continual daydreams. The book was never completed and was eventually given up in favor of psychoanalytical work.

Although there were fundamental differences in the age, temperament, and background of the two women, only once does a disagreement become apparent. Andreas-Salomé had helped Anna Freud's first work to a good start. Her criticism of the finished book, *Introduction to the Technique of Child Analysis* (1927), meant a lot to Anna Freud. She anticipated a negative reaction when she wrote: "I was not at all sure that you would be satisfied, especially because they are children, whom I always want to change, while you prefer to leave them as they are." As a matter of fact, both women thought and felt entirely different in this regard. During her whole life, Andreas-Salomé had always done exactly what she wanted. She did not need to be subservient to a father who worshiped her, nor to her friendly and kindhearted brothers. She could remove herself from her stiff and strict Hamburg mother. In contrast, Anna Freud had voluntarily placed herself in the service of her father and had taken over many responsibilities of the psychoanalytic movement. It seems that Andreas-Salomé had tried to influence Anna Freud through a kind of conversion. Anna had been so overjoyed at Andreas-Salomé's general commendation of her book that Andreas-Salomé thought she expected always to be reprimanded for what she was doing. The truth is that Anna Freud appreciated Andreas-Salomé for accepting her as she was and not having any set expectations about her, as many people did. The matter was so important that Anna Freud was unable to correspond with Andreas-Salomé for half a year; even after that, her letters became scantier and shorter. Her first book made Anna Freud independent, and Andreas-Salomé's role as a mentor would have ended at this point anyway.

The interesting thing about Anna Freud's letters is the early appearance of ideas about ego psychology, which was later dealt with extensively in her book *The Ego and the Mechanisms of Defense* (1936). As early as 1924, she had quite clearly formulated her thoughts on the question of sociopathic personality disorder in contrast to neurosis, for which August Aichhorn's experience with "wayward youth" formed the basis (see pp. 179–80). Antisocial behavior was seen here to be the result of a distorted development of the ego in the same way that neurosis was viewed as the result of diverted infantile sexuality. Failure of the first object relationship as a result of external factors—for example, in orphans and foundlings—as well as difficulties in the early object relationship lead to a distorted or at least very problematic development of the ego, which can result in antisocial behavior. In 1934, during the immediate preparatory phase for *The Ego and the Mechanisms of De-*

fense, she wrote quite clearly: "By Christmas I want to complete my first serious work on the mechanisms of defense, actually a type of psychology of the ego." The psychology of the ego, which dominated émigré psychoanalysis for a long time, was very early part and parcel of Anna Freud's thinking.

For quite some time, Anna Freud was rather critical toward the emigration movement of psychoanalysts. When Helene Deutsch went to the United States, she felt "actually very upset" at her for having left so easily. Even when Max Eitingon, who was quite close to her, went to Palestine, she complained vividly about the loss that meant for European psychoanalysis. In the same manner she made critical remarks concerning the emigration of Franz Alexander, Sándor Radó, and others who had accepted a lot "over there" and lost a lot of what they took along with them. However, it is clear that Anna Freud's remarks were not politically motivated. At that time she was mainly concerned about the preservation of psychoanalysis, her own humanitarian ideas, her therapy, and her organization. The political developments that ushered in the Nazi era are hardly ever mentioned in her correspondence with Andreas-Salomé. Personal issues were more important to the two women.

Although Rainer Maria Rilke is not mentioned very often, she does lay a special emphasis on him. In 1921, Andreas-Salomé sent her some handwritten poems that Rilke had dedicated to herself, and Anna Freud for many years afterward thought them to be a copy of the *Duino Elegies*. In reality, these were the original elegies, which had not been completed or published at this point. When Andreas-Salomé asked for the manuscript in 1935, Anna Freud did not understand the sense of the request. As she explained later, the elegies had remained obscure to her as well as to other people. The poetry of *The Book of Pictures* and *The Book of Hours*, which she knew almost by heart, remained her fondest of Rilke's works. She had always hoped to get to know Rilke personally through his friendship with Andreas-Salomé; she regretted that Rilke visited the Freud household only once and never wanted to return. Apparently Andreas-Salomé did not discuss Rilke's neurosis—or whatever could have been taken for it—but she did refer to her own advice against psychoanalytic treatment for him. Anna Freud understood but could not accept these arguments. She was convinced that analysis would have helped Rilke and would have complemented his powers of creativity rather than hamper them.

Those who would like to know more about the love life of Anna Freud will find the correspondence rather disappointing. Merely the fruitless courtship of Hans Lampl is mentioned here. His later wife, Jeanne Lampl-de Groot, became a close friend of Anna Freud's. If one wished, one might see in this a good example of "altruistic departure."

As a young woman, Anna Freud was too close to Andreas-Salomé to be able to write about her. But she did just that in her later letters to Ernst Pfeiffer. After being stimulated by reading *The Freud Journal of Lou Andreas-Salomé*,[2] she portrayed her friend as sincere, innocent, and pensive; one who was very quick to grasp important matters and ignore the unimportant. Andreas-Salomé is also described as being ready to add something new to what she had already learned. Even one year before she died, Anna Freud attempted to express the uniqueness of Andreas-Salomé's personality. People, she said, are unprepared to accept the fact that the uniqueness of human nature is expressed in ordinary values such as honesty and frankness, the absence of weaknesses, self-assertion, or self-obsession, and the refusal to use anything as a weapon or a defense. When Anna Freud adds that she had learned a lot from Andreas-Salomé, this should be taken literally.

Her description of Andreas-Salomé's personality is almost fully applicable to herself. This, too, becomes evident from her letters, where she presented herself as she really was throughout her life, and all who seek anything else will be disappointed. As she wrote to Andreas-Salomé: "I cannot show myself in any way other than I really feel."

UWE HENRIK PETERS

Spring 1984

Preface

In 1971 Arnold R. Rogow, professor at the City University of New York, published a survey conducted among psychiatrists and psychoanalysts in which they were asked to name their most outstanding colleagues.[1] Both psychiatrists and psychoanalysts mentioned Anna Freud more often than anyone else.

Psychiatrists	Votes	Psychoanalysts	Votes
Anna Freud*	44	Anna Freud*	21
Karl Menninger	37	Heinz Hartmann*	20
Erik H. Erikson	26	Erik H. Erikson	16
Heinz Hartmann*	21	Phyllis Greenacre	7
Lawrence Kubie*	19	Rudolph Loewenstein*	7
Erich Fromm*	10	René Spitz*	7
"The Menningers"	10	Robert Waelder*	6
Roy R. Grinker, Sr.	8	Karl Menninger	4
Jules Massermann	8	Edward Glover*	3
Manfred S. Guttmacher*	7	Roy R. Grinker, Sr.	3
Harold F. Searles	7	Don D. Jackson*	3
René Spitz*	7	Edith Jacobson	3
Franz Alexander*	6	Bertram D. Lewin*	3
Eric Berne*	6	D. W. Winnicott*	3
Don D. Jackson*	6		
Sándor Radó*	6		
Silvano Arieti	5		
Jerome D. Frank	5		
Robert Waelder*	5		
Francis Braceland	4		
Helene Deutsch	4		
Edward Glover*	4		
Judd Marmor	4		
William Menninger*	4	*Psychiatrists and psychoanalysts	
S. A. Szurek*	4	since deceased	

Among the 109 names on the list, Anna Freud's was also the only one for whom there was such unanimous agreement. While this is understandable among the psychoanalysts who were interviewed, it is remarkable that Anna Freud—neither a physician nor therefore a psychiatrist, and, moreover, a woman—should also head the list of psychiatrists. What other male-dominated profession has named a woman as its leading representative?

It is also interesting that the two relatively short lists include the names of three of Anna Freud's colleagues: Heinz Hartmann, Robert Waelder, and Helene Deutsch.

Such a list, if it existed in the German-speaking world, would be quite different. In West Germany, Anna Freud's name raises at most the question of her possible connection with Sigmund Freud. A smaller and better-informed group sees in her a remote, almost mythical figure who has already taken on historical dimensions. There is no doubt that in German and Austrian psychiatry Anna Freud is not considered a prominent personality, though she lived and worked in Vienna until 1938 and then for more than forty years continued her work in nearby London.

Anna Freud's appearance at international conventions was always a climax. She received honorary doctorates from many universities, primarily American ones, as well as one from the University of Vienna, but neither a West German nor an East German university awarded her such a distinction.* Anna Freud was an honorary member of the American Psychoanalytic Association; of the psychoanalytic societies of Boston, Cleveland, Detroit, New York, Philadelphia, San Francisco, Topeka, and Western New England. But she belonged to no German association. She thus seems to belong primarily to American and English intellectual history, although her intellectual roots developed within German culture.

Anna Freud represented the history of psychoanalysis in both her person and her age. As old as psychoanalysis, she was the living representative of her father's work. She occasionaly received honors intended for him, and she also bore animosities aimed at him. Her own significant work is now widely disseminated in English.

There has hardly been a personality in this century who has led such an intensely public life while revealing so few of its private details. Personally, Anna Freud always withdrew behind psychoanalysis, as well as behind her own and her father's work. A description of her work together with her life would therefore be incompatible with her sensibility. In this she was not very different from her father. When Dr. Roy Winn of Sydney asked him to write a "more intimate biography," Sigmund Freud replied: "I don't think anyone would learn much from such a publication. Personally I ask nothing more from the world than that it should leave me in peace and devote its interest to psychoanalysis instead."[2]

From the scattered information I have gathered on Anna Freud I have sketched the history of her life and introduced her principal works. I hope that with

*Until 1981; see p. xi above.

this effort I have rendered Anna Freud's life and work more familiar, especially to the younger generation. In particular, I want to reestablish those connections with historical developments which the Hitler regime and World War II severed.

The idea for this book was suggested to me by Helmut Kindler in 1976, while I was spending several days on the beach at Santa Monica, California, organizing, reading, and rethinking my notes. I was traveling in the United States, tracing the paths of German-speaking emigré psychiatrists as part of an intensive program sponsored by the German Research Association. At that time I also began reading Anna Freud's war reports from the Hampstead Nurseries, where she described her experiences with children sheltered from air raids in those homes. The descriptions evoked in me extremely vivid memories of my own childhood experiences during the war.

At the insistent urging of Nina and Helmut Kindler, and with the encouragement I received from Helene Deutsch, Martin Grotjahn, and other known psychoanalysts with whom I discussed the subject, I finally set to work.

UWE HENRIK PETERS

ANNA FREUD

1895, The Year of Anna Freud's Birth

Anna Freud's first name and the year of her birth at once evoke associations: she was born on December 3, 1895, the same year that Sigmund Freud's and Joseph Breuer's *Studies on Hysteria*[1] marked the beginning of the history of psychoanalysis. During the weeks following her birth, Freud also did the creative preliminary work for *The Interpretation of Dreams*,[2] although the final manuscript did not become available until the summer of 1899. It was characteristic of Freud's working method to complete a work in his mind long before he actually wrote it down, so that the writing proceeded—as it did for Mozart—smoothly and required hardly any emendations. Freud's main work thus already existed at the time of Anna Freud's birth, even if only in the author's mind. It is not an exaggeration, then, to define 1895 as the fateful year for psychoanalysis.

Anna was the youngest of Freud's six children, born over a period of eight years. Contrary to frequent assumptions, she was not his favorite daughter. It was the frail and often sickly Sophie, two and a half years older than Anna, who held that place.[3] After Sophie's death during the great influenza epidemic of 1920, Freud transferred his affection to her little son Heinele, after whose premature death he was inconsolable. Freud's relationship to Anna, on the other hand, was from the very beginning approving, untroubled, and happy. Even later on in life, he never complained about her or found fault with her.

Anna was born during Freud's intense and still unclouded friendship with Wilhelm Fliess. (Self-analysis, in which Fliess was to play a difficult part, did not begin until two years later.) We find the first report of Anna Freud's existence in Freud's correspondence with Fliess. On the day of her birth, Freud wrote to Fliess in one of his shortest letters on record:

> If it had been a son I should have sent you the news by telegram, as he would have been named after you. But as it is a little girl of the name of Anna, you get the news later. She arrived today at 3:15 during my consulting hours, and seems to be a nice, complete little woman. Thanks to Fleischmann's care she did not do her mother any harm, and both are doing well. I hope it will not

be long before similar good news arrives from you, and that when Anna and Pauline meet they will get on well together.[4]

One could conclude from this letter that Freud wanted a son, whom he would have named Wilhelm out of his attachment to Fliess. However, Anna Freud thinks it unlikely that her father would have preferred a son, since he already had three.[5] Freud's comment perhaps indicates only the then common attitude of valuing a son's birth more than a daughter's. The effort Freud made to bring his friend Carl Fleischmann, one of Europe's most famous gynecologists, to his home to attend the birth bespeaks his self-esteem, which remained unscathed despite his obscure professional status at that time.

Several weeks after Anna Freud's birth, the Fliesses had a son who was given the name initially intended for Anna—Wilhelm—as his middle name. The later dispute between Freud and Fliess did not move Freud to prevent Robert Wilhelm Fliess from becoming a productive and internationally acclaimed psychoanalyst.

It cannot be precisely determined to whom Freud's youngest daughter owed her name. The Freuds had the habit of giving names not according to family traditions but after people they admired. Mathilde, the eldest (b. 1887), was named after Breuer's wife; Jean Martin (b. 1889) after Jean Martin Charcot; Oliver (b. 1891) after Oliver Cromwell; Ernst after Ernst Brücke, Freud's great Academy teacher; while Anna Freud was supposedly named after the daughter of an old schoolteacher, Anna Hammerschalg Lichtheim. Anna Lichtheim, the sister of Breuer's son-in-law, was one of Freud's favorite patients who later became a welcome guest at the Freud house on Sundays. But the name of Freud's sister was also Anna. Moreover, the name brings to mind Anna O., a pseudonym for Bertha Pappenheim, who is considered the actual inventor of the talking cure. The first hysterical patient treated by Breuer, she inspired Freud to formulate his first psychoanalytic thoughts and interpretations.[6] Anna O.'s case history was Breuer's only contribution to Freud's *Studies on Hysteria*.

Anna Freud was born during the period of Freud's greatest social isolation, which was, however, his most productive time. In addition to *The Interpretation of Dreams*, the volumes *Jokes and Their Relation to the Unconscious* and *The Psychopathology of Everyday Life*[7] also were nearing completion, and have now become his most significant as well as his most popular works.

Since 1892 the family had lived in a spacious, upper-middle-class apartment at 19 Berggasse, which today houses the Sigmund Freud Museum. Besides Freud, his wife, Martha, and their six children, the household included a cook, a maid, and a cleaning woman. A governess was in charge of the older children, while a nanny took care of the younger ones. Aunt Minna Bernays, his wife's sister, joined the household following Anna's birth and helped in raising the children. Later she emigrated with the family to London, where she died. After Freud's death, Anna Freud lived with her mother and aunt in the same house in London. Compared to current living conditions, the Freuds lived in quite an extended family and employed a relatively large staff. In those times, however, such seeming luxuries were hardly extraordinary and even compatible with a way of life that was rather modest in other respects. Not only were living space and household staff relatively inexpensive then, but we must also bear in mind that homemaking was a much more arduous task without the technological conveniences we take for granted today. Martha Freud had her hands full with the management of the large home; Freud was free to devote himself entirely to his patients and studies.

Vienna, 1895

Anna Freud was born into a complex world of oppositions, whose intellectual trends, both positive and negative, were to dominate the entire twentieth century. Although many of the ideas that are influential in today's society originated in Vienna around the turn of the century, two world wars have triggered such profound upheavals that we find it difficult to imagine the nineteen years between Anna Freud's birth and the outbreak of World War I.

As a result of the pogroms in Eastern Europe, the number of Jewish residents was constantly on the rise in Austria, where Emperor Franz Joseph offered them his special protection. In thirty-three years the Jewish population had increased from 1.3 percent in 1857—one year after Freud's birth—to 12 percent in 1890. There was a high number of poor and destitute Jews who were hardly able to earn a subsistence. But there was also a growing class of educated and successful Jews in the business world, in influential state positions, and in scientific, artistic, and academic professions. At the University of Vienna Medical School for example, which flourished during the last decades preceding World War I, 48 percent of the faculty were of Jewish descent in 1889–90.

At the same time anti-Semitism increased, assuming an alarmingly radical form. Christian-Socialist politicians and their Austrian constituencies agitated with virulent speeches and pamphlets. The Christian-Socialist Party, founded in 1887 and whose *Illustrierte Wiener Volkszeitung* proudly carried the subtitle *Das Organ des Antisemitismus* ("The Journal of Anti-Semitism"), became at once the standardbearer of anti-Semitism. The prominent Christian-Socialist politician Ernst Schneider called publicly for the extermination of Jews. Members of the All-German League, a radical–right precursor of National Socialism, wore "hanged Jews" on their watchchains. One of the central figures was Dr. Karl Lueger, leader of the Christian-Socialist Party and Freud's enemy, whom Hitler later praised in *Mein*

Kampf as his great teacher. Lueger became mayor of Vienna in 1897, after Emperor Franz Joseph had declined four times to ratify his nomination. Thus, the ideological foundations of the processes that were to evolve into mass murder with the rise of Hitler had already been laid down at the time of Anna Freud's birth.

Accordingly, Anna Freud's youth was marked on the one hand by pronounced tolerance toward Jews, owing to the Austrian emperor's protection. Many Jewish citizens attempted to loosen or even dissolve the ties with their own religion and frequently aimed for complete integration into the intellectual and cultural life of the country. (Circumstances were similar in Prussia, the other German "superpower.") On the other hand, Vienna's Jewish residents were exposed to barbarous Austrian anti-Semitism. These extremes of Jewish assimilation and anti-Semitism characterized Anna Freud's youth.

E. Stransky, a well-known Viennese psychiatrist with a "pan-German" disposition who had converted to Judaism in his early youth, commented on the year of Anna Freud's birth in his as yet unpublished memoirs:

> During my first three years of medical school, I witnessed the sudden political change in Vienna. In 1895, the fledgling anti-Semitic Christian-Socialist movement led by Karl Lueger moved victoriously into City Hall after several years of leading—from both inside the parliament and muncipalities, and outside them—a noisy, embittered, and often brutal campaign against the dominant Liberals. As a thoughtful contemporary, I may well be able to shed some light on this historically trenchant and portentous shift which would deeply affect Vienna's academic life.[1]

It is Stransky's opinion that "anti-Semitism had in fact begun to conquer a part of the middle-class intelligentsia, but not the masses of Vienna's lower-middle class." The Jewish population had found almost no economic base in small trades or the lower-middle class. This led to a "snowballing infiltration of the fields of journalism, law, and, later, medicine by a section of the Jewish residents."[2]

The mood in this multinational state may best be rendered by Joseph Roth's *Radetzky March.* It is the melancholy mood of an unremitting historical process—the decay of the Hapsburg Empire—a mood Freud succumbed to as well, claiming in connection with the decline of the imperial monarchy that his entire libido was attached to Austria-Hungary.[3] It is a mood that acknowledges the brittleness, decay, and injustice of this unequal government structure, lamenting at the same time the disappearance of promising possibilities arising out of the many disparate currents whose lines of force had converged in Vienna.

People who become scientifically or artistically creative absorb and preserve the intellectual currents of their childhood and youth. They need not be conscious of this; traces and causal connections are often visible only decades later, a phenomenon that calls for further research. It is no doubt significant for Anna Freud's life that during her early years, as during the initial phases of her father's psychoanalytic work, the Jugendstil—Art Nouveau—was the dominant artistic current.

The Jugendstil began to develop at the time of Anna Freud's birth. Only today, and perhaps transfigured, is its significance as a lifestyle emphasized again. The Jugendstil owes its name to the periodical *Jugend*, founded by Georg Hirth in 1896 in Munich. Vienna's young artists felt awakened to a "sacred spring," and so two years later named their periodical *Ver Sacrum*. Hermann Bahr (1863–1934), at that time well known in Austria as a writer and comedy playwright, wrote in its first issue about the three maxims to be observed by those who wanted to achieve something in Vienna. To be sure, the maxims referred to the new artistic trend, but they were no less relevant to the young practice of psychoanalysis: "The first is: To achieve something in Vienna, one may not fear ridicule. Every powerful idea and all those who have finally triumphed here have first had to endure many years of ridicule. In Vienna things don't seem to work any other way. Since the Viennese respect only those they loathe, one must know how to become loathsome. And third: One must refuse to be pacified."[4]

The Jugendstil, which until shortly before World War I developed its particular forms and textures, with its curvilinear and fabulous ornamentation, pervaded everything, even shaping the small objects of daily life—glass, porcelain, books, furniture, script, signs, and houses. Artists who adopted this genre united and in 1897–98 erected the Secession building in Vienna.

It was above all Gustav Klimt (1862–1918) who combined a refined realism with the floral ornaments of the Jugendstil.[5] He painted dreams, which he filled, like many of his other paintings, with a plethora of symbols that could only be understood through close examination and consideration of a variety of traditions. The content of many Jugendstil illustrations—and even more so, the literature of this period—was determined by symbolism.

The symbolist period immediately preceded Anna Freud's birth. Her father may have learned about French symbolism in 1885, when he spent several months in Paris. In any case, it was not until more than a decade later that its effect on him bore fruit, particularly in *The Interpretation of Dreams*. The fundamental concept of symbolism involves a rebellion against the predominance of naturalism and the thinking modes specific to natural sciences. It goes back to German romanticism and Anglo-Saxon literature, for example to Edgar Allan Poe. The symbolist artist attempts, among other things, to grasp the soul's mystery through figurative and metaphorical signs that tie together objects and subjective dispositions. But the artist cannot arbitrarily choose the symbols that are to be utilized as stylistic devices. They must be inserted as they are found in tradition, above all in the Christian heritage, since it is only the connection with tradition that enables us to understand the symbolism of an image. At the same time the artist must vary the symbols creatively to allow them to unfold their multiple layers and afford new insights.

We can easily recognize that the same is true of Freud's symbolism. Freud was evidently not conscious of how immersed he was in this cultural current. He believed he had discovered symbols in his patients' dreams first, and only later in the cultural tradition. In actuality, the dreamer makes use of symbols that are already culturally familiar. Freud writes:

> In the course of investigating the forms of expression brought about by the dream-work, the surprising fact emerged that certain objects, arrangements and relations are represented, in a sense indirectly, by "symbols," which are used by the dreamer without his understanding them and to which as a rule he offers no associations. Their translation has to be provided by the analyst, who can himself only discover it empirically by experimentally fitting it into the context. It was later found that linguistic usage, mythology and folklore afford the most ample analogies to dream-symbols.[6]

Symbolic variations render the decoding of the proper "meaning" difficult for both dreamer and analyst. Hence it is important to define the rules that the encoding of the dream symbol, like its decoding, obey. We will later see that this is one of the most significant arguments in the controversy between Anna Freud and Melanie Klein, since Klein for the most part interprets the symbols for actions "wildly," that is, without considering rules.

The most important representatives of symbolism in French literature are Baudelaire, Verlaine, Rimbaud, and Mallarmé; in England they are predominantly Arthur Symons and W. B. Yeats. Russian symbolism, which received little attention mostly because of language difficulties, is best represented by Alexander Blok and Andrei Bely, who, in developing their own linguistic modes, clearly revealed the limitations that had to be observed in the choice and variation of symbols.[7]

Among German writers, Stefan George (1868–1933), the Viennese poet Hugo von Hofmannsthal (1874–1929), and Rainer Maria Rilke (1875–1926) adopted the tendencies of French symbolism. Anna Freud was deeply and affectionately attached to Rilke's work and, through her later friend Lou Andreas-Salomé, to him personally. It is interesting to note that the aforementioned developments were soon reversed: it was Freud's symbolism as he had laid it down in his early work that began to inspire literature. We can find Freud's symbolism in Hugo von Hofmannsthal, in Hermann Hesse (in *Steppenwolf*, for example), and in the little-known C. Spitteler, whose novel *Imago* (1906) provided the title for the psychoanalytical periodical that today survives as *American Imago*. Finally, another Viennese poet of Anna Freud's youth was Arthur Schnitzler (1862–1931), whose personal relationship with the Freud family we will turn to later.

Childhood and Youth

At home Anna Freud experienced the political and artistic influences of an upper-middle-class milieu. To be sure, a family tradition was still missing, since her father had only recently reached this social status. The lifestyle the family adopted and which Anna Freud preserved throughout her life involved a sheltered childhood, early experiences with a governess, and, later, an upper elementary school for the middle class.

Freud used one of Anna's earliest dreams three times in his work. He mentioned it first in *The Interpretation of Dreams* (1900), written during her early childhood.

> My youngest daughter, then nineteen months old, had had an attack of vomiting one morning and had consequently been kept without food all day. During the night after this day of starvation she was heard calling out excitedly in her sleep: "Anna Fweud, stwawbewwies, wild stwawbewwies, omblet, pudden!" At that time she was in the habit of using her own name to express the idea of taking possession of something. The menu included pretty well everything that must have seemed to her to make up a desirable meal. The fact that strawberries appeared in it in two varieties[1] was a demonstration against the domestic health regulations. It was based upon the circumstance, which she had no doubt observed, that her nurse had attributed her indisposition to a surfeit of strawberries. She was thus retaliating in her dream against this unwelcome verdict.[2]

Freud was so struck by his little daughter's oneiric expression that he referred to it a second time in *The Interpretation of Dreams*.[3] And in the 1916–17 edition of *Introductory Lectures on Psychoanalysis*, Freud once again quoted the entire dream, without directly indicating that it was his daughter's, to illustrate how dreams, reacting to internal somatic stimulation, function as wish fulfillments.[4]

Besides the wish fulfillment and the father's obvious fascination with the manner in which the child "handles" it in her dreams, what interests us here is the nurse's care and close attention to the little girl's health and sleep, which she was then able to report to the father.

When Anna was almost three years old, Freud mentioned her again in a letter to Fliess: "Little Anna describes, not inappropriately, a small Roman statuette I bought in Innsbruck, as 'an old child.' "[5] Freud, who affectionately called his daughter "Annerl" (little Anna), admired her expressiveness even then. We do not know which statuette Freud was referring to, but it presumably belonged to his collection, which he was able to save and move to London, and where it remained in Anna Freud's home until her death.

The vacation of the following year gave Freud further occasion to write about Anna in a letter to Fliess. The entire family was staying in Berchtesgaden, where Freud was busy writing *The Interpretation of Dreams*.

> There are mushrooms here, though not many yet. The children naturally join in the fun of looking for them. The housewife's [Martha Freud's] birthday was celebrated on a big scale, among other things by a family outing to Bartolomäe. You should have seen little Anna on the Königssee.[6]

Gathering mushrooms was one of Freud's favorite pastimes. He excelled here too, and even the children could not compete with him.

Of all his children, Freud mentioned Anna most often in his letters. If he wrote about the others generally, he wrote about Anna in detail, or at least mentioned her first. This does not necessarily imply favoritism. Anna was after all the youngest, a little wag allowed to be bold, cheering everyone up. A short comment to Fliess sheds light on this: "The children and their mother are at last well again. Little Anna woke up one morning and was suddenly cured, and since then has been delightfully cheeky."[7]

Anna's insolence—or, as she later preferred to call it, her "naughtiness"—obviously never met with harsh judgment from her family, but was always received with enthusiasm. Freud wrote: "Recently I was told that little Anna said on Aunt Minna's birthday: 'On birthdays I am usually rather good.' "[8] And several weeks later: "Little Anna is positively beautified by naughtiness."[9]

Anna entered first grade in 1901, at the usual age of barely six years. During the first two years, between 1901 and 1903, she attended the private Elementary School I in Tuchlauben, and between 1903 and 1905 the elementary school on Grünentorgasse in the 9th district, which was only two blocks from Berggasse, a distance she could walk comfortably, accompanied by older siblings. She began fifth grade at this school, but completed the year in the elementary school of the Cottage Lyceum, where she later also taught. That same year she transferred to the lyceum's high school.[10] Located on Gymnasiumstrasse in the 19th district, this school was also close to Berggasse. It had been established as a private school in 1902 under the direction of Dr. Salka Goldmann, a widely admired woman. Contrary to what has sometimes been written, the Cottage Lyceum was not a Jewish school. The principal was indeed Jewish, as were more than half of the students; however, as several students who are still alive now recall, there were hardly political or "racial" reasons for this fact. The Cottage Lyceum was merely a very expensive private school with the legal provisions of a public school, including the right to impose final examinations. Affluent Jews, especially those who lived in the Freud's neighborhood, could afford to send their children to this prestigious school.

We know from Gertrud Baderle, a schoolmate and friend of Anna's, that Anna was a very bright student who, with the exception of this friend, sought little contact with other students and lived in her own fantasy world. She was a serious student who helped Gertrud with her homework, or simply dictated it to her. Anna's verbal facility and gift for expression drew attention in school no less than at home. In a course in French essay writing, the children once had to describe their room. Anna, who shared her room with her sister Sophie, described it as "having three walls," Sophie being the fourth wall. This ability to use language creatively deeply impressed her schoolmates.

During that time, not quite an adult, Anna Freud was apparently still as vain as other girls of her age. Gertrud Baderle vividly remembers a velvet coat with a blue silk lining that Anna wore and her female schoolmates admired. Anna Freud herself refuted this story tenaciously: "It is not true that I was concerned with my clothes at that time. Nor do I remember a velvet coat with a silk lining. On the contrary, my sister Sophie and I used to wear our brothers' worn-out reefers."[11] After sixty years it is difficult to determine which of the two friends had a better memory. Both versions seem plausible. Nevertheless, Anna Freud showed in one of her examples, the case of a young governess (see pp. 19–21 below), that an early wish to make oneself attractive and to be liked because of one's beautiful clothes can be reversed. The adult Anna Freud certainly showed no vanity whatsoever with respect to her attire.

In 1963, at the age of sixty-eight, Anna Freud herself mentioned her school days briefly. In a publication on infantile regression, she told of an episode from 1912, her last year in school:

> Actually, my first encounter with such manifestations happened much earlier, when I was still *in school*. I remember vividly being myself a member of a class of sixth formers who were overstrained due to a timetable which arranged for a series of difficult subjects in succession without sufficient intervening breaks. Eminently sensible and attentive as we were at the beginning of the morning, this invariably broke down in the fifth or sixth hour when even the most innocent words uttered by anybody produced wild outbursts of giggles and uncontrolled behavior. The male teachers who had the misfortune to take the class at this time would indignantly denounce the whole roomful of girls as "a silly flock of geese." I realized that we were tired and it puzzled me that this should make us silly, but the connection between fatigue and ego-regression was at that time beyond my reach![12]

The entire Freud family spent the summer vacation of 1909 in the Allgäu Ammerwald, a small region in the Ammer mountain chain. On August 19, Freud left for Bremen by way of Oberammergau and nearby Munich. In Bremen he embarked with Carl Gustav Jung and Sándor Ferenczi for the United States, where he gave five lectures at Clark University in Worcester, Massachusetts. Here he was awarded the title of Doctor *honoris causa*, his first mark of official recognition. Freud's family did not remain in Ammerwald, but crossed the Alps southward to settle in Riva on Lake Garda.[13]

In 1910, the Freuds spent part of the summer separately. Aunt Minna Bernays traveled with the unmarried daughters Sophie and Anna to Bielitz, at the foot of the Carpathian Mountains in Austrian Silesia (now Bielsko-Biala, Poland). The women took up quarters in Ludwig Jekels' sanatorium: it was once customary to spend vacations in the private sanatoriums of physician friends. Ludwig Jekels was one of the first psychoanalysts to be closely connected with Freud. Later he sold his sanatorium and moved to Vienna to be analyzed by Freud and to practice psychoanalysis himself. After the Nazi annexation of Austria to Germany, he emigrated with many other psychoanalysts to the United States.

In late July, the entire Freud family met in Nordwijk, Holland, where they spent a happy month by the North Sea. They parted in late August. Freud traveled with Ferenczi to Paris, Florence, and Rome. Ernst and Anna Freud had to return to Vienna. The rest of the family journeyed to The Hague.

In 1911, at the relatively early age of fifteen, Anna Freud completed her high-school education with the then usual Matura diploma. She spent the summer vacation with her mother in Klobenstein (Collalbo) in the Dolomite Mountains, where Freud joined them in early August. Ferenczi came on August 20 and stayed for two weeks, until Freud had to leave for the memorable Weimar congress that was held September 21–22. Since Anna Freud was not yet involved in psychoanalysis, she did not accompany her father to Weimar.

During the following year, Anna Freud continued her intensive training privately. Freud arranged an eight-month trip to Italy for her as a reward for her hard work during the previous year and in order for her to "see something beautiful while she was still young." Nothing came of this plan, however, because the engagement of her sister Sophie in the summer of 1912 to Max Halberstadt made other tasks more urgent. Aunt Minna, who was meant to accompany Anna to Italy, was needed in the Berggasse household, while Mrs. Freud and Sophie were in Hamburg preparing the apartment for the young couple.[14]

In the summer of 1912, the family again went to the Dolomites. Freud and his wife—who had first vacationed with Sophie in Karlsbad—came in August to Bolzano, where they met the rest of the family. They settled in the Hotel Latimar on Lake Carezza, twenty-four kilometers northeast of Bolzano. A well-known photograph from this period showing Anna Freud and her father is one of the most carefree and serene pictures of the young Anna. We see her at sixteen years old, in a long dirndl dress, knapsack on her back, arm in arm with her father in a meadow at the edge of a forest. Freud, with a knapsack on his back, a pipe in one hand and a walking cane in the other, is wearing a proper walking outfit, including boots.

It was decided that Anna would spend the winter in Merano (Meran), valued then, as it is today, for its mild winter weather, and where Marie Rischavy, the sister-in-law of Anna's eldest sister, Mathilde Hollitscher, was living. While she was staying in Merano, Anna received two letters from her father. The first arrived on the occasion of her seventeenth birthday on December 3, 1912, the first birthday she spent away from home. The second followed two weeks later.

My dear Anna,

I haven't been able to write to you before because since your departure, which already seems ages ago, life here has been hectic; and the Sunday in Munich—with the night journeys before and after, conversations in between lasting from 9 A.M. till 11:40 P.M.—wasn't exactly a rest cure. In any case I know the ladies of the house keep you regularly informed about anything worth hearing. Today's letter, however, is meant as a birthday congratulation. As you know, I am always premature on such happy occasions. Today I gave Heller an order which I trust will arrive in time and be what you want. Your monthly allowance will reach you in your new home via the post office savings bank.

I have no doubt at all that you will put on more weight and feel better once you have grown accustomed to idleness and the sunshine. You might as well abandon the knitting until after the wedding; it probably isn't very good for your back. Otherwise keep well and enjoy all that is offered you by the winter in Meran and the care of your sister-in-law, Frau Marie.

I don't think I shall be going away for Christmas; as a matter of fact I am expecting Dr. Abraham to visit me here. As you know, I am no longer master of my free time, a condition, however, that I quite enjoy.

I don't think you have seen my room since it was refurnished, or have you? It has turned out very well. Before you return for good we will do your room too; writing table and carpet are in any case assured.

I send you fond greetings, wish you everything good for your seventeenth (hard to believe that I too was once so young!) and please give my kind regards to Frau Marie and Edith.

Your
Papa[15]

My dear little Anna,

I hear you are already worrying again about your immediate future. So it seems that putting on $3\frac{1}{4}$ pounds still hasn't changed you much. I now want to set your mind at rest by reminding you that the original plan was to send you to Italy for eight months in the hope that you would return straight and plump and at the same time quite worldly and sensible. Actually we hadn't dared to hope that a few weeks in Meran would achieve this transformation, and so had already prepared ourselves at your departure for not seeing you at the wedding or so soon afterward in Vienna. I think you must now slowly accustom yourself to this terrible prospect. The ceremony can be performed quite well without you, for that matter also without guests, parties, etc., which you don't care for anyhow. Your plans for school can easily wait till you have learned to take your duties less seriously. They won't run away from you. It can only do you good to be a little happy-go-lucky and enjoy having such lovely sun in the middle of winter.

So now, if you are reassured that your stay in Meran won't be interrupted in the immediate future, I can tell you that we all enjoy your letters very much but that we also won't be worried if you feel too lazy to write every day. The time of toil and trouble will come for you too, but you are still quite young.

Give my kind regards to Frau Marie and Edith and feel as well and happy as

Your Father
wants you to be.[16]

In the birthday letter Freud voices his concern about his daughter's health and well-being. He wishes her to gain weight so that she might feel better. He warns her to give up knitting because the sustained posture it requires is harmful to her slightly bent back. She disregarded these admonitions or gave them only hasty consideration, but managed, on the other hand, to gain three pounds during this period. Freud's concerns proved to be groundless. Anna Freud was always very slender, and even if she never "straightened" her back, nor gave up her passion for knitting, she remained in excellent health into advanced age.

Freud's letters also shed light on Anna's mental and emotional disposition. She already showed herself to be conscientious and responsible, tending rather toward intellectual matters. Freud repeatedly had to urge her to accept idleness and pampering, because on her own she was evidently not inclined to self-indulgence. The birthday present ordered from Freud's publisher Hugo Heller, a Viennese book dealer who was temporarily a member of the Psychological Wednesday Society, consisted of books, though they were not about psychoanalysis.[17] Anna Freud's concerns about her immediate future involved her desire to become a teacher. That a woman should wish to practice a profession was rather unusual before World War I, though the training of women teachers was relatively common. Freud did not object to his daughter's plans, but he wanted to avoid rash actions.

The significant year of 1913 began with Sophie's wedding on January 14 at 19 Berggasse. Anna had remained in Merano. During the first half of the year Freud worked on *Totem and Taboo*,[18] and on March 21 he was able to leave for northern Italy for a brief Easter trip. Anna met him in Bolzano on March 22, after completing her five-month sojourn in Merano, and accompanied him to Italy. They made a brief stopover in Verona and then left for Venice, where they stayed at the Hotel Britannia for four days. Freud wanted to show his daughter this magnificent city he himself had already seen. On their way back they passed through Trieste, which then belonged to Austria, and on March 27 they were again in Vienna. This first brief trip together was not without significance, as one of Freud's remarks in a letter to Oskar Pfister indicates: "I am looking forward to Easter, which I am going to spend in Venice with my small and now only daughter."[19] Anna was *still* the little one, and after Sophie's wedding the only one remaining at home.

There were frequent allusions to this. In a letter to Ferenczi on July 20, 1912, Freud remarked in connection with the engagement of his daughter Sophie that this event bore on a theme he was then working on: Lear's three daughters.[20] A year later, in another letter to Ferenczi, Freud returned to the subject: "My closest companion will be my little daughter, who is developing very well at the moment (you will long ago have guessed the subjective condition for the 'Choice of the Three Caskets')."[21]

Cordelia and Antigone

It seems accurate to apply Freud's brief essay "The Theme of the Three Caskets," first published in 1913, to the author himself. In it Freud studied a familiar motif from myth and literature, according to which a man must choose among three women and always chooses the youngest. In Shakespeare's *Merchant of Venice* it is literally a choice among three caskets. In *King Lear* the father chooses among three daughters, but Freud demonstrates that this variation is only a displacement of the same motif. His interpretation reveals, surprisingly, that Lear's youngest daughter represents the death goddess and that "eternal wisdom, clothed in primaeval myth, bids the old man renounce love, choose death and make friends with the necessity of dying."[1]

According to this interpretation, then, it would have been his youngest daughter, Anna, who loved him silently, though most deeply, while he mistook the feelings of the two elder daughters for the most intense love. A psychoanalytic examination of Freud's treatment of the theme of the three caskets permits the conclusion that he withdrew part of his libido from his two married daughters to direct it to the youngest. It is equally understandable that the *memento mori*, the reminder of life's finiteness, which steals upon every parent when the grown-up children leave home, should overcome the fifty-seven-year-old Freud. This is the first time that Freud fully developed the second principal theme of his life—the death instinct (the first having been the libido). Finally, Freud and his youngest daughter developed a relationship during this period which was to endure for the rest of their lives. If one bears in mind the reversal Freud thought was necessary, Anna's role during her father's long cancer illness bears similarities to Cordelia's role in *King Lear*.[2]

Extrapolated inferences and interpretations, applied to Freud himself rather than to the theme he conceived, appear to this author contrived and inappropriate. This is also true of a detailed essay Heinz Politzer wrote, shortly before his own death, on "The Theme of the Three Caskets."

In Freud's case the situation can again be reversed and thus the denouement restored. In 1912 he became aware that he would lose to his "crown prince," Carl Gustav Jung. What he could very well have wished but couldn't have known yet, in the year he wrote "The Theme of the Three Caskets," was that he would attract in his Cordelia the executor of his will and the incarnate heir of the psychoanalytic movement.[3]

But this reiterated identification of Anna with Cordelia does violence to the actual circumstances, despite its beautiful consonance with the Lear saga. Even if Anna Freud assumed an increasingly important place in her father's life, and soon also achieved a great reputation in the psychoanalytic movement, this author doubts that Freud consciously discerned these connections. Freud allowed all his children, including Anna, to pursue their own inclinations. Nor can Anna Freud be seen as "the incarnate heir of the psychoanalytic movement," for this would imply a disregard of her own outstanding achievements.

Freud often compared Anna to another mythological figure, Antigone.[4] Oedipus, King of Thebes, fathers Antigone by Jocasta, unaware that the latter is his mother. Later Antigone not only cares and provides for her old father, but follows him in exile to Colonus, in Attica, and after his death returns to Thebes. Here too there seems to be an obvious connection, which Freud himself also had in mind. Since Antigone represents the ideal of selfless love in the Greek saga, especially toward her father and siblings, the relationship between Anna Freud and the discoverer of the Oedipus complex seems to bear out this even deeper interpretation, in particular because it points toward the future. The comparison is thoroughly apposite. Even if Anna Freud never gave up London as her home after she emigrated, she nonetheless visited Vienna, her intellectual home, in 1971, thus again becoming a part of it. At the instigation of the Viennese psychoanalyst Eva Laible, Anna Freud received a medallion on this occasion on which Freud's Anna–Antigone saying had been engraved. This gift attests not only to great psychoanalytic acumen but to a deep historical understanding, for at that moment the mythological circle was closed.

It seems insufficient, however, to consider the father–daughter relationship merely from the paternal point of view. What did he mean to her? Most people take a daughter's devotion to her father for granted, hence hardly worth consideration. What then is the daughter's relationship to her siblings, who normally compete for their parents' love? In the case of Anna Freud, the question must focus particularly on her sister Sophie, who was closest to her in age.

While the father and others lavished loved on Sophie because she was beautiful, delicate, and feminine, and perhaps also because she was sickly, the youngest daughter had to make a constant and overt effort to win her father's love and affection. We saw that little Anna delighted her father with unusual expressions and by being funny and naughty. Her father appeared as a central intellectual figure in her life, even during her school years. Once, when the teacher asked Anna if she was related to Professor Freud, her face beamed as she answered: "He is my father."[5]

Around that time she began to work on a never-ending story, making meticulous entries in large, black notebooks every day for years, and informing her friend Trude Baderle daily about its progress. It was the story of a large family with many children, no doubt fictional, but very realistically described. At that time Anna Freud had a favorite song she sang with her friend, and which she could still recite by heart seventy years later. It is called "The Grenadiers," with lyrics by Heinrich Heine and set to music by Robert Schumann.

THE GRENADIERS

Toward France there wandered two grenadiers;
In Russia they had been taken,
And as they reached the German frontiers,
Body and spirit were shaken.

For there they learned the tragic tale
That France had been lost and forsaken;
The army had suffered to no avail,
And the Emperor, the Emperor was taken.

They wept together, those two grenadiers;
To one thing their thoughts kept returning.
Alas, said one, half choked with tears,
That old wound of mine keeps burning.

The other said, This is the end,
With you I'd gladly perish.
But there is the homeland to defend,
And wife and child to cherish.

What matters wife? What matters child?
With far greater cares I'm shaken.
Let them go beg with hunger wild.
My Emperor, my Emperor is taken!

And, brother, this is my only prayer,
When I am dying, grant me:
You'll bear my body to France and there
In the soil of France you'll plant me.

> The cross of honor with crimson band
> Lay on my heart that bound me,
> Then put the musket in my hand
> And strap my saber around me.
>
> Then I will lie and listen and wait,
> A sentinel down in the grass there,
> Till I hear the roar of the guns and the great
> Thunder of hoofs as they pass there.
>
> The Emperor will come and the columns will wave,
> The swords will be flashing and rending,
> And I will rise full-armed from the grave,
> My Emperor, my Emperor defending![6]

The content of the song provoked discussions among the two friends, who identified with the two soldiers. The girls seem to have completely missed the exaggerated political overtones. Although Sigmund Freud was still alive at that time, it is not difficult to identify Freud the father with the emperor whom the soldiers are to protect even from their graves. The debates between the young girls revolved mostly around the lines "What matters wife? What matters child?/With far greater cares I'm shaken," which Anna Freud especially liked. Trude Baderle was not only horrified that a girl would identify with the most masculine of all male professions—military life—but it seemed equally incomprehensible and shocking to her that family life would be renounced for the sake of higher goals. Life later fulfilled the "life plan" expressed by the song and the friends' discussions. Anna Freud dedicated her life to high goals, which included defending her father. Her friend, on the other hand, opted for husband, child, and a middle-class existence.

Anna Freud showed interest in her father's work rather early. Their walks along Lake Garda, when Anna was fourteen years old, were the first occasion for long "professional conversations." Freud spoke to his daughter about psychoanalysis, and also about single case histories which impressed her so deeply that she told her girlfriend about them in detail.[7] During the following years Anna Freud became increasingly close to her father, especially because of psychoanalysis.

The relationships of the two sisters Anna and Sophie to their father were therefore of an entirely different nature. Sophie stirred boundless admiration in Anna with the same qualities that captivated others: her beauty and femininity. If one looks at the sisters' photographs from that period, however, the discrepancy between their beauty is not as apparent. It is possible that the calm regularity of Anna's features adumbrated the intellectual figure in her, conveying more than Sophie's photographs. Opinions on this matter were very different then, particularly those of Anna Freud herself. She exacted, in all earnestness, a promise from her girlfriend that the latter would take care of Sophie in case something happened to Anna. She later extended this concern to little Heinele, Sophie's son and Freud's beloved grandchild. Yet Anna Freud's wish sounds strangely like a premonition of Sophie's and Heinele's premature deaths.

The relationship between the two sisters will remind those familiar with Anna Freud's writings of the motif of "altruistic surrender," which she described much later as a form of ego defense whose roots obviously lie partly in self-observation. Indeed, one of the case histories of "altruistic surrender," though it cannot be identified definitely as self-description, may be generally applicable to Anna Freud. The young teacher was merely transformed into a young governess.

A young governess reported in her analysis that, as a child, she was possessed by two ideas: she wanted to have beautiful clothes and a number of children. In her fantasies she was almost obsessionally absorbed in picturing the fulfillment of these two wishes. But there were a great many other things that she demanded as well: she wished to have and to do everything that her much older playmates had and did—indeed, she wanted to do everything better than they and to be admired for her cleverness. Her everlasting cry of "Me too!" was a nuisance to her elders. It was characteristic of her desires that they were at once urgent and insatiable.

What chiefly struck one about her as an adult was her unassuming character and the modesty of the demands which she made on life. When she came to be analyzed, she was unmarried and childless and her dress was rather shabby and inconspicuous. She showed little sign of envy or ambition and would compete with other people only if she were forced to do so by external circumstances. One's first impression was that, as so often happens, she developed in exactly the opposite direction from what her childhood would have led one to expect and that her wishes had been repressed and replaced in consciousness by reaction formations (unobtrusiveness instead of a craving for admiration and unassumingness instead of ambition). One would have expected to find that the repression was caused by a prohibition of sexuality, extending from her exhibitionistic impulses and the desire for children to the whole of her instinctual life.

But there were features in her behavior at the time when I knew her which contradicted this impression. When her life was examined in more detail, it was clear that her original wishes were affirmed in a manner which seemed scarcely possible if repression had taken place. The repudiation of her own sexuality did not prevent her from taking an affectionate interest in the love life of her women friends and colleagues. She was an enthusiastic matchmaker and many love affairs were confided to her. Although she took no trouble about her own dress, she displayed a lively interest in her friends' clothes. Childless herself, she was devoted to other people's children, as was indicated by her choice of a profession. She might be said to display an unusual degree of concern about her friends' having pretty clothes, being admired, and having children. Similarly, in spite of her own retiring behavior, she was ambitious for the men whom she loved and followed their careers with the utmost interest. It looked as if her own life had been emptied of interests and wishes; up to the time of her analysis it was almost entirely uneventful. Instead of exerting herself to achieve any aims of her own, she expended all her energy in sympathizing with the experiences of people she cared for. She lived in the lives of other people, instead of having any experience of her own.

The analysis of her infantile relations to her mother and father revealed clearly the nature of the inner transformation which had taken place. Her early renunciation of instinct had resulted in the formation of an exceptionally severe superego, which made it impossible for her to gratify her own wishes. He penis wish, with its offshoots in the shape of ambitious masculine fantasies, was prohibited, so too her feminine wish for children and the desire to display herself, naked or in beautiful clothes, to her father, and to win his admiration. But these impulses were not repressed: she found some proxy in the outside world to serve as a repository for each of them. The vanity of her women friends provided, as it were, a foothold for the projection of her own vanity, while her libidinal wishes and ambitious fantasies were likewise deposited in the outside world. She projected her prohibited instinctual impulses onto other people. . . . The patient did not dissociate herself from her proxies but identified herself with them. She showed her sympathy with their wishes and felt that there was an extraordinarily strong bond between these people and herself. Her superego, which condemned a particular instinctual impulse when it related to her own ego, was surprisingly tolerant of it in other people. She gratified her instincts by sharing in the gratification of others, employing for this purpose the mechanisms of projection and identification. The retiring attitude which the prohibition of her impulses caused her to adopt where she herself was concerned vanished when it was a question of fulfilling the same wishes after they had been projected onto someone else. The surrender of her instinctual impulses in favor of other people had thus an egoistic significance, but in her efforts to gratify the impulses of others her behavior could only be called altruistic.

This passing on of her own wishes to other people was characteristic of her whole life and could be traced very clearly in the analysis of little isolated incidents. For instance, at the age of thirteen she secretly fell in love with a friend of her elder sister who had formerly been the special object of her jealousy. She had an idea that, at times, he preferred her to her sister and she was always hoping that he would give some sign of loving her. On one occasion it happened, as it had often happened before, that she found herself slighted. The young man called unexpectedly one evening to take her sister for a walk. In analysis the patient remembered perfectly distinctly how, from having been at first paralyzed with disappointment, she suddenly began to bustle about, fetching things to make her sister "pretty" for her outing and eagerly helping her to get ready. While doing this, the patient was blissfully happy and quite forgot that it was not she, but her sister, who was going out to enjoy herself. She had projected her own desire for love and her craving for admiration onto her rival and, having identified herself with the object of her envy, she enjoyed the fulfillment of her desire.

She went through the same process when frustration rather than fulfillment was in question. She loved to give the children of whom she was in charge good things to eat. On one occasion a mother refused to give up a particular tit-bit for her child. Although the patient herself was, in general, indifferent to the pleasures of the table, the mother's refusal made her furiously indignant. She experienced the frustration of the child's wish as if it were her own, just as in the other case she had rejoiced vicariously in the fulfillment of her sister's desires. It is plain that what she had made over to other people was the right to have her wishes fulfilled without hindrance.[8]

More than twenty years of life experience lay between the formative years of youth and the writing of this case history. Let us therefore return to the chronological order of events.

After the 1913 trip to Italy with her father, Anna Freud was again at home, where she pursued her private studies in preparation for her first teachers' examination. In the summer she traveled again with Freud, joined this time by her mother and her Aunt Minna. On July 13, 1913, all four left Vienna for Marienbad, Bohemia, then under Austrian rule, to settle in the Villa Taube. Freud, who couldn't bear to stay there for very long, blamed the cold and humid climate. Later Anna Freud told Ernest Jones that that was the only time she had ever seen her father depressed.[9] On August 11, Freud went again to the Dolomites, this time to San Martino di Castrozza.

At Easter 1914, Freud wanted to take Anna along to Arbe to meet Sándor Ferenczi. However, she had been running a temperature and finally came down with whooping cough, a childhood disease she had to suffer at the age of eighteen. In her place, Freud took along his student and colleague Otto Rank. They traveled to Brioni and four days later returned to Vienna. Jones aptly remarks that they had gone a rather long way to catch some sea air.

In July, Freud vacationed in Karlsbad, Bohemia. He allowed Anna to go to England on July 18. This trip, several days before World War I broke out, was noteworthy because England—where the Freuds had relatives and which later was to become Anna Freud's home—here played a part in her life for the first time. The signs of war were already visible. On June 28, 1914, the Austrian crown heirs were murdered at Sarajevo. Fear of a large-scale war was pervasive, though most European leaders did not want one. Anna Freud left Vienna on July 18; only five days later Austria-Hungary presented the ultimatum to Serbia. A general mobilization was ordered in Russia on July 29 or 30. Anna Freud experienced these developments in England, and her family feared she might be detained there. But the protection of the Austrian ambassador enabled her to return with him to Vienna in the third week of August, by a detour through Gibraltar and Genoa.[10]

■

The Beginning of World War I

Even those who were born and grew up in this century all too easily forget what an immense crisis World War I represented for Europe. It is not so much a matter of the war's immediate consequences, though they were painful for those involved. But as a result of the war Vienna completely lost its significance as the intellectual center of a multinational state.

Traveling from one country to another entailed no difficulties before World War I, as indicated by the trips the Freuds took. Psychoanalysis had thus been able to grow into an international movement during the first fifteen years of this century. These connections did not collapse immediately. Ernest Jones later wrote: "I see from one of my letters of that time that I had volunteered to escort [Anna Freud] to the Austrian frontier 'by one of the numerous routes available,' such was one's innocence in those happy days of what governments could do in blocking the old freedom of travel."[1]

During the war, Freud was able to write to Herbert and Loe Jones in England, thanking them for having taken care of Anna in London. The letter, which he sent via a neutral country, could bear neither signature nor date:

> My dear friends,
>
> These wretched times, this war, which impoverishes us as much in spiritual as in material goods, have prevented me from thanking you earlier for the clever and practical fashion in which you returned my little daughter and for all the friendship that lies behind it. She is very well, but I suspect she sometimes pines for the country of our enemies.
>
> I was very pleased to hear via an obvious channel that all is well with you and that you are about to move into a new home, which I would like to bless with the most heartfelt good wishes for you both. Till we meet again, God alone knows when!
>
> Your faithful
[unsigned][2]

In June 1914, Anna Freud took her first teachers' examination and, to fulfill the requirements for the second one, began a two-year preparatory period in an elementary school. She was, by then, the only one of the six children still living with her parents. Her brothers Martin and Ernst entered the military rather quickly. Oliver received his engineering diploma on the same day that Anna passed her teachers' examination, and throughout the war was involved in the construction of tunnels and barracks.

Anna Freud spent the first two years of the war as a candidate for a teaching position. One of her former students tells in a letter how much the students loved her as a teacher.

> One day we children were electrified: a young, slender woman, dark-haired and with interesting eyes, was introduced to us and immediately took over the direction of the class. I can't recall too many details, but this young woman—her name was Miss Freud—had us much more under control than the older "aunties." Standing by her table, her right arm propped up by the left at the elbow, she had only to look at us firmly and seriously to keep us in order. She was such a marvelous and simple figure that I loved her deeply at that time.[3]

For Anna Freud, this was a period of manifold significance. She ambitiously pursued a systematic training program which, as her first professional activity, traced a firm guideline for the rest of her life. After the second teachers' examination in 1917, she continued teaching, until 1920, at the elementary school of the Cottage Lyceum, the same school she had graduated from a few years before. It was later the opinion of some that she had hardly any other opportunity but to teach in a Jewish school, since state schools denied her access. This is incorrect because, as has been said earlier, the Cottage Lyceum was not a Jewish school and was licensed by the state. Anna Freud's connection with this highly regarded school was of an older and different kind.

Her students from that period remember her with enthusiasm. One of them, Gerda Schöler, took her entrance examination with Anna Freud. As a child during World War I, she had studied at an Italian school in Fiume. Shortly before the end of the war, the girl came with her parents to Vienna. On September 14, 1918, when she was sitting in front of Anna Freud to take her entrance examination for the second grade, Anna Freud asked her first whether she could sing a song. At first, nothing came to the mind of the seven-year-old Gerda, but when she finally sang a popular Italian song, Anna Freud leaned back in her chair laughing loudly, joined in, and thus won the child's trust. The beginnings of the "warming-up technique," which Anna Freud later introduced into the methodology of child analysis, are already visible here. When the examination ended, the girl had done very well.[4]

Even today there are former students of Anna Freud's in Vienna who recall her unequaled talent for inspiring children with enthusiasm for the material. Given her early and unique comprehension of the experiential world of young people, such memories are understandable even if one bears in mind the blurring effects time may have had on her former students, and that friendly memories about Anna Freud tend to result from her reputation, which, after so many years, has finally penetrated *her* Vienna as well. There were significant episodes during her teaching period. It is told how Anna Freud brought little statuettes from her father's collection to school to show them to the children. Another story describes her as Santa Claus who distributed gifts to the children at the house at 19 Berggasse. It is not easy to imagine the small and delicate Anna Freud as a convincing white-bearded Santa Claus with a sack on her back. She herself remarked drily: "I consider the Santa Claus story a fantasy. I remember nothing of that sort".[5] A photograph showing her among her students—in her idiosyncratic posture—conveys something about her as a teacher.[6] Lili Schnitzler, the daughter of the poet Arthur Schnitzler with whom Anna Freud was connected through family friendship, was also one of her students.[7]

The five years of educational practice during which Anna Freud gained extensive experience with children and adolescents strongly determined the path she later pursued. Henceforth she would always be concerned with children and adolescents. Later she often referred to this period as one that reaffirmed her conviction that the psychoanalyst returns to his original profession after he completes his special training.

Thirty-two years later, in 1952, Anna Freud led a discussion on the role of the teacher with a number of prospective teachers at the Harvard Graduate School of Education, during which several participants took notes.[8] Before introducing the audience to the psychoanalytic insights necessary in the education of both younger and older children, she spoke of her own teaching experiences. She stressed the extraordinary importance of contact with children of every age, since each stage in a child's development represents only a transition period. Still, Anna Freud questioned the teacher's uncritical acceptance of a child's imaginary and experiential world, because it could thwart the teacher's relationship to the adult world, into which the child must ultimately grow. Twelve years later, in 1964, when Jefferson Medical College in Philadelphia awarded her an honorary doctorate, she returned to this point:

> Clinical experience—practical contact with human beings, as it was called at that time—which was demanded from every analyst, was supplied for me by teaching school, a five-year contact with young children. This proved important for me, . . . since in later life analysts usually return to, and single out for application, the very fields in which they had their first, preanalytic, practical experience.[9]

During her first years as a teacher, Anna Freud was eagerly reading poetry and, concomitantly, attempted some writing herself. Freud wrote to Lou Andreas-Salomé on April 1, 1915, about Anna Freud's passion for Rilke's poetry: "Please tell Herr R. M. Rilke that I also have a nineteen-year-old daughter who knows his poems, some of them by heart, and who envies her brother in Klagenfurt the greetings he received."[10] Andreas-Salomé had written on the previous day from Munich where she was visiting Rilke. In a brief postscript, the latter had sent greetings for Freud and his son Ernst who was staying in Klagenfurt at that time, but he did not mention Anna Freud. The younger generation saw in Rilke, then as well as later, the embodiment of the poet, and he enjoyed enthusiastic reverence. The period of Andreas-Salomé's intimate involvement with him had long since passed, and her connection with Freud and his daughter was just being forged. When Anna Freud returned to Vienna at the age of seventy-six, she still quoted Rilke to express her innermost feelings and thoughts.

During that period Anna Freud evidently perfected her passion for handicrafts. Freud had written to her in Merano to give up knitting temporarily, but she paid as little attention to this warning as she did to others. One could assume that such typically feminine, domestic activity was not to be taken for granted in a woman with overriding intellectual interests and with so highly productive a mind. To be sure, we know today that intellectuality and femininity do not necessarily conflict with one another. We now see emancipated women who knit everywhere, in lecture halls, at conventions and meetings. To compare Anna Freud with them is rather inappropriate, since she never pretended to be emancipated in the usual sense. In any event, she never lost her passion for knitting and handicrafts. She knitted for the dolls of children who were in therapy with her, and her friends occasionally received from her something she herself knitted. Helene Deutsch tells that she always honored such gifts and that, even as an older woman, on special occasions she wore a black blouse Anna Freud had crocheted for her at the beginning of their friendship.[11] Throughout her life, Anna Freud sewed her own clothes. She also practiced weaving. There was a loom in her London house as well as in her country house on the Irish coast. There may be an element of restlessness behind these activities, which never let her hands be idle, but calmed her and allowed her to pursue her thoughts.

While still active as a teacher, Anna Freud became increasingly engaged in psychoanalysis. At first this entailed mostly reading psychoanalytic literature, as Freud briefly hinted in a letter he wrote to her on August 1, 1915, from the health resort of Karlsbad. She had evidently written to him and asked about the meaning of "transference." The letter shows, moreover, that Freud was able to be quite exuberant even during the war, at least during its first years. This letter also contains one of Freud's few "poems," whose collectors' value the "weighing-booth man" mentioned in the letter obviously did not know.

Karlsbad, August 1, 1915

My dear Anna,

I want to reply quickly to your letter so that your mind may be set at ease. We are both well again and have given up Marienbad but not you. We are now planning, on Dr. Kolisch's advice, to extend our stay here until the 15th, then to go to Ischl to a hotel and spend the birthday and the rest of the summer either in Ischl or in Aussee, wherever we find something suitable. This should certainly satisfy you.

Your desk mishap is not unique. During her first days here, the good and strong girl threw your picture on the floor and the glass had to be replaced. Unfortunately this wasn't sufficient warning for me. Several days later she hurled an ashtray so that it broke; she evidently regrets it was only the porphyry and not the nephrite ashtray I left home. Now I have regained my energy. After several arguments I showed her a large strip of paper I had fastened with thumbtacks to the desk and which said:

Do not touch! Under penalty!

That seems to have worked.

I have had occasion here for another literary work. In front of the friendship room where we breakfast stands a man with a weighing booth, who for years has been inviting people to use it with the following ghastly stanza:

As God's eyesight is true,
So each guest's weight is too,
In the friendship room he should not neglect
To let his changing weight be checked.

I finally took the liberty of asking the man where he had found the poem, to which he replied that it was his own creation, though he knew it was not without flaws. Moved by such modesty, I undertook to provide a substitute for this absurd piece, and the next day I gave him the following verse containing his own ideas:

As his heart and eyes are true,
So is the weight of each guest too,
But in becoming a problem it will not fail
Unless in the booth he gets on the scale.

He praised it very highly and promised to use it next season.

I must have written to you that by yesterday Ernst will have left. From Martin a postcard came yesterday in which he speaks of a ten-day vacation.

Several days ago the brothers played a game of tarok together for the first time.

"Transference" is a technical term referring to the patient's transference of his latent tender or hostile feelings to the doctor. Despite the bad times—one gets used to everything—we have resumed contact with Mrs. Schapira. After much insistence Mama had her pearls reset and finally enjoys them. For Grandma we found a showy old brooch; for you a trifle made of opal, now being worked on; and I am bargaining for a nephrite bowl which is marvelously beautiful, but, strangely, it has a small old German coin inlaid in its center. We still haven't reached an agreement on it.

Many warm greetings from
your Papa[12]

Anna Freud later pointed out that no comprehensive psychoanalytic training program such as those widely known today existed then. The formal decision to become a psychoanalyst was not really necessary. Those who were interested became involved in the new field until they were absorbed into a group of psychoanalysts, or else they dropped their pursuit after a certain time. The minutes of the Psychological Wednesday Society reveal that a considerable number of interested people participated temporarily in the psychoanalytic debates, but then dropped out, not necessarily as the result of a dispute. Their interests had simply found another focus.

In "Curriculum Vitae of a Lay Analyst," presented on the occasion of her award from Jefferson Medical College, Anna Freud expressed her own view on this matter:

> I share, in fact, with all other lay analysts the lack of a medical education. I also have in common with a few remaining analysts of my generation the circumstance that our analytic training took place at a period before the official psychoanalytic training institutes came into being. We were trained by our personal analysts, by extensive reading, by our own, unsupervised efforts with our first patients, and by lively interchange of ideas and discussion of problems with our elders and contemporaries.[13]

One can discern in this brief description a development that lasted for years and finally permitted Anna Freud to describe herself as a trained psychoanalyst. Those were years of unlimited openness during which she absorbed a great deal, thought about issues, and worked them through without actually participating in discussions. Today, when many young people believe they must contribute to every discussion, even if they are quite unfamiliar with the subject, Anna Freud's reserve seems especially attractive.

During the war Freud had continued, if intermittently, to lecture at the psychiatric clinic. The catalogue of the University of Vienna listed Freud's lecture course "Introduction to Psychoanalysis" for the winter semester of 1914–15, which Anna Freud then heard for the first time. The lecture was scheduled for Saturdays from 7:00 to 9:00 P.M., a rather late hour but convenient for interested persons who were not free at other hours. There was at that time no weekend as we now know it. It was customary in the medical profession, as it still was a few years ago, to work Saturday evenings and Sundays until noon. On June 9, 1924, Freud wrote to Oskar Pfister that he had stopped lecturing in 1918, that is, at the relatively early age of sixty-two.[14] Anna Freud could therefore attend her father's lectures—his last—for only a few semesters.

Anna Freud's thought and work were determined not only by education and psychoanalysis, but also by literature, which she absorbed extensively. Unlike her father, she did not have a university education. As a result, she used mythological images and comparisons only as they were already available in psychoanalytic literature, where they had been introduced mainly by her father.

Ward Rounds at the Vienna Psychiatric Clinic

For two years between 1915 and 1918, Anna Freud regularly joined Paul Schilder and Heinz Hartmann on their ward rounds at the Psychiatric Clinic of the Vienna General Hospital in order to expand her knowledge of her future field. Julius Wagner-Jauregg, then the clinic's director, had given her this unusual permission. We will dwell briefly on these three personalities, since each of them is in his own way significant to the history of psychoanalysis. Anna Freud later referred often to these rounds.

Julius Wagner-Jauregg

Julius Wagner, Knight of Jauregg, and Sigmund Freud were almost the same age. They had met during their training and internship, and valued each other highly. Wagner-Jauregg was eminently successful in his academic career. In 1893, at the age of only thirty-six, he was given the University of Vienna's professorial chair for psychiatry and neurology, the only truly coveted teaching chair in psychiatry in Austria. He thus had a considerable scientific and social advantage over Freud, whose academic career ended when he settled into private practice in Vienna. Even today, a private practice is not as highly respected as an academic position. Further-more, in 1927 Wagner-Jauregg received the only Nobel Prize ever awarded to a psychiatrist, for his "Malaria Therapy of Progressive Paralysis." Anna Freud ac-knowledged this therapy as late as 1967, by calling attention to the first successful cases of malaria therapy she had been able to observe during her rounds.[1] Helene Deutsch, who enjoyed Wagner-Jauregg's special trust, had the privilege of injecting the patients with the malaria serum while working at the Wagner-Jauregg Clinic between 1912 and 1918. It must have been charming to observe Anna Freud and Helene Deutsch, the two psychoanalysts and friends, in their simultaneous efforts with paralyzed patients receiving malaria therapy.

Unlike Freud's, Wagner-Jauregg's reputation has faded considerably, despite the Nobel Prize. His scientific achievements are hardly mentioned, and malaria therapy is no longer used in progressive paralysis cases, which today rarely exist anyway. It is difficult, therefore, to envisage the glamour once attached to Wagner-Jauregg's name.

Since the middle of the nineteenth century, psychiatry has been widely influenced by natural sciences, incorporating theories from their various branches, including biology. Karl Ludwig Kahlbaum, for example, proposed a model that assumed identical causes, an identical clinical picture, identical therapy, and identical pathological/anatomical evidence for each particular psychic illness.[2] Half a century later, when assiduous research culminated in the discovery of the syphillis germ, the *Treponema pallidum*, the entire psychiatric world became enthusiastic when the idea of the "medical model of madness" showed itself to be useful in the treatment of the general paresis of the insane. The enthusiasm reached a climax when Wagner-Jauregg, with the assistance of Gerstmann who later emigrated to the United States, successfully introduced malaria therapy.

The therapeutic principle consisted in applying *one* specific therapy to *one* specific illness: malaria was injected into *every* paralytic patient. This achievement remained the guiding idea for several decades, in the hope that all psychic illnesses—and schizophrenia in particular—would finally be understood by means of the same principle and would prove amenable to specific therapeutic methods. Only after decades did this idea lose its appeal, although many scientists still defend it.

Freud had nothing to contribute in this area. Although he too postulated a biological origin of emotional and mental disorders and remarked that somatic causes of neuroses may one day be determined, his own thoughts increasingly diverged from such goals. According to Anna Freud, the assumption that Freud postulated biological causes in the aforementioned sense is altogether mistaken. Rather, she saw in Freud's remarks an indication of the possibility of treating neuroses chemically, that is, an anticipation of current psychopharmacotherapy.[3] F. J. Sulloway's reinterpretation of Freud's "biological" theories[4] confirm Anna Freud's views. Freud knew that physicians were "brought up to respect only anatomical, physical and chemical factors. They were not prepared for taking psychical ones into account and therefore met them with indifference or antipathy."[5] Further, "If someone succeeded in isolating and demonstrating the hypothetical substance or substances concerned in neuroses, he would have no need to worry about opposition from the medical profession."[6]

It is understandable, then, that Wagner-Jauregg, whose ideas did not differ from those of other physicians, did not take a deep interest in psychoanalysis, with which he familiarized himself nonetheless. Toward Freud as a person, he maintained a friendly and liberal attitude; he put the clinic's lecture hall at his disposal and inquired from time to time whether difficulties had arisen in administrative matters. When Emil Raimann, a close co-worker of Wagner-Jauregg, drew attention with his unremitting hostility toward Freud, Wagner-Jauregg stopped it.

Wagner-Jauregg maintained this liberal attitude toward Freud's daughter Anna as well. Thus, he gave her permission to accompany Schilder and Hartmann on their rounds at the clinic—a privilege other psychiatrists would have probably refused, out of fear of "infecting" their coworkers with psychoanalytic thought. Indeed, some hesitation would have been appropriate, since Anna Freud, not a physician, had to acquire knowledge that involved professional esotericism and medical confidentiality. But one should not assume that Wagner-Jauregg's support of Anna Freud went beyond this permission. He remained for the most part invisible to her.

In 1917, we still find ourselves in the strict hierarchical system of the Austro-Hungarian monarchy. Next in line after the clinic's director came, in hierarchical order, the first assistant, Paul Schilder; then the second assistant, Heinz Hartmann. Speaking in 1964 of her rounds with them, Anna Freud said:

> The ward rounds, especially when led by Schilder, were highly instructive, and what they taught was never forgotten by me. We all listened spellbound to the revelations made by the patients, their dreams, delusions, fantastic systems, which the analytically knowledgeable among us fitted into a scheme.[7]

Paul Schilder

Paul Schilder, so clearly brought to the fore by Anna Freud, was one of those universal minds that can hardly be fit into current narrow categories. To classify him as either neurologist or clinical psychiatrist, as psychoanalyst or philosopher, is difficult, since he made outstanding contributions in all these fields. He died, regrettably, in 1940 at the age of only fifty-four, following an accident.

Schilder was trained in psychiatry in Halle under Gabriel Anton and in Leipzig under Paul Emil Flechsig. In 1912, in Leipzig, at the age of twenty-six, he published the description of *encephalitis periaxialis diffusa*, today known as Schilder's Disease, which made him famous as a neurologist all over Europe. He had also studied in Halle with Wilhelm Wundt's students Neumann and Krueger, both proponents of holistic psychology; at that time psychology and philosophy were not yet separate fields. When Schilder became an intern at Wagner-Jauregg's clinic in 1918, where he was hired as an academic lecturer as early as 1919, he was not yet a psychoanalyst in the current sense. He had indeed attended several of Freud's lectures while he was a student, but, as he later admitted, these had not impressed him very deeply. Although his orientation was biological at that time, he was invited to join the Vienna Psychoanalytic Society in 1919. His incredibly fast reception of psychoanalysis is demonstrated by the 1925 publication of his *Introduction to a Psychoanalytic Psychiatry*, the first book in which he tried to amalgamate clinical psychiatry and psychoanalysis.[8] The book is still read today.

It is not clear who had a more enduring influence on whom. Anna Freud already had considerable theoretical knowledge of psychoanalysis when she met Schilder, but she was only at the beginning of her psychoanalytic practice. In 1918, Schilder had clinical experience but was relatively unfamiliar with psychoanalytic methods. Anna Freud did not think her influence on Schilder was very great: "I was a novice then, much too diffident to 'influence' someone, and certainly not Schilder, who was far ahead of me."[9] With her usual modesty she may, even in retrospect, have underestimated her intellectual importance during that period. Schilder's enthusiasm was evidently easily stirred, and he was also capable of inspiring enthusiasm in others. It is understandable, then, that Anna Freud should speak so warmly about her Vienna memories fifty years later.

Schilder removed himself from Vienna's psychoanalytic community fairly early on. In 1928, he spent a brief period in New York, where he settled in 1930. He was critically injured in a car accident after visiting his second wife, Lauretta Bender, who was in a clinic recovering from childbirth. Several days later he died.

There had been growing tensions between him and the Vienna Psychoanalytic Society because Schilder had trained psychoanalysts at the University Hospital on his own, disregarding the training rules of the Society. Later he was refused membership in the New York Psychoanalytic Society because he himself had not been analyzed. Still, he had occupied an important place in the Vienna Psychoanalytic Society while he was in Austria. He introduced into the psychiatric clinic not only Anna Freud, but also other, later famous, psychoanalysts, such as Wilhelm Reich, Jeanne Lampl-de Groot, and finally Heinz Hartmann. He was thus a crucial link between clinical psychiatry and psychoanalysis. Anna Freud had been fascinated not only by Schilder's personality, but by the manner in which he roused patients to speak and showed interest in their dreams, thoughts, and feelings—gifts that opened to her a world which otherwise would have remained closed.

Heinz Hartmann

The resident physician Anna Freud joined on his rounds at the psychiatric clinic was Heinz Hartmann. He was only one year older than she, and in 1915 was at the beginning of his career as an academic psychiatrist and psychoanalyst. Therefore he could not yet impart much knowledge to her. Like Schilder, Hartmann became a psychiatrist who deftly combined clinical psychiatry and psychoanalysis. He worked at the Vienna Psychiatric Clinic for fourteen years (1920–34), and from 1926 to 1939 he was a lecturer at the Vienna Medical School although he never received the necessary permission from the government to lecture because he insisted on having no membership in a church. At the same time, Hartmann occupied a leading position in the Vienna Psychoanalytic Society, where he became a training analyst as soon as this position was created. From 1932 to 1941 he was editor of the *Internationale Zeitschrift für Psychoanalyse*, and from 1951 until 1957 he was president of the International Psychoanalytic Association. Forced to emigrate in 1938, Hartmann went first to Paris, where he worked as a training analyst, then to Switzerland, finally settling in New York in 1941. He very soon became one of the most influential psychiatrists in new American psychiatry. In the United States, the following decades were marked by a close affinity between clinical psychiatry and psychoanalysis. Nearly all the professors in leading clinical positions were psychoanalysts.

In the 1950's and 1960's, ego psychology became prominent in psychiatric and psychoanalytic discussions. In 1939, Hartmann published a book on this subject, *Ego Psychology and the Problem of Adaptation*,[10] to which later discussions repeatedly referred. Anna Freud said that Heinz Hartmann believed her to be his "silent critic." He felt that although Anna Freud was critical of his ego psychology and the rest of his psychoanalytical theory, she would not speak out against him.

Hartmann's seventieth birthday, which the New York Psychoanalytic Society celebrated on November 4, 1964, was an occasion for clarification. For this event, Anna Freud wrote not only a speech of appreciation, but also a detailed article, "Links Between Hartmann's Ego Psychology and the Child Analyst's Thinking."[11] In this essay she spoke briefly about her personal acquaintance with Hartmann. She did not mention the rounds at the Vienna clinic, possibly because they preceded the scientific reputation of both. Anna Freud indicated, however, that they joined the Vienna Psychoanalytic Society at almost the same time, and referred to him as her slightly older brother or stepbrother, because—from the psychoanalytic point of view—in a certain sense they indeed shared the same father. Hartmann was analyzed by Freud—in fact for free—who was also Anna Freud's training analyst. The relationship between Anna Freud and Heinz Hartmann was, however, limited to a professional one. She related that both had begun to work in ego psychology at the same time, but that she had not shown adequate understanding for Hartmann's critique of the first two chapters of her book *The Ego and the Mechanisms of Defense*.[12] Hartmann wanted to consider the ego in facets other than just its defense mechanisms and its struggle against the id. In her tribute, Anna Freud pointed out the many connections and parallels between her and Hartmann's writings.[13]

The End of the War

Let us glance once again at the opening scene of this excursus in which Schilder, Hartmann, and Anna Freud are going together from bed to bed, discussing issues among themselves and with patients. Let us remember that each of them would later make significant contributions to psychoanalysis, though in careers that widely diverged. No one would have been able to predict these developments at the time, the patients least of all.

The war was thus a period of intensive learning for Anna Freud, in education as much as in psychoanalysis, during which she acquired formative practical experience. At 19 Berggasse it was quieter then than in previous years. The elder sisters had left home to live with their own families, and the brothers had been drafted. Freud had fewer patients; other issues engaged his attention, and, as often happened under such circumstances, he used the time to work intensively on his writings.

Despite the war the Freuds did not give up their vacation trips. A letter from Freud to Lou Andreas-Salomé on July 30, 1915, informs us that Anna Freud was in Ischl with Freud's eighty-year-old mother. In 1918, Anna Freud and her father again went to Steinbruch, in Hungary, where they spent several days at the house of Anton von Freund and his sister, Katá Levy. They combined this trip with attendance at the Fifth International Psychoanalytic Congress, held on September 28–29, 1918, at the Academy of Sciences in Budapest, and whose subject was war experiences from a psychoanalytic perspective. It was the first congress Anna Freud attended, and her mother and brother Ernst were also on the guest list.

Five days after the congress, Austria-Hungary accepted the truce of the German government, which precipitated the collapse of Austria-Hungary within only five weeks. On October 21, 1918, revolution broke out in Vienna. Hungary became an independent country. Czechoslovakia was declared a new nation; as a result, the connection with Bohemia and Moravia, Freud's home, was severed. The southern Tyrol and the Italian regions of Tarvisio (Tarvis) and Idrija (Idria) were relinquished. Finally, the last Austrian emperor, Karl, abdicated on November 11, 1918, and went into exile in Switzerland. A small, truncated republic, "German-Austria," remained. Although these historical events have often been described, it is difficult today adequately to imagine the changes.

The Austrian population did not have time to reflect on the political changes, since a financial and economic collapse immediately followed. Moreover, an influenza epidemic claimed 2.6 million victims in Europe alone and 20 million worldwide—more victims than World War I.

Those who could withdraw into their work and their family during such radical changes were fortunate. Despite inevitable sporadic interruptions, Anna Freud pursued her psychoanalytic training undisturbed. It was finally possible to restore the international connections that the war had interrupted. The fate of Anna Freud's brothers, all three of whom had been active in the war, was uncertain for some time, but they returned home unscathed.

Freud's practice dwindled even more toward the end of the war and finally came almost to a standstill. He was advised to emigrate, possibly to Hungary, Switzerland, or Holland. Ernest Jones's first offer from England had already come, and twenty years later Freud was forced gratefully to accept the second. In 1919, Freud again had ten patients daily. But economic difficulties and bad nutrition in particular remained onerous. For weeks there was no meat; during the last two years of the war, food scarcities had become more and more common. Sándor Ferenczi and Max Eitingon especially were able to send food from Hungary to the Freud family until the war's chaos severed the connections with that country.

Training Analysis and the Postwar Period

Between 1918 and 1921, Anna Freud studied psychoanalysis with her father. This process later occasioned lively comment. Paul Roazen, for example, remarked maliciously that "this may be the most obvious example that Freud arrogated to himself special rights for which he would have probably sharply censured other analysts."[1]

Such an attitude misrepresents the status psychoanalytic training had at that time. Training analysis in the current sense was not yet common. Physicians and nonphysicians alike came to Freud or to other analysts as patients, and later became practicing analysts themselves. Today therapeutic analysis is something quite different. The sharp distinction between therapeutic and training analysis has technically disappeared, since psychoanalysts presuppose that every human being suffers from some kind of neurosis. During Freud's time, on the other hand, analyst and analysand either did not discuss personal problems when the analysand was "healthy," or they spoke about them while taking a walk. That is how Max Eitingon became a psychoanalyst after taking many walks with Freud.[2] There was often only a mutual exchange of dreams, which the participants analyzed to the best of their abilities— as, for example, Freud and C. G. Jung did on their boat trip to America. It is well known that this exchange of dreams brought about the first discord between them.

Hermann Nunberg was the the first to propose that each analyst should himself be analyzed, at the Budapest congress of 1918:

> At the Congress of the International Psycho-Analytic Association in Budapest in 1918, Freud suddenly announced that I had an important statement to make. Taken by surprise, I had to improvise, and made the motion that every analyst be analyzed. This was opposed by [Otto] Rank and [Viktor] Tausk. I was puzzled by their opposition; the motives behind it still remain unknown to me. It was only in 1926, at the Congress in Bad Homburg, which was chaired by Karl Abraham, that this motion was carried. It was then that training analysis was introduced. From then on it became obligatory for anyone who wanted to carry out analytical treatment himself.[3]

These comments, taken from Nunberg's memoirs, to which Anna Freud wrote a preface in 1968, clearly characterize the situation of that period. Since there was no training analysis before 1926, in 1918 Freud could not have violated regulations that did not yet exist. The training analysis of one's own child, especially one of the opposite sex, is certainly problematic. The necessary transference cannot occur during analysis with a member of the analyst's own family constellation, hence the Oedipal relationship cannot be analyzed.

Freud did not consider training analysis to be as strict an issue as today's Freudians do, although he defended it unambiguously in the last letter he wrote to Edoardo Weiss in 1935, which has frequently been quoted since. Freud was replying to Weiss's question of whether he should analyze his son.

Dear Doctor,

I am glad that you could give me much better news about the chances for your publications.

Concerning the analysis of your hopeful son, that is certainly a ticklish business. With a younger, promising brother it might be done more easily. With [my] own daughter I succeeded well. There are special difficulties and doubts with a son.

Not that I really would warn you against a danger; obviously everything depends upon the two people and their relationship to each other. You know the difficulties. It would not surprise me if you were successful in spite of them. It is difficult for an outsider to decide. I would not advise you to do it and have no right to forbid it.

With cordial greetings,
Yours, Freud[4]

The letter dissuaded Weiss from analyzing his son. That the analysis of Freud's daughter was successful cannot be doubted. None of Anna Freud's critics could ever reproach her for unconsciously seeing her own problems in her patients.

In her theoretical discussions about the problems of training analysis, Anna Freud later acknowledged not only its indisputable advantages but also its shortcomings. For example, some of the shortcomings pertain to an incompletely resolved transference situation: "It is well known that many analysts suffer from . . . undissolved ties to their training analysts . . . or defend themselves violently against dependence by means of theoretical innovations which bear the character of rationalizations."[5]

A great deal of absurd "loyalty" as well as many superfluous innovations could be avoided if the problem were adequately dealt with. The problems of "orthodoxy" on one hand and of "dissidence" on the other, which have so often eclipsed the history of psychoanalysis, are also related to the problem of training analysis. Anna Freud pointed out that the training analysand does not resolve his relationship with the analyst as a patient does. On the contrary, the former enters the analytic world, becomes a member of the association his training analyst belongs to, and eventually even becomes his colleague. No one can determine whether this is the result of a resolved or an unresolved transference.

The postwar period also coincided with Anna Freud's preparations for her teachers' examination. Since elementary-school teachers were required to be able to sing, she took voice lessons with Hedwig Hitschmann. The lessons were also meant as a kind of therapy, to help Anna Freud overcome her dread of public speaking. Hedwig Hitschmann was a singer at the Vienna State Opera, one of the world's best opera houses during that period, and gave numerous concerts. Since her marriage in 1913 to Eduard Hitschmann, one of Freud's oldest and most loyal supporters, she had gradually converted to the occupations of voice teacher and speech therapist. We now know the potential psychotherapeutic significance of speech lessons and breathing techniques. At any event, the lessons were very successful, inasmuch as Anna Freud passed her examination and became a brilliant lecturer. The bulk of her printed work consists of her lectures.

The postwar period, especially the years 1920 and 1921, was marked by the oppressive economic situation and cheerless prospects for the future. Friends still provided the Freud family with food. As soon as it was again possible, Eitingon sent food from Hungary, as he had during the early years of the war. Since 1926, Eitingon had been in Miskolc, Ferenczi's hometown, working as the head physician of the psychiatric division of a military hospital. After the war he moved to Berlin, where he was able to acquire food from Poland. At that time Freud thought that the fate of psychoanalysis would be determined in Berlin. Further developments confirmed his conjecture, since during those years Berlin became, even if briefly, the center of German-speaking culture.[6] Following a proposal by Eitingon, the Berlin Psychoanalytic Society opened a polyclinic on July 19, 1919, one of the few rays of hope to light up that year. However, the economic situation became dire in October 1919. Freud wrote to Eitingon that all his savings would be spent in about a year and a half. That Freud thought he might even have to move to England, where his two brothers were buried and where he later would suffer the same fate, rings almost as a premonition.[7] But we only wish to show here that the thought of England as a country of refuge arose twenty years before Freud emigrated: he entertained the thought of emigrating to England relatively early and, given his personal reasons, ultimately could consider no other country for this purpose. On the other hand, the fact that he stayed in Vienna so tenaciously reveals how attached he was to the city that had become his home very early in life. Only the massive pressure of the Nazis was able to persuade him to leave.

As always, Eitingon acted very responsibly in Freud's difficult situation. He first sent food to the Freuds by his own parents, who were passing through Vienna. In November 1919, Freud also received from Eitingon 3,000 Swedish crowns as a safe deposit in hard foreign currency, a considerable sum and a princely present in those times. In a detailed acknowledgment, Freud described to Eitingon the conditions in his home, where his three sons and the three women—his wife, his sister-in-law, and Anna—were again united:

> As I was busy with four analyses in the morning, I had no time to think about it, and read the letter out loud at luncheon during which, apart from my wife, three sons and our young daughter (whom you know) were present. It had a strange effect: the three boys seemed satisfied, but the two women were up in arms and my daughter declared—evidently she can't stand the demolition of her father complex—that as a punishment (!) she wouldn't go to Berlin for Christmas.[8]

The Eitingons had invited her to spend several days with them in Berlin. When she finally did decide to go to Berlin for Christmas, a railroad strike interfered with her plans, but she made up for it in 1920, when she visited the Eitingons twice.

Another ray of hope in the grim year of 1919 was the establishment of the Internationaler Psychoanalytischer Verlag, at the beginning of the year. This publishing house was made possible by a generous gift from the industrialist Anton von Freund. Its function was to publish psychoanalytic books and journals. During the war it had often seemed that the psychoanalytic journals would have to be discontinued. Now the house took charge of the *Internationale Zeitschrift für Psychoanalyse* and *Imago*. Anna Freud was active in the house from its inception. But the joy that independence from other publishers brought was soon troubled, since Anton von Freund's funding capital dwindled following the rapid currency devaluation. At the beginning of 1920, Eitingon, who had always been willing to sacrifice what he had, saw that further financial support was needed. One of his brothers-in-law from New York was in Berlin at that time, and Eitingon stirred his enthusiasm for psychoanalysis. As a token of appreciation, he donated $5,000 after he returned to New York, an enormous sum at the time, which Eitingon put at Freud's free disposal. Freud used part of the money to raise the salaries of Otto Rank and Theodor Reik, who worked as editors at the publishing house. In May 1920, Eitingon insisted that another worker at the publishing house be adequately compensated—namely, Anna Freud.

When Anna Freud visited the Eitingons in Berlin in 1920, she delivered to Eitingon Freud's personal Committee membership ring: "Anna is finally bringing you the ring you have long since been entitled to. I took it off my finger because I find nothing to be beautiful in this impoverished time. You deserve it more than anyone else; you could also wear it in my memory, for you have become a valuable friend and a precious son to me."[9]

The Committee, founded as early as 1913 at the suggestion of Ernest Jones, after Alfred Adler, Wilhelm Stekel, and C. G. Jung had withdrawn from the psychoanalytic movement, gained significance again in 1920. Originally the Committee was a body accessible only to initiates. Its functions were to prevent or settle disputes, and to keep quarrels out of Freud's radius. In particular, it was to protect

Freud against all external attacks and thus allow him to pursue the building of psychoanalytic theory undisturbed. Jones's detailed description of the Committee's creation and history informs the reader, among other things, about the close connection between two areas of psychoanalysis still considered important: theory and organization (psychoanalytic therapy would be the third area). The purpose of the meetings was to further the consolidation of theory and to defend it against unwarranted attacks.

The first Committee members were Ferenczi, Abraham, Jones, Hanns Sachs, and Rank. In 1913, each of them received an antique Greek gem from Freud's collection, which they then set in gold rings. During the war, the Committee had to suspend some of its activities. Anton von Freund was to be accepted as its sixth member in 1919. But his illness and death cancelled the plan, and Eitingon was accepted instead. That Anna Freud delivered the ring to Eitingon was not fortuitous. In the same year she had also received the Committee membership ring from her father, and in 1924, after Rank's withdrawal, she "officially" became a member.

Despite its external difficulties, 1920 was a crucial year for Anna Freud. Henceforth her life would be insolubly bound to psychoanalysis. If until 1920 she had been primarily a teacher and secondarily a student of psychoanalysis, now, at the age of twenty-four, Anna Freud had to be considered fully a psychoanalyst. On January 26, 1920, her sister Sophie Halberstadt succumbed to the influenza epidemic that was then raging in Europe. The words in which Freud communicated his feelings and the event to Ferenczi have often been quoted since in similar situations: "As a confirmed unbeliever I have no one to accuse and realize that there is no place where I could lodge a complaint. . . . Deep down I sense a bitter, irreparable narcissistic injury. My wife and Annerl are profoundly affected in a more human way."[10]

These words are certainly appropriate. The shock the mother and sister felt differed from the father's; it was more human, hence finally surmountable. Given the adverse circumstances, only the eldest sister, Mathilde, and her husband, Robert Hollitscher, were able to attend the funeral in Hamburg. The usual railroad traffic had been halted, but they were able to board another, so-called children's train.[11] Sigmund and Anna Freud were able to visit Halberstadt in Hamburg only after the August vacation. Eitingon joined them there later to travel with them to The Hague.

The Sixth International Psychoanalytic Congress was held in The Hague in September 1920. Participants from Budapest, Vienna, and Berlin had difficulties meeting the travel expenses. But the necessary money could be taken from the donation of Eitingon's brother-in-law, and Anna Freud was thus able to attend, even after a short stopover in Hamburg.

At this conference, attended by fifty-seven participants, the question of a psychoanalytic diploma was first discussed. The necessity for a diploma arose because a great deal of "wild analysis" was being practiced under the name of psychoanalysis, particularly in the United States. It is interesting that at such an early stage of its international reputation, psychoanalysis had to be protected against misuse. There is a widespread assumption today that other forms of psychotherapy lean on psychoanalysis—as either friend or foe—because it had gained such high recognition. For example, while psychodrama and Gestalt therapy claim to be the most significant psychotherapeutic lines working *alongside* of psychoanalysis, an explicit antipsychoanalytic hostility exudes from behavior therapy. The fact that "wild analysis" began so early indicates that the theoretical edifice of psychoanalysis must have harbored seductive impulses from the very beginning.

The Hague congress was Anna Freud's first opportunity to meet other analysts. Jones reports that, at a dinner the English group gave for Sigmund and Anna Freud, the latter suprised the participants with "a graceful little speech in very good English."[12] During the second half of her life, English became the language in which she wrote, taught, and practiced therapy.

After the congress Anna Freud had planned to travel to England for the second time. As a result of the war, however, she was unable to obtain a visa. Father and daughter traveled instead through Holland in the company of Jan van Emden and Johann H. W. van Ophuijsen, and on September 28, 1920, the Freuds parted in Osnabrück. Freud returned to Vienna via Berlin, while Anna Freud traveled again to Hamburg to help her widowed brother-in-law for some time with the household. On her way back she stopped, for the second time that year, in Berlin at the Eitingons', where she remained for several weeks; in October 1920, Eitingon's father called on the Freuds in Vienna on his way to Palestine.

Max Eitingon

Max Eitingon's substantial significance for psychoanalysis, especially its organizational aspect, has usually been underestimated even by psychoanalysts. On the one hand, he bears the charge of meager scientific originality; on the other, he is envied for the indisputable appreciation Freud showed for him. Finally, he is saddled with the claim that Freud's affection was based foremost on the extensive financial support Eitingon made available to the Freuds. Among these claims, it is true only that Eitingon's theoretical work was not very significant. Only sixteen of his forty-five published works address specific psychoanalytic issues; the rest consist of work reports and birthday and memorial addresses.

Eitingon was born on July 26, 1881, in Mogilev, Russia. Because he stuttered, he was not even able to pass the Abitur examination and therefore could only choose a limited number of courses at the University of Leipzig, but he was finally able to study medicine in Heidelberg, Marburg, and Zurich. He officially graduated in Zurich in 1909 under Eugen Bleuler, but C. G. Jung was actually his advisor and drew Freud to his attention. Eitingon always put his business and organizational talents unselfishly at the disposal of the psychoanalytic movement, and bore resulting family discords without complaint.

After World War I, Eitingon founded and financed the Berlin Polyclinic. In 1921 and later, he often rescued the almost bankrupt Internationaler Psychoanalytischer Verlag. He laid down plans for a uniform international training program for psychoanalysts, and in 1925 he became the first president of the International Training Commission.

Forced to emigrate in 1933, he chose Jerusalem for his new home. There he founded the psychoanalytic institute that today bears his name, using the Berlin institute as a model. Throughout those difficult times, Eitingon correctly perceived the economical and political situation. When problems nonetheless arose, it was most often because his advice had not been followed. Freud, who had both theoretical and organizational talents—as the two thousand letters he wrote to Rank will fully disclose when they are published—indeed valued Eitingon's gift for organization and always followed his advice, even after his emigration to England. Eitingon died in Jerusalem on July 3, 1943.

First Independent Works

In 1921, Anna Freud actively confronted psychoanalytical problems for the first time. During that year she translated from English a book by Julien Varendonck, *The Psychology of Daydreams*.[1] A rather forgotten author now, Varendonck worked on the psychology of court witnesses at the beginning of World War I. Influenced by Freud's writings, he wrote several essays and books after the war, of which *The Psychology of Daydreams* was his first psychoanalytical work. In this relatively unassuming book, Varendonck described how he inadvertently came upon Freud's *Interpretation of Dreams* while serving as an interpreter in the English army. He was at once inspired and attempted to analyze his own daydreams as Freud had analyzed his (night) dreams. The originality of the book lies in its unabashed communication of his own wishful dreams—which breaks off, however, when the stream of thought veers toward sexuality.

Anna Freud not only proved to be a masterful translator—the book reads as if it had been written in German—but her treatment of the German language was equally exemplary. Thus, she corrected Varendonck's quotation of Alphonse Maeder with a sharp-witted footnote. By omitting in the German edition the "synthetic part" that constituted half of the English volume, she spotlighted the more original first part of the book. Her interest in daydreams persisted, and in the following year she published her first essay, which focused essentially on daydreams.

Anna Freud spent the summer vacation of 1921, from mid-July to mid-August, with her mother on the Salzkammer estate in Aussee, while Freud traveled with his sister-in-law Minna to the Badgastein health resort. On August 14, the family was united again in Seefeld, Tyrol, where Anna Freud was present during the visits of van Emden, whom she had met in Holland, of A. A. Brill from the United States, and of Ferenczi from Hungary.

During the same year, Anna Freud also worked on "Beating Fantasies and Daydreams," her first independent manuscript. At the same time she met two personalities who were to become important later in her life: Lou Andreas-Salomé and August Aichhorn. Each had a different significance for her first work. Anna Freud maintained a deep bond with both.

Lou Andreas-Salomé

Freud evidently welcomed a friendship between Lou Andreas-Salomé and his daughter Anna. He had met Andreas-Salomé when she first visited Vienna, from October 1912 until April 1913, and had been in correspondence with her since. Both Freud and Andreas-Salomé frequently mentioned Anna Freud in their letters, mostly to suggest that a meeting between the two women would be desirable. In 1917, Andreas-Salomé wrote:

> The tone of your letter gave me to hope that your anxiety on behalf of your three sons is somewhat less acute at this moment—may it remain so! I am sorry that I did not get to know your youngest daughter in 1912/13—I was about to do so on one occasion, but, alas, she escaped me. Perhaps she has become your poet-translator from foreign tongues? Or perhaps even a poetess on her own account? That would be the finest translation of her father's psychoanalysis into a feminine medium. [1]

Before the congress at The Hague in 1920, Freud wrote: "I intend to take my daughter Anna with me to The Hague; she has long been anxious to meet you." [2]

Again Andreas-Salomé wrote, "Warmest greetings to you all, among whom I include of course your daughter Anna, whom I have so long wanted to meet."[3]

When Lou Andreas-Salomé visited Vienna again in September 1921, she was a guest at 19 Berggasse. She had already expressed her joy at that prospect with her particularly contagious exuberance: "And now like a wish-dreaming teenager I picture to myself every day a little of what it will be like when I shall really and truly be your guest."[4]

For Freud, the meeting between Andreas-Salomé and his daughter was so important that he wrote, "My daughter will let her projected journey to Hamburg depend on your arrangements."[5]

On November 8, 1921, Andreas-Salomé finally left Göttingen for Munich. She arrived in Vienna the following day, where Anna Freud and a servant, Fräulein Betti, met her at the train station.[6] Since it was an evening when the Wednesday Society of Viennese psychoanalysts convened, the two women went straight to the meeting.

On her second visit to Freud's Viennese circle, Andreas-Salomé was sixty years old and already surrounded by a European legend whose stereotypical aspects have survived unaltered. Friedrich Nietzsche had loved her when she was twenty-one, but she had refused his marriage proposal. Later she was Rilke's longstanding friend. She had met Nietzsche and Rilke at a time when their reputations were still obscure. Freud, on the other hand, was already a mature figure at the height of his creativity when he met Lou Andreas-Salomé in 1912.

Much has been written about this woman; most often she has been considered a "femme fatale,"[7] and her feminine gifts were more trusted than her intellect. She has even been saddled with a secret love affair with Freud, yet she was not the woman to keep such a love affair secret had it existed. As one of the great intellectual inspirations of the nineteenth and twentieth centuries, she has remained undiscovered. What was it about her that attracted great minds so irresistibly? She was unquestionably an intelligent and well-educated woman. And even if the 20 books and 123 essays she published were not of enduring value, her intellectual reflections on her friendships with great men such as Nietzsche,[8] Rilke, and especially Freud[9] are still enlightening. One can infer from these writings what her gift actually consisted in: she asked those questions that men who outranged her intellectually needed in order to clarify and articulate their own ideas. This would explain her friendship with significant men who, in a certain sense, worshiped themselves in her. Andreas-Salomé had a keen sense for the creative, which she was able to arouse, but she was also able to detect genius long before the world and sometimes even before its possessor recognized it.

Men's irresistible attraction to Lou Andreas-Salomé is part of her legend. Yet she affected women with promising intellect with equal intensity. One of them was Edith Weigert, the great psychoanalyst, who did her training analysis with Andreas-Salomé (as did Weigert's sister and the latter's husband).[10] Anna Freud was another, though the literature has paid little attention to this fact.

Andreas-Salomé's visit in 1921 must have been extraordinarily inspiring for Anna Freud; the two women were together for almost the entire time. On December 7, 1921, they attended the dress rehearsal of Arthur Schnitzler's play *Living Hours*, four one-act pieces which had first been produced in Berlin in 1902 and were now being performed at the German Popular Theater in Vienna. A week later, on December 15, they were both invited to dinner at the poet's house. A legendary party gathered that evening: Lou Andreas-Salomé, Anna Freud, Arthur Schnitzler.[11] What could they have talked about? Human comedy? Human tragedy? About the decadence of the upper-middle class of fin-de-siècle Vienna? About the physician as a writer—Schnitzler was a physician—and about Schnitzler's relationship to Sigmund Freud?

Perhaps they talked about Anna Freud's first independent psychoanalytic work, which appeared a year later, in 1922, under the title "Beating Fantasies and Day-dreams" and whose starting point was a 1919 essay by her father, " 'A Child Is Being Beaten': A Contribution to the Study of the Origin of Sexual Perversions."[12] In it, Freud investigated the phenomenon that hysterical and obsessive-compulsive people often report from their fantasies: "a child is beaten"—a pleasure-arousing fantasy most often followed by masturbation. Andreas-Salomé had also shown interest in Freud's essay, and, a year earlier, had expressed her views in a detailed letter:

> I was still more absorbed by the discussion in V, 3 (has 4 not appeared at all?) on "A Child is Being Beaten," on which I have a few brief comments to make. The first is occasioned by a questionnaire put to a class of girls, which was conducted by Helene Stöcker. The answers revealed that a large majority of the girls in playing with their dolls found pleasure in beating the doll-chil-dren, and in every case this applied *only to their favorite dolls*. But the answers also revealed that the girls imagined that they were providing *plea-sure* in this way, not only for themselves, but also to some extent for the dolls—so that beaters and beaten both enjoyed the experience. Both sadism and masochism in their original identity play their part in this. It is my view, in general, that as products of the *unconscious* they are in fact identical in their oppositeness, and when they later become more strongly differentiated they are already influenced by the ego-tendencies of the conscious personal-ity. When that stage has been reached, sadism can, it is true, express pure *Schadenfreude* [pleasure at another's harm] and satisfaction (without any ac-tual sexual pleasure), as in the first phase that you mentioned concerning the sight of a child being punished; or else masochism can arise on the basis of a sense of guilt, because the ego has overreached itself. But this would be a secondary masochism and mixed in its emotional content, and would also lack the original purely sexual excitation.
>
> I cannot get rid of the feeling that primary masochism is a pre-sadistic one, which is then resuscitated secondarily, after this has been made possible

by the small portion of ego-consciousness which was necessary to produce the sadism. In the primary stage there is an identity of outer world and self, where memory does not exist. It can however survive this stage, and can play its part when pain is inflicted on the ego by the hand of a loved object, and there revives the blissful memory of that primal undifferentiated state, where no distinction is felt between the ego and the non-ego, in which indeed one has not yet acquired an ego. Unfortunately, a theme like this cannot be dealt with satisfactorily in correspondence, but there is something there about which I would gladly unburden myself, to be sure that I was at one with you on the subject.[13]

Even if Andreas-Salomé's comments are neither very clear nor particularly original, it is nonetheless obvious how her questions stimulated her partner to think. If one bears this in mind, her diary also becomes more understandable. About her visit to Vienna and her conversations there, she wrote:

> On November 8 left for Munich.
> Reached Vienna evening 9th November; train was late. Anna and Frl. Betti recognized me; Freud himself would have come to the station had there not been a [Wednesday] Society meeting that evening. I have only just remembered that. Almost as soon as we had reached the Berggasse Anna and I set off again for the meeting. Stormy; long wait for a bus; late. But how happy and cheerful was our arrival there. Freud unaltered; 50 people; one was missing (Viktor Tausk). I looked for him everywhere, so that it seemed to me that all the old familiar faces were missing. Three of us together returned home late; I took up my quarters in my magnificent room with its verandah and its rosewood bed.
> When I fell asleep in this bed, which generally happened very late, I still went on talking with Freud in my dreams; and often too, because I realized that he was overburdened with analyses during the day and could not remember what we had been discussing, I settled many problems for myself in my dreams. Indeed when we went out late at night for a walk (often the only time in the day when he can get out) we talked now and then on quite different matters and he frequently analysed Vienna, as it were; the streets under their wintry snow reminded him of the city's remotest past. One sensed how easily such a re-creation of the past came to him and one was reminded of the antique objects in his study and that the archaeologist had created the psychoanalyst in him.
> Anna and I used to sit with him in the evenings in his back room to talk about our theme in which we were immediately and involuntarily absorbed. From then on I always spent the mornings in Anna's room; she would wrap me up in a wonderful rug and squat down herself by the stove. Freud would come in for a few moments and talk with us and share in our work. I still often think

of these minutes and of my walks with him and of the evening hours spent in his company.

I always found him in a serene mood, never grumpy. Fundamentally he remains, no doubt, a man of pessimistic tendency, as I have always know him, but it is not merely self-control that strikes one in him, but his very passive attitude towards life, his cheerfulness and his kindness. And this attitude of serene well-being struck me as characteristic of the entire Freud family. It even characterized his mother at eighty with her wonderful inner vigour and it endowed her sister Rosa [Graf] with a charm which defied both ear-trumpet and old age. Both Freud's daughters, Anna and Mathilde, have it in abundance. Mathilde still remains today the good, wise elder daughter, always ready to help, while Anna, though her development has been on deeper and more difficult lines, is a person of the kindest disposition.

I also always admired Frau Freud's ability to fulfil her part unerringly in things that concerned her. She was always devoted and always ready to make decisions, but she did not take it upon herself to interfere in tasks which she considered her husband's; she was always sure of herself and never a mere spectator. It was doubtless through her that the upbringing of the children remained remote from psychoanalysis, yet this was certainly not due to any indifference on Freud's part. But he did derive a certain satisfaction, I now see, in knowing that his domestic circle was far removed from any public conflict and his wife's part in this was a source of pleasure to him. In any case their domestic life made a deep impression on me and I began to reflect on the false distinction that is usually drawn between being "free" and being "tied to one's family." It is usually a grain of "morbidity" that disturbs the potential balance between freedom and social obligations (which include the obligations of family ties).

Through our acquantance with [August] Aichhorn, Anna and I thought about the problem from the other side, i.e., from that of abnormal children. [In the margin:] (How amused Freud was when I specially asked that Aichhorn should be invited to the house during my visit: "Out of 75 analysts you have inexorably picked out the one non-Jew.") Aichhorn is without a doubt a tremendously valuable find for us. We also learnt a great deal from [Siegfried] Bernfeld and I am grateful to him for the mornings which he devoted to our discussions.

It was only rarely that Anna and I went out, but we did visit Eugenie Schwarzwald several times, and with regard to her I must confirm that one cannot have everything in life; for if one leads as social a life as she does it leaves one no time for reflection or for individual contacts. Apart from these visits we only went to see [Richard] Beer-Hofmann (Salten, Schnitzler), and this relationship was as it always has been and always will be. Zemek [Dr. Friedrich Pineles] I visited on my own. On the very last day that my ticket was valid I left early in the morning, accompanied by Anna, who was not allowed beyond the ticket barrier, but then when I was already in my carriage she appeared.

Listening to Anna talk about her father; about picking mushrooms when they were children. When they went collecting mushrooms he always told them to go into the wood quietly and he still does this; there must be no chattering and they must roll up the bags they have brought under their arms, so that the mushrooms shall not notice; when their father found one he would cover it quickly with his hat, as though it were a butterfly. The little children— and now his grandchildren—used to believe what he said, while the bigger ones smiled at his credulity; even Anna did this, when he told her to put fresh flowers every day at the shrine of the Virgin which was near the wood, so that it might help them in their search. The children were paid in pennies for the mushrooms they had found, while the best mushrooms of all (it was always Ernst who found it) got a florin. It was the quality and not the quantity of the mushrooms that mattered.[14]

It is therefore out of the question that Andreas-Salomé participated in the writing of "Beating Fantasies and Daydreams," but with her questions and tendency to relentless discussion she no doubt assumed a midwife's role, and the mode of discussion clearly encouraged Anna Freud immensely. Anna Freud prefaced the German publication of her essay: "This paper was written on the basis of several discussions I had with Frau Lou Andreas-Salomé, to whom I am very grateful for her interest and participation."[15]

Freud's part in the manuscript was limited to the ten-minute conversations he was able to squeeze in between his analytic sessions. "The magnificent room with its verandah and its rosewood bed" must have been the family's former dining room, a large, somewhat dark room with a veranda in front and a passage to the master bedroom on one side, which E. E. Engelman redesigned as a living room (1938 plan).[16] The other two doors led to Freud's dressing room and to the hall.[17]

Andreas-Salomé mentioned above two important persons in Anna Freud's life: Aichhorn and Bernfeld. To the first, as has been mentioned, Anna Freud remained loyal in both mind and soul. With the latter—and with Willie Hoffer, who must not be omitted in this context—she maintained a lifelong connection. In the Freud lectures she delivered in Vienna at the age of eighty-four, she still mentioned these two people with kind words. Anna Freud made a direct connection between the Baumgarten Nursery in Vienna, which Siegfried Bernfeld and Willie Hoffer founded in 1919, and the Hampstead Nurseries in London, which she founded in London during World War II.

A small but frequent error must be rectified in connection with Lou Andreas-Salomé. It has been claimed that Anna Freud completed her training analysis with Andreas-Salomé, and a passage from a letter Freud wrote on December 20, 1921, is quoted as evidence:[18]

Frau Lou left this morning, so this evening is the first moment I have had to answer yours of November 30–December 7, with its good news. She was a charming guest and is altogether an outstanding woman. *Anna discussed analytic topics* and visited a number of interesting people *with her*, and enjoyed being with her very much. [My italics.][19]

Even Hans Lobner, an expert in the history of psychoanalysis who turned to Anna Freud for information, was dissatisfied with her answer: "Oh, this was purely a friendly relationship." He thinks that "it may be said in support of the written version that half a century has since passed."[20] I think, however, that Anna Freud's answer is unequivocal, and the letter can therefore refer only to the many discussions between Anna Freud and Andreas-Salomé, including the intense discussion on "Beating Fantasies and Daydreams," in which Freud himself played a peripheral part.

We may claim that both the most important persons in Anna Freud's life and the themes she did not abandon for the rest of her life were already visible during these years. It was therefore a formative period. Anna Freud developed one of the few intimate friendships of her life with Lou Andreas-Salomé, and often visited her in her Göttingen house, "Loufried." We will of course know more about the discussions between the two women when the correspondence between them is published.* The correspondence between Sigmund Freud and Andreas-Salomé reveals that Freud—probably urged by Anna—twice gave hard currency to her. In 1922, Freud sent her 20,000 marks, to be sure at the low exchange rate of 1922;[21] another time he sent her U.S. $50 through Eitingon.[22] During that period Freud in fact had a good income from his analyses of several foreign patients, who paid him in highly desirable foreign currency, particularly American dollars. Abraham Kardiner, who had come to Vienna in October 1921 to spend six months in training analysis, was one of these clients.

In his memoirs,[23] Kardiner speaks at length of the rumors that circulated in the psychoanalytic circles of Vienna in 1921. Vienna has always been rife with spicy gossip, and the claim that someone was having a love affair with So-and-so was not necessarily slanderous, but was often meant—entirely or in part—as a special form of recognition. I know of significant Viennese figures who purposely do not deny false rumors about an alleged affair. Yet only a genuine Viennese can distinguish between a rumor's defamatory or complimentary tone.

That the almost twenty-seven-year-old Anna should be drawn into such rumors is quite understandable. Indeed, it would be quite astonishing had she not been linked with this or that person. Gossip connected Anna Freud alternately with Siegfried Bernfeld, Hans Lampl, Max Eitingon, and most obstinately with the unmarried Otto Rank, yet strangely enough not with August Aichhorn, although he would have been at least as appropriate a candidate. Each of these men was personally close to Anna Freud. Nevertheless, there was nothing to feed such suspicions.

*See above, pp. xii–xv.

Lecture at the Society

Anna Freud resumed her travels at the beginning of 1922. On March 2, she visited Eitingon's parents in Leipzig, where she met Esther Elkuss, Eitingon's youngest sister, whose daughter had just been born. Max Eitingon, always on the move, also came for a brief visit from Berlin. Anna Freud then left for Berlin and Hamburg, and between April 25 and May 5 she visited Lou Andreas-Salomé for the first time at "Loufried" in Göttingen. Anna returned home for her father's birthday on May 6, and brought a birthday letter from Göttingen in which Andreas-Salomé alluded to some of the feelings Anna Freud had stirred in her. Max Eitingon and his wife also arrived in Vienna to congratulate Freud.

On May 31, Anna Freud delivered her lecture "Beating Fantasies and Day-dreams" at the Vienna Psychoanalytic Society. Participants report that she had attended the sessions since about 1918, though without participating in the discussions. Similarly, Kardiner mentioned Anna Freud's silence with evident disapproval; she, on the other hand, stressed in the introduction to her lecture, and later as well, that it had been her intention *to learn*. Later she added that young people should not immediately elbow their way into discussions, but should listen first instead. That she now began to step forward and express herself meant that her learning stage in psychoanalysis was in her view completed.

The lecture, in which she mentioned colleagues we already know—Andreas-Salomé, Aichhorn, Bernfeld, and finally Freud himself—was significant foremost as a symbolic marker. Anna Freud now definitively established herself as a psychoanalyst and began her long series of lectures and writings.

The subject of her first lecture was equally significant. She gave an account of a girl who had the type of fantasies Freud described in his essay "A Child Is Being Beaten." The girl ended each of those beating scenes with masturbation. Anna Freud now expanded on what Freud had mentioned only marginally: that daydreams develop around the beating fantasies, assuming an important role for the person. The girl derived her ongoing stories from a book for boys in which a fifteen-year-old boy is kept captive by a feudal lord. In the fantasy, the feudal lord seems always on the verge of injuring the boy. But the denouement is not only positive; the feudal lord lavishes favor upon favor on the boy, and this arouses in the girl—at the climax of the scene—feelings of pleasure. Anna Freud pointed out that the progress in the stages of the beating fantasy and the daydream was always identical: in the beating fantasy, there was first an infliction of pain (beating) followed by an orgasm through masturbation; in the daydream, the feudal lord inflicted harm (for example, confinement in a dungeon), but then granted favors that triggered a feeling of pleasure similar to that brought about by masturbation, which was here avoided. Furthermore, Anna Freud showed that the girl knew nothing about the parallel operations of those processes. The daydream and the beating fantasy therefore had the same structure, and the psychoanalytic therapy consisted in bringing the girl to this insight. It is noteworthy that Anna Freud used the word "structure" here ("But this structure also contains the important analogy between the nice stories and the beating fantasy which our daydreamer did not suspect"),[1] though Freud himself did not use the word in the same context. It was not until the past decade that A. Lorenzer described working out such repeated structures as essential to psychoanalytic work.[2]

In this relatively small work, we see that Anna Freud already grasped the essence of psychoanalytical processes. In her subsequent works she articulated the particulars of the psychoanalytic process with increasing clarity. The aforementioned case of a girl on the threshold between childhood and adolescence was the only example she used in her presentation. Henceforth Anna Freud would dedicate her life to psychoanalytic work with children and adolescents, and her ability to disentangle the complexities of a problem gradually became her strength. Thus, the image she presented during her first lecture already adumbrated the entire future character. To be sure, closer acquaintance with her later developments makes this even more apparent.

We know that every psychologist uses some of his personality as a source of knowledge and perception. What Anna Freud disclosed here about herself is therefore an apposite question. Given the case history's protagonist (a girl) and its themes (the girl's sexuality), as well as the significance of the Oedipal situation (the need to compete with siblings for the father's exclusive love), perfunctory observation would argue that Anna Freud had described herself and her own daydreams. But nothing confirms that such assumptions are even partly correct. Moreover, it is hardly probable that Anna Freud would have described her own life so unreservedly, or that she was so unaware of her writing as to offer the reader an intimate self-description. As plausible as it may seem that Anna Freud did speak of herself in some parts of the essay, these are nonetheless difficult to locate. In any event, the source of the notes on the fiteen-year-old girl remains unexplained. The case certainly did not come from her father's practice, since this would imply that Freud analyzed daydreams as part of his work. The idea that he may have is clearly refuted by Andreas-Salomé's reference to the origins of the essay. Nor could it have come from Anna Freud's own practice, because two years later, on March 23, 1923, Freud wrote to Andreas-Salomé: "Anna has *now* also joined the practicing analysts, but at least has started off cautiously and still enjoys her work." [My italics.][3]

At the business meeting of June 13, 1922, Anna Freud was accepted as a member of the Vienna Psychoanalytic Society. In his correspondence with Andreas-Salomé, Freud expressed special joy at the event. At the urging of the new member—Anna Freud—Andreas-Salomé was also accepted as a member at the very next meeting, held on June 21, 1922. On the same evening Anna Freud wrote to her friend, informing her of the acceptance. Andreas-Salomé effusively expressed her gratitude for being exempted from an admission lecture.[4] Although always ready for a discussion, she proved strangely incapable of giving a lecture. In his next letter, Freud alluded to the exemption, and, to vindicate Andreas-Salomé, claimed that she had in any case influenced his daughter's lecture: "Shortly beforehand your shadow was to be seen flitting across the stage in the shape of Anna's really excellent lecture."[5]

While Freud traveled to Badgastein on June 30, Anna Freud went to Göttingen, where she arrived on July 6 to spend the summer vacation again with Andreas-Salomé. Her mother stopped briefly in Göttingen on August 3 and 4, and mother and daughter then traveled to Obersalzberg. Freud had moved to lodgings in the Hochgebirgskurheim on August 1, and most of his family gradually joined him.[6] At the end of September they arrived in Berlin, where the Committee met on September 23 and the International Psychoanalytic Congress was held on September 25–27. Anna Freud attended the congress in Lou Andreas-Salomé's company, but did not present a paper.

Beginning an Independent Practice

In 1964, Anna Freud briefly described her early psychoanalytic practice. Her first patients suffered from: 1) *globus hystericus*; 2) a fully developed compulsion neurosis: an adolescent girl surrounded her mother with compulsive care and almost killed her by wrapping her in warm shawls (finally the police had to be called to release the mother); 3) work disturbance; and 4) phobia. Later Anna Freud listed more disturbances: psychic traumas, seduction, perversion, delinquency, mania, and schizophrenia, which had been referred to her with the diagnosis of "neurosis."[1]

The beginning of Anna Freud's analytic practice also prompted a rearrangement of the apartment at 19 Berggasse. She received her own consulting room, which was located next to her bedroom and across from her father's consulting room. She had given up teaching at the elementary school of the Cottage Lyceum to devote herself entirely to psychoanalysis.

But the joy she found in her independent practice and in discovering the causes of the psychic disturbances of her patients, until then known to her only from professional literature or case descriptions, was soon to be clouded. From March 23, 1923, until the end of the month, she was able to visit Lou Andreas-Salomé in Göttingen again to continue verbally their written exchange of thoughts. But in August Freud's illness broke out, entailing many operations and bringing about a total conversion in the family's lifestyle, finally resulting in Freud's death sixteen years later.

Ernest Jones, Felix Deutsch, Hans Pichler, who was Freud's physician later that year, and especially Max Schur, who had been Freud's personal physician since 1928, have frequently and vividly described the history of Freud's illness and the duties it imposed on Anna Freud. On April 20, the growth in Freud's mouth was incompletely excised in the first operation. Freud was not fully informed about the diagnosis. Neither he nor his physician—Markus Hajek at the beginning—had clearly informed the family about the surgery and the reasons for it. Only after the surgery and following a heavy hemorrhage was the family notified and requested to bring several belongings, since Freud had to remain in the clinic overnight. Quoting Ernest Jones, Schur revealed Hajek's highly dangerous negligence and irresponsibility in Freud's case, as well as the unpredictable changes Anna Freud had to handle from hour to hour:

> Upon their arrival at the hospital, "Frau Professor" Freud and Anna found Freud sitting on a kitchen chair, covered with blood. There was no nurse or physician in attendance. What follows now is the description pieced together by Jones from information supplied by Deutsch, Freud, and Anna Freud:
> "The ward sister sent the two ladies home at lunch time, when visitors were not allowed, and assured them the patient would be all right. When they returned an hour or two later they learned that he had had an attack of profuse bleeding, and to get help had rung the bell, which was, however, out of order; he himself could neither speak nor call out. The friendly dwarf, however, had rushed for help, and after some difficulty the bleeding was stopped; perhaps his action saved Freud's life. Anna then refused to leave again and spent the night sitting by her father's side. He was weak from loss of blood, was half-drugged from the medicines, and was in great pain. During the night she and the nurse became alarmed at his condition and sent for the house surgeon, who, however, refused to get out of bed. The next morning Hajek demonstrated the case to a crowd of students, and later in the day Freud was allowed to go home."[2]

The results of the tissue test showed epithelial cancer. On October 4 and 12, and finally on November 12, Pichler performed the necessary radical surgery, removing considerable parts of the upper and lower right jaw, of the right soft gum, and of the mucous membrane of the cheek and tongue. The required prosthesis became an unremitting torture for Freud, and only Anna completely mastered the extremely complicated technique of insertion and removal.

The family suffered a further heavy blow of fate when Heinele—Anna Freud's nephew and the son of Sophie, who had died four years earlier—died of tubercular encephalitis in Freud's apartment on June 19. Freud had developed an intimate attachment to his grandchild, as he indicated to Katá and Lajos Levy in a very moving letter punctuated by repeated attempts at self-detachment. No doubt, the ever-present fact of life's transience was borne in on the Freud family with horrible clarity during the summer of 1923, in fact *after* Freud had written his most important works on his theory of the death instinct. Such was the first year of Anna Freud's independent practice as a psychoanalyst.

We have run somewhat ahead of events. The summer between the first excision and the radical surgery should have been a period of recovery and relaxation for Freud as much as for his wife and daughter. Indeed, Anna traveled with her father to Badgastein and from there to Lavarone in the southern Tyrol, where they stayed at the Hotel du Lac. Freud's condition deteriorated so much, however, that his daughter urged him to send for Felix Deutsch, who immediately made the correct diagnosis and initiated all the necessary arrangements for what was to take place later that year. The Committee had meanwhile convened nearby in San Cristoforo; Anna Freud and Felix Deutsch walked there and back together. Though obviously suspicious, Anna Freud didn't yet know what her father's illness was. We are indebted to Jones for the account of how, on their way back from San Cristoforo, Anna Freud attempted to get more precise information from Felix Deutsch. She tested him by hinting that she could extend the visit to Rome, which she and her father had planned for that month. When Deutsch vehemently objected and insisted that she cancel the trip, Anna Freud knew the truth.[3]

The trip to Rome, originally planned for 1912, had always held symbolic significance for Freud. Jones suspected that Freud considered this his last opportunity to show Rome to his daughter, and therefore decided to take the trip despite his doctor's severe reservations. If Jones was correct, then Freud was indeed right. Except for small outings to Vienna's surroundings and several indispensable professional and medical trips to Berlin, the trip to Rome was his last before he was forced by the Nazis to emigrate to England. Father and daughter traveled in early September to Verona, which they had already visited together. From there they took the night coach to Rome. The incident in the train, often mentioned later, again clearly showed what Anna Freud's new duties were. When a stream of blood gushed from Freud's mouth, probably because a piece of tissue had loosened, she courageously helped stop the bleeding. This second and last long trip bound father and daughter to one another irrevocably, precisely also because both were able, notwithstanding their distress, to abandon themselves entirely to the charm of the city. In the notes to the correspondence between Sigmund Freud and Lou Andreas-Salomé, there is an excerpt from a letter Anna Freud had written to her older friend that conveys their surprisingly cheerful mood:

> Papa was much better than in Lavarone and he could really enjoy everything. Just in the last two days his mouth has been giving him trouble again. He has introduced me to everything so well, and made me feel at home among all the beauties, antiquities, and other sights, that now after the second week I feel that I quite belong, and as if I had been with him on all the other numerous occasions that he has been here.[4]

From Rome, Freud wrote a very brief letter to Andreas-Salomé in a similar tone: "So I am in Rome again and I note that it will do me good. I realize here for the first time what good company my little daughter is."[5]

They returned to Vienna on September 21. Several days later, Freud wrote to Eitingon: "Rome was very lovely, especially the first two weeks before the sirocco came and increased my pain. Anna was splendid. She understood and enjoyed everything, and I was very proud of her."[6]

Eight days later the series of radical surgeries began, which considerably impaired Freud's speaking ability. Just before Christmas, while strolling through Vienna with his wife and Anna, he met the poet Arthur Schnitzler, who made the following entry in his diary: "December 19, 1923: Errands in town, met Professor Freud with wife and daughter; he spoke, after his surgery, only with much difficulty!"[7]

The difficulties and concerns of that year did not hinder Anna Freud from publishing a small essay in *Imago,* rather insignificant at first glance, entitled "A Hysterical Symptom in a Child of Two Years and Three Months," which she had first presented at a session of the Vienna Society on March 4, 1923. The concise and clear language makes its complete quotation worthwhile.

> The little incident which I shall report here did not come under my observation. The child's mother, Hilda Sissermann, told me about it and gave me leave to publish it. She vouches for the correctness of the observation. Her story is as follows:
>
> At the time the incident occurred she and her children were living in a house with a courtyard in which there was a deep well. She had repeatedly told all the children that they were not to go near the well by themselves or even to play by it and, in order to deter them from doing so, she had vividly described to them the danger of falling in. One day she happened to be standing near the well with one of the children, a little boy of $2\frac{1}{4}$ years, when a full bucket of water which had just been drawn broke away from the chain and crashed down into the well. The incident obviously made a profound impression on the boy. He spoke of it as follows (as far as he could speak plainly at all): "Bucket was naughty; bucket fell into the well." He continued to talk of it with excitement,

making the bucket into a child, and finally he himself became the child that fell in.

After his mother and he had gone back into the house, while she was beginning to take off his little coat, he suddenly began to scream and cry, calling out that his arm hurt him, that they must not touch it, for he had "broken it to bits" when he fell into the well. His mother was convinced that it must be simply a fantasy and tried, first gently and then sternly, to make him obey her, but without success. At last she became frightened at the look of his arm, which he kept rigidly bent, so that the baby fat bulged out all over and made it look swollen. She began to wonder if, in leading him in, she could really have strained or sprained his arm, and so she sent for the doctor.

He was a clever physician, experienced in the ways of children. He gave it as his opinion that there was no evidence of a fracture, but was inclined to think that there was a very painful strain, and prescribed poultices. While the arm was being examined the child screamed as if in torments. His little coat had been cut away. He was put to bed and sat up in his cot and played, without ever moving his arm; when anyone tried to touch it he screamed. When he was asleep in the afternoon his mother tried to touch the arm, and immediately he woke up. Nevertheless she still felt a doubt about the reality of the injury. When the boy woke up from his afternoon nap, she sat down by his bed with a friend and played with him so long and in such a diverting way that he gradually became more lively and forgot everything, and finally stretched, lifted, turned, and dropped both arms, while playing at being a bird and flying. From that moment nothing more was heard of his arm hurting him.

This is the mother's account, and she adds that in his later development the child never again showed a tendency to symptom formation of this sort.

I think that in this case a large part of the mechanism of symptom formation is plainly evident. Probably the little boy had often wished to disobey his mother and go near the tempting well. On the basis of this wish feelings of guilt arose, which enabled him to put himself in the place of the bucket and to transfer to himself what he imagined to be the bucket's punishment.

But I think we may venture to supplement this with a further stage in the mechanism. We are probably justified in supposing that the feelings of guilt, which related to playing by the well, were reinforced by other, more serious feelings arising from the actual, and not merely fantasied, transgression of a prohibition; I refer to the prohibition of masturbation. If this were so, what the child saw happen at the well—the breaking away of the bucket from the chain and its fall into the depths of the water—must have signified to him a symbolic execution of the threat of castration: the loss of a guilty and highly prized bodily organ—first of all the penis itself, and then, by a process of displacement, the arm and the hand which had shared the forbidden activity.

From this point of view the child's symptom had a double meaning. The stiffness and immobility of his arm would represent the influence of moral tendencies, since these symptoms would constitute a direct punishment for masturbation and a renunciation of the habit. The way in which he held his arm tightly pressed to his body and anxiously shielded it from every interference from outside would represent a defense against the instinctual wish and a precautionary measure against the castration which he feared.

Of course, from a distance and without any possibility of testing one's supposition, it is impossible to decide how far the explanation I have suggested is really correct.[8]

Not only the vivid description of the small boy seems to me significant in this essay; the succinct and clear interpretation is especially noteworthy. It demonstrates convincingly that the child's paralysis can be interpreted like any other symptom of conversion hysteria—namely, as the immediate symbolic expression of a present conflict. Anna Freud showed very succinctly that this small, easily removable symptom was already multiply determined, and that scorned sexuality was already at this stage the predominant theme of symbol displacement. The objection Anna Freud raised at the end concerning her interpretation is actually insignificant and bears only on the absence of information on dreams, associations, or slips of the tongue normally used as supporting evidence. Hence the interpretation had to rely essentially on general experience, which, however, remained unaltered. This unpretentious observation shows above all that a twenty-seven-month-old child at a rudimentary stage of linguistic development displays essentially the same symptoms as a hysterical adult. Psychoanalytic theory—and no less technique—therefore requires no or only very slight changes to be applicable to a child. This inescapable conclusion, though not yet clearly articulated, would become the center of Anna Freud's psychoanalytic teachings.

One should also bear in mind that this was the case of a child, although Anna Freud was treating mostly adults at that time. She had evidently already found what was to be her life's main pursuit.

The Beginnings of Child Psychoanalysis

The year 1924 began under altered though normal circumstances. Freud was finally able to resume his practice on January 2. He paid as little attention as possible to the problems raised by his illness, and on January 4, 1924, he wrote to Oskar Pfister, "I also thank you for saying so little about my illness, which during the past few months has been taking up too much space in our lives."[1]

That Anna Freud had moved into the role of the privileged or—if you will—the especially burdened nurse from the very beginning is all too understandable, and has often been emphasized. It was Jones who most clearly described her new role as an expression of her strong bond with her father:

> From the onset of his illness to the end of his life Freud refused to have any other nurse than his daughter Anna. He made a pact with her at the beginning that no sentiment was to be displayed; all that was necessary was to be performed in a cool, matter-of-fact fashion, with the absence of emotion characteristic of a surgeon. This attitude, her courage and firmness, enabled her to adhere to the pact even in the most agonizing situations. [2]

Indeed, Anna Freud accepted the duty fate had clearly intended for her, and for sixteen years fulfilled it without any hesitation. During this rehabilitation period, the genuinely extraordinary and good relationship between Sigmund and Anna Freud matured in its historical depth and significance, and became decisive for Anna Freud's life. If we describe her as the favorite daughter in this context—which she actually was not—we in fact minimize her real merit. She not only became a nurse, but put herself entirely in the service of her father's scientific work. She took dictation, wrote manuscripts, and presented Freud's lectures at congresses. After the onset of his illness, Freud did not attend any psychoanalytic congresses, and attended only one meeting of the Vienna Psychoanalytic Society. For the most part he became invisible to the public, which caused a number of curious psychoanalysts who visited Vienna to complain, since they had hoped to meet him. When written contact was insufficient, and personal, verbal comments were required, Anna Freud became her father's mouthpiece. Out of consideration for his state of health, she did not even attend the International Psychoanalytic Congress in 1924, although the meetings were held, from April 21 to April 23, in nearby Salzburg. Freud had influenza and to recover spent Easter at the Semmering rest house on Vienna's outskirts. As indicated a letter he wrote to Lou Andreas-Salomé on March 14, 1924, Freud had planned to attend this congress.

Notwithstanding the difficult situation, Anna Freud was able to pursue her own scientific work. Even if she had merely receded behind her father personally and devoted herself exclusively to the management and publication of *his* work, her personal worth would not have suffered. World literature tells of many wives and daughters of famous men who gained high recognition by devoting decades of their lives to the augmentation of their husband's or father's fame. Dostoevsky's second wife, Anna, published a diary on her life with Dostoevsky. [3] Tolstoy's daughters took over the management of their father's work. [4] Erika Mann is another example of a daughter who, for the sake of her father's work, set her own talents aside.

Anna Freud's attitude to her father and his work invites a clear comparison. Robert Byck, who compiled Freud's essays on cocaine in one volume, [5] laid bare their historical development and added other works on the subject. (Central in this work was the discovery of cocainization, discovered through the anesthesia of the eye prior to surgery—considered an important finding even today.) We recall that Freud had done extensive research on cocaine, but that it was his friend Carl Koller who successfully applied the anesthesia while Freud was staying at his young wife's house in Hamburg. Both men had daughters who pursued their father's profession, and to both Byck grants ample room to speak. Hortense Koller-Becker highly and affably extolled her father's significance—this was his only scientific accomplishment—thereby underscoring herself as well. Anna Freud remained objective, sober, almost overly sparing, and allowed herself no effusive or personal words in her commentaries on the significance of her father's works on cocaine. She placed herself in the background.

In a sense, it is no wonder that Anna Freud is often viewed exclusively as "Freud's daughter," because she always accepted her duties willingly and without a trace of objection. Later she bore with the fact that many of the honors awarded to her were meant—overtly or not—for her father rather than for her personally, although her own work deserved no less honor. Her achievement was in child psychoanalysis; her reward was the deep penetration of the child's experiential and emotional world.

Anna Freud frequently remarked that she was not the first psychoanalyst to focus on children, and others have readily accepted this statement. To be sure, Anna Freud's child psychoanalysis evolved not only from the psychoanalysis of her father and his students but also from currents contemporaneous with her psychoanalytic activity. What she found, however, had only a very limited range of use and has therefore been preserved only as reflected in her own work. In 1964, in a brief retrospective survey on the beginnings of child psychoanalysis, she mentioned a number of persons she felt indebted to,[6] and we will therefore refer to each separately. The reader is already familiar with some names; others are less known to the general public: Siegfried Bernfeld, August Aichhorn, Isidor Sadger, Paul Federn, Alexander Staub, Hermine Hug-Hellmuth, Berta Bornstein, Melanie Klein, Ada Müller-Braunschweig, Steff Bornstein, and Alice Balint. Anna Freud did not mention Maria Montessori, probably because the educator, though well appreciated by her was not a psychoanalyst. In another historical retrospective of 1970, Anna Freud listed as early child analysts Hug-Hellmuth, Klein, the Bornstein sisters, and herself.[7] Only very few figures were truly pivotal in the history of child psychoanalysis, and only one had preceded Anna Freud in her field: Hermine Hug-Hellmuth.

Hermine von Hug-Hellmuth

Hermine von Hug-Hellmuth was unquestionably the only truly outstanding figure from the period when psychoanalysis was first used with children. Hardly anything is known about her except that she was murdered on September 9, 1924, at the age of fifty-three, by her nephew, Rudolph Hug. The main reason for the lack of biographical information stems from her own desire to erase the traces of her memory. The following obituary appeared in the professional journals:

> On September 9, 1924, in her fifty-third year, Frau Dr. Hermine Hug-Hellmuth, a member of the Vienna Society, of whose merit, especially in the field of child psychology, our readers need no reminder, was murdered by her eighteen-year-old nephew, Rudolph Hug. In a will made a few days before her death, she expressed the desire that no account of her life and work should appear, even in psychoanalytical publications. Dr. Siegfried Bernfeld, Secretary.[8]

Her last wish, which sounded like a premonition of her imminent death, was respected. Today, Hermine von Hug-Hellmuth is virtually forgotten. Her name is mentioned—if at all—in connection with *A Young Girl's Diary* (1919), the English translation of which was still available a few years ago.[9] This is not basically a psychoanalytic book, and Hermine von Hug-Hellmuth described herself only as the editor of the manuscript, which a young girl had given to her. It is the animated diary of a pubescent, upper-class Viennese girl, in whom the gradual awakening of sexuality is quelled. It was suspected from the very beginning that the editor and the diarist were one and the same person, and that the book was a revision of Hermine Hug-Hellmuth's own diary.[10] For this reason, publication of the book was discontinued after the third edition.

The investigations that led to the arrest of her nephew nonetheless brought to light some facts about her life and work. Like her sister, Antonie Hug-Hugenstein, Hermine Hug von Hugenstein—this was her real name—remained unmarried and received a Ph.D. in philosophy from the University of Vienna. She worked as a teacher in the elementary schools of Vienna, but then retired with a good pension which enabled her to lead a life free of economic worries. Since 1914, she had been living in a small, meticulously clean apartment at 10 Lustkandlgasse, which consisted of a room, consulting room, anteroom, and kitchen. She was also able to afford a servant to manage the household. The tenants of the building hardly noticed Hug-Hellmuth, who was small, frail, and graying at the temples, because she evidently made an effort to draw as little attention as possible to herself. She was indeed friendly and charming, but had no contact with the people in the building and received hardly any visitors except for Isidor Sadger, who was a frequent guest. He was also the guardian of her nephew and later the executor of her will. She was not known as a psychoanalyst since she did not practice therapy, but enjoyed a reputation as a highly revered healing educator. Many parents entrusted her with the education of their retarded children, and she taught them in their own homes. Hug-Hellmuth also gave courses and lectures on child education, which were very well attended, and with the publication of her work she became well known as a writer.

From the very beginning, Hug-Hellmuth had a special relationship with her nephew, Rudolph (Rolf) Hug. He was the illegitimate son of her only and beloved sister. Nothing is known about his father except that he was a private teacher. Both sisters devoted themselves to the education of the child with an openness and intensity that were rare during those times. Since they were educators and writers in this field, they considered his education an important task.

Contrary to occasional claims, Rudolph was not in psychoanalytic therapy with his aunt or any other therapist. But, in a series published in *Imago* beginning in 1912,[11] Hug-Hellmuth described her observations. In the same series, she also described the relationship of the two sisters to the child and her own role as a father surrogate.

> My nephew disliked it—at the age of seven as much as at the age of two—when his mother played the piano. He already rejected singing toy birds, et cetera, in this early period, and a set of bells interested him only if another person had acquired the same—that is, sheer envy was his motive for an occasional preference for sounds. The boy's mother, an excellent piano player, had enjoyed music intensely as a child. For both of them, their personal relationship to their mother played a significant role. The extremely lively boy experienced the constraint of keeping busy alone and without too much noise when his mother played the piano as a curtailment of maternal affection. Even at the age of six, he would suddenly weep quietly and, asked for the reason, would explain sobbing: "I can't stand it when Mommy plays the piano; the stupid piano-playing!" The mother herself had always seen in *her* mother's play a token of love, which she often requested at dusk.
>
> Though we may try to understand the countless affectionate words of children, we lack the knowledge of the secret threads by which the child's soul binds its deepest inner life with the external world. Only sometimes does some understanding of the connection flash before us. My nephew, who from very early on was quite strongly attached to me, at the age of six often omitted in his speech the address "Aunt," transformed the name Hermine first into "Hermun," then into "Hermann"; when told that it was a boy's name, he replied: "It doesn't matter, you are quite a man." (But this is impossible, I am a woman.) "Yes, but for me you are quite a man; a Herr-Mann [Mr. Man], so you are twice a man." Here the unconscious expresses the wish of the father-less child: the aunt, whom he asks for advice in questions concerning his architecture—the erection of mills and "electrical plants" ("Mommy doesn't know this!")—is expected to replace his absent father.[12]

The boy's mother died of tuberculosis in 1915 in Bolzano, and in her will entrusted her sister with her son's education. The boy had never been denied any wish since early childhood, and, as usually happens in such cases, great difficulties arose during puberty. The demands he made on his aunt increased, and she finally had to refuse some of his wishes. He then proceeded to rob her, and she always forgave him. When she was at her wits' end, however, she put him in the Sankt

Veit children's shelter. Even then she yielded to his requests for money, but became increasingly afraid of him and lived with the fear he would injure her. She made her will and remarked to her acquaintances: "One day he will stand before me and strangle me. If only it would happen quickly!" Indeed, one night he stole into her apartment through an open window, probably not to kill her but only to steal money and valuables she had previously refused to give him. That night, however, she happened not to be sleeping in her bedroom but on a couch under the very window through which he climbed in. She immediately woke up and began to scream. Her nephew first held her mouth, and when she continued resisting, he squeezed her throat more and more tightly until her body collapsed, lifeless.

The act and its previous history reveal the convergence of several circumstances that finally led to Hermine Hug-Hellmuth's violent death. One of them was the mother's but also her sister's poor child-raising methods. They granted him unbridled satisfaction of his wishes, perhaps out of a misunderstanding of the Montessori theories, and thus created in him what we would call today a low threshold of frustration tolerance. Hence his increasingly aggressive attempts at fulfilling his wishes.

Hug-Hellmuth was indeed an enthusiastic follower of Freud's psychoanalysis and tried to apply information on childhood derived from psychoanalysis to her educational observations. But she cannot be defined as a child psychoanalyst. What she sought was an educational practice based on psychoanalytic principles. She recorded her experiences and observations in a few writings in which she strove foremost to familiarize parents, teachers, educators, school physicians, kindergarten teachers, and social workers with Freud's psychoanalytic theories.[13] With the children and parents themselves, she primarily practiced counseling. Until her death she also supervised the Psychoanalytic Educational Advisory Board of Vienna, where counseling was psychoanalytically oriented but did not involve actual psychoanalytic treatment of children. Even her lecture "On the Technique of Child Analysis," delivered at the Sixth Psychoanalytic Congress at The Hague in 1920, in which she spoke in detail about her own methods, does not constitute psychoanalytic *counseling* from a current perspective.

Although Hug-Hellmuth approached some problems in the same manner as later psychoanalysts, she developed neither her own psychoanalytic theory of the child nor her own psychoanalytic technique. Now we remember her only as an educator enthusiastically oriented toward psychoanalysis, who was deeply interested in children. All the rest still remained to be done.

Siegfried Bernfeld and the Baumgarten Nursery

The precursors Anna Freud listed had been active in the field of juvenile education. But, their connection with psychoanalysis notwithstanding, they cannot be described as child and juvenile psychoanalysts. Among them, Siegfried Bernfeld occupied a salient place.

Bernfeld had been attending the sessions of the Vienna Psychoanalytic Society since 1913, but he was mainly interested in the youth movement and the urgent problems of the youth of his time. Bernfeld was an eminently imaginative author and a gifted organizer. He inspired and fascinated those around him with new ideas and projects which even today would be viewed as modern. Helene Deutsch vividly described him in her memoirs:

> This man seemed to be the very incarnation of the Don Quixote type, even in his external appearance. He was tall and gaunt, with an ugliness that impressed one as beauty. His fanatical adherence to his Zionist ideals misled him at times into opportunistic actions, but also made him a spellbinding speaker who converted many enthusiastic young followers to his ideology. In the field of analysis he very soon became a collaborator of Anna Freud, and achieved what no other member of the analytic group had done: he became a training analyst without having had regular analytic training himself.[14]

In 1913 Bernfeld founded an archive for youth culture. In 1914 he published *Women and the New Youth* and in 1920 "Psychoanalysis in the Youth Movement."[15] He established an Institute for Juvenile Psychology and Sociology in the same year. In 1919 he had founded the Baumgarten Nursery, where Willie Hoffer was temporarily employed. Unfortunately, this establishment was destined to only a brief existence, but it endures as a historical model.

Vienna's Baumgarten Nursery, a Jewish community school located in a former war hospital at 299 Linzerstrasse, and which Anna Freud linked with the founding of the Hampstead Nurseries, lasted only from August 1919 until April 1920. Before World War I, Bernfeld had already investigated possibilities for accommodating as many children as possible from among the twenty thousand homeless and orphaned Jewish children who were then roving through southeastern Europe. It was his intention to rectify the neglect they had suffered by applying the new, liberal educational theories of Maria Montessori, Berthold Otto, and Gustav Wyneken. When he found five well-preserved barracks and a financial sponsor, the American Joint Distribution Committee for Jewish War Sufferers, he seized the opportunity. Three hundred children between the ages of three and sixteen were admitted to the boarding school.

Teachers and assistants, and Bernfeld in particular, were passionate in their educational theories:

> The general formula could be: unconditional love and respect for children; ruthless constraint of one's appetites for power, vanity, dominating, and educating. As old as this requirement actually is, and as modern as it is today under the slogan of relations of camaraderie between teachers and students, only rarely is it realized, even in its obvious aspects.[16]

To be sure, Bernfeld warned against the educator's frequent permissiveness:

> The criterion [for relations of camaraderie] would first be perhaps a negative one: camaraderie must not mean setting oneself on the children's level, for

in this case the adult becomes childish; and it does not mean wanting to be liked by the children, for in this case he becomes hypocritical and aimless.[17]

Current education is paying ever greater attention to the model of the Baumgarten Nursery. Many of the present trends had already been realized there, even if for a brief period. Bernfeld, like many other educators, considered himself a socialist, but certainly not in the contemporary sense.

The well-functioning school, which turned three hundred neglected children into civilized human beings within a few months, failed as a result of mismanagement. The Joint Distribution Committee, which managed the money that flowed in from Jewish aid organizations in the United States, strongly interfered with the educational program, and modern techniques could therefore no longer be implemented. Bernfeld resigned and withdrew altogether. It was Anna Freud's opinion that Bernfeld became a skeptic after the Baumgarten Nursery failed.[18]

Only in 1921, after the Baumgarten Nursery was dismantled, did Bernfeld begin to practice psychoanalysis and treat patients. He nonetheless remained unusually interested in all public events and wrote about them, not scientifically, but with a light hand and a personal and honest touch.

During her youth, Anna Freud had allowed herself to be fascinated by Bernfeld, and over the decades kept alive the spirit that emanated from him and the Baumgarten Nursery. On no occasion did she forget to mention him and his achievements, yet she criticized his writings[19] as speculative. Bernfeld emigrated in 1934, first to the south of France, where he did not receive a work permit, and then to the United States, where he was accepted, as were so many other Europeans, by the Menningers in Topeka (see pp. 221–24 below). Later Bernfield was predominantly interested in history. He wrote a series of books about the young Freud which are still widely read. His ideas ranged from the student movement and education to the potentialities of psychoanalysis. But to describe him as a child psychoanalyst would be a mistake.

Ada Müller-Braunschweig; Alice Balint; Isidor Sadger

The only two essays in psychoanalysis Ada Müller-Braunschweig wrote appeared in 1928 and 1930,[20] and hence cannot be regarded as a contribution to the foundations of Freudian theory. Anna Freud imparts a great deal of honor to this woman by including her among the precursors of her own field.

Almost the same can be said about the few essays of Alice Balint, the first wife of Michael Balint. Born in 1898, Alice Balint was Anna Freud's contemporary. After World War I, she completed her training in Berlin, and in 1923 became a member of the German Psychoanalytic Society. Later she moved to Budapest, where she was close to Ferenczi until his death. Her essays concern educational psychology and ethnology. By managing exchange lectures among child analysts from Vienna and Berlin, she achieved a certain merit in the area of child analysis. She died on August 9, 1939, at the age of forty-one, shortly after her emigration to England.[21]

That Anna Freud should include Isidor Sadger among early child psychoanalysts is surprising. Sadger was a very prolific writer who published a number of works every year. His specialty, however, was sexual pathology, and he described case histories of the utmost perversion, not always without moral indignation. It is known that Freud was not entirely happy with Sadger's zeal in this respect. Freud once wrote to Jung of "Sadger, that congenital fanatic of orthodoxy, who happens by mere accident to believe in psychoanalysis rather than in the law given by God on Sinai-Horeb."[22] And in 1919, in planning a yearbook of psychoanalysis and psychopathological research, to which Sadger contributed two essays,[23] Freud wrote with unusual coarseness: "Sadger's writing is insufferable, he would only mess up our nice book."[24] Sadger suffer a tragic fate. Though he withdrew from the Vienna Psychoanalytic Society as early as 1934, he did not emigrate but remained in Vienna throughout the period of Nazi despotism. He has been considered missing since World War II.

Anna Freud referred to Isidor Sadger's early works, in which he discussed test anxiety and student suicide, the problems of unloved children, early childhood anxieties, and sexuality.[25] Again, the issue was not child psychoanalysis, but observations and reflections derived from the application of Freud's theories to certain subjects.

The Bornstein Sisters

We know rather little about the Bornstein sisters, who so often received honorable mentions from Anna Freud, mainly because they almost never expressed opinions about their own work. Even about Berta ("Bertl") Bornstein, the better known of the two, there is scarcely any information. She was born in September 1900 and moved with her family from Krakow to Berlin in the 1920's. She became a social worker and, under the influence of Otto Fenichel, became acquainted with psychoanalysis. She and her younger sister Steff became well known as "the Bornsteins." They belonged to the Berlin group and worked not only with Otto Fenichel, but with Edith Jacobson and Annie Reich, and with the latter two conducted a "child seminar," similar to the one Anna Freud later led in Vienna. Anna Freud and Berta Bornstein met in Berlin when Anna Freud, due to her father's illness, spent several long periods of time there. Berta Bornstein then moved to Vienna and participated in Anna Freud's seminars there. Berta Bornstein's special talent lay in her communication with children less than three years old. According to Anna Freud, her special merit was her teaching—against Anna Freud's own recommendation—the implementation of the "warming-up" technique (i.e., the introductory stage of child analysis) in psychoanalytic method. Unlike Melanie Klein, Berta Bornstein stressed that the child's play was important for the analyst not as an interpretive vehicle, but as a means of understanding the child. Never did she *interpret* the play, much less symbolically. In 1938, Berta Bornstein moved to New York, where she became, as a nonphysician, an associate member of the American Psychoanalytic Association. Her work is not extensive: between 1930 and 1953 she wrote thirteen essays in which she recounted her experiences with small children and developed thoughts largely inspired by Anna Freud's conceptions. The writings nevertheless include what is considered one of the few "great" case histories in psychoanalytic literature, which Heinz Hartmann justly compared to Freud's case histories.[26] Berta Bornstein died in Rockland, Maine, on September 5, 1971.

By mentioning these names, Anna Freud evidently wanted to convey the impression that child psychoanalysis had preceded her in both theory and practice. In reality, it was she who had to lay the foundations of child psychoanalysis.

The turn of the century was rife with educational innovations, which Anna Freud absorbed very quickly. One of the most important is credited to Maria Montessori. As a medical student at the psychiatric clinic of the University of Rome, she turned from observations of behavioral disturbances in children to educational questions concerning the healthy child.

Maria Montessori

Born on August 31, 1870, Maria Montessori was a generation older than Anna Freud.[27] Not only did she expound her new theory in both her main work, *The Montessori Method*,[28] first published in 1919, and in other books, but she traveled frequently through Europe and America to disseminate the then revolutionary ideas in vivacious, though not always scientifically sound, lectures. The public appearance of this attractive Italian woman who bore the title of M.D., then so rare among women that it was always accompanied by a stir of publicity unbelievable even according to today's standards, must have fascinated a wide and uncritical audience as much as it produced skepticism among critics.

Maria Montessori's intellectual roots can be traced back to the psychologist Wilhelm Wundt and the philosopher Johann Friedrich Herbart, who also influenced Freud. Herbart taught that the psychology of a child corresponds to the child's physical makeup, and from this Maria Montessori derived a practical science of education. Considered an independent person, the child must be able freely to choose both his activities, according to natural inclinations, and the instructional method by which to perfect them. At the same time, Montessori assigns the important role of guidance to parents and educators. It is the educator's task to familiarize the child with forms of socially acceptable interaction, with a sense of order, and with the need for self-control and bodily hygiene. Anna Freud also stressed the educator's double role of fully recognizing and respecting the child's personality, on the one hand, and guiding and training it on the other.

In a letter he wrote to Montessori, Freud alluded to his daughter's attitude:

My dear Frau Montessori,

It gave me great pleasure to receive a letter from you. Since I have been preoccupied for years with the study of the child's psyche, I am in deep sympathy with your humanitarian and understanding endeavors, and my daughter, who is an analytical pedagogue, considers herself one of your disciples.

I would be very pleased to sign my name beside yours on the appeal for the foundation of a little institute as planned by Frau Schaxel. The resistance my name may arouse among the public will have to be conquered by the brilliance that radiates from yours.

Yours very sincerely
Freud[29]

Mrs. Schaxel, Willie Hoffer's future wife, was first mentioned during the conversations between Anna Freud and Lou Andreas-Salomé. Hoffer himself later worked with Anna Freud in London at the Hampstead Nurseries.

The Children's House, a Montessori prekindergarten, had been opened in Vienna as early as 1922 under the leadership of the very active Lilli Roubiczek. From a well-to-do Prague family, she had originally come to Vienna with the intention of studying psychology with Karl Bühler. The Montessori philosophy fascinated her so much that she generously financed the school with her own money. It was at her urging that Montessori came to Vienna in 1923 and gave lectures for teachers. The minutes of the Vienna Psychoanalytic Society indicate that on November 18, 1931, Roubiczek gave a guest lecture on both Montessori and psychoanalytic education, and that Anna Freud participated in the discussion.

In the introduction she wrote to Rita Kramer's biography in 1976, Anna Freud again acknowledged the merit of Maria Montessori's fundamental principles:

As a contemporary of Maria Montessori and her work, I can, from my own experiences, confirm the grateful enthusiasm described in this book [. . .] and that, in a children's "Montessori House" (like the one created in Vienna), the child is for the first time master, as in his own home; that for the first time he is able freely to develop his interest in the available material, instead of being integrated in a prescribed group activity, as in the usual kindergarten; that for the first time, not the praise and rebuke of adults, but the enjoyment of success in one's own work becomes the appropriate incitement; above all, that the educational principle was not authoritarian discipline but freedom within carefully defined limits. [30]

Maria Montessori is often saddled with the concept that children ought to be granted *complete* freedom. Anna Freud examined this problem in 1932:

One [point of view among educators] claims that whatever the child has as native endowment is good. We must respect it, and leave it alone, a point of view which Rousseau formulated and which in modern education is sponsored especially by Montessori. According to this attitude the child is always right in what he wants; adults only cause trouble when they interfere.[31]

We recognize, however, that Montessori's influence on Anna Freud was in fact limited. Furthermore, on the basis of psychoanalytic theory and her accreting experiences, Anna Freud had to attribute special if not pivotal importance to the development of childhood sexuality. Montessori, on the other hand, evinced no understanding for this idea. Her point of view adhered closely to those of her own generation.

When we introduced those persons Anna Freud and others mentioned in the context of early psychoanalysis, we necessarily touched on events that, in 1924, were yet to happen. Let us return then to the events of 1924.

For the summer the Freuds planned a trip to Flims, a country house in Graubünden, where Freud intended to spend six or seven weeks with his family. The plan had to be cancelled, however, since Freud needed to remain within reach of his surgeon. As a result, the family spent the summer from July 8 to September 27 at the Villa Schüler in Semmering, from where they could easily travel to Vienna.

Freud had long entertained the idea of turning Vienna into a center for psychoanalytic training. Through the efforts of Abraham and Eitingon, Berlin had unmistakably become the center for these activities. In 1924, plans to establish a psychoanalytic clinic in Vienna, as well as Ferenczi's plans to move definitively to Vienna, were shattered. But, at Helene Deutsch's suggestion a training institute, modeled after the one in Berlin, was established in Vienna in October 1924. Training was in fact already practiced at the General Hospital's Ambulatorium, which was established on May 23, 1922, and where the psychoanalytic training of physicians presented no major difficulties. The Training Institute was designed to solve the problems that arose when educators and kindergarten teachers sought psychoanalytic training. Helene Deutsch became director; Siegfried Bernfeld, vice director; and Anna Freud, secretary. Lay analysis, which Anna Freud always regarded as the psychoanalytic training of school and kindergarten teachers, arose here for the first time. It still concerns the psychoanalytic movement today.

Anna Freud was now drawn into issues of teaching and training. Henceforth these subjects would remain part of her life's work and purpose.

1925

The new Training Institute was in accordance with the particular stage psycho-analysis had reached in its development. During the years following World War I, psychoanalysis showed a considerable advance. The psychoanalytic debates that had persisted since the beginning of the century gathered momentum (and have continued ever since, for the most part with traditional arguments) above all in Austria and Germany. A generation of extremely active, innovative, but often not uncomplicated people—among them medical students and young physicians dissat-isfied with psychiatry—turned to psychoanalysis. While education and psycho-analysis were beginning to intersect in Vienna, academic psychologists remained on the periphery. Not only did official psychology dismiss psychoanalysis, but the latter did not even become a melting pot for dissatisfied psychologists. Connections between psychology and analytical psychotherapy were forged only much later.

Among those interested in psychoanalysis, many were very eager to be trained. If personal instruction—in addition to the study of Freud's writings—had first been considered sufficient for the purpose of psychoanalytic practice, now much more was necessary, and courses were designed to satisfy new requirements. The Ambu-latorium, which had existed in Vienna since 1922, was now at crosspurposes with the authorities because it had admitted a large number of nonphysicians.

> As a controlling authority, the municipal Board of Health assured itself through repeated inquiries that nonphysicians were not working at the Ambu-latorium. But this had never been the case; only specialized physicians and physicians with complete theoretical training in psychoanalysis were allowed to practice treatment. Supervised training analyses, training courses, and anal-yses were continued as established at the beginning of the Ambulatorium; they have been part of the activities of the newly established Training Institute since January 1925.[1]

It cannot be sufficiently stressed how significant the training institutes of Vi-enna and Berlin were in the further development not only of psychoanalysis but of psychiatry as well. Every psychoanalytic institute, and even the schools for psycho-therapy that have rebelled against psychoanalysis, were modeled after these two. The history of the proliferation of psychoanalytic training institutes, exemplary as they are, remains to be written. Nor is there, even today, a uniformly organized and mandatory training program for the psychiatric specialist. In Germany and Austria, this lack is redressed by individual guidance given by trained teachers in university clinics, but large psychiatric hospitals offer hardly any individual training. Each psychiatrist is more or less an autodidact. In the United States, where the European model of university clinics does not exist and large distances often hinder the concentration of staff, psychoanalytic training institutes were the first instance of a systematic training of psychiatrists. This also accounts for the rapid spread of psychoanalysis in the United States during the 1930's and 1940's. The first attempts in Berlin and Vienna at setting up appropriate training programs for psychoanalysts were evidently successful, since they have remained virtually unchanged. The following excerpt outlines the purposes of the Vienna Training Institute:

> The purpose of the institute is first to train future psychoanalysts and, further, to disseminate knowledge of psychoanalytical theory, especially in relation to questions of education. The training of psychoanalysts includes (1) their own analysis for purposes of instruction; (2) theoretical training by means of lectures, seminars, demonstrations, and the use of the institute's library; (3) practical training by conducting analyses under the supervision of the institute. . . . The course covers two years.[2]

The emphasis on education corresponded to the particular circumstances in Vienna, as well as Anna Freud's proclivities. Eight courses of fifteen hours each, two of which were mandatory, were designed for the first fifteen auditors. Several guests also attended these courses ocasionally. From the very beginning, Anna Freud exercised a decisive influence on the direction of psychoanalytic training—and not simply when, after Helene Deutsch's emigration, she herself became head of the institute.

Anna Freud was not left idle during the vacation of 1925. On June 30, the family again stayed at the Villa Schüler in Semmering. Since Freud's condition did not permit the difficult trip to Bad Ischl, Anna Freud traveled in his place in mid-August to congratulate Freud's mother on her ninetieth birthday. Lou Andreas-Salomé came to Semmering for two weeks to visit Freud and his daughter. Later, on her way to the Ninth International Psychoanalytic Congress, which was held September 3–15 in Bad Homburg, near Frankfurt, Anna Freud traveled with Andreas-Salomé to Vienna and then to Munich. There, Robert Hollitscher, Anna Freud's brother-in-law, met them and took them to Eva Rosenfeld's home, where they spent an evening with Siegfried Bernfeld. They then parted, Andreas-Salomé for Göttingen while Anna Freud boarded the train to Frankfurt-am-Main.[3]

Anna Freud had not prepared her own paper for this congress, but read instead Sigmund Freud's "Some Psychical Consequences of the Anatomical Distinction between the Sexes,"[4] which was received by the 190 participants, according to the congress reports, "with cheerful gratitude." The lecture had actually not been planned, and it occurred to Anna Freud to present it at the last moment.[5] Karl

Abraham's personal report on the congress to Freud elucidates the effect the lecture had on the audience:

> But now I come to the best part of the whole Congress. The news that Miss Anna would read a paper of yours evoked spontaneous applause at the beginning of the Congress which I wish you could have heard for yourself. *Her extremely clear way of speaking did full justice to the contents.* [My italics.][6]

The business sessions focused on issues of training and lay analysis. A motion was accepted to introduce training programs in other countries, which would be as similar as possible to the original program. Training thus reached an international scope such as existed in no other field. It was agreed to create both local and international training commissions and Eitingon was elected as their president. Anna Freud became secretary of the Vienna commission, Helene Deutsch chairman, and Siegfried Bernfeld her representative.

At the December 9, 1925, session of the Vienna Psychoanalytic Society, Anna Freud presented two "litte reports" on child psychoanalysis, "An Observation of a Child" and "Jealousy and the Desire for Masculinity."

The year 1925 ended with Abraham's unexpected death in Berlin on December 25. Abraham had complained about health problems at the congress in Bad Homburg and had been receiving treatment from Wilhelm Fliess, but his death nevertheless came as a surprise. Freud must have experienced Abraham's death as a heavy blow to psychoanalysis, because Abraham had represented psychoanalysis in Berlin since 1910. Freud in Vienna and Abraham in Berlin were the personification of psychoanalysis, and both men had always been able to maintain a cordial and congenial relationship. On January 6, 1926, Freud attended the obsequies for Abraham held during a session of the Vienna Psychoanalytic Society. But surgery had impaired his speaking ability, and it was his daughter who read his brief memorial address.[7]

Freud at Seventy

Contrary to the custom observed in previous years, the Freuds took an early vacation from March 5 to April 2, 1926, at the Cottage Sanatorium, where Anna Freud slept in the room adjacent to her father's. She undertook his care for half of each day, alternating with her mother and her Aunt Minna.

The greatest event of the year 1926 lay ahead: Freud's seventieth birthday, when congratulations streamed in from all over the world to celebrate and affirm his role in intellectual life.

At the B'nai B'rith Association, of which Freud had been a member since 1895 and where he had occasionally lectured, Professor Ludwig Braun held an encomium which Freud unfortunately could not attend. However, Anna Freud and a large number of family members who had come to Vienna for May 6 were present. A letter Freud wrote to Marie Bonaparte reflects the spirit of these events: "My wife, who is fundamentally quite ambitious, has been very satisfied by it all. Anna, on the other hand, shares my feeling that it is embarrassing to be publicly exposed to praise."[1] No doubt, Freud aptly described Anna Freud's characteristic attitude. A letter to their common friend Lou Andreas-Salomé, which Anna Freud typed as her father dictated, vividly describes the birthday's afterpains: "We sit, Anna and I, every evening answering letters, or rather intending to do so, but sometimes we find it hard and give up again."[2]

In 1925, while in Semmering, Anna Freud had acquired a German shepherd named Wolf, and he was meant to accompany her on her walks through the woods. Henceforth until the mid-1930's, Freud frequently mentioned the dog in his letters. Even in a letter to Abraham, Freud commented on the animal's behavior: "Some adventures with Wolf, whom you have not met yet—with his passionate affection and jealousy, his mistrust of strangers, and his mixture of wildness and tractability, he is an object of general interest."[3]

While Anna Freud's German shepherd got along well with Freud's chow chow, the patients at 19 Berggasse sometimes had to contend with Wolf's wilder side. Anna's dog always gave occasion to jokes between father and daughter. On Freud's seventieth birthday, Anna Freud wrote a poem on the dog's body, had it photographed, and presented Freud with the photograph as a birthday card. As a precaution, however, Wolf stayed with his previous owners during the actual birthday celebration.[4]

Introduction to the Technique of Child Analysis

With the establishment of the Psychoanalytic Training Institute in 1925, Anna Freud became involved in teaching activities, and, in the process, prepared herself for issues in both education and psychoanalysis. She was able, as a result, effectively to combine teaching and research. She articulated new and unfamiliar subjects simply but precisely, making them accessible to a larger audience. Her first book, *Introduction to the Technique of Child Analysis*,[1] is simply a series of lectures she gave at the Vienna Training Institute in 1926–27, where she introduced innovation as the most self-evident thing in the world.

The innovation was child psychoanalysis.

We will try to approach this new field from several angles, first through the young patients Anna Freud introduced, and then through her theory. Finally, we will continue to examine developments in child psychoanalysis prior to and contemporaneous with her.

The Devil-Girl

Anna Freud always refused to illustrate her ideas with single case histories comparable to Sigmund Freud's famous cases: Dora, the Wolf-Man, or even Little Hans.[2] Still, her frequent references to the same patients when expounding her ideas allow a fairly complete picture of single cases to be assembled. Her first example, a six-year-old girl with a compulsion neurosis, occupies a prominent place. In the course of analysis, the girl learned to communicate with the analyst on two levels, as we would say today. Or, as the child herself more vividly expressed it, she allowed the devil to speak up from within her. Anna Freud not only learned much from the little girl, but she developed a deep and enduring relationship with her. To be sure, it is not entirely clear whether this girl is identical to the adolescent girl Anna Freud referred to in 1964 as her second case of compulsion neurosis.[3] (Anna Freud wrote: "No, these two cases have nothing in common, they were as different as possible. The six-year-old girl was American and had grown up in a family of five children. The adolescent girl came from Vienna's middle class, the only child of separated parents, and had been referred to me by the Vienna Psychiatric Clinic. The first was a private patient, the second was not.")[4] We can further conclude that the Devil-Girl is identical with the second of Dorothy Burlingham's four children.

The Devil-Girl occupies more space in the book than all other cases together. Anna Freud often apologizes to the reader for treating this case in detail, betraying her own commitment with phrases such as: "I would not have expatiated on this example if . . ." and "I would not have adduced so many details from this fantasy if it had not. . . ." We can now assemble from the detailed descriptions—against the author's own intentions—the picture of a remarkable case revealing both Anna Freud's narrative talent and her personal style of interacting with the girl.

> I am reminded of the case of a little 6-year-old girl who was sent to me last year for three weeks' observation. I had to determine whether the difficult, silent, and unpleasing nature of the child was due to a defective disposition and unsatisfactory intellectual development, or whether we had here a case of an

especially inhibited, dreamy, and withdrawn child. Closer observation revealed the presence of an obsessional neurosis, unusually severe and well-defined for such an early age, together with acute intelligence and keen logical powers.

In this case the introductory process proved very simple. The little girl already knew two children who were being analyzed by me, and she came to her first appointment with her slightly older friend. I said nothing special to her, and merely let her become familiar with the strange surroundings.

The next time, when I had her alone, I made the first approach. I said that she knew quite well why her two friends came to me: one because he could never tell the truth and wanted to give up this habit, and the other because she cried so often and was angry with herself for doing so; and I wondered whether she too had been sent to me for some such reason. Whereupon she said quite straightforwardly, "I have a devil in me. Can it be taken out?"

I was for a moment taken aback at this unexpected answer. Certainly it could, I said, but it would be no light work. And if I were to try with her to do it, she would have to do a lot of things which she would not find at all agreeable. (I meant, of course, that she would have to tell me everything no matter how unpleasant.)

She became quite serious and thoughtful before she replied, "If you tell me that this is the only way to do it, and to do it quickly, then I shall do it that way." Thereby of her own free will she bound herself to the fundamental analytic rule. We ask nothing more of an adult patient at the outset. But further, she fully understood that a lengthy time period would be required.

When the three trial weeks were up her parents were undecided whether to leave her in analysis with me or to make other provisions for her care. She herself, however, was very disquieted, did not want to give up the hope I had awakened that she could be cured, and insistently demanded that, even if she had to leave me, I should rid her of her devil in the remaining three or four days.

I assured her that this was impossible and that it would take a long time of working together. I could not make this intelligible to her in the usual way, for although she was of school age, she had as yet no knowledge of numbers on account of her numerous inhibitions. Thereupon she sat herself down on the floor, pointed at the pattern of my oriental rug, and said, "Will it take as many days as there are red bits? Or even as the green bits?" I showed her the great number of appointments that would be necessary by referring to the many medallions in the pattern. She fully grasped the point, and in the imminent decision did her part in persuading her parents of the necessity for a very long time of working with me.

Not all dreams occurring in the analysis of children present so few difficulties in interpretation. But on the whole my little obsessional neurotic was right when she would announce to me a dream of the preceding night as follows: "Today I have had a funny dream, but you and I will soon find out what it all means."

The 6-year old obsessional patient lived at the beginning of her analysis with friends of her family. She had one of her fits of naughtiness, which was much criticized by the other children. Her little girlfriend even refused to sleep in the same room with her, which upset her very much. In the analysis, however, she told me that because she had been so good, the nanny had given her a present of a little toy rabbit; at the same time she assured me that the other children liked sleeping with her very much. Then she recounted a daydream which she had suddenly had while she was resting. She did not even know whether she was making it up.

"Once upon a time there was a little rabbit, whose family was not at all nice to him. They were going to send him to the butcher and have him slaughtered. But he found it out. He had a car which was very old, but it could still be driven. He went for it at night and got in and drove away. He came to a dear little house in which a little girl [here she used her own name] lived. She heard him crying downstairs and came down to let him in. Then he stayed to live with her."

Here the feeling of being unwanted, which she would willingly be spared in my eyes and her own, shows itself quite transparently. She herself is twice present in the daydream—as the little unloved rabbit and as the little girl who treats him as well as she herself would like to be treated.

Here and there, and more frequently than these deliberate and invited associations, others, unintentional and uninvited, come to our help. I again take the little obsessional neurotic as an example. At the climax of her analysis it became essential to confront her with her hatred of her mother, against the knowledge of which she had previously protected herself by the creation of her "devil," the impersonal representative of all her hostile impulses. Although until then she had cooperated readily, at this point she became quite reluctant and resistive. At the same time, however, she relapsed at home into all manner of defiant behavior, from which I daily proved to her that one could only hate a person whom one treated so badly. Finally, confronted with these constantly recurring proofs, she gave way, but now she wanted me to tell her why she would have such hostile feelings for her mother whom she professed to love very much. Here I declined to give further information, for I too was at the end of my knowledge. Thereupon after a moment's silence she said, "You know, I believe it is the fault of a dream I once had [some weeks earlier] that we never understood." I asked her to repeat it, which she did:

"All my dolls were there and my rabbit as well. Then I went away and the rabbit began to cry most dreadfully; and I was so sorry for it." She now added:

"I believe I am always copying the rabbit now, and that is why I keep crying like it did."

In reality of course it was the other way round—the rabbit copied her, not she the rabbit. In that dream she herself had taken the mother's place and treated the rabbit as she had been treated by her mother. With this dream idea she had finally found the reproach which her consciousness always shrank from making against her mother: that she had always gone away just when the child needed her most.

Some days later she repeated the process a second time. When after a momentary sense of liberation her mood became quite gloomy again, I urged her to try to contribute more on the same subject. She could not do so, but said suddenly in deep thought, "It is so lovely at G., I should like so much to go there again." On closer questioning it became apparent that during a holiday in that place she must have passed one of her unhappiest times. Her elder brother who had had whooping cough had been sent back to town to his parents, and she was isolated with a nanny and two younger siblings. She added spontaneously, "The nanny was always cross when I took the toys away from the little ones." Thus at that time the nanny's actual preference for the younger children was added to the parents' supposed preference for the brother. She felt herself neglected on all sides and reacted in her own way. Once again she had found one of her deepest reproaches against her mother through a recollection, this time of the beauty of the countryside in G.

In what follows I present a detailed example of a positive transference fantasy from the 6-year-old obsessional girl mentioned several times. The external occasion for this fantasy was furnished by myself, for I had visited her in her own home and stayed for her evening bath. She opened her hour on the next day with the words, "You visited me in my bath and next time I'll come and visit you in yours."

A little later she told me a daydream which she had composed in bed before going to sleep, after I had left. I add her own explanatory asides in brackets.

"All the rich people did not like you. And your father who was very rich did not like you at all. [That means I am angry with your father, don't you think?] And you liked no one and gave lessons to no one. And my parents hated me and so did John and Billy and Mary and all the people in the world hated us, even the people who did not know us, even dead people. So you liked only me and I liked only you and we always stayed together. All the others were very rich, but we two were quite poor. We had nothing, not even clothes because they took away everything we had. There was only the couch left in the room and we slept on that together. But we were very happy together. And then we thought we ought to have a baby. So we mixed a big job and a little job to make a baby. But then we thought that was not a nice thing to make a baby out of. So we began to mix flower petals and other things and that gave me a baby. For the baby was in me. It stayed in me quite a long while [my mother told me that babies stay quite a long time in their mothers]; and then the doctor came and took it out. But I was not a bit sick [mothers usually are, my mother said]. The baby was very sweet and cute and so we thought we'd like to be just as cute and changed ourselves to be very tiny. I was 'so' high and you were 'so' high. [I think that is because we found out that I want to be as small as Billy and Mary.] And since we had nothing at all, we started to make ourselves a house out of roseleaves, and beds out of roseleaves and pillows and mattresses all out of roseleaves sewn together. Where the little holes were left we put something white in. Instead of wallpaper we had the thinnest glass and the walls were carved in different patterns. The chairs too were made of glass, but we were so light that we were not too heavy for them. [I think my mother does not appear at all because I was angry with her yesterday.]"

Then there followed a detailed description of the furniture and all the other things that were made for the house. The daydream was obviously spun out in this direction until she went to sleep, laying special emphasis on the point that our initial poverty was finally made up for and that in the end we had much nicer things than all the rich people she had mentioned at the beginning.

At other times, however, the same little patient related how she was warned against me from within. The inner voice said, "Don't believe Anna Freud. She tells lies. She will not help you and will only make you worse. She will change your face too, so that you look uglier. Everything she says is not true. Just be tired, stay quietly in bed, and don't go to her today." But she always told this voice to be silent and said to it that it should wait for the next session to tell me all these things.

I will give one last example to illustrate how necessary it is for the analyst to be in control of the relationship between the child's ego and his instincts.

After I had brought my young obsessional patient to the point of allowing her "devil" to speak, she began to communicate to me a large number of anal fantasies, hesitatingly at first, but soon with ever-increasing boldness and detail when she realized that no expressions of displeasure on my part were forthcoming. Gradually the analytic hour was given over to anal confidences, and became the repository of all the daydreams of this kind which otherwise oppressed her. While she talked in this way with me the constant oppression was relieved. She herself called the time with me her "rest hour." She once said, "My time with you, Anna Freud, is my rest hour. I don't have to restrain my devil. But no," she went on, "I have another rest period, when I am asleep." Apparently during analysis and sleep she was free of what would be equivalent to the adult's constant expenditure of energy in maintaining repression. Her relief showed itself above all in an altered, attentive, and animated manner.

After a time she went a step further. She began to display something of her hitherto strictly guarded anal fantasies and ideas at home as well; for example, when a dish was brought to the table, she made a half-audible comparison or a "dirty" joke to the other children. I was asked by the adults what to do about this. Inexperienced as I was, I took the situation lightly, advising that one should neither acquiesce in nor reject such minor misbehavior but simply let it pass unnoticed. The effect was unexpected.

In the absence of external condemnation, the child lost all moderation, carried over into her home all the ideas previously expressed only during analysis, and completely revelled, as she had with me, in her anal preoccupations, comparisons, and expressions. The other members of the household soon found this intolerable; especially on account of the child's behavior at the dinner table, they lost all appetite and one after another, children as well as adults, left the room in silent disapproval. My little patient had behaved like a pervert or a mentally ill adult, and thereby put herself beyond the pale of society. Since she was not punished by being removed from the company of others, the consequence was that they removed themselves from her. During this period she abandoned all restraints in other respects as well. In a few days she had become transformed into a cheerful, insolent, and disobedient child, by no means dissatisfied with herself.

The adults returned to me to complain. They said the state of affairs was unendurable. What ought they to do? Should they tell the child that talking of such things was not in itself wicked, but ask her to give it up at home for their sake? I did not agree to this suggestion. I had to acknowledge that I had made a mistake, in crediting the child's superego with an independent inhibitory strength which it did not possess. As soon as the important people in the external world relaxed their demands, the child's superego, previously strict and strong enough to bring forth a whole series of obsessional symptoms, suddenly had turned compliant. My relying on the obsessional structure had been incautious and had not even furthered the analysis itself. I had changed an inhibited, obsessional child into one whose "perverse" tendencies were liberated. But, in doing so, I had also ruined the situation for my work. This liberated child now had her "rest hour" all day long, lost her enthusiasm for our joint work to a considerable degree, and no longer brought me the proper material because this was now spread over the whole day instead of being reserved for the analytic session; moreover, she had temporarily lost [the] insight that anything was wrong with her and needed help. The classical maxim that the analytic work can be carried out only in a state of abstinence has even greater application to the analysis of children than to that of adults.

Fortunately, the situation was not so bad as it looked and in practice was easy to solve. I asked the family to do nothing except have patience. I would deal with the child's behavior but could not promise how soon the result would show. In the child's next session I acted energetically; I said all this was a breach of our agreement; I had thought she had wanted to tell me about these dirty matters in order to be rid of them, but now I saw that this was by no means so, that she wanted to tell them to everybody, for the pleasure of doing so. I had nothing against that, but in that case I could not see that she needed me; we could simply give up our hours together and let her have her pleasure. But if she stuck to her first intention, she must tell these things only to me and to no one else. The more she kept to herself at home, the more would occur to her during her hour; and the more I would know about her, the easier it would be to rid her of it. She must now decide and choose.

She went very pale and reflected for some time, and then looked at me and said, with the same thoughtful comprehension as on the first occasion, "If you say that that is how it is, I will not talk like that anymore." With that her obsessional conscientiousness returned. From that day on no mention of the objectionable topic crossed her lips at home. She was retransformed, but she had again turned from a naughty and perverted child into an inhibited and apathetic one.

We had to accomplish similar transformations several more times in the course of her treatment. Whenever the analytic work succeeded in liberating her from her unusually severe obsessional neurosis, she always escaped to the other extreme; then all I could do was once again to restore the neurosis and the already vanished "devil" to his place; naturally each time this occurred with diminished intensity and I used greater precautions and gentleness than had been used in her previous upbringing. Finally we succeeded in getting her to steer a middle course between the two extremes.

But in contrast listen to another example, this time from the analysis of a 6-year-old obsessional little girl. . . . In her case as well—as always—we are dealing with the impulses of the oedipus complex, and here again the idea of killing plays a part. The little girl had, as the analysis disclosed, gone through a period of early passionate love for her father, and in the usual way had been disappointed in him by the birth of the next sibling. Her reaction to that was extraordinarily strong. She surrendered the barely achieved genital phase in favor of a full regression to anal sadism. She turned her hostility against the new arrival. Having turned her love almost completely away from her father, she made an effort to retain him at least by incorporation. But her endeavors to feel herself a man came to naught in her rivalry with her elder brother whom she recognized to be better equipped bodily for this role. The result was an intensified hostility toward her mother—hatred of her, because she had taken the father from her; hatred, because she had not made her a boy; and, finally, hatred, because she had borne the child whom my little patient herself would willingly have brought into the world.

But at this point—somewhere in her fourth year—something decisive occurred. She perceived dimly that through these hate reactions she was about to lose entirely any good relationship to her mother whom from early childhood on she had after all loved dearly. And in order to rescue her love for her mother, and still more her mother's love for her without which she could not live, she made a mighty effort to be "good." She split off, as it were with one stroke, all these hatreds, and with them her whole sexual life with its anal and sadistic habits and fantasies; and set them in opposition to her own personality as something foreign to it, no longer belonging to it, something "devilish."

What was left behind was not much: a diminished and restricted personality whose emotional life was not fully at her disposal, and whose great intelligence and energy were occupied in forcefully keeping the "devil" in the state of repression imposed on it. Very little indeed was left for the outside world: she had at best only lukewarm feelings of tenderness toward her mother, not strong enough to bear even the slightest strain, and otherwise an almost complete lack of interest.

In addition, however, even with the greatest expenditure of energy, she was not capable of maintaining this split. The devil occasionally overpowered her for a short time, so that it might happen that without any real external reason she would throw herself down on the floor and shriek, in a fashion which in earlier times would certainly have been deemed "possessed"; or she would suddenly yield and revel with full satisfaction in sadistic fantasies, imagining that she wandered through her parents' house from top to bottom smashing all that she found and throwing the pieces out of the window, and striking off the heads of all the people she met. Such victories of the devil were always followed by anxiety and remorse.

But the split-off evil had yet another way of manifesting itself, even more dangerous. The "devil" liked excrement and dirt; she herself began gradually to develop a particular anxiety as to the punctilious observance of the precepts of cleanliness. Beheading was a matter dear to the devil's heart; she then at a certain time in the morning had to creep to the beds of her brothers and sisters to ascertain whether they were all still alive. The devil transgressed every human law with zest and relish; she, however, developed a fear of earthquakes which came on in the evenings before going to sleep—for someone had given her the idea that earthquakes are the most effective means God uses to punish people on the earth.

Thus her daily life was increasingly taken up with reaction formations, acts of contrition, and reparation for the deeds of the split-off wickedness. We might say that the ambitiously conceived and urgent effort to retain her mother's love and to be socially conforming and "good" had failed miserably; it had simply resulted in an obsessional neurosis.[5]

Anna Freud's Theory of Child Analysis

It is rather obvious that the observation of children provides insights into those stages of psychological development that dreams and free association make accessible only after painstaking effort: the child's libidinal tendencies, the various sexual and partial instincts in his daily behavior (in particular the Oedipus complex and its immediate effects), the primary processes of the pleasure principle in the unconscious which impel the child to seek satisfaction and to avoid pain, and, finally, the child's extreme dependence on the persons surrounding him. In 1970, Anna Freud was still surprised that not all psychoanalysts had plunged eagerly into this field of knowledge.

Objections were directed exclusively toward technical problems. A child does not independently turn to a psychoanalyst because of certain neurotic complaints. Instead, the parents bring him to a psychoanalyst or psychologist because of alarming behavior. "Common sense," then, may resist the idea that a child is amenable to psychotherapy. The analyst cannot lay the child on the couch, sit behind him with equable attention, and expect him to reach insights on the basis of his interpretable dreams. It is inconceivable that a child can be made to accept, either willingly or by the use of force, the renunciation an adult is capable of in analysis. Freud himself had thought so for a long time. Still, except for the case of "Little Hans" (1909), he did not have to confront the problem practically.

Almost fifty years later, Anna Freud showed that the average analyst finds it difficult

> to accept a technique in which free association is nonexistent; in which transference is shared with the parents; in which there is a minimum of insight on the patient's part, coupled with a maximum of resistance; where the patient's treatment alliance is unstable and precarious and needs parental assistance in times of stress; where action takes the place of verbalization; and where the analyst's attention cannot be concentrated on the patient exclusively but needs to be extended to his environment.[1]

What is extraordinary about Anna Freud's achievement lies precisely in her demonstration that, all these obstacles notwithstanding, only slight changes in the techniques of adult psychoanalysis are necessary to yield a psychoanalysis apposite for children. These changes are often only shifts in emphasis: i.e., what is important for an adult becomes peripheral for a child, and vice versa.

Anna Freud very clearly spelled out that the goal of psychoanalytic work with children, as with adults, consists in making unconscious processes conscious. Since a discussion of the many similarities between child and adult psychoanalysis is superfluous here, I will limit myself to a description of the differences.

Extensive space in Anna Freud's work is taken up by the description of the preliminary phase of analysis, that is, the phase in which the child's cooperation with the psychoanalyst is elicited. The dilemma is that "the analyst, as the child knows, is commissioned and paid by the parents; that means that he is in an awkward position if he takes a stand against his clients, even if this is ultimately in their own interest."[2]

The techniques and suggestions Anna Freud offered to resolve this problem convey an impressive picture of her talent and her ability to interact with children. We can picture her squatting with the six-year-old Devil-Girl on the carpet and counting its little medallions. For a boy, she "wrote letters for him on the type-writer, was ready to help him with the writing down of daydreams and self-invented stories of which he was proud, and made all sorts of little things for him during his hour with me."[3] During the sessions with a little girl, "I zealously crochetted and knitted . . . and gradually clothed all her dolls and teddy bears."[4] We have already mentioned Anna Freud's passion for knitting and crocheting, which were not limited to doll clothes. To avoid misunderstandings, we would like to remind the reader that this activity had nothing to do with psychoanalysis. Its purpose was to "make the child analyzable," i.e., to create a "working relationship," as we would say today. To be sure, such a working relationship is no less necessary in adult analysis, though it is usually less difficult to establish.

Once the child's analysis has been channeled in this direction, only a few particulars need to be considered. As the case of the Devil-Girl shows, *dreams* as an analytical means can be used equally well with children or adults. In keeping with her own interest in daydreams, Anna Freud also emphasized the use of *daydreams*.

Drawing became another important resource, which "in three of my cases . . . almost took the place of all other communications for some time."[5] Sigmund Freud was not familiar with drawing as a therapeutic means, but today it is so common in adult therapy that it no longer seems a technique specific to child analysis, although its use is more prevalent in child therapy.

The analytical technique of *free association*, a fundamental rule of psycho-analysis which has almost no substitute, is clearly inapplicable to children. A child does not quite know what to do with questions such as: "What comes to your mind here?" It was this difficulty in particular that perplexed analysts vis-à-vis children. Anna Freud recommended asking the child "to see pictures" and using the sponta-neous associations the child offers in therapy. But on the whole, free association can hardly be considered.

Another problem is *transference*, which in adult analysis is defined as the analysand's projection of his early childhood, wishes, attitudes, and feelings toward parents and other close persons on the analyst. The child, however, cannot develop this type of transference relationship because he is still surrounded by primary persons—father, mother, et cetera. Or, as Anna Freud put it: "Unlike the adult, the child is not ready to produce a new edition of his love relationships, because, as one might say, the old edition is not yet exhausted."[6] The analyst does not supplant a primary person for the child, but "enters this situation as a new person, and will probably share with the parents the child's love or hate."[7] The therapeutic situation of child psychoanalysis corresponds therefore to adult therapy insofar as the child develops feelings of affection and hostility toward the therapist. But no transference neurosis occurs, and no transference symptoms focused on the analyst replace the child's previous symptoms. Nor does the analyst assume the passive role of "empty screen" on which the adult projects psychic pictures, cinematically as it were. The child "continues to display his abnormal reactions where they were displayed before—in the home."[8] This unavoidable idiosyncrasy of child psychoanalysis demands special consideration in psychotherapy. "Because of this the child analyst must not only take into account what happens under his own eye but also direct his attention to the area where the neurotic reactions are to be found—the child's family."[9]

Anna Freud also described her participation in the daily life and care of children who were in therapy with her. She was present, for example, during their bath, and then incorporated this common experience into therapy. If the home environment was hostile toward the child, the therapy evidently required another setting. For such cases Anna Freud demanded that independent institutions be established, as she herself later did in Hampstead.

The main difference between adult and child psychoanalysis lies, according to Anna Freud, in the relationships between ego ideal and superego. The demands of the infantile ego ideal—that is, the child's identification with central figures—are weak and dependent. In older children they tend to be less dependent, but are directed, time and again, particularly on occasions of insecurity, toward the central figures, hence first of all toward the commandments and prohibitions of father and mother. Anna Freud speaks of the virtual "double standards" of the child, who can behave as expected in the presence of adults, e.g., show shame and disgust, which entirely disappear among peers who don't impose such constraints. Hence the child, and by implication his neurosis, remains dependent on environmental demands. The work of the child analyst is thus always double; it is both therapeutic and educational:

> He has to analyze and educate, that is to say, in the same breath he must allow and forbid, loosen and bind again. If the analyst does not succeed in this, analysis may become the child's charter for all the ill conduct prohibited by society. But if the analyst succeeds, he undoes a piece of wrong education and

abnormal development, and so procures for the child, and whoever controls his destiny, another opportunity to improve matters."[10]

On another occasion Anna Freud examined this difference from another angle:

Our task with the childish superego[11] is a double one. It is analytic and proceeds from within in the historical dissolution of the superego, so far as it is already an independent structure, but it is also educational (in the widest sense of that word) in exercising influences from without, by modifying the relations with those who are bringing up the child, by creating new impressions, and revising the demands made on the child by the environment.[12]

The insistent reference to the educational function of the child analyst has not always received due attention; often it was even deliberately dismissed, owing to differences in point of view. Thus quite a few cases came to failure.

It seems understandable, then, that a child's resistance (against making conscious its unconscious processes, against removing the disturbing behavior) can assume forms different from those in adults. This is evident in the fact that parents are involved, and because the child can play father and mother against each other.

He may play off analyst against home, and use the conflicts existing between them as a means to escape from all demands in both cases.

This situation also becomes dangerous when the child, in a phase of resistance, induces in the parents such a negative attitude toward the analysis that they will break off the treatment. Then we lose the child at the very worst moment, in a state of resistance and negative transference, and can be sure that he will exploit in the most undesirable ways what the analysis has liberated in him.[13]

This was Anna Freud's extraordinary achievement: she proved that a special theory of child psychoanalysis is *not* necessary. All psychoanalytic insights—which have always used the child's developmental stages as a guide—can also be applied to children. We find in the child, as in the adult, dreams and daydreams, transference and resistance, and much more. If digressions from adult psychoanalysis occur at all, they result from the child's specific, age-determined situation in the family and society. These data must determine the psychoanalyst's choice of behavior and technique. Yet Anna Freud never succumbed to the temptation of denying the child's totality and therefore treating it wrongly. Rather, she respected the child as an independent person, as an adult, while showing—more than anyone before her—a more precise and meaningful reverence for the various idiosyncrasies of each developmental stage.

The lectures in which Anna Freud definitively formulated the problems of child psychoanalysis first appeared in book format in 1927, and it soon became a classic. The reviews that rapidly followed unanimously praised, among other aspects of the book, Anna Freud's clear and articulate language, which distinguished her later writings as well. Heinrich Meng, who was then in Vienna (later he worked in Basel), wrote: "Anna Freud's work is written in a clear and very finely articulated language which makes it comprehensible to physicians, parents, and educators."[14]

In Berlin, Sándor Radó, who later worked in New York, wrote a particularly extensive review in which he also stressed Anna Freud's clear language and thought: "Her description is of exemplary clarity. . . . Thanks to the meticulous cleanliness of her methodology, in her technical provisions it is always clear in what psychological situation, with what expectations, and with what actual results this methodology was undertaken. One may say—and this factor makes the reading particularly pleasurable—that she has thoroughly rationalized her technical procedures." Radó further emphasized that Anna Freud successfully and "*appropriately* applied adult analysis to child therapy."[15]

It is worthwhile to consider briefly the circumstances under which Anna Freud established herself in the psychoanalytic—hence scientific—world. Unlike most pioneers in science, she enjoyed great advantages that furthered her career. She was born into psychoanalysis in the most literal sense. While still young she was introduced to her father's complicated theoretical system and was able to absorb it without difficulties. From the very beginning she thus treated Freud's theoretical constructs (such as the unconscious; the id–ego–superego—the economical, dynamic, and topographical system of the psyche) to some extent as real data, as if they were palpable objects rather than theory. In contrast to so many other young scientists, Anna Freud did not take long detours to reach *her* subject, *her* profession. Sigmund Freud had devoted considerable time to zoology, neuropathology, and neurology before he formulated the thought system he called psychoanalysis. Anna Freud, on the other hand, was able to become productive in psychoanalysis at a much earlier age. And, if she asked for his criticism of her work, it was a matter of course that she could rely on him to protect her from grave errors.

Whether the possibility of using her father's name facilitated or complicated her entrance into the psychoanalytic world, with its familial structure, we do not know. But we may perhaps assume that her father's friends and students accepted her activities and writings, to the extent that he had approved of them, with a certain generosity.

But these advantages also entailed many drawbacks. First, no one would have been surprised if Anna Freud—to use an image—had added little leaves here and there to the completed tree of psychoanalysis, which was already standing upright with trunk, branches, twigs, and leaves. That was the road many "orthodox" psychoanalysts took, even famous ones such as Ernest Jones and Marie Bonaparte. Instead, Freud's daughter created a new tree of psychoanalysis, identical to the old one in its system of logic, but nonetheless independent. It seems to me that Anna Freud's originality was underestimated precisely because she was Freud's daughter. Even with her I would have argued in favor of this view, since I am not certain whether she was aware of it.

The necessity, on the one hand, to use the extant psychoanalytic theory and, on the other, to create something independent has raised difficulties for a number of psychoanalysts. If we consider the many systems of depth psychology that were created alongside or in opposition to Freud, whether they call themselves neoanalytic, dasein-analytic, fate-analytic, et cetera, we will often be astonished at how slightly they differ from Freudian psychoanalysis. Psychoanalysts who value originality can thus claim, to quote a frequent example, that all of Freud's ideas were correct except for his assumption that penis envy existed. On the basis of such objections, one can then build a parapsychoanalytic theory and practice. Or, by shifting the Oedipus complex to an earlier stage of development, as Melanie Klein has done, one gives it a new direction. These small changes dismiss the fact that only single knots have been relocated in the vast net of psychoanalysis. Freud always resisted such changes, as Anna Freud did later.

It is true that Freud viewed such changes as a very personal affront, and sometimes they were indeed meant as such, given the familylike relations among early psychoanalysts. But this should not mislead us. What matters here is that the theoretical system of psychoanalysis, within which all parts relate logically to one another, does not permit peremptory changes without being completely changed. Unless, of course, we wanted to reject the entire logical structure.

Anna Freud always remained within the logical system of psychoanalytic theory. This is most probably the reason why her independence has not been fully recognized and honored. As shown even as her first book appeared, she had to brook comparisons with her father throughout her life.

Anna Freud's first book clearly renders her thinking. In it she developed—as she did later—her own thoughts in front of an audience. Almost all her works consisted of lectures, and they were all ready for print. They were clear, comprehensible, and vivid because Anna Freud always adjusted her language to her audience's level of understanding. Even the relatively rare cases of publications that were not printed speeches or reports referred to her lectures. They were thus always directed to a very specific public—as for example the Hampstead reports written during the war to her financial sponsors.

One of the reasons why Anna Freud is known to the German-speaking audience mainly through her early writings—and even here almost as a historical figure—may lie in the fact that she never addressed a German audience after she was forced to leave her home.

In her method of working, Anna Freud clearly differed from her father. He developed his thoughts in his correspondence, tested their effect by presenting them to his interlocutor in an imaginary discussion, and then wrote them down at one stroke, virtually without corrections. Even the few lectures Freud gave were written in this manner.

Melanie Klein

In reporting on the history of child psychoanalysis, one typically mentions Melanie Klein and Anna Freud in the same breath. Melanie Klein thus takes on the status of an adversary. Although both women came from Vienna and spent most of their professional life in London, some see in Klein the founder of a second—or even the first—school of child psychoanalysis, and often contrast the English school (Melanie Klein's) and the continental school (Anna Freud's). Such a simplistic scheme does not do justice to the matter; we should try to understand developments on the basis of their origins. The biography of Klein has yet to be written,[1] hence the following detailed information.

Although often thought of as Hungarian, Melanie Klein, née Reizes, was born on March 30, 1882, at 8 Tiefer Graben in Vienna,[2] where she grew up. The house was in Vienna's elegant first district, only a few blocks—almost at a stone's throw—from the Freuds' apartment. Her father, Moriz Reizes, who came from an Orthodox Jewish family in Poland, had broken with family traditions to study medicine in Vienna, where he later practiced maxillary surgery. Her mother, Libussa Deutsch, was the daughter of a rabbi. The family was able to afford a French governess for their daughter's education, with whom she remained in contact until the beginning of World War II. She studied for three years at Vienna's Gymnasium. She left in 1899 at the age of seventeen, having received her Matura diploma, to become engaged to her second cousin, Dr. Arthur Klein. This had been a young love and, like many early relationships, was not destined to last a lifetime. Arthur Klein was an industrial chemist who had also studied medicine for a few semesters. Melanie Klein studied art and history in Vienna, but left the university without graduating.

They married in 1903. Melitta Klein, the first child, was born on January 17, 1904, in her grandparents' house in Rosenberg, Hungary. She also became a psychoanalyst, practiced child psychoanalysis, and helped her mother in the editing of her work. In professional circles she became known as Melitta Schmideberg, and was considered intelligent, amusing, and interesting. In 1935 she broke all professional and personal ties with her mother, and in 1963 she withdrew from both British and international psychoanalytic associations[3] and closed her psychoanalytic practice.

Melanie Klein's first son, Hans, was born in 1907 and died in a climbing accident in the High Tatras in 1934. Erich Klein, who was born in 1914, today lives in London under the anglicized name Eric Clyne. He was evidently his mother's favorite son.

Shortly before World War I, the family moved to Budapest because Dr. Arthur Klein was offered an executive position at Count Henkel-Donnersmarck's paper mills. One of his colleagues was a certain Mr. Ferenczi, whose brother Sándor Ferenczi was already known in the psychoanalytic world.[4] It is possible, though not certain, that this was Melanie Klein's first contact with psychoanalysis. In any event, while her husband was serving in the Austro-Hungarian army during World War I, she went into psychoanalytic treatment with Ferenczi. The relationship, however, never became more personal; as letters from Willie Hoffer have made clear, it maintained its professional basis. Like Anna Freud, Melanie Klein was in the audience at the psychoanalytic congress held in Budapest on September 28–29, 1918. After the war Arthur Klein took a position in Sweden, while his wife remained with her three children at her father-in-law's house in Rosenberg, which had since been annexed to Czechoslovakia under the name of Ružomberok. Melanie Klein's address at the time of her admission to the Hungarian Psychoanalytic Society in July 1919 was therefore: c/o Director J. Klein, Savings Bank, Ružomberok, Czechoslovakia. In 1920, Melanie Klein published her first, rarely mentioned work, "The Family Novel in Status Nascendi,"[5] in which she reported several rather naive observations of her son Erich, whom she mentioned by name. Today the story can hardly be considered psychoanalytical, even if Melanie Klein in the conclusion alluded to her and Ferenczi's opinions about the possibility of a psychoanalytic interpretation. It is nevertheless a revealing work, since a comparison with her later ideas clearly indicates that Klein gathered all her early analytical experience from her own children. A comparison of different texts admits almost no conclusion other than that Fritz and Felix, the protagonists of her publication, are identical with her own sons, Erich and Hans respectively. Her first publication consists essentially of descriptions of her own children. The following juxtaposed excerpts from "The Family Novel in Status Nascendi" (1920) and "The Development of a Child" (1921) support this conclusion:

Erich Klein (1920)	*Fritz* (1921)
My son Erich, now five years old, is a healthy, strong child, of normal though somewhat slow mental development. He did not begin to speak until the age of two, and was more than three and a half years old before he was able to express himself coherently. But even at that stage, particularly remarkable expressions, such as one occasionally hears from gifted children quite early on, were	The subject is a little boy, Fritz, the son of relatives living in my immediate neighborhood. I thus had the opportunity to spend a great deal of time with the child without restraint. Since, moreover, the mother followed all my recommendations, I was able to strongly influence his education. The boy, now five years old, is a healthy, strong child, of normal men-

not noticed in him. Still, in his appearance and in his nature he gave the impression of being an alert and intelligent child. Very slowly he acquired a few concepts. He was already over four years old when he learned to distinguish between colors, and almost four and a half when the concepts of "yesterday, today, tomorrow" became clear to him. In practical matters, that is, as far as the development of his sense of reality was concerned, he was decidedly behind other children of his age.

tal development. He did not begin to speak until the age of two, and was more than three and a half years old before he was able to express himself coherently. Even at that stage, particularly remarkable expressions, such as one occasionally hears from gifted children quite early on, were not noticed in him. Still, in his appearance and in his nature he gave the impression of being an alert and intelligent child. Very slowly he acquired a few concepts. He was already over four years old when he learned to distinguish between colors, and almost four and a half when the concepts of "yesterday, today, tomorrow" became clear to him. In practical matters, that is, as far as the development of his sense of reality was concerned, he was decidedly behind other children of his age.

There is much more evidence that Erich and Fritz were identical; we here quote the end of the description:

Suddenly, after saying good morning, Erich turned to me with the question: "Mama, please tell me, how did you come into the world?"

. . . that on the next morning he asked his mother, after saying good morning: "Mama, please tell me, how did you come into the world?"

Evidence that "Felix" is in fact Klein's son Hans is not as ample and unequivocal. But whenever Klein referred to the age difference between "Felix" and his younger brother "Fritz," she indicated exactly seven years, that is, the same as between Erich and Hans. "Fritz" and "Felix" played the pivotal role in Melanie Klein's early writings, in which she reported on their expressions and behavior more as a mother would.

There is nothing extraordinary about a psychologist's use of his own personality or immediate environment as a source of observation and scientific knowledge. We have seen that in his work Freud often used one of Anna's dreams. Jean Piaget wrote entire books on the observation of his own children. Klein's use of such material is nonetheless different. Here the subject is psychoanalysis conducted by one of the two most important primary persons—the mother. An evaluation of the processes of such analysis and of the analyst's inferences cannot dismiss the fact that the analyst is the mother and that the Oedipal entanglements, as well as other problems, are thus brought into play. Yet the same Melanie Klein specifically calls for the removal of children from the home for purposes of therapy, precisely because the "Oedipal entanglement" must be avoided.

In "The Psychoanalytic Play Technique: Its History and Significance," Klein wrote in 1955:

My first patient was a five-year-old boy. I referred to him by the name "Fritz" in my earliest published paper. To begin with I thought it would be sufficient to influence the mother's attitude. I suggested that she should encourage the child to discuss freely with her the many unspoken questions which were obviously at the back of his mind and were impeding his intellectual development. This had a good effect, but his neurotic difficulties were not sufficiently alleviated and it was soon decided that I should psychoanalyze him. In doing so, I deviated from some of the rules so far established, for I interpreted what I thought to be most urgent in the material the child presented to me. . . . I sought advice from Dr. Karl Abraham. He replied that since my interpretations up to then had often produced relief and the analysis was obviously progressing, he saw no ground for changing the method of approach. I felt encouraged by his support and, as it happened, in the next few days the child's anxiety, which had come to a head, greatly diminished, leading to further improvement. *The conviction gained in this analysis strongly influenced the whole course of my analytic work.* [My italics.]

The treatment was carried out in the child's home with his own toys. This analysis was the beginning of the psychoanalytic play technique, because from the start the child expressed his fantasies mainly in play, and I consistently intepreted its meaning to him, with the result that additional material came up in his play. That is to say, I already used with this patient, in essence, the method of interpretation which became characteristic of my technique.[6]

A bit later she adds:

More important still, I found that the transference situation—the backbone of the psychoanalytic procedure—can only be established and maintained if the patient is able to feel that the consulting room or the playroom, indeed the whole analysis, is something separate from his ordinary home life. For only under such conditions can he overcome his resistances against experiencing and expressing thoughts, feelings, and desires, which are incompatible with convention, and in the case of children felt to be in contrast to much of what they have been taught.[7]

It must again be emphasized that precisely the so-called Kleinians have reproached Anna Freud, not for having been in therapeutic analysis with her father for serious neurotic disturbances resulting from the Oedipus conflict, but for having been in training analysis with him. Surprisingly, Klein treated her own sons for neurotic disturbances, a fact she at first admitted, but later quite successfully camouflaged. Nowhere in the available literature was I able to find evidence for this noteworthy circumstance.

Klein was not satisfied with the mere analysis of her sons, but even drew the material of her early publications largely from these analyses, which provided the basis for her entire play therapy and her rejection—justified, to be sure—of child analysis in the home environment. Her daughter Melitta was evidently not included as a detailed psychoanalytic case, but occasionally appeared as an extra in the reports on "Fritz." She was the older, sensible sister who went for walks with the little boy or answered one of his many questions objectively after careful deliberation. In 1921, Melitta was already seventeen, past the age that interested her mother as a psychoanalyst. Klein may have referred to her in one or another example in her early works, but this cannot be verified. Perhaps her own ambivalent relationship to her daughter also comes to the fore here—in any event, she seems to have been much more attached to her sons.

About Melitta Schmideberg, we know that she attended sessions of the Hungarian Psychoanalytic Society as early as 1919, at the age of fifteen.[8]

In 1920, Melanie Klein was a guest at the psychoanalytic congress at The Hague, where she met Freud. But this remained a fleeting acquaintance. Klein spent the turn of the year 1920–21 in the Tatras and then traveled to Berlin, where her husband had meanwhile built a house at 19 Auf dem Grat in Dahlem, which survived World War II and today houses the Egyptological Institute of the university. Through Karl Abraham, Melanie Klein received immediate entrée into the Berlin psychoanalytical group. Her marriage, which she described warmly in her early writings, did not survive the separation imposed by World War I, and the couple divorced in 1924. Unlike before, when her husband's wealth had permitted her to limit her psychoanalysis to her own children and those of neighbors, she now concentrated more seriously on her work, in order to attain greater financial security.

In 1925, Ernest Jones invited her to give several lectures on child psychoanalysis in London, and she arrived there in July 1925 for the first time. Until then, she had published only five smaller works, among them the already mentioned story about her own family. "On the Genesis of Tics"[9] appeared later in 1925, with "Fritz" and "Felix" again the main protagonists. The term "play therapy" first appeared in 1927 in "The Psychological Principles of Infant Analysis,"[10] although, as we have already seen, Klein had long since been playing with *her* children and interpreting the play's processes. In October 1924, she gave a lecture at the First Conference of German Psychoanalysts, held in Würzburg, on a case of infantile compulsion neurosis whose subject was clearly "play therapy." This lecture was not published or preserved in its original format, but later, under the title "An Obsessional Neurosis in a Six-Year-Old Girl," constituted the basis of Chapter 3 of *The Psychoanalysis of Children* (1932). This chapter—or rather, revised and published lecture—is the only source in Melanie Klein's early writings where she discusses details of her technique. Anna Freud must also have been familiar with the contents of the Würzburg lecture.

Klein did not yet use the term "play therapy" in this lecture, in which she discussed the 575 therapy sessions of a six-year-old girl with a compulsion neurosis. The girl was brought into therapy because she repeatedly beat her head on her pillow, vigorously sucked her thumb, constantly masturbated, and suffered from sleep disturbances. Whether these were genuine compulsive symptoms remains moot, since there is no information on the ideas the child associated with these activities. One would in fact expect the child to express an opinion on her compulsive symptoms.

During therapy sessions, Klein allowed children to do what they wanted. It is therefore not true that a child, abetted by those who witness his play, acts out a constructive or even destructive *game*. It would be more correct ot speak of *acting*, which in a child often assumes playful forms and which Klein interpreted step by step. "The *lessening* of *affects* or even their dissolution is brought about by *interpreting the present situation* together with the *original* one."[11] This procedure almost exclusively entails symbolic interpretations, a selection of which will be quoted further below.

Strangely enough, the best and clearest source of information about Melanie Klein's early theories can be found in Anna Freud's *Introduction to the Technique of Child Analysis,* which refers not to a specific work but to Melanie Klein's works in general, though mostly to the 1924 Würzburg lecture. Surprisingly, even Klein and her editors refer to Anna Freud when they present Klein's early throughts.[12] Considering later developments, it is noteworthy that the only early description of what became the famous play therapy came from Anna Freud, who was the first to make it accessible to a broader psychoanalytic audience. Reading Anna Freud's book without appropriate preparation gives the impression that she was discussing in careful detail an already well-known and accepted form of psychoanalytic therapy for children. She used Klein's description of the therapeutic process to expound on her own technique. If Klein thought that each disturbance in a child's emotional and mental development could be removed or favorably affected, and that even normal and inconspicuous children could benefit from analysis, Anna Freud claimed, on the contrary, that analysis was meaningful only in the case of infantile *neuroses.* Essentially, the problem was how to manage in child analysis without the free associations that are so important in adult analysis. Anna Freud introduced Klein's *play technique* here (and on this occasion evidently coined the term):

> Instead of taking the time and trouble to pursue [the child] in his home environment, we establish at one stroke the whole of his known world in the analyst's room, and let him move about in it under the analyst's eye—at first without any intervention. In this way we have the opportunity of getting to know the child's various reactions, the strength of his aggressive impulses or of his affections, as well as his attitude to the various objects and persons repre-

sented by the toys. To observe the child thus at play also has other advantages over watching him in his home background. The toys are easily manipulated by the child and subject to his will, so that he can carry out with them all his actions which in the real world are banned and remain confined to phantasy.[13]

Anna Freud fully concurred with the technique of observing a child's play in such an artificially constructed environment, but she rejected Klein's view of the child's acts as free associations, as the latter interpreted them.

She assumes that these play actions of the child are equivalent to the free associations of the adult patient, and persists in translating every action that the child performs into the corresponding thoughts; that is to say, she attempts to find the symbolic content underlying each single move in the play. If the child overturns a lamppost or a toy figure, she interprets this action, e.g., as an aggressive impulse against the father; a deliberate collision between two cars as evidence of the child having observed sexual intercourse between the parents. Her procedure consists of accompanying the child's activities with translations and interpretations which—like the interpretation of the adult's free associa-tion—exert a directing influence on the further course of the patient's inner processes.[14]

Above all, Anna Freud criticized Klein for interpreting *all* of the child's acts symbolically:

Instead of being invariably invested with symbolic meaning, it may sometimes admit of harmless explanations. The child who upsets a toy lamppost may have witnessed some such incident in the street the day before; the car collision may be reproducing a similar happening; the child who opens the handbag of a lady visitor is not necessarily, as M. Klein maintains, expressing his curiosity whether his mother's womb conceals another baby; he may be repeating an experience of the previous day when a similar visitor brought him a present in a similar receptacle.[15]

The question of symbolic interpretation is of fundamental significance for early psychoanalysis and the public criticism it incurred. We know that Freud was able to show that dream content often expresses symbolically something unaccept-able to waking consciousness. Slips of the tongue, errors, misreadings, slips of the pen, and hysterical symptoms operate on the same principle. The meaning of the symbol always remains hidden from the consciousness of the affected person, and even the analyst does not understand it immediately. The psyche adopts greatly varied symbolic forms to represent its unconscious content in condensed form. We know that this concept has proved extraordinarily fertile and has made possible a broad understanding of otherwise incomprehensible connections. Understandably, early psychoanalysis extended this finding to every conceivable phenomenon and thus no doubt often exaggerated it. The reports of the Vienna Psychoanalytic

Society show that, even within this first psychoanalytic association, imaginative, but often ungrounded and even arbitrary symbolic interpretations were presented. Wilhelm Stekel in particular excelled in this. It goes without saying that the most conspicuous contents of dreams—namely, sexual organs and sexual acts—time and again had to bear the brunt of "wild" symbolic interpretation.

These exaggerations provoked particularly vehement rejections of psychoanalysis, and criticism itself lost all measure. The pervasive sexual content of symbolic interpretations often lured analysts into interpreting all elongated objects as a penis, all roundish objects as a vagina, and bushes and trees as pubic hair—all at great cost to the reputation psychoanalysis had attained. Freud himself was never guilty of such exaggerated symbolic interpretations; rather, he had been quick to recognize the danger. His criticism of Stekel mainly concerns Stekel's "wild" symbolic interpretations. The rule that an almost unlimited number of real objects and even of abstract concepts can be transformed into symbols is certainly valid, but its pertinence to each case must be verified by means of various "techniques."

When Anna Freud warned against the dangers of an immediate and exclusively symbolic interpretation of a child's acts, her critique was taking into account the dangers of an insufficiently verifiable symbolic interpretation. The information given is often a matter of a mere recollection, which carries no symbolic value. The example Anna Freud quoted from Melanie Klein was aptly chosen and could have been taken from the jokes on psychoanalysis: A child runs to meet a female visitor and opens her purse to see "whether his mother's womb conceals another baby." Indeed, the purse often symbolizes female genitalia, but from the child's act alone we can conclude nothing about the validity of this symbolic interpretation.

Klein adduced numerous similar incidents from the case history of the six-year-old girl with the "obsessional neurosis."

> Erna used very often to play at being a mother. I was to be the child, and one of my greatest faults was thumb-sucking. The first thing which I was supposed to put into my mouth was an engine. She had already much admired its gilded lamps, saying, "They're so lovely, all red and burning," and at once put them into her mouth and sucked them. *They stood to her for her mother's breast and her father's penis.* [My italics.]

> Once, instead of the father, a magician came along. He knocked one child on the anus and then on the head with a stick, and as he did so a yellowish fluid poured out of the magic wand. On another occasion the child—a quite little one this time—was given a powder to take, which was "red and white" mixed together. This treatment made the little child clean, and it was suddenly able to talk, and became as clever as its mother. *The magician stood for the penis, and knocking with the stick meant coitus. The fluid and the powder represented urine, feces, semen and blood, all of which according to Erna's phantasies, her mother put inside herself in copulation through her mouth, anus and genitals.* [My italics.][16]

Klein later rejected the criticism that she invariably interpreted a child's acts as symbols. Her own examples, however, permit no other conclusion, since her interpretations immediately followed her descriptions, and, except for a few vague explanations (according to which "the material as well as other cases supports this interpretation"), she nowhere explained how she reached this interpretation. It was precisely these vague explanations that Melitta Schmideberg later sharply criticized, surely not as a daughter, but in her capacity of psychoanalyst. Since Klein offered no exact evidence to justify each particular interpretation, enemies of psychoanalysis can find in her a fertile ground for their criticism.

During her 1925 visit to London, Klein made many new contacts and, urged by Ernest Jones, moved to England in 1926, where she rapidly began to play a signficant role, apparently for rather personal reasons. Jones, indisputably a central figure in the British Psychoanalytic Society, entrusted her with the therapy of his children. But Klein also fascinated the relatively large number of female members of the society, many of whom later became her disciples.

To sum up: The development of Melanie Klein's thought can be well traced in her early writings. In "The Family Novel in Status Nascendi" (1920), she openly relates information about her sons Erich and Hans, as well as incidents from her family life. In "The Development of a Child" (1921) and its sequel, "Infant Analysis" (1923),[17] Klein describes the education of her two sons under the pseudonyms Fritz and Felix, but the essays are mostly about Erich/Fritz and his sexual development. We do *not yet* find here any form of psychoanalysis, as Klein herself expressly stated. She still emphasized the educational perspective here, and "for that purpose wish[es] to apply the term 'education with an analytical hint.'" Evidently dissatisfied with her educational achievements in her work with her sons, she completely turned to therapy at the end of "Infant Analysis":

> On the one hand, then, we must not rate too highly the importance of so-called analytical up-bringing, though we must do everything in our power to avoid mental injury to the child. On the other hand, the argument of this paper shows the necessity of analysis in early childhood as a help to all education. We cannot alter the factors which lead to the development of sublimation or of inhibition and neurosis, but infant-analysis makes it possible for us, at a time when this development is still going on, to influence its direction in a fundamental manner.[18]

The basic outline of play analysis, or play therapy, finally became distinct in "An Obsessional Neurosis in a Six-Year-Old Girl."

Such was the situation at the time of the symposium held in London after the publication of Anna Freud's *Introduction to the Technique of Child Analysis.*

The London Anti–Anna Freud Symposium

On May 4 and 18, 1927, Anna Freud attended a symposium on child analysis organized by the British Psychoanalytic Society. The point was not, as is common in scientific symposia, to exchange experiences and thoughts, but to criticize and disparage Anna Freud's book, *Introduction to the Technique of Child Analysis.* Speakers were those who later belonged to the Melanie Klein school: Joan Riviere, M. N. Searl, and Ella Sharpe. Edward Glover, who was Ernest Jones's representative, and Jones himself were the closing speakers. The rejoinders, of which Melanie Klein's lecture alone constituted three-fifths, were almost as long as Anna Freud's book itself. Still, Klein's lecture differed from her early writings in many respects. With a transparent style that distinctly conveyed the technique of child psychoanalysis, she reached a level she never mastered again.

Even if we wonder whether Jones might not have lent a hand, we must nonetheless understand that it was Anna Freud's book that first stimulated Klein to felicitously present her own ideas.

Klein opened the symposium with a historical introduction, pointing out that the history of child psychoanalysis began with Sigmund Freud's case of Little Hans. In making this presentation, she falsely claimed that Little Hans's father knew nothing about his son's psychoanalytic therapy. Anna Freud herself asked: "How could such error have occurred? The patient's history clearly shows that the father himself carried out the analysis, i.e., provided the interpretations."[1] The father, Max Graf, not only knew about his son's analysis, but was even a member of the Vienna psychoanalytic group, though he himself never practiced psychoanalysis. Klein then mentioned the merits of Hermine Hug-Hellmuth and finally those of her own work, referring to her essay of "The Development of a Child" (1921) as her *first* publication, although it was, in fact, her second.

According to Klein's statements, then, Anna Freud was not a pioneer but a latecomer to child psychoanalysis. All subsequent authors accepted this version, and we have already seen how Anna Freud, by preferring to keep her work and herself in shadows, reinforced this historical view.

Klein then proceeded to tear Anna Freud's statements to pieces, using psychoanalytic principles to expose their alleged falseness. Klein repeatedly quoted Sigmund Freud against his daughter, and charged her with the violation of acknowledged psychoanalytic regulations. This accusation must have indirectly stricken Freud himself, since it is quite inconceivable that Anna Freud would have published something of which he had not approved. In the entire lecture one looks in vain for even a single passage that would show, at least out of esprit de corps, some respect for Anna Freud's merits. Even in the concluding sentence, usually used as a polite bow, Klein shot a final, especially sharp arrow: "If, however, he [the child analyst] does this [fearlessly analyzes to the very core], he will discover the signficance of the second principle, which I posit in contrast to Anna Freud: namely, that we must analyze completely and without reservations the child's relationships to its parents and its Oedipus complex."[2]

Here lies, if deftly hidden, the reproach that Anna Freud is not even competent to analyze the Oedipus complex because, having been analyzed by her father, her own unresolved relationship to him left her caught in the complex. It was left to Ella Sharpe to repeat this reproach even more indelicately.[3] The claim, she said, that a child is too young for analysis and that a fusion between analysis and education is therefore advisable (what Anna Freud required) stems "probably from the fact that in the insufficiently analyzed analyst, as in the child, a deeply moored superego, condemnatory of sexuality, is at work."[4]

In simple language, this means: Anna Freud's analysis—with her father—was unsatisfactory, for otherwise she would not have developed such views; her "superego, condemnatory of sexuality," and her own unanalyzed Oedipus complex were therefore to be blamed for her inapposite theories. It may even have made her incapable of having a sexual love relationship. No one would believe that the charges were accurate if he knew that the five-year-old child through whose analysis Klein demonstrated the feasibility and importance of the analysis of the Oedipus complex was her own son Erich. But who knew that? She certainly did not mention it in her lecture: "During my analysis of a five-year-old boy, I found (as was confirmed by all my later analyses) that it is easily possible as well as remedial to probe the Oedipus complex to its depths, whereby results can be obtained that are at least as valuable as those of adult analysis."

She referred therefore to a procedure she held against Sigmund Freud and his daughter Anna: analysis by a parent of the opposite sex. The other speakers concurred, even if less vehemently, with Klein and Sharpe. There was not a single word of recognition for Anna Freud's work. Ernest Jones, who spoke last, at least refrained from personal attacks, but essentially agreed with the previous speakers. He emphasized that he had no experience in child psychoanalysis and that he substantiated whatever opinion he had on the matter with his close observation of several analyses of younger children by outstanding specialists in the field. What he meant was no doubt the analysis of his own children by Klein.

Unquestionably, this tribunal was meant as an attack not only on the young Anna Freud, but also at least as strongly on Sigmund Freud, who now normally remained outside of the ongoing controversy because of his illness and age. The entire debate also revealed Jones's ambiguous character, already deplored by Freud and Jung in their correspondence,[5] which was rectified only in his old age. Even if he did not stage the symposium, as was alleged, it may still have been in his power to prevent the malicious imputations. At the least, he should have fulfilled his obligations and said a few words of recognition about Anna Freud's work.

In an examination of the *factual* content of the arguments that were raised, the contrasts in views no longer seem significant enough to have necessitated such violent disputes. First, Klein and her followers always spoke about children of under six years, whereas Anna Freud treated children in the latency period, that is, over six years old. This constitutes a considerable difference in psychoanalysis. Second, they always insisted on "analyzing through" the Oedipus complex, as if Anna Freud had claimed that it was forbidden. In fact, Anna Freud only indicated that the child's linguistic development could not be disregarded. The Melanie Klein group also claimed that the devices for the introductory phase, lovingly described by Anna Freud, were not only unnecessary but even detrimental. Still, as Anna Freud extensively argued, because the subject here was not psychoanalysis but the preparation for it, various paths should be possible.

The question then arose as to what could supplant the associations that a child lacks. Klein insisted on replacing them in every case with what she now labeled "play technique." Anna Freud had rigorously pursued this question. In this context Klein denied for the first time the reproach of prematurely interpreting a child's acts symbolically (note the example of the child who looks for the sibling in the mother's purse, i.e., her genitalia). She interpreted symbolically, she now claimed, only if this was justified by reiterations and further evidence. This sounds plausible, but the cases Klein had published at that time do not display this rigor.

Klein rejected Anna Freud's conviction that children do not develop a full transference neurosis because the "first edition" (of the primary relationships) is not yet out of print. The absence of a transference neurosis, she contended, would be attributed, among other things, to the devices the Anna Freud school used in the introductory phase. Klein insisted as well that the Oedipus complex appears much earlier than Freud had assumed.[6] Hence, the superego also has to develop much earlier. This view would have surely required a complete revision of the then current psychoanalytic paradigm of the stages of early child development. We have already heard that Freud objected to such revisions, and they have still not been carried out.

The last essential attack was aimed at the connection between psychoanalysis and education propagated by Anna Freud and acknowledged by the entire Viennese circle. This attack is the least understandable today, since Anna Freud's views have prevailed on a worldwide scale. Klein insisted that such a connection is impossible, because analysis tolerates instincts that education condemns. According to Klein, special educational measures are superfluous in the complete analysis of the Oedipus complex she calls for.

Anna Freud's 1928 report on the symposium to the Vienna Psychoanalytic Society was not published. It was not only at that time that she decided against a rejoinder—to both personal reproaches and objective differences—but even later rarely let drop a critical word. Had she defended herself, a schism between continental European and English psychoanalysis would have been inevitable. In any case, time worked, even if very slowly, in Anna Freud's favor. As always, she accepted personal injury as simply an important and regular part of life's experience.

Ernest Jones's Role in Child Psychoanalysis

Ernest Jones deserves a special place in early child psychoanalysis, although he himself never treated children. It was Jones who brought Melanie Klein to England. At his suggestion, she analyzed both his children and his wife, and this example was followed by many London analysts. At the London Anna Freud symposium in 1927, he obviously sided with Klein, even if less demonstratively than others, but as politely as always. In his biography of Freud he alludes to the meeting only briefly, cautiously avoiding details and pointing merely to a disagreement that arose on this occasion between him and Freud. Finally, he quotes Freud's conciliatory letter on the proceedings:

> I do not estimate our theoretical differences of opinion as slight, but so long as there is no bad feeling behind them they can have no troublesome results. I can say definitely that we in Vienna have not infused any ill will into the contradiction, and your amiableness has repaired the way in which Melanie Klein and her daughter erred in this respect toward Anna. It is true I am of [the] opinion that your Society has followed Frau Klein on a wrong path, but the sphere from which she has drawn her observations is foreign to me so that I have no right to any fixed conviction.[1]

A small, rather insignificant error found its way into Freud's letter, but it should be corrected nonetheless: Melanie Klein's daughter Melitta Schmideberg was still in Berlin at that time and did not attend the London symposium.[2] Later in his text Jones almost apologizes for the fact that Freud did not side with Melanie Klein: "In a long discussion with Freud I defended Melanie Klein's work, but it was not to be expected that at a time when he was so dependent on his daughter's ministrations and affections he could be quite open-minded in the matter."[3]

According to Jones, then, Freud would have approved of the Kleinian views had he not been, owing to his illness, dependent on his daughter for physical care. Jones's comment disguises an inimical judgment about both Anna Freud's psychoanalytic work and Freud's competence to evaluate it. The partiality was actually in Jones, whose clear analytic intellect would presumably not have been impressed by Klein's somewhat obscure and blurred ideas had he not been affected by her evidently fascinating personality. Elsewhere in his biography of Freud, he treats the subject with almost the same words. In the report on the year 1927, he writes:

> In September Freud sent me a long letter complaining strongly about a public campaign I was supposed to be conducting in England against his daughter Anna, and perhaps therefore against himself. The only basis for this outburst was my having published in the *Journal* a long report of a discussion on child analysis. It was a topic that had for years interested our Society, which contained so many women analysts, and it had been further stimulated by Melanie Klein's coming to England the year before. I wrote a comprehensive account of the whole matter to Freud, and he replied: "I am naturally very happy that you answered my letter so calmly and fully instead of being very offended by it." But he remained sceptical, and possibly prejudiced, about Melanie Klein's methods and conclusions. I had later several talks with him on the subject of early analysis, but I never succeeded in making any impression on him beyond his admitting that he had no personal experience to guide him.[4]

Freud, on the other hand, was more than appropriately reserved, most probably to avoid the reproach of defending his daughter. In his work Freud refers to Melanie Klein only once—disapprovingly—when he discusses her "Shift of the Oedipus Complex to an Earlier Stage." Freud no doubt rejected Klein's conception of child analysis. He found many of her claims too extravagant and unfocused; fundamentally they fit poorly into his psychoanalytic theory. Klein's case could be brought up as an index of Freud's tolerance. Had Freud unequivocally expressed his views on the matter, he might have brought about—after such vehement discussions—a schism in the British Psychoanalytic Society and perhaps even provoked an irreconcilable discord with Jones, his later biographer. It was after all Jones who brought Freud and Anna into exile in England, where Klein and her followers were active. Moreover, his care for both Sigmund and Anna Freud is unequaled in the history of psychoanalysis and in the history of emigré German-speaking psychiatrists. Perhaps out of gratitude for this assistance and out of consideration for English hospitality, Anna Freud refrained from ever clearly asserting her point of view in the dispute with Klein.

Only after the first edition of Freud's biography was published did Anna Freud express her opinion about Jones in these matters more clearly:

> Nevertheless, while work continued, professional harmony did not do the same. With the arrival of Melanie Klein in London under the sponsorship of

Ernest Jones, scientific differences made their appearance. Ernest Jones disapproved strongly of my early lectures on child analysis and complained in a letter to my father of their publication. He was, I believe, eager at that time to prevent the disagreements from increasing and, for scientific discussions of their causes, he advocated the establishment of exchange lectures between London and Vienna. He visited Vienna to give one of these; Robert Waelder went to London for the same purpose. Nevertheless, the controversies grew and deepened, without, though, ever touching or altering the bonds of friendship between us. We merely agreed to disagree.[5]

She adds:

> I have never ceased to be grateful to the British Society for their attitude [the rescue of Viennese analysts] at this crucial moment, and the memory of it influenced many of my later actions. Above all, I was always careful that none of my later activities in England should in any way constitute an embarrassment to our hosts.[6]

Finally, Anna Freud also described how Freud's biography had been written and her contributions to it. It is one of the very few passages in which she indulged in slight irony:

> What happened then was a most exciting event, namely, Ernest Jones' undertaking to write a biography of my father. I do believe that in the beginning he approached the task with some hesitancy, or even fear. However, this changed quickly and made itself felt as an intense and pleasurable preoccupation. There were some inaccurate, and even ludicrous statements made about this in some places. I remember a rather malicious American author asserting that this was done under my direction, and that I carefully scrutinized every page which he wrote. Whoever knew Ernest Jones personally knows very well that this was wholly fictitious. No one ever directed Ernest Jones, or gave him permissions, or even criticized him to his face. It was always the other way round. With this labor to which he had devoted himself as well, he was entirely his own master, choosing what to use, what to discard, how to arrange matters to achieve maximum information for the reader. His aim was to be factual and to adhere strictly to the truth. I would not be surprised to be told that his biography is one of the few ever written which achieved this aim.
>
> His collection of material was simple and direct. He used to appear at our house empty-handed and depart with armfuls of documents, letters, handwritten notes, etc. It made little difference whether we were always willing to part with them. They went and found their place in Ernest Jones' study. They did not even always return. My brother Ernst recovered some of them after Ernest Jones was gone; others found their way into the library of the British Society and Institute as gifts donated by Mrs. Jones. Some may still be floating around somewhere.[7]

Indeed, some are still floating around, and rumors purport that Paul Roazen acted very much like Jones. At any rate, Roazen, a specialist in psychoanalytic gossip, had access to the documents Jones had acquired and used them extensively, not always to the satisfaction of those involved.

In her later publications, Melanie Klein did not merely discuss problems of child psychoanalysis but completely restructured psychoanalytic thought. We cannot further contend with Klein in this book on Anna Freud, but it should be remembered that Klein's later writings, even if they no longer incited disputes, nonetheless stood in the most sharply conceivable contrast to Anna's as well as to Sigmund Freud's thought. The ideas Klein developed on the paranoid-schizoid and depressive states, projective identification, manic resistance, and the early stages of the Oedipus complex remain strangely blurred and obscure and have nothing in common with the psychiatric concepts of schizophrenia, depression, or mania. These concepts could also have provoked a schism in the British Psychoanalytic Society, since they did not deserve to be called psychoanalytic. But Jones's authority on the one hand and Anna Freud's unflagging consideration on the other prevented an open conflict here as well.

The spate of Kleinians has grown and commands a number of closed-membership groups, in the United States as well as Europe. Even after Klein's death in London on September 22, 1960, at the age of seventy-eight, her followers pursued the direction she had laid down. In these times of professed rationality, it is precisely the obscure theories that exert their magnetism even on intelligent and critical people. Still, clarity and lucidity, as they have again and again been achieved and preserved by Anna Freud, have been widely acclaimed and, with ever-growing effectiveness, have reached a considerable audience, foremost in the United States.

Psychoanalysis and Education

Gradually, Vienna became the psychoanalytic center for education. Maria Montessori's ideas gained firm footing. Siegfried Bernfeld established the Baumgarten Nursery, and August Aichhorn embraced the cause of neglected adolescents. As previously mentioned, Anna Freud later observed that some psychoanalysts, following their psychoanalytic training, show a strong tendency to return to their original profession, where they then apply the psychoanalytic knowledge they have gained. This was certainly true of Anna Freud herself, who had to ask herself to what extent psychoanalytic ideas on normal and abnormal child development could be incorporated into education.

The consulting center that had been established earlier in the Vienna Ambulatorium concentrated on educational problems, and Aichhorn, who soon became the counselor for education at Vienna's Youth Welfare Department, was influential in this area. The Vienna Society had already held well-attended seminars and courses for educators and social workers. Among the subjects that concerned the society, where Anna Freud often participated in discussions, was "Psychoanalysis and Education." The first issue of the *Zeitschrift für Psychoanalytische Pädagogik* (Journal for Psychoanalytic Education) appeared at last in October 1926, edited by Heinrich Meng in Stuttgart and by Ernst Schneider in Riga. The new journal, put out by Hippokrates Verlag in Stuttgart, soon faced financial difficulties and had to be discontinued as early as May 6, 1927, following "work fraught with many sacrifices." To continue its publication, however, an independent publishing house for the *Zeitschrift für Psychoanalytische Pädagogik* was set up at 3 Andreasgasse, Vienna VII, the private address of Vienna Society members Eric Hiller and A. J. Storfer.[1]

The journal set as its aim to publish works that

> are taken from practice, that is, are experience- and observation-oriented. Here we think first of the application of psychoanalytical procedures to children and adolescents, or to adults whose childhood has become the object of analytical inquiry. The experiences to be considered, then, are those the psychoanalytically oriented educator culls from his various educational achievements in the school and at home, from institutional, therapeutic, and nursing education, from teachers' training, from educational and professional counseling, from characterological investigations (psychodiagnosis), et cetera.[2]

After its first year, the journal was published with the help and contributions of August Aichhorn, Paul Federn, Anna Freud, Josef Friedjung, and Willie Hoffer. The Viennese circle, busy with educational questions, had thus become a determinant force. To be sure, aspirations varied among the editorial staff from the very beginning. Heinrich Meng wanted to transform the journal into an instrument for the popularization of psychoanalysis. He had already helped to establish the journal *Hippokrates* while working at Hippokrates Verlag, where he had also edited *The Popular Book of Psychoanalysis,* and later wrote several popular scientific works on psychoanalysis.[3] Paul Federn, who had analyzed Heinrich Meng, represented the same tack in Vienna. Anna Freud, Aichhorn, and Hoffer, on the other hand, pursued a more scientific line and wanted the journal to be an organ for discussion of psychoanalytic education. Only in 1932 did these contrasts collide, when Paul Federn asked Freud for permission either to revise difficult articles for a wider public or to reject them. Freud replied that the essays had to be printed in their original form or rejected.[4] Following this dispute, Federn resigned from the editorial staff.

In 1928, circumstances were particularly propitious for the revival of educational concerns, and enough members of the psychoanalytic camp were available to satisfy this need. August Aichhorn and Anna Freud had already spoken several times before nursery-school teachers. Inspector Jalkotzky now invited Anna Freud to teach an introductory course in psychoanalysis for educators. The four lectures of this course were subsequently published in 1930 in book format under the title *Psychoanalysis for Teachers and Parents*.[5] The fourth lecture, "The Relation between Psychoanalysis and Education," published in 1929 in the *Zeitschrift für Psychoanalytische Pädagogik*, had been the first to appear. Another essay, "The Role of Bodily Illness in the Mental Life of Children,"[6] first published in 1952, was added to later editions. In the educational psychoanalysis presented here, Anna Freud was not interested in developing her own thoughts and theories, but in dispelling the prejudices of educators by introducing them to psychoanalysis for their own professional purposes. She suspected that the psychoanalytic theory of instincts bore the brunt of their prejudices:

> The theory of the child's instinctual development is the most important part of the new psychoanalytic discipline, it is also the reason for most of its unpopularity. Very likely this is also the explanation why many of you have until now stayed away from analytic teachings.[7]

It was precisely this part of educational psychoanalysis that later prevailed on a worldwide scale. Anna Freud also expounded the psychoanalytic theory of development. The first lecture, "Infantile Amnesia and the Oedipus Complex," thus addressed the familial Oedipal situation, the child's dependence on the mother's care and love, and rivalry between siblings. The second lecture, "The Instinctual Life of Early Childhood," described the psychoanalytic model of stages, that is, the division of the child's development into oral, anal, and phallic stages. The third lecture, "The Latency Period," continued the description of the developmental theory, clarifying the concepts of resistance, the castration complex, and the libido. The significance of the latency period in intellectual development was also precisely explained. In the conclusions Anna Freud drew in the last lecture, she proposed mandatory training analysis for educators.

She asserted that already at this time psychoanalysis made possible in education:

1. a critique of existing forms of education;

2. the educator's broader knowledge of people, in particular an understanding of the child's developmental steps;

3. a therapeutic method to counter harm inflicted on a child during the educational process.

Even if Anna Freud aimed solely at presenting already familiar psychoanalytical theories in an accessible form, she could not altogether prevent the intrusion of her own thoughts and observations. Thus she models in the round the "misdemeanors" of children, one of her favorite themes:

Education . . . struggles with the child's demeanor, or, as the adults see it: his misdemeanors. . . . Children are frightfully inconsiderate and egotistic; they are concerned only with getting their own way and satisfying their own wishes whether this hurts others or not. They are dirty and messy; they do not mind touching the most disgusting matters or even putting them to the mouth. They are quite shameless so far as their own body is concerned and very curious about the things that other people wish to conceal from them. They are greedy and crave sweets. They are cruel to all living creatures that are weaker than they themselves and take great pleasure in destroying inanimate objects. They engage in an abundance of bad habits as far as the body is concerned: they suck their fingers, bite their nails, pick their noses, and play with their sexual organs; and they do all these things with intense passion, bent on gratifying every one of their wishes, and are quite intolerant of even the slightest postponement.

There are two chief complaints raised by parents. One is a feeling of hopelessness; scarcely have they broken the child of one bad habit than another takes its place. The other is a sense of bewilderment. They cannot understand where all this comes from. Certainly not from the parents' examples; and they have been careful to keep their own child away from contact with children known to be depraved.[8]

As a precaution, Anna Freud defended herself from the very beginning against the reproach that she was advancing an "indictment" of children. The list of "misdemeanors" was to be viewed merely as a random heap of idiosyncrasies whose particular meaning could be learned only step by step.

Even more crucial were Anna Freud's remarks on correct educational standards, which must take into account the reciprocity between society and education, an insight viewed as rather contemporary. Educators, she explained, that is, "the adults to whom the child belongs always want to make of him what suits them, i.e., they have aims which differ according to the century, position, class, political affiliation, etc."[9] Anna Freud was acutely aware of the tendency to try to adjust children to opportune models in the course of their education.

If one considers how much harm one can inflict on one's own child through an incorrect upbringing, one perforce comes to think of giving up instructive intervention altogether. This consideration has resurfaced in the 1970's in some socialist children's centers. But to return to Anna Freud:

A small girl developed an excessive pleasure in her naked body, showed herself naked to her brothers and sisters, and delighted in running through the rooms stark naked before going to bed. Education stepped in and the child made a great effort to suppress her desire. This resulted in intense feelings of shame and modesty which continued in later life. When the question of choosing a career arose, somebody suggested an occupation which would necessitate her sharing a room with companions. Unhesitatingly she replied that this was not for her. Behind the apparently rational motivation she ultimately revealed the fear of undressing in the presence of others. What profession to choose was less important than the prohibition carried over from childhood.[10]

She concluded:

> The analyst to whom all this is apparent resolves, so far as he is concerned, not to participate in such efforts, but to leave his own children free rather than to educate in this way. He decides to risk their being somewhat unruly rather than enforcing on them such crippling of their personalities.[11]

All so-called liberal theories of education could therefore refer to Anna Freud, who here again made her loyalty to Montessori's ideas clear. But she was equally aware of the possible damages of an excessively liberal education. To support her claim, she quoted several examples from Aichhorn's *Wayward Youth*.[12] Aichhorn tells of

> a boy who from about his sixth year onward had been offered every kind of sexual gratification by his mother, and finally, after reaching sexual maturity, had regular sexual intercourse with her. He had thus actually experienced what other children wish for in their fantasy. But this boy, too, with all restrictions removed, by no means developed into a self-reliant, harmonious, vigorous human being.
>
> What had occurred in his development was a kind of "short-circuiting." By the actual fulfillment of his childhood wishes he was saved the necessity of traversing the whole laborious path toward adulthood. He did not need to become a grown man in order to attain all the possibilities of gratification permitted to a man. But whatever he had escaped, he paid for by giving up all further development.[13]

That is, the extreme freedom of being sexually involved with one's mother must also be paid for with disturbances that later enormously impair social adjustment. Even if the demand that society abolish the incest taboo were fulfilled, this could not lead to a normal development, because necessary developmental steps would thereby have been skipped. Therefore, "The task of upbringing based on analytic understanding is to find a middle road between these extremes—that is to say, to find for each stage in the child's life the right proportion between drive gratification and drive control."[14]

Early psychoanalytic educational theory nevertheless raised the hope that it was possible to raise conflict-free people, if only disturbing influences—in particular those of family and environment—were eliminated or rectified early enough through child psychoanalysis. This inadmissibly simplified idea held the family, especially the mother, responsible for every disturbance and change in the child. The mother was thus expected to raise her child to be an emotionally well-balanced person. Anna Freud later explained that those were unrealistic and unrealizable expectations and that it was fundamentally impossible to reach this goal.

Lay Analysis and the Scope of Psychoanalysis

All arguments for and against lay analysis had already been raised in public before an acceptable resolution was sought at the Tenth International Psychoanalytic Congress at Innsbruck, which was held September 1–3, 1927. The psychoanalytic community hoped that Freud would be able to make the short trip from Vienna, but he was forced once again to forgo attendance. In keeping with what had by then become tradition, Anna Freud opened the congress by reading one of his lectures, "Humor."[1] She also read one of her own papers for the first time, "The Theory of Child Analysis,"[2] which was later inserted in *Introduction to the Technique of Child Analysis*. At this congress, Anna Freud was formally elected general secretary of the International Psychoanalytic Association (she had taken on the tasks a year earlier, when Eitingon replaced Abraham as president following the latter's death), thus assuming the first of many positions she was to occupy within the organization.

The business sessions revolved chiefly around lay analysis, that is, around the question of whether psychoanalysis may be practiced by nonphysicians. It seemed obvious, on the one hand, that those who had studied and mastered psychoanalysis should be allowed to practice it. But once examined in detail, the argument raised more questions than it answered. Anna Freud had always been concerned with the problem of nonmedical psychoanalysis, since she was a lay analyst herself and frequently had to express her views on the subject.

The question of lay analysis is worth discussing in greater depth, partly because the controversy has been rekindled today.[3] Debates have focused on three themes: 1) psychoanalysis' range of applicability; 2) diagnosis prior to psychoanalytic treatment; and 3) protection against wild analysis and quacks by means of regulated and organized training. Reading through them, however, one is surprised to discover that in the last fifty years, not one fresh argument has been added to this question.

In his essay "The Question of Lay Analysis" (1926),[4] as well as in personal conversations, Freud vigorously defended lay analysis. It has been claimed that he intended in this way to help his daughter. Such an insinuation is absurd because, had it been the case, Freud would have certainly persuaded his daughter either to study medicine or to give more weight to important ideas than to her personal destiny. Freud saw the future of psychoanalysis as dependent on lay analysis. That is why, during the last decades of his life, no problem concerned him more than that of lay analysis.

Although psychoanalysis developed out of psychopathology, Freud had realized early on that the applicability of psychoanalytic insights as explanatory theories extended far beyond psychiatry and the treatment of neuroses. Indeed, historical developments have fully confirmed his expectation that nonmedical areas—i.e., those that have nothing to do with clinical treatment—would become far more significant for psychoanalysis than medicine. Today, psychoanalysis is certainly not irrelevant to medical treatment, but its significance has clearly ebbed compared to anthropology, mythology, ethnology, literature, sociology, law, and education. Freud saw great danger in relegating psychoanalysis exclusively to the medical profession, which could not be expected to provide cultural analyses in addition to its own services. Nevertheless, he acknowledged that those who are competent to make such cultural analyses certainly should not be denied access to the experiences psychoanalysts gain in therapy.

There are, nevertheless, counterarguments to this. It seems reasonable that, after having been trained in psychoanalysis for a certain period, "culture psychoanalysts," if we may use this term, would return to their original profession, where they would benefit from the knowledge they had acquired. Practice, however, teaches again and again that this simple principle does not work. Once conversant with psychoanalysis, many choose to practice psychoanalytic therapy, though the original field of interest may act as a guideline for their work. As a result, their profession loses members who, as nonmedical therapists, are as much mere therapists as are psychoanalytically trained physicians. Among the many examples of such cases we can mention Lou Andreas-Salomé, who spent the last decades of her life practicing psychoanalytic therapy.

On the other hand, there is a group of analysts who do return to their original profession; among them, Géza Róheim and Ernst Kris. Both were lay analysts who made important contributions to their scientific fields after they had completed their training in analysis. Among nonphysicians we also find those interested in psychology, who acquire their entire knowledge from books, that is, from the comprehensive and sometimes excellent literature of psychoanalysis. Even so, these producers and interpreters of culture suffer from the disadvantages imposed by the abstract, intrinsically logical, yet practically inapposite theories in which they tend to lose themselves. Thus, they gradually withdraw from psychoanalysis or make indefensible claims based on their theoretical view. Without clinical experience, without the contact with patients who seek therapy, it is virtually impossible to truly understand psychoanalysis.

Finally, some psychoanalysts, whether trained in medicine or not, are both interpreters of culture and practitioners. Freud belonged to this group, and so did Anna Freud, insofar as her writings diverged from mere clinical questions. Another prominent example is Alexander Mitscherlich, who popularized psychoanalysis in Germany after World War II and whose book *The Inability to Mourn*, written with Margarete Mitscherlich, offers a cultural interpretation from the psychoanalytic point of view.[5] Although this group was clearly the most significant, it did not solve the dilemmas that had been raised because, whether the subject be medical or nonmedical psychoanalysis, these writers and practitioners had to fulfill two functions at once, each of which claimed unswerving dedication. The workload imposed on them was far too great and could hardly be reconciled with quite a number of psychohygienic principles. We will have to admit, then, that a few exceptions aside, lay analysis is fundamentally an inadequate means for applying psychoanalytic insights to general cultural problems.

It seems obvious that nonmedical psychotherapists, and certainly their patients, should be protected from the possible harm of a false diagnosis. That is why Freud vehemently insisted on the analysand's medical examination prior to the beginning of analysis. But the lay analyst Hanns Sachs has pointed out that under certain circumstances this precaution may be insufficient, e.g., when diagnosis can be determined only in the course of psychoanalytic treatment. Also, physical symptoms may appear that so perfectly fit the psychic clinical picture that a somatic illness is not even suspected. Moreover, neurosis may exploit an already existing somatic illness.

Such objections are no doubt serious. Both the medical and the nonmedical analyst can make errors. But it also happens quite often that a psychic or psychosomatic disturbance is misconstrued as somatic illness. Freud remarked sarcastically that even physicians who dabble in psychoanalysis without appropriate training should be viewed as quacks. "Taking my stand on this definition, I venture to assert that—not only in European countries—doctors form a preponderating contingent of quacks in analysis."[6]

But here as well the dilemma remains ultimately insoluble, even if medical quacks are common among psychoanalysts, as Jones claimed was true in Austria, but not in England or America.[7] We will always hold a physician responsible for having overlooked a somatic illness, and even sue him for negligence and reprehensible conduct. On the other hand, we cannot demand that a lay analyst notice a somatic illness. Freud and most analysts took it for granted that the prospective psychoanalyst should receive thorough, high-quality training. Freud recommended that the curriculum include cultural history, mythology, psychology of religion, and literary criticism, because without good preparation in these fields the analyst will confront a large part of the material without understanding it.[8] Because of its scientific, materialistic orientation, Freud saw in medicine dangers rather than advantages. We must remember that today, even more than in the past, no training imposes as many sacrifices as psychoanalysis, and that psychoanalysts were the first to organize a comprehensive training system. But it should also be added that the training of the lay analyst lasts only a quarter of the time required of the psychiatrist. Thus, since Freud's day, postanalytical methods have again and again developed, whose attractiveness consists foremost in their lower training requirements.

Some analysts, above all Jones, opposed Freud on this question. Jones did not shrink from statements that were surprising in this proverbially polite Englishman. "There are passages in the book in question where professor Freud does not fully reach his exceptional standard. . . . [Freud's arguments] are presented deftly and perspicaciously, but contain nothing new, omit many important points, and are obviously biased."[9] Jones's trenchant criticism is all the more astonishing because lay analysis was less prevalent in the Vienna group than among London psychoanalysts. before World War I, there was only one lay analyst in Vienna—Hermine Hug-Hellmuth—and she worked with children. The initial illusion that psychoanalysis was easier to practice with children than with adults obviously had to be dismissed. Still, the interweaving of education and therapy should have aroused more generosity from the very beginning. Even in America, where the attitude toward lay analysis was particularly hostile, lay analysis was temporarily permitted with children in 1929. Otto Rank, who later became Vienna's first lay analyst, even apologized to Jones for analyzing only children.[10] We have already spoken about other lay analysts, such as Siegfried Bernfeld and August Aichhorn, and their work with children and adolescents; Theodor Reik and Robert Waelder were among the other few lay analysts.

Circumstances were completely different in London. Forty percent of the members of the British Psychoanalytic Society were not physicians. Joan Riviere, Ella Sharpe, and Barbara Low, as well as Melanie Klein and others who had heavily attacked Anna Freud, were lay analysts and, moreover, enjoyed Jones's special protection. It is difficult to explain why Jones became the spokesman for the opponents of lay analysis, and why he defended this position even in his biography of Freud.[11] But inconsistency apparently belonged to Jones's character.

In 1927, it became clear that there would be no agreement on the question of lay analysis. Opinions diverged too widely, and both sides were all too able to raise cogent arguments.

A. A. Brill, who represented and popularized psychoanalysis in the United States, announced to the New York Psychoanalytic Society that he would break relations with Freud if Vienna's psychoanalytic community maintained its positive attitude toward lay analysis. In 1926, lay analysis was even declared illegal in New York. Finally, in 1927, the New York Psychoanalytic Society rejected lay analysis altogether.

Each country could have made allowances for different regulations if European analysts had not already gone to the United States, where they understandably sought admission to psychoanalytic organizations. Even if they had not studied medicine, Americans received their psychoanalytic training in Europe without difficulty, and were welcome as members in the local organizations of Vienna and Berlin. Upon their return to the United States, however, organizations of their own country denied them membership. It was therefore imperative to seek a resolution to this problem.

Anna Freud, who as general secretary had drawn up the report on the Innsbruck debate, described it as "extremely lively." Jones later spoke about a "heated discussion, often with several speakers talking at once."[12] The congress finally accepted Sándor Radó's proposal to delegate the International Training Commission to set up general mandatory guidelines (Radó did not know that four years later he would become training supervisor at the New York Psychoanalytic Institute). Although it seemed innocuous, this directive marked not only a victory for the adherents of lay analysis, but showed moreover that American organizations could be forced to permit lay analysis despite their established regulations.

The International Training Commission was headed by Eitingon, who had been elected president of the International Psychoanalytic Association at the Innsbruck congress. Three years earlier, the Berlin Institute, under Eitingon's leadership, had set up training rules that admitted lay analysts in principle, but declared such admission to be an exception, since medicine was still a prerequisite for training in adult analysis. "Exceptions can be allowed only in special cases,"[13] and only the child analyst was permitted to substitute academic for medical training. But where Eitingon was concerned, one could safely presume that he would finally adopt Freud's point of view. In his lecture at the Innsbruck congress, Eitingon had already cautiously withdrawn his point of view: "All those well trained in analysis, well equipped for their particular speciality in the profession, and who apply analysis in their research and work, using the correct methodology, will promote analysis as a science."[14] To be sure, Eitingon also stressed that those trained in medicine were better equipped for analytical practice than those who felt at home in other professions.

The congress therefore passed the resolution first presented to the participants of the preliminary conference:

> I. The congress enjoins the training committees of the branch societies to request that candidates seeking training in psychoanalytic therapy have or complete medical training, without, however, rejecting candidates with special abilities and the appropriate scientific preparation but who lack medical qualifications.
>
> II. Within this basic position, each branch society can independently determine the admission requirements. In the case of foreign candidates, the training committees must consider, in addition to their own regulations, those regulations effective in the candidate's homeland. The training committee of the candidate's homeland is to be informed of a candidate's admission. Eventual objections are to be addressed to the International Training Commission.[15]

The acceptance of Radó's proposal, in which the American representatives were outvoted, clearly overruled the existing regulations. Consequently, there was a good chance that the American psychoanalysts would make good their threat to sever relations with Freud and the European organizations. Anna Freud immediately understood the danger of this extremely critical moment and prevented a confrontation:

> Things looked distinctly unpleasant at the meeting when suddenly above the hubbub a girlish voice rang out with the words: "Gentlemen, I think we are committing an injustice." It was this intervention of Anna Freud's which saved the situation. She pointed out that we were legislating for America on an occasion when there were only three Americans present, and that we should not take advantage of this minimal representation.[16]

Anna Freud revealed her true nature here. There could have been no doubt about her own positive attitude toward lay analysis, not only because she was a lay analyst herself and her father had expressed his unequivocal opinion on the subject, but also because she had always kept in mind the importance of maintaining the widespread influence psychoanalysis enjoyed around the world. With this intervention she clearly meant—even at the expense of her own convictions and interests—to prevent a schism between European and American psychoanalysis.

In 1933, German psychoanalysts began to emigrate, and were soon followed by those from the rest of continental Europe. The outbreak of World War II brought the debate on lay analysis to a standstill. With the exception of those in England, there was scarcely a psychoanalyst left in Europe in 1945. American psychoanalysis, on the other hand, as well as American psychiatry, reached a supremacy they have maintained ever since. No longer could anyone think of challenging the Americans on the question of lay analysis.

Today, however, psychoanalytic institutes confront entirely different problems. The number of students desiring entry into the field has decreased considerably. Since many psychoanalytic institutes cannot thrive only on young medical doctors, doors that had previously been locked are now open.

A Calm Year

The year 1928 was to be less turbulent for Anna Freud than the previous one. There was neither a symposium against her, nor were there heated discussions on lay analysis. On February 5, 1928 she gave a lecture at the Budapest Psychoanalytic Society where she dealt again with the special relationship between psychoanalysis and education. Soon thereafter she traveled to Berlin, where a discussion on the psychoanalytic training of teachers took place. With Siegfried Bernfeld, she reported on it to the Vienna Society in May. Next she had to travel to Paris, where Jones had organized a meeting of the Committee.[1]

In reality the Committee in its old format no longer existed. Rank, one of its most reliable members and among the guardians of the theory, had resigned. And Abraham, psychoanalysis' strongest supporter next to Freud, had died. There remained a heterogeneous group consisting of Jones, Ferenczi, Eitingon, Andreas-Salomé, and Anna Freud. Ernst Simmel joined at the end of 1928, and Freud, urged by his daughter, gave him the ring that members of the most intimate circle wore.[2] Since the distance to Paris was too great for Ferenczi, and in the end Jones himself could not come either, only Anna Freud and Eitingon met in Paris, although they could have talked matters over equally well in Vienna. What they discussed or what issues they were to have addressed has not been recorded.

In May, Eitingon, in his capacity as representative of the International Training Commission, assigned the drafting of a psychoanalytic training program for educators to Anna Freud and August Aichhorn, a project Anna Freud had time and again called for. They were also to establish guidelines for the training of child analysts that would enable these to be later considered an independent professional group. But Eitingon had also assigned the same task to the London group (Barbara Low, Melanie Klein, Nina Searl, Susan Isaacs, and Ella Sharpe), and agreements could not have been expected.

In August, Anna Freud joined her father for a vacation which they again spent in nearby Semmering. On August 30, they took the difficult—but, for Freud, necessary—trip to Berlin where Professor Schroeder replaced the old, badly functioning, and uncomfortable prosthesis. They stayed at the Tegel Palace sanatorium, whose director was Ernst Simmel. On September 30, they took advantage of the opportunity to attend the inauguration festivities for the new home of the Berlin Psychoanalytic Institute, which, like the first building, had been designed by Ernst Freud. Anna Freud gave a brief speech and, as was customary on such occasions, spoke of "a new and consistent stage of development through which our analytic organization expects to fulfill its hopes for the future."[3]

Visitors came to Berlin-Tegel, among them Lou Andreas-Salomé. Anna and Sigmund Freud did not return to Vienna until the end of October, and during the winter of 1928–29 Anna Freud held a seminar on "The Technique of Child Analysis"—as we know, the subject closest to her heart. This seminar, where cases of child analysis were continually reported on, gained historical significance. Anna Freud herself later recalled it with fondness. The seminar was taught until the 1938 emigration, and was then resumed in London. Many well-known people attended it: Berta and Steff Bornstein, Editha Sterba, Jenny Waelder-Hall, Dorothy Burlingham (who was living in Vienna at this time), Edith Buxbaum, Erik Erikson (Homburger), Hedwig and Willie Hoffer, Annie Angel-Katan, Marianne Kris, Anna Maenchen, Margaret S. Mahler, Esther Menaker, Edith Jackson, Marian Putnam, and Helen Ross. At the Vienna Training Institute, it was Willie Hoffer who introduced the training for educators.

The Frankfurt Psychoanalytic Institute

For Anna Freud, 1929 was to be another year of travels, as outlined by Freud in a letter to Oskar Pfister on February 16, 1929:

> Dear Dr. Pfister,
>
> I have discussed with Anna the possibility of her attending the congress at Elsinore (August 8–22) but found her very loth, I think with good reason. She has to give a lecture in Frankfurt very soon, she is going with me to Berlin in March, is meeting Eitingon, Jones and Ferenczi in Paris in April, and of course cannot miss the congress at Oxford [in July], so you will see that she has enough travel in store for this year and is reluctant still further to restrict the summer after a hard year's work. With Aichhorn it would be different, I mean it would be if I had not already spoken to him, there would be nothing to stop his travelling. But I know that he is an official who lives on a limited budget and cannot afford the expense of such a journey. Also I wonder whether you do not overestimate the importance of this congress and its attitude to analysis. In one eventuality I should myself embark on the trip to Elsinore in spite of all my infirmities, that is, if you could persuade Prince Hamlet to appear in person and confess in a lecture that he indeed suffered from the Oedipus complex, which so many people refuse to believe. But even you will not be able to manage that, so I shall have to stay at home.[1]

The congress mentioned in the letter was the World Conference on New Education held in Elsinore, Denmark, which Anna Freud did not attend. The letter also sheds light on the particularly cordial relationship both father and daughter had with Aichhorn. But Aichhorn could not attend the conference either. Psychoanalysis was represented by Gertud Behn-Eschenburg from Zurich, who spoke about the analysis of the young child, and by Nelly Wolfheim from Berlin, who lectured on "The Kindergarten and Psychoanalysis."[2] Pfister also gave his own course on psychoanalysis in Elsinore.

Anna Freud's traveling season began in February. She traveled first to Frankfurt-am-Main to the opening of the Frankfurt Psychoanalytic Institute, which had been founded by the Southwestern German Psychoanalytic Society. Headed by Karl Landauer, who was later murdered by the Nazis, the Southwestern German group was indeed impressive despite its small size. Heinrich Meng resigned from his position as chief physician in Stuttgart to assume the direction of the institute with Landauer. In 1934, Meng emigrated to Basel. Frieda Fromm-Reichmann, who later distinguished herself in the United States as a psychoanalyst of schizophrenics, also taught at the institute. During that time, Fromm-Reichmann also had her own psychoanalytic practice and clinic in Heidelberg. Since 1926 she had been married to Erich Fromm—a problem, according to Landauer, because Fromm, ten years younger than his wife, was her former analysand. Fromm spent most of his time in Berlin, but was the principal link with the Frankfurt Institute for Social Research, which put its library at the disposal of analysts and where at first courses in psychoanalysis were also taught. Fromm was both a member of the Psychoanalytic Institute and, as a specialist in psychoanalysis, a member of the Institute for Social Research,[3] with which Meng and Landauer also maintained close contacts. Many discussions took place with Max Horkheimer, Friedrich Pollock, and Theodor Adorno until the Institute for Social Research moved to the United States.[4] S. H. Fuchs also taught at the institute; after he emigrated to England, he became one of the first world-famous group psychoanalysts under the anglicized name Foulkes.

A new center for psychoanalysis thus developed in Frankfurt-am-Main. It was presumably Meng who maintained contact with Anna Freud, who—like Siegfried Bernfeld, Hanns Sachs, and Paul Federn—was invited to give a public reading on psychoanalysis. Anna Freud spoke on education and, according to Landauer's report,[5] both she and the subject of her lecture received wide attention in the Frankfurt press. The *Frankfurter Zeitung* described her appearance and bearing:

> Anna Freud, an elementary-school teacher from Vienna, daughter of Sigmund Freud, a slender young woman with dark hair surrounding a clear and relaxed face, stood yesterday on the podium of the small concert hall where all seats to the very last one had been sold out, so that many who wanted to hear her were not allowed in. Moreover, this was the first time Anna Freud spoke in front of a large audience. Her manner of lecturing is so perfectly modest and clear, so far from rhetorical pretension in its objectivity, that to listen to her is an esthetic pleasure: intellectual grace which effortlessly captivates.[6]

It had been Landauer's plan to use the establishment of the Frankfurt Psychoanalytic Institute to arouse interest in psychoanalysis among Frankfurt's broader public. He managed to persuade the *Frankfurter Zeitung* to publish three articles under the title "The Consequences of Psychoanalysis," which presented psychoanalysis in generally comprehensible terms. Landauer and Oskar Pfister wrote on psychoanalysis and medicine, as well as on psychoanalysis and sociology. Bernfeld wrote an article on the significance of psychoanalysis for education, in which he very briefly outlined a program: "Aimed at the child's creative, independent activities, at the dismantling of authority and punishment, the newer education will defend itself with decisive arguments drawn from psychoanalysis."[7]

This also conveys Anna Freud's position. A very sympathetic review appeared in November 1929, which included an excerpt from Anna Freud's forthcoming *Psychoanalysis for Teachers and Parents.*[8]

On March 11, 1929, Anna Freud again accompanied her father to Berlin, where Schroeder adjusted the prosthesis. They stayed at Simmel's little Tegel Palace again, but remained only two weeks. During this time, Lou Andreas-Salomé came to Berlin from Göttingen twice to visit father and daughter. As Freud later wrote, at these visits he was forced to leave the conversation mostly to Anna, not only because he had difficulty speaking but because he had lost some of his hearing.

Andreas-Salomé sent Freud a letter of good wishes for his seventy-third birthday on May 6, 1929,[9] in which, probably to comfort and cheer him up, she described his condition in Tegel in positive terms. The letter also reflects her relationship with Anna Freud, who had evidently proved to be pleasantly attentive to her.

Dear Professor,

This is to pay you a little letter-visit for the day after tomorrow, in order to discharge a large load of affection at your door. I still rejoice when I think of how fresh and rejuvenated you seemed in March at Tegel, and I can only hope that you were not too disappointed by the terribly unseasonable weeks that followed. Here at least we are still confronted with a bleak and rigid winter landscape, and only yesterday it was adorned with a garment of white which the most friendly eye could hardly mistake for fruit blossom. I comforted myself by eating oranges one after the other—Anna's splendid Jaffas, and you must please tell her how gratefully I thought of the donor at each mouthful. And now both of you have long been hard at work again, and it is a long time till the holidays. I wonder if in the meantime you have found somewhere to go among the lakes and mountains?[10]

A few days after Freud's birthday, Anna Freud again attended to plans for the summer vacation. She went to Berchtesgaden with Dorothy Burlingham to see whether "Schneewinkellehen," a house not far from Königssee, would be suitable for her father.[11] The entire family moved to Berchtesgaden as early as June 18, where Freud received visits from Jones, Ferenczi, and A. A. Brill in succession, as well as from René Laforgue and Joan Riviere.

At the end of May, Anna Freud traveled to Paris, where the Committee finally met a year later than scheduled. The meeting served as a preliminary session of the Eleventh International Psychoanalytical Congress scheduled for July in Oxford, that is, on English territory for the first time. The subject of lay analysis was again on the agenda, and acute conflicts were expected, mainly with the Americans. Jones reported on vehement disputes between Ferenczi and Anna Freud at this meeting, but we can only guess at their contents. Perhaps Anna Freud tried to convince Ferenczi of the importance of lay analysis; perhaps she tried to attenuate his radical attitude toward the Americans. Eitingon as usual tried to act as mediator.

The Eleventh Congress was held on July 27–31, 1929, in Oxford. On her way to Oxford, Anna Freud stopped over in London for several days to attend, as Freud's "messenger," the festivities for Jones's fiftieth birthday. Jones had already turned fifty on January 1, but the celebration held by the British Psychoanalytic Society had been scheduled for July 24 to allow him to attend it before the Oxford congress. Two years had passed since Anna Freud had last visited London, on the occasion of the turbulent symposium on child psychoanalysis. The London group had not pursued the polemic, Freud had written an encomium, and in a private birthday letter to Jones he brooked past "disagreements" as family quarrels.

Anna Freud did not read one of Freud's introductory lectures at Oxford, but instead gave her own lecture, "A Counterpiece on Animal Phobia in Children." With two case histories she demonstrated that the same elements that trigger an animal phobia (for example, the fear of horses in "Little Hans") can also provoke an animal fantasy "which compensates for the fear of the father by transforming it into its opposite."[12]

The business sessions of the congress again revolved around the question of lay analysis, but a resolution was postponed. That is, the only action taken was the formulation of a new committee that attempted to cover as many international theoretical nuances as possible. Hence no agreement could be expected, despite the brilliant names of its members: Marie Princess Bonaparte (Paris), Abraham Arden Brill (New York), Helene Deutsch (Vienna), Max Eitingon (Berlin), Sándor Ferenczi (Budapest), Anna Freud (Vienna), Ernest Jones (London), Smith Ely Jelliffe (New York), Hans Sachs (Berlin), J. H. W. van Ophuijsen (The Hague), and Philipp Sarasin (Basel). Nevertheless, Eitingon's proposal to officially include child psychoanalysis and the psychoanalytic training of educators was now formally suspended, though even in these two areas it was not expected that an agreement could ever be reached. Anna Freud presented the decisions of the Vienna commission (Anna Freud and August Aichhorn), and Melanie Klein presented those of the London commission (Barbara Low, Melanie Klein, H. F. Searles, Susan Isaacs, Ella Sharpe). The two proposals were neither discussed nor published. The question of a special, psychoanalytically oriented training for the "nursing personnel of the mentally ill" was raised for the first time by Paul Federn, but the congress took no note of it. Behind the scenes, however, the same questions were so vehemently debated that a schism again threatened the International Psychoanalytic Association. Eitingon nevertheless remained its chairman, and Anna Freud was again elected general secretary. The Oxford days were obviously very exhausting for Anna Freud. She wired daily reports on the congress to her father, who was still in Schneewinkel. Freud made mention of this in a letter to Lou Andreas-Salomé from this period:

Anna is having a rather hard time in Oxford; by this evening she will have given her paper and will then, I hope, take things more easily. As to the accommodation, she writes, as one might expect: "More tradition than comfort." I expect you to know that the English, having created the notion of comfort, then refused to have anything more to do with it. Like Wolf, I can hardly wait for her return. I write, and he spends half the day lying apathetically in his basket.[13]

From Oxford, Anna Freud returned to the Schneewinkel house in Berchtesgaden to resume her interrupted vacation with her father. He had meanwhile written the larger part of *Civilization and Its Discontents*, one of his most important books, but one that he himself did not particularly like.[14] From September 15 to October 20, 1929, Anna Freud accompanied her father to Berlin to see Schroeder for the second time that year. Again they stayed at the Tegel Sanatorium, where the American diplomat William C. Bullitt visited them and discussed with Freud plans for a historical-psychoanalytical study of Woodrow Wilson. (In 1938, in his capacity as American ambassador to Paris, Bullitt later interceded to bring the Freud family out of Vienna, and welcomed them in Paris.)

It was also in 1929 that, at the prompting of Marie Bonaparte, Max Schur became Freud's personal physician. Working closely with Anna Freud, he attended to her father's medical care until Freud's death.[15]

At the end of 1929, Anna Freud took her last trip for that year, the only one meant exclusively for her pleasure: a visit to Lou Andreas-Salomé in Göttingen.

The Goethe Prize for Sigmund Freud

Nineteen thirty began auspiciously, yet brought a number of distressing and crucial events in its course. For Anna Freud, everyday life now consisted of caring for her father, traveling as his messenger, working with her own patients, and, finally, the pursuit of child psychoanalysis. At thirty-five, she had thus established a routine in her life that would endure until disturbed by external circumstances. Unlike previous years, long hikes were no longer possible during the extended summer vacation, and father and daughter enjoyed instead walks through the woods accompanied by their dogs. Work with patients followed the morning walk. Father and daughter shared a waiting room but had separate consulting rooms. The entire family gathered around the table for midday dinner. Therapy was continued throughout the afternoon, usually into the early evening. Later in the evening they either sat at their desks or worked together. During these evenings, as well as during the day (mostly between analysis sessions), Freud attended to his extensive correspondence, of which only a small part has thus far been published. Anna Freud herself had also become a diligent letter writer and replied promptly to her mail. Like her works, her letters strike the reader with the same concise though always exhaustive treatment of a subject. She did not give in to the world's curiosity to read this correspondence. Though Anna Freud stood in the public limelight by 1930, she was always intent on leaving her personal life in the background.

Anna Freud's life had settled, the family's economic situation had improved, and the consequences of World War I and inflation had been largely overcome. Still, gloomy clouds gathered on the horizon. The calm of daily work could not mitigate Anna Freud's concern over the progress of her father's illness. Moreover, political developments smothered every optimistic feeling. Unemployment escalated by leaps and bounds, and the considerably declining birthrate further pointed to generally grim prospects for the future. The clamor of the Nazis became louder and louder in Germany, and even more so in Austria. The geographical focal point of the historical evolution toward violence, terror, and murder having shifted since then, one tends to forget that Hitler—at that time not yet a naturalized German—was in fact from Upper Austria, and that the National Socialists enjoyed a far greater popularity in the Austrian states than in German-speaking areas in the north. The initial field of tension of the barbarously brutal National Socialism with its salient anti-Semitic agitation lay between Vienna and Munich—that is, in Freud's immediate proximity. In 1930 the German Reichstag showed an astounding rise in Nazi-held seats, from 12 to 107.

Omens had darkened in Russia as well. At first Soviet ideology had exerted a powerful attraction on Western intellectuals. Even Freud was well disposed toward it. Yet despite impressive progress in art and science in the Soviet Union, the tyranny became noticeably more cruel around 1930. Wilhelm Reich, with whom Anna Freud was professionally albeit not personally connected, was still attempting at that time a synthesis between psychoanalysis and Marxism, and with much distress reported to the Vienna Psychoanalytic Society on the status of psychoanalysis in the Soviet Union. Psychoanalysis had at first been promoted there, but was soon suppressed. At the same time Reich presented a brilliant psychological analysis of National Socialism, but the bulk of his numerous lectures delivered to the Vienna Psychoanalytic Society addressed primarily purely clinical psychoanalytical problems. Two years later, Reich would completely break with other psychoanalysts.

On February 26, 1930, Anna Freud delivered her 1929 Oxford lecture, "A Counterpiece on Animal Phobia in Children," to the Vienna Psychoanalytic Society. On March 26, she spoke on the methods of case description before the Hungarian Psychoanalytic Society in Budapest. These lectures stemmed from her aforementioned Vienna seminar on child psychoanalysis, which was now held on Mondays.

At the end of April, Anna Freud accompanied her father to the Cottage Sanatorium in Vienna, because he had heart and intestinal problems. These finally proved to be harmless, and—since Freud then gave up smoking after all—they disappeared within a few days. This rash reaction shows the fear about Freud's health that was constantly hovering over the family. On May 4, father and daughter again traveled to Berlin, where Schroeder had to assemble another prosthesis for Freud. Freud's birthday on May 6 was celebrated at the Tegel Sanatorium in Berlin. This sojourn, liberally estimated to take six weeks, ended up stretching over a three-month period. During this time the friendship between Freud and Bullitt became closer. At the end of May, they took a three-day trip from Berlin to Hiddensee, the island lying near Rügen, where Anna's brother Ernst, who owned a house in Berlin, had acquired a small fishing cabin. That Freud had on this occasion boarded an airplane for the first time in his life for a round-trip flight—there is even a photograph of the event— indicates that his general condition had improved.

Freud's illness involved several longer trips with Anna Freud to Professor Schroeder in Berlin, precisely during the years of the portentous rise of Nazism. They were thus able to actually observe the political developments from close by, a circumstance that has thus far been neglected in the literature.

After the three months in Berlin, the Freud family set out to spend their summer vacation in Rebenburg-am-Grundelsee, in the Salzkammer district, where their friend Dorothy Burlingham (we shall later devote more attention to her) had also arrived. Several days later, Freud received the news that he had been awarded the Goethe Prize, worth 10,000 marks, by the city of Frankfurt. We may assume that the opening of the Frankfurt Psychoanalytic Institute and Anna Freud's assistance there during the past year may have had a bearing on the selection of the winner. To be sure, available documents offer no evidence of this, but there had evidently been vehement disputes before the prize was awarded to Freud. Contrary to the rules, it became known that Freud would be the recipient of the prize before it was actually handed to him. According to Heinrich Meng, a member of the board of trustees, the lyricist and playwright Alfons Paquet, with whom Meng had long since been in close contact, also played a key role. The physician and writer Alfred Döblin also supported the selection of Freud.[1] Since Freud himself could not travel, Anna Freud had to represent him again. The festive presentation took place on August 28, 1930—Goethe's birthday—in the reception room of Goethe's parental home in Frankfurt. A small crowd of guests had gathered. As an introduction, Alfred Höhn played the largo from Chopin's Opus 58. The Lord Mayor of Frankfurt, Dr. Landmann, then honored the recipient. Anna Freud, who received the prize for her father, read her father's acceptance speech. Höhn closed with the *Polonaise* in A flat major by Chopin. A souvenir photograph was taken, but it was soon lost.[2] The great, even astonishing effect this honor had on Freud is revealed in the 1935 Postscript to An Autobiographical Study: "A little later my daughter Anna, acting as my proxy, was given a civic reception in the Rathaus at Frankfurt-on-Main on the occasion of my being awarded the Goethe Prize for 1930. *This was the climax of my life as a citizen.*" [My italics.][3]

The reader will chuckle to notice that Freud misplaced the celebration from the Goethe House to the Frankfurt City Hall.

Only a few days following the presentation of the award, on September 12, 1930, Freud's mother died in Vienna at the age of ninety-five. She had lived in Ischl during the last years of her life but had been brought to Vienna during the days preceding her death because of the intense pain rampantly spreading gangrene in her leg was causing her. Freud, surprisingly, remained at the health resort while Anna Freud represented him at her grandmother's funeral in Vienna. Freud wrote to Ernest Jones: "Again Anna represented me as at Frankfurt. Her value to me can hardly be heightened."[4]

How deeply her grandmother's suffering moved Anna Freud is evident in a letter Lou Andreas-Salomé wrote to Freud: "[Anna] wrote to me about the death of her grandmother: why, oh why had so long a life to end with weeks of torment? Do not our wretched laws make man inexpressibly cruel to his fellow men?"[5]

After the funeral, Anna Freud went to Switzerland and Italy with Dorothy Burlingham.

Dorothy Burlingham

Dorothy Burlingham, who lived with Anna Freud at 20 Maresfield Gardens, London, until her death on November 19, 1979, came into Anna Freud's life in 1925. She concealed herself from public view even more than Anna Freud, so that only scanty personal information has become available. It is known that she came from the well-to-do Tiffany family, and was thus able to enjoy solid financial security. She left her husband, who was considered "mentally disturbed," early on and moved with her four children to Vienna, where she was analyzed first by Theodor Reik and then by Freud. Her children were among Anna Freud's first patients. Anna Freud not only analyzed all of them but, as a family friend, also assumed an educator's role. This became her first opportunity to practice psychoanalytic education over an extended period. From the very beginning, Burlingham had accepted Anna Freud's conception of analysis and always defended her position in the great controversy with Melanie Klein.

After Burlingham terminated her analysis, her personal ties with the Freuds became even firmer, and from 1928 until the emigration she lived at 19 Berggasse, one floor above the Freuds, and belonged to the most intimate circle of family friends. It was she who gave Freud the chow chows he is seen with in photographs from his last years. In January 1929, Freud wrote to Ludwig Binswanger: "Our symbiosis with an American family (husbandless), whose children my daughter is bringing up analytically with a firm hand, is growing continually stronger, so that we share with them our needs for the summer."[1]

In 1930, the two women traveled together for the first time. At the end of that year, they bought a small farm cottage at Hochrotherd, near Breitenfurth, which still exists. Breitenfurth is a small rural settlement in the immediate vicinity of Vienna. Hochrotherd is so small that it is not marked even on larger maps. A passage in a letter Anna Freud wrote to Lou Andreas-Salomé mentions the purchase: "Dorothy and I have bought a little cottage with three acres of land. It is in Hochrotherd near Breitenfurth, in the neighborhood of Mauer, but high up. It is all still very shabby, but we are fixing it up."[2]

Not only the two women and Dorothy Burlingham's children used the house for their enjoyment and recreation. Like everything else the Freud family owned, it was viewed within a larger frame and used by the entire family, which had drawn into its midst a close circle of friends, some of whom were explicitly treated as family members. Freud also let himself be taken to Hochrotherd, and on May 8, 1932, he wrote to Arnold Zweig from the house that had meanwhile been renovated and furnished:

> Dear Arnold Zweig
>
> Where am I writing from? From a farm cottage on the side of a hill, forty-five minutes by car from the Berggase, which my daughter and her American friend (she owns the car) have acquired and furnished for their weekends. We had expected that your return home from Palestine would take you through Vienna, and then we would have insisted on your seeing it.[3]

Felix and Helene Deutsch also visited the Freuds in Hochrotherd, and Helene Deutsch described the visit in her memoirs:

> From time to time Felix (also a devoted friend of Anna's) and I would visit "Hochroterd" [sic], Anna's little farm near Vienna, where she enjoyed a modest kind of farming. The Sundays we spent with her are perhaps even clearer in my memory than our work in the service of psychoanalysis. For my husband and me, "Hochroterd" was the seed of our love for our own American farm, "Babayaga."[4]

In 1932, Dorothy Burlingham became an associate member of the Vienna Psychoanalytic Society. She began to practice analysis with children and adults in 1934. Her lecture of admission to the society carried the title "The Urge to Communicate and the Compulsion to Confess." Burlingham was finally elected to the Committee, receiving the ring from Freud, and in 1937 became a full member of the Vienna Psychoanalytic Society. She joined the Freuds when they emigrated to London, where she and Anna Freud continued to work together and publish joint writings.[5] Beginning in 1940, both women managed the Hampstead Nurseries and, from 1952 on, the Hampstead Child Therapy Course and Clinic.

Shortly after Anna Freud and Burlingham returned from their trip to Italy, Freud's health deteriorated. On October 10, he had to undergo more minor surgery. A week later, he was ill with pneumonia and had to stay in bed for ten days. Now more than ever he was dependent on his willingly self-sacrificing daughter, to whom he dictated his correspondence from bed. It seems that Anna Freud occasionally augmented his letters.[6] Only a few analyses had been continued during the vacation, and it was not until November, after a seven-month interruption, that both were able to resume work with patients.

The Shadows of the Future

Except for Freud's seventy-fifth birthday, 1931 passed without major events. Life went on, and Anna Freud published nothing that year. Freud, celebrating his jubilee, received numerous honors from all over the world. A historical marker was hung on the house where he was born in Freiberg (now Príbor), Moravia. Freud had left Freiberg at the age of three and returned for a visit only once, at the age of sixteen. Anna Freud, who had never been there before, went with Federn and Eitingon to read Freud's brief letter of appreciation. No one attributed special significance to the event. But one annoying detail cropped up: the Freiberg birth registry had entered Freud's birthday as *March* 6, 1856, and the ensuing controversy lasted until 1969, when May 6 was proven to be the correct date.

The shadows of the future hovered over the year 1931. Psychoanalysts, who had meanwhile reached modest prosperity, were increasingly affected by the general economic crisis. Health insurance did not yet pay for psychoanalytic therapy. The number of those who could afford analysis, which was expensive owing to the necessary sacrifice in time, decreased. Even those who had sufficient funds refused to spend them on analysis. Considering the importance emotional balance and the relief of psychosomatic suffering have for the development of the human being, such an attitude seems hardly sensible or appropriate. But psychoanalytic therapy has always been viewed as somewhat of a luxury.

The financial losses incurred in 1931 were so great that the psychoanalytic congress scheduled for that year had to be cancelled. It was feared that most psychoanalysts would not be able to meet the travel expenses. Even Eitingon could no longer support the Berlin Psychoanalytic Institute and the psychoanalytic publishing house. It was his task as president and Anna Freud's as general secretary of the International Psychoanalytic Association to cancel the congress originally scheduled for September "due to the difficult economic situation in Germany whose extent and effect could not be estimated."[1]

Within the Vienna Psychoanalytic Society, Anna Freud assumed an increasingly distinguished role. On October 7, she was elected secretary in place of Hermann Nunberg, a position she continued to hold for the rest of her life. She had entirely lost her diffidence during discussions, which some outsiders had never understood. The reports after that time nearly always designate her as a participant in discussions.

The year 1932 seemed to promise that the difficulties would be surmounted. Intellectual and economic life had become somewhat more animated. The congress that had been cancelled the previous year was held in Wiesbaden on September 3–7, 1932.

> It proceeded, despite warnings about the inauspicious time and place for scientific events, very harmoniously and was stimulating. . . . On the preceding evening, September 3, the participants already present were welcomed by the German Psychoanalytic Society. On the free afternoon of the 6th, everyone came along for a very lovely ride on the Rhine from Mainz to the Lorelei cliff.[2]

C. P. Oberndorf reported, however, that only a part of those present agreed to appear in the traditional group photograph, because they feared unfavorable consequences.[3]

Anna Freud spoke on "The Neurotic Mechanisms under the Influence of Education," an old theme by now, which she broached, however, from a new angle. During the business sessions, the question of lay analysis was of course discussed, but no progress was made; nor was a schism brought about. The committee formed at the last congress, in which Anna Freud was active, established "Guidelines for the Admission and Training of Candidates," which determined, among other things, "that no foreign candidates should be admitted to training without prior approval of their own country's training commission."[4] In simple language this meant that the prevailing—and diverse—practices should essentially be maintained, but that those societies which refused to admit lay analysts (mainly the American) should have the option of preventing the training of lay analysts, even abroad.

In 1931, Anna Freud wrote an essay, entitled "The Psychoanalysis of the Child" for the American *Handbook of Child Psychology*, in which she described Freud's theory of psychoanalysis as based on the age of a child, but did not discuss practical child analysis, which she distinguished from adult analysis mostly on the basis of technical problems.[5] In "The Educator and Neurosis,"[6] an essay she wrote for the *Zeitschrift für Psychoanalytische Pädagogik*, she vehemently defended lay analysis, especially for educators, who should, in her view, not only *educate* according to psychoanalytic principles, but also *practice therapy*. She included a brief and very clear synopsis of child psychoanalysis:

Only a decade ago, attempts at direct psychoanalytic work with children were isolated curiosities. Today a large number of analysts are more or less exclusively engaged in this field. In the course of work and research, two orientations—rather sharply distinct from each other in their technique—evolved in child analysis, one represented and taught by Melanie Klein in London, the other by me in Vienna.[7]

Anna Freud here again distinguished between two schools, though both could be labeled psychoanalytic. In this essay she also summarized her book on child psychoanalysis. Furthermore, she stressed that training in child psychoanalysis should supplement training for adult analysis:

> To circumvent general analytic training in the specialized training for child analysis is as impossible as, say, to circumvent general medical training in the specialized training of pediatrics. Training in child analysis is an addition to, not a substitute for, analytic training. In the treatment of infantile neuroses, the child analyst needs all the theoretical and practical knowledge required by the treatment of adult neurosis.[8]

In 1932, Melanie Klein published *The Psychoanalysis of Children*, a book that bore the same title in German as Anna Freud's essay of the previous year.[9] It appeared first in German, and shortly thereafter in English. Intended essentially as a rebuttal to *Introduction to the Technique of Child Analysis*, it at least avoided diatribes against Anna Freud. It consisted chiefly of a collection of lectures Klein had given in England, some of which had already been published. The book added nothing new to the ongoing controversy between Klein and Anna Freud.

Franz Alexander of Chicago used the book's publication as an occasion to expose again the weaknesses of Klein. He drew what seemed an apposite, yet thus far tacit, conclusion: that Klein's therapeutic success resulted from what she denied to be the educational influence her personality exerted on the child, rather than from the accuracy of her theories. This was "certainly inevitable, given the child's immense suggestibility and elasticity."[10]

Anna Freud spent the vacations of 1931 and 1932 with her father and the rest of the family in Pötzleinsdorf, just outside Vienna. The distance between vacation and city residences was even smaller than in previous years.

The family moved to their summer house as early as May 14, and remained there until after the Wiesbaden congress. That year Anna Freud's analytical practice expanded even more. She was now also active on the Ambulatorium's Psychoanalytic Educational Advisory Board, which had been founded by Hermine Hug-Hellmuth. Her interest there was aimed particularly at children and adolescents from the poor segments of the population, who had been referred by physicians, schools, and foster homes, or privately. Psychoanalysis was conducted when deemed indispensable; otherwise the staff tried to provide adequate counseling. August Aichhorn, Willie Hoffer, and Editha Sterba also worked there. In those times, when complete health insurance did not yet exist, those in the therapeutic professions saw it as their duty to use the freedom provided by the fees of well-to-do patients to make the same help available to poorer patients. Psychoanalysis was also provided free of charge. Social consciousness among therapists was more pervasive then than it is today; one was still ready to make personal sacrifices.

It was at this time, even before the National Socialists came to power in the "German Reich," that the emigration process set in among the intellectual elite, of which psychoanalysts represented a relatively small group. No one could have imagined then the proportions this movement was to assume in the following years. One of the most productive and flourishing intellectual movements practically disappeared from the German-speaking world within six years and was virtually forgotten during the following decades. Only today, from a historical perspective, does one begin to fathom the results of this loss in creative power.

First the Berliners emigrated. Franz Alexander moved to Boston and then to Chicago. Karen Horney and her daughter, later known as Marianne Horney von Eckhardt, moved to New York in 1932. Hanns Sachs also left Germany that year, first representing Franz Alexander in Boston and then teaching in Chicago, where several analysts who had been trained in Europe had meanwhile founded a psychoanalytic institute. Two years later, the German Psychoanalytic Societies had lost half of its members through emigration.

1933, Germany's Fateful Year

One finds it astonishing today that almost all psychoanalysts—the majority of whom were Jewish—understood relatively early that National Socialism would eclipse all other fascist forms of government in its inhumanity, while so many Jews in other academic professions and in business, out of their love for Germany, refused to believe what was approaching. At that time psychoanalysis was already one of the few truly international scientific organizations with a lively exchange of ideas. It was therefore easier for German-speaking psychoanalysts to recognize the imminent dangers and act accordingly.

When Hitler came to power in Germany in 1933, organizational changes took place within the Vienna Psychoanalytic Society. Anna Freud became its second vice chairman at this time. This ostensibly harmless title obscures the fact that the actual functions of chairman had been handed over to her. Thus far, the group had not had a second vice chairman; Freud was its chairman, but for some time he had been holding this office only in an honorary capacity, since he was no longer able to handle the daily affairs. Paul Federn, who enjoyed great respect in Vienna as one of the oldest and best analysts, had been vice chairman since 1924. But he was sixty-two years old, rather uninterested in organizational management, quite cautious, and hardly the man to steer the psychoanalytic ship through dangerous waters.[1] He was not spared the fate of emigration either, and after World War II he shot himself, on May 4, 1950, in New York, at the age of almost eighty.

No one had spoken out against Federn in Vienna, nor were there disputes involving him. Hence there was no reason not to reelect him, which he would have taken as a personal insult. It was characteristic of him, in his capacity as vice chairman, to withdraw from difficult situations, and it would have been appropriate now to urge him to perform the functions of his office. Yet these withdrawals were at times merely tactical, to elicit Freud's reconfirmation. In order not to hurt Federn, a second vice chairman was elected. Federn himself proposed the necessary changes in the statutes, which were unanimously accepted. Anna Freud thus combined three important functions of the psychoanalytic organization, serving as secretary of the Vienna Society, general secretary of the International Association, and member of various committees.

Political events unfolded with frightening rapidity. They affected not only Jewish psychoanalysts but the entire psychoanalytic movement, which was denounced as a Jewish invention. A few weeks after the seizure of power in Germany on January 30, 1933, decrees were issued prohibiting the active participation of foreigners in the executive committees of scientific organizations. This affected Eitingon, who had opted for Polish citizenship after World War I. His voluntary withdrawal would not only imply an acknowledgment of the authority of National Socialism, but would entail leaving the Berlin Institute and the German Psychoanalytic Societies—models for all psychoanalytic organizations—to Felix Böhm and Harald Schultz-Hencke, whose divergent views had already created problems. On May 6, 1933, Eitingon nonetheless saw himself forced to resign the chairmanship of the Berlin Society. That year he emigrated to Palestine, where he founded a new institute modeled after the Berlin Institute.

The Seventh Congress of the German Society for Psychotherapy was scheduled to take place in Vienna on April 6–7, 1933. This organization included psychoanalysts and psychotherapists representing various views. The theme of the congress was to be "The Psychotherapy of Maturational Processes." Ernst Kretschmer (who was then president), Paul Schilder, Heinz Hartmann, Anna Freud, and Charlotte Bühler had been nominated as principal lecturers. But due to the recent political events, Kretschmer had to withdraw from the congress at the end of March, and on April 6, scheduled to be the first day of the congress, he resigned the presidency. C. G. Jung followed him as president and wrote texts congenial to the Nazis. Perceived as such even then, they are still held against him.

The emigration question gained pressing importance for Freud and his family, although one could still feel relatively safe in Austria. There must have been various attempts immediately after the seizure of power in Germany to convince Freud of the necessity to emigrate, a thought he rejected but which—how could it not?—preoccupied him nonetheless. On March 16, 1933, he wrote to Marie Bonaparte: "In our circles there is already a great deal of trepidation. People fear that the nationalistic extravagances in Germany may extend to our little country. I have even been advised to flee already to Switzerland or France."[2]

Even the seriously ill Ferenczi, with whom Freud was having a series of disagreements at the time, almost begged Freud to move to England with his family, and perhaps with several patients as well. Freud had yet to decide, since neither he and his family nor the Vienna Society were in immediate danger. It is interesting that the question was nevertheless already being discussed. At the general book-burning in Berlin at the end of May 1933, Freud's books were among those burned. Thomas Mann entered the event in his diary on June 2, 1933:

> Wiegand wrote from Levici about the burning of Freud's works in Dresden, done as a protest against the "soul-rending overrating of instinctual life, and for idealism." What ignorance and mendacity in the word combination of "soul-rending overrating"! Yet instinctual life is actually sacred to this "dynamic," antirational movement. One might want to protect oneself from soul-rending, this makes sense, but to inveigh at the same time against overrating is idiotic. A kindly but sullen lower-middle-class sensibility always conflicts here with a barbaric, dynamic, irrational ambition.[3]

It began with the burning of books, it ended with the burning of people. Freud wrote to Marie Bonaparte: "This world seems to me to have lost its vitality and to be doomed to perdition."[4] Bonaparte had invited him to St. Cloud, but Freud declined the invitation.

The Freud family had extremely close ties with the Germany of the Reich. Ernst Freud had moved to Berlin and become a German citizen; Oliver also lived in Berlin, though he returned to Vienna after he lost his job in 1932. Ernst Freud left Germany at the beginning of April 1933 and was soon the first of the family to settle in London, where he remained until the end of his life. There were other family members in Germany as well, and the Freud family was therefore directly affected by the first persecutions.

An International Psychoanalytic Congress could understandably not take place in 1933. Nor did Anna Freud publish a new work that year. The family could not spend its vacation in Pötzleinsdorf, which they had grown fond of, but found something adequate in Döbling, another suburb of Vienna.

The Lucerne Congress

The year 1934 brought no scientific high points. The expulsion of psychoanalysts from the German Reich continued, clearly revealing how dependent the psychoanalytic movement had been on German societies. A congress was held that year in Lucerne, which kept mainly organizational questions in the foreground.

We have already mentioned that by 1934 the German Psychoanalytic Societies had lost half of its members as a result of emigration—primarily, though not exclusively, Jewish members. In that year, however, Jews were no longer permitted to emigrate as easily as previously. In his introductory speech at the Lucerne congress, Jones was right in saying, "The mere mention of the [following] names is sufficient to show what losses the German organization has suffered." Those were names the majority of which gained considerable significance in exile: Franz Alexander, Jenö Hárnik, Karen Horney, Melanie Klein, Melitta Schmideberg, Siegfried Bernfeld, Max Eitingon, Otto Fenichel, Karl Landauer, Annie and Wilhelm Reich, Theodor Reik, Ernst Simmel, Steff Bornstein.

Following the departure of so many analysts, the Internationaler Psychoanalytischer Verlag, in unremitting financial difficulties anyway, gradually lost its main market. This was of great significance, given the limited editions that could—with few exceptions—be published in psychoanalytic literature.

The Thirteenth International Psychoanalytic Congress, held in Lucerne August 26–31, 1934, under the presidency of Ernest Jones, was the outstanding event of the year. It showed that the focal point of the discussions had gradually shifted during the previous years from scientific psychoanalytic subjects to organizational questions, partly because the psychoanalytic movement had grown into an international organization, with the difficulties typical of such a scope.

Anna Freud gave a lecture "On the Problem of Puberty," whose content she rendered laconically in her report: "The parallels between the instinctual constellations of early childhood and those of puberty are further pursued and discussed." This was another study toward the book she was writing, *The Ego and the Mechanisms of Defense* (1936).

Anna Freud was unusually active during the business sessions, where the question of lay analysis time and again stood in the foreground. Now, when so many European emigrés without medical training faced difficulties practicing psychoanalysis in the United States, a resolution of the problem had become urgent. But no progress was made this time either.

The journals were so endangered by the closing of the publishing house that Jones suggested that each member of a psychoanalytic organization be required to subscribe to two professional periodicals to insure a certain level of circulation. The Americans and the French objected, the first because there was not yet an official journal in the United States, the latter because they could read psychoanalytic literature in French only, which provoked Jones to remark caustically that his suggestions should be particularly welcome as a remedy for such an "obvious flaw." A consensus was reached, however, and a committee formed, with Anna Freud among its five members. She was also elected as one of the two members of the International Training Commission. On the other hand, she lost the position of general secretary of the International Psychoanalytic Association and was elected instead to the rather nominal post of member of the central executive committee. These changes, which were justified because of her heavy workload, were in accordance with Jones's particular wishes. The new general secretary was Edward Glover, Jones's representative in the British Psychoanalytic Society, who assured him of a congenial and smooth working relationship. (Only much later did difficulties with Glover arise.) Thenceforth, the president's right to appoint a general secretary of his own choosing became an accepted rule.

Another disturbing event at the Lucerne congress was Wilhelm Reich's withdrawal from the International Psychoanalytic Association, mentioned by Jones in his biography of Freud with the brief sentence: "It was on this occasion that Wilhelm Reich resigned from the Association."[1] The act was subsequently clouded by rumors. Until then, Reich had been a respected member of the Vienna Society and had shown a great deal of initiative as a teacher, lecturer, and participant in discussions. Since 1922, he had headed the Vienna seminar for psychoanalytic therapy, and in this way had come into extensive contact with Anna Freud. To be sure, this was quite some time before his withdrawal. Like other colleagues from the Vienna circle, Reich had moved to Berlin in 1930, but had to escape after the Reichstag fire on February 28, 1938, because of his Marxist sympathies. He returned to Vienna, but two months later left for Denmark, finally going to Norway. Disagreements with other analysts persisted, since Reich had removed himself from mainstream psychoanalysis not only by his Marxist sentiments, but also, as Freud said, because of his personal psychoanalytic theories. On August 1, 1934, Reich received a letter from Carl Müller-Braunschweig, who had succeeded Eitingon as president of the Berlin organization, informing him that his name had been struck from the membership list of the Berlin Society,[2] but that it was assumed he would be admitted to the Scandinavian Society, which had been formed in Lucerne. This action was quite reasonable, since the Berlin Society, hoping to rescue at least a few persons during the Nazi period, could not assume the burden of Wilhelm Reich's name. Reich, however, sensed other animosities, no doubt real, but which had nothing to do with his exclusion. He wrote to Anna Freud in her capacity as general secretary that he could not accept this decision; she replied that she knew nothing of the omission of his name and would refer the matter to Jones, the president of the International Psychoanalytic Association. David Boadella reports that pressure had nonetheless been exerted on Norwegian psychoanalysts not to admit Reich, and that his exclusion was even a stipulation for the recognition of the group as a psychoanalytic society. This, to be sure, has not been documented. At any event, the Norwegian Society was recognized in Lucerne. Reich attended a session in Lucerne, chaired by Anna Freud, at which it was suggested that he resign from membership. He refused, because he viewed his work as a consistent and legitimate development of psychoanalysis. During another session, which Reich could not attend, Jones, Federn, and Eitingon openly brought charges against him, while the remark "a great injustice has been done here" is credited to Anna Freud, who was never involved in calumnies against him. It was resolved that Reich, much against his will, would no longer be a member of any psychoanalytic society, which prompted him to introduce the lecture he was permitted to give with the words: "After fourteen years of membership, I am speaking today for the first time as a guest of the congress."

A rumor arose at this congress and has persisted since: that Reich was mentally ill—paranoid and schizophrenic. If one reads today contemporary as well as later reports, it becomes evident that Reich never suffered from schizophrenia or any other mental illness. Still, it is true that since the time of the Lucerne congress he entertained an exaggerated conviction that he and his ideas were being persecuted and that his theories were misinterpreted and discriminated against.

In conversations Reich had on October 18 and 19, 1952, in Rangeley, Maine, with K. R. Eissler,[3] another psychoanalyst who was a native of Vienna, he hinted at another very private motive to explain the rejection he had met with in Lucerne: in 1933, Reich divorced Annie Reich, an equally outstanding psychoanalyst, and during the Lucerne congress he was living with Elsa Lindenberg in a tent on Lake Lucerne. His colleagues censured him for carrying on this relationship so openly. It also happened that he had a "powerful genital relationship" with Emmy Radó, by which Reich obviously did not mean genital contact. At any rate, it was said that out of jealousy Sándor Radó planted the rumor about schizophrenia and that it was first snatched up by Otto Fenichel. It is conceivable that Reich's genital theory and his behavior were misunderstood, and that he was found eccentric and peculiar. Still, it is difficult to imagine why so many malicious intrigues were spun against a man who, after having been driven from his home, was also robbed of his intellectual home. Reich's later fate was widely written about.

In Vienna, the numerous and difficult organizational tasks Anna Freud had to solve within the International Psychoanalytic Association increased still more. In the election on October 17, 1934, she was confirmed as vice president. She was no longer secretary but vice chairman of the training committee, while Helene Deutsch continued to head the executive committee. A change occurred in the

Training Institute in October 1934, when Anna Freud left the beginning seminar on child psychoanalysis to Editha Sterba in order to lead the advanced seminar on "The Technique of Child Analysis."

Anna Freud again spent the summer vacation with her parents on the outskirts of Vienna, this time in Grinzing, where they rented a house with a large garden. During this year she published a small essay, "Psychoanalysis and the Upbringing of the Young Child,"[4] where she again discussed the application of psychoanalytic theories to educational practice and, referring to Maria Montessori's new theories, stressed how imperative it was to find the right balance between freedom and educational influence.

The Ego and the Mechanisms of Defense

Anna Freud spent all of 1935 and the first months of 1936 working on *The Ego and the Mechanisms of Defense*, which was published in May 1936, on Freud's eightieth birthday. The extensive preliminary work for it consisted of the unpublished congress lectures she had given over the last years. The 1929 Oxford lecture, "A Counterpiece on Animal Phobia in Children," appeared again in the book's fourth chapter. The Wiesbaden lecture, "The Neurotic Mechanisms under the Influence of Education," was integrated into the section "Examples of the Avoidance of Objective Unpleasure and Objective Danger." Finally, the Lucerne lecture, "On the Problem of Puberty," can be found in the section "Defense Motivated by Fear of the Strength of the Instincts." One notices here the economy of Anna Freud's intellectual work, that is, the consistency with which she steers toward a goal over an extended period. Still, work on the book exacted so much effort that she began to fear she would never complete it. The clarity and lucidity she finally achieved are thus the result of long and strenuous work.

In February 1935, Anna Freud first presented a summary of her manuscript at the Vienna Society where—entirely without precedent—three full evenings had been set aside for the lecture and discussion of one essay alone, "The Application of Analytic Technique to the Study of Psychic Institutions."[1] Freud could therefore write to Arnold Zweig proudly: "I must remind myself that my daughter Anna is now making good analytic discoveries and, according to everyone, reports on them masterfully."[2]

In a letter to Lou Andreas-Salomé several weeks earlier, he expressed his satisfaction with his daughter's work, as well as a concern for her future and his lack of self-deception about the nature of some analysts:

My one source of satisfaction is Anna. It is remarkable how much influence and authority she has gained among the general run of analysts—many of whom, alas, have derived little from analysis as far as their personal character is concerned. It is surprising, too, how sharp, clear, and unflinching she is in her mastery of the subject. Moreover, she is truly independent of me; at the most I serve as a catalyst. You will enjoy reading her most recent writings. Of course there are certain worries; she takes things too seriously. What will she do when she has lost me? Will she lead a life of ascetic austerity?[3]

This was one of Freud's last letters to Andreas-Salomé. This woman had not only encouraged but undoubtedly had also participated in the writing of Anna Freud's important new book—surely not with her own theories, but with her unusual gift for raising vital questions about the subject, as well as by insisting that the book be finished. With the keen intuition that had always been her special gift, she suspected the great significance this book would have.

The Freuds moved to the Grinzing house in April 1935 and remained until mid-October. Freud's oppressive illness was particularly agonizing during these months. On his birthday, Anna Freud and Max Schur could not even insert his prosthesis.

From June 8 to June 10, Austrian psychoanalysts and their colleagues from three neighboring countries, Hungary, Czechoslovakia, and Italy, convened in Vienna. Anna Freud read a lecture by Helene Deutsch, who had meanwhile emigrated to the United States, and actively participated in all the discussions.

On August 1, Anna Freud met with Eitingon for the third time. He had now established the Palestinian Psychoanalytic Society, whose first honorary member was not Sigmund but Anna Freud. In Paris, she untiringly again discussed questions of training with Jones, though without making any progress. She was now in charge of writing the report of the training committee of the Vienna Society and had to take over Helene Deutsch's many other functions and tasks.

A report by Jones on that period, meant to attest to Freud's tolerance, shows instead how involved Anna Freud was with the problems of psychological "defense."[4] Ludwig Eidelberg, a psychoanalyst who won considerable esteem in American exile with his popular book *Take Off Your Mask* and with his scientific *Encyclopedia of Psychoanalysis*,[5] had written a manuscript in Vienna, "The Study of Slips of the Tongue," which he presented on March 11, 1935, to the Vienna Society. But the *Internationale Zeitschrift für Psychoanalyse* refused to publish the essay. Eidelberg therefore gave the manuscript to Anna Freud, who immediately responded.

In *The Psychopathology of Everyday Life*, Freud had shown that errors can be viewed as a compromise between two incompatible tendencies. He defined one, the unconscious tendency, as "harmless." This harmless tendency is disturbed by a second, harmful tendency. In an example Freud gives of a timid young man who would like to see a young woman home, the "harmless" (subsequently disturbed) tendency "to see the lady home" (*die Dame begleiten*) is now disturbed by another, aggressive—that is, harmful—tendency: "to insult" (*beleidigen*). The fusion of both tendencies yields the compromise *begleitigen*, a Freudian slip of the tongue.

Eidelberg's thoughts concerned the expression "harmless," since he believed he had good reason to assume that the first tendency could not be so fortuitous—hence "harmless"—either. Eidelberg suspected that "to see the lady home" had, in addition to the conscious and harmless meaning ("now what is objectionable about someone wishing to see a lady home?"), another, unconscious meaning. This meaning could be transcribed as, say, the scorned instinctual desire to take advantage of the situation by making a forbidden sexual overture to the woman. The disturbing tendency "to insult" (which can also be understood as sexual, a "violent insult") served here as the resistance or "defense" of a second, unconscious, and by no means harmless tendency embedded in the harmless tendency.

But that was precisely the point with which Anna Freud argued most intensively. She immediately understood that in no way was this a critique of Freud's theory, although Eidelberg had more than once been misunderstood, but a valuable complement to it.

Eidelberg's study showed precisely that the ostensibly innocent concept "to see home" could contain other meanings besides those already explained by Freud; that is, it was multiply determined. Anna Freud therefore wrote to Eidelberg and approved of his analysis, invoking Freud's authority:

> Your criticism of the word "harmless" for the trend that is disturbed is thoroughly justified, and further investigation of the apparently "harmless" is undoubtedly important. He suggested that the relation of the two tendencies is probably a variable one. Further investigation along these lines would probably be very rewarding.[6]

Anna Freud saw to it that Eidelberg's study received attention at the next international congress and that it was published, first in *Imago* and then in the *International Journal of Psychoanalysis*.[7]

It is astonishing that Anna Freud was able to write her main work, *The Ego and the Mechanisms of Defense*, during such a difficult period, when not only were Freud's health and strength increasingly waning, but the threat of anti-Semitism was constantly on the rise. The book offers a comprehensive and effective description of human defense processes. In itself, "defense" was nothing new. Freud had already introduced the concept in his very early "The Neuro-Psychoses of Defense"[8] (1894) and *Studies on Hysteria* (1895), in which he named and described some of the various means the psyche uses to prevent unwanted ideas from entering the consciousness. But since about 1900 Freud had added nothing new to this concept, nor did he pay much attention to the defense processes that had been described by others.[9] As a result, these had virtually disappeared from psychoanalytic discussions; they were brought up again after Freud introduced the "layer theory" in 1923, which structures the psyche into the layers of id, ego, and super-ego. Defense could now be seen as essentially the ego's function and task, and the concept of defense therefore needed to be reexamined in its relation to these layers. This explains the presence of the two main concepts in the book's title, *The Ego and the Mechanisms of Defense*. Freud himself had taken up the theme in "Inhibitions, Symptoms and Anxiety"[10] (1926), but even he had not written a thorough treatise on the subject of defense.

An essential yet hardly noticed innovation Anna Freud introduced consisted of steering the analyst's eye from the id toward the ego. In early analysis, repressed instinctual impulses had understandably stood at the center of interest. It was the analyst's work to track down and expose them. Freud devoted his attention to this goal for a quarter of a century. Anna Freud showed in this book that it is sensible to draw conclusions from the form of repression about the content that has been repressed. Defense forms are easily accessible to observation and perforce raise the question first of just what has been repressed. To be sure, Anna Freud countered the tendency to pay less attention to the id's processes by saying that the analyst "directs his attention equally and objectively to . . . all three institutions"—id, ego, superego.[11]

Anna Freud used "Inhibitions, Symptoms and Anxiety" as a point of departure to explain all the defense forms known thus far. She discussed their significance in neurosis and psychoanalytic therapy from every conceivable angle. But she also defined two new defense forms, which she labeled altruistic surrender and identification with the aggressor.

In altrusitic surrender, one actively seeks to fulfill one's own vital and unsatisfiable desires by satisfying them in others. Anna Freud illustrated altruistic surrender with an example from literature, *Cyrano de Bergerac* by Edmond Rostand (first produced in Paris in 1897 and for a long time one of the most popular of French plays). The comedy refers to a historical figure, Cyrano de Bergerac, famous for his adventures and his long nose:

> The finest and most detailed study of this altruistic surrender is to be found in Edmond Rostand's play *Cyrano de Bergerac*. The hero of the play is a historical figure, a French nobleman of the seventeenth century, a poet and officer of the Guards, famous for his intellect and valor but handicapped in his wooing of women by a peculiarly ugly nose. He falls in love with his beautiful cousin, Roxane, but, conscious of his ugliness, he at once resigns every hope of winning her. Instead of using his formidable skill as a fencer to keep all rivals at a distance, he surrenders his own aspirations to her love in favor of a man better looking than himself. Having made this renunciation, he devotes his strength, his courage, and his brains to the service of this more fortunate lover and does all he can to help him attain his desire. The climax of the play is a scene at night, under the balcony of the woman whom both men love. Cyrano whispers to his rival the words with which to win her. Then he takes the other's

place in the dark and speaks for him, forgetting in the ardor of his wooing that he himself is not the wooer and only at the last moment falling back into his attitude of surrender when the suit of Christian, the handsome lover, is accepted and he goes up to the balcony to embrace his love. Cyrano becomes more and more devoted to his rival and in battle tries to save Christian's life rather than his own. When this vicarious figure is taken from him by death, he feels that it is not permissible for him to woo Roxane.[12]

Since Anna Freud surprisingly omitted the end of the story, we would like to offer it here. Roxane enters a convent, where Cyrano visits her every Saturday, but he is unable to reveal to her how her heart was deceived. It is not until he is lying in her arms dying from a gunshot wound fifteen years later that he confesses his love for her and reveals the truth about the wooing. Only his impending death lent him the force to break his resistance to revealing the truth.

Anna Freud gave a further interpretation of this literary example:

That the poet is depicting in Cyrano's "altruism" something more than a strange love adventure is clear from the parallel which he draws between Cyrano's love life and his fate as a poet. Just as Christian woos Roxane with the help of Cyrano's poems and letters, writers like Corneille, Molière, and Swift borrow whole scenes from his unknown works, thus enhancing their own fame. In the play Cyrano accepts this fate. He is as ready to lend his words to Christian, who is handsomer than himself, as to Molière, who is a greater genius. The personal defect which he thinks renders him contemptible makes him feel that the others who are preferred to himself are better qualified than he to realize his wish fantasies.[13]

The concept of altruistic surrender has often been useful in explaining life-shaping determinant forms of behavior that would otherwise have remained incomprehensible.

In the other defense form, which Anna Freud called "identification with the aggressor," the subject assimilates the qualities, behavior, thoughts, forms of aggression, or power symbols of a person seen as an enemy. This entails, according to Anna Freud, processing the actual anxiety experiences that are considered "a by no means uncommon stage in the normal development of the superego."[14] She illustrated this with the example of a six-year-old boy she frequently mentioned. To present the entire case and convey how uniquely gifted Anna Freud was in sensitively capturing a child's nature, we will quote below the entire case history compiled from various parts of the book:

I was told that this used to be a favorite game of one of my child patients, who, when I knew him, would fall into a state of extreme ill humor whenever he saw an unusually tall or powerful man. He used to put on his father's hat and walk about in it. As long as nobody interfered with him, he was contented and happy. In the same way, during the whole of one summer holiday he went about with a full rucksack on his back. The difference between him and the little boy who plays at being a big man is simply that my small patient's play was earnest, for, whenever he was forced to take off the hat indoors, at meals or when he went to bed, he reacted with restlessness and ill humor.

On being given a peaked cap which had a "grown-up" appearance, the little boy repeated the behavior originally associated with his father's hat. He carried the cap everywhere with him, clutching it convulsively in his hand, if he was not allowed to wear it. Of course, he constantly found that he wanted to use his hands for other purposes. On one such occasion, when he was anxiously looking around for somewhere to put his cap, the possibilities of the flap in front of his leather breeches dawned upon him. Without more ado he thrust the cap into the opening and so had his hands free and concluded to his great relief that now he need never be parted from his treasure. Clearly it had arrived at the place where, according to its symbolic significance, it had always belonged: it was in immediate proximity to his genitals.

When I was analyzing the little boy whom I introduced in the previous chapter as "the boy with the cap," I was able to observe how his avoidance of unpleasure developed on these lines. One day, when he was at my house, he found a little magic drawing block, which appealed to him greatly. He began enthusiastically to rub the pages, one by one, with a colored pencil and was pleased when I did the same. Suddenly, however, he glanced at what I was doing, came to a stop, and was evidently upset. The next moment he put down his pencil, pushed the whole apparatus (hitherto jealously guarded) across to me, stood up, and said, "You go on doing it; I would much rather watch." Obviously, when he looked at my drawing, it struck him as more beautiful, more skillful, or somehow more perfect than his own, and the comparison gave him a shock. He instantly decided that he would not compete with me any more, since the results were disagreeable, and thereupon he abandoned the activity which, a moment ago, had given him pleasure. He adopted the role of the spectator, who does nothing and so cannot have his performance compared with that of someone else. By imposing this restriction on himself the child avoided a repetition of the disagreeable impression.

This incident was not an isolated one. A game with me in which he did not win, a transfer picture which was not as good as one of mine—in fact, anything which he could not do quite as well as I could was enough to produce the same sudden change of mood. He lost all pleasure in what he was doing, gave it up, and automatically, as it seemed, ceased to be interested in it. On the other hand, he would become obsessed with occupations in which he felt himself to be my superior and would spend unlimited time on them. It was only natural that, when he first went to school, he behaved just as he did with me. He steadily refused to join the other children in any game or lesson in which he did not feel quite sure of himself. He would go from one child to another and "look on." His method of mastering unpleasure by reversing it into something pleasurable had undergone a change. He restricted the functioning of his ego and drew back, greatly to the detriment of his development, from any external situation which might possibly give rise to the type of unpleasure which he feared most. Only when he was with children much younger than himself did he get rid of these restrictions and take an active interest in their doings.

The six-year-old patient to whom I have several times alluded had to pay a series of visits to a dentist. At first everything went splendidly; the treatment did not hurt him and he was triumphant and made merry over the idea of anyone's being afraid of the dentist. But there came a time when my little patient arrived at my house in an extremely bad temper. The dentist had just hurt him. He was cross and unfriendly and vented his feelings on the things in my room. His first victim was a piece of India rubber. He wanted me to give it to him and, when I refused, he took a knife and tried to cut it in half. Next, he coveted a large ball of string. He wanted me to give him that too and painted me a vivid picture of what a good leash it would make for his animals. When I refused to give him the whole ball, he took the knife again and secured a large piece of the string. But he did not use it; instead, he began after a few minutes to cut it into tiny pieces. Finally, he threw away the string too, turned his attention to some pencils, and went on indefatigably sharpening them, breaking off the points, and sharpening them again. It would not be correct to say that he was playing at "dentists." There was no actual impersonation of the dentist. The child was identifying himself not with the person of the aggressor but with his aggression.

On another occasion this little boy came to me just after he had had a slight accident. He had been joining in an outdoor game at school and had run full tilt against the fist of the games master, which the latter happened to be holding up in front of him. My little patient's lip was bleeding and his face tear-stained, and he tried to conceal both facts by putting up his hand as a screen. I endeavored to comfort and reassure him. He was in a woebegone condition when he left me, but next day he appeared holding himself very erect and dressed in full armor. On his head he wore a military cap and he had a toy sword at his side and a pistol in his hand. When he saw my surprise at this transformation, he simply said, "I just wanted to have these things on when I was playing with you." He did not, however, play; instead, he sat down and wrote a letter to his mother. "Dear Mummy, please, please, please, please send me the pocketknife you promised me and don't wait till Easter!"[15]

Anna Freud added a further interpretation:

Here again we cannot say that, in order to master the anxiety experience of the previous day, he was impersonating the teacher with whom he had collided.

Nor, in this instance, was he imitating the latter's aggression. The weapons and armor, being manly attributes, evidently symbolized the teacher's strength and, like the attributes of the father in the animal fantasies, helped the child to identify himself with the masculinity of the adult and so to defend himself against narcissistic mortification or actual mishaps.[16]

The description of this case shows, quite incidentally, that Anna Freud was again using experiences from her practice of child psychoanalysis. The title of her book could have led to the assumption that she had abandoned child psychoanalysis in favor of adult psychoanalysis. But while in her two earlier books she showed that adult psychoanalysis could be applied to children with only slight changes, she showed here, on the other hand, how experiences with children and adolescents can provide generally valid insights relevant to adults as well.

Another remarkable case in this book again shows how Anna Freud employed her early experiences from "Beating Fantasies and Daydreams." The points in question are denial and its transformation into its opposite, and the ego's means of avoiding objective displeasure and objective fear:

Here is another animal fantasy, produced by a ten-year-old patient. At a certain period in this boy's life, animals played an immensely important part; he would pass hours at a time in daydreams in which they figured, and he even kept written records of some of his imaginary episodes. In this fantasy he owned a huge circus and also was a lion tamer. The most savage wild beasts, which in a state of freedom were deadly enemies, were trained to live together in amity. My little patient tamed them, i.e., he taught them first not to attack one another and then not to attack human beings. When taming them, he never used a whip but went about among them unarmed.

All the episodes in which the animals figured centered in the following story. One day, during a performance in which they were all taking part, a thief who was sitting among the public suddenly fired a pistol at him. Immediately the animals banded together to protect him and dragged the thief out of the crowd, being careful not to hurt anyone else. The rest of the fantasy was concerned with the way in which—always out of devotion to their master—they punished the thief. They kept him a prisoner, buried him, and triumphantly made an enormous tower over him out of their own bodies. They then took him to their den, where he had to stay for three years. Before they finally released him, a long row of elephants beat him with their trunks, last of all threatening him with uplifted finger (!) and warning him never to do it again. This he promised. "He won't do it any more, as long as I am with my beasts." After a description of all that the animals inflicted on the thief there was a curious postscript to this fantasy, containing the assurance that they fed him very well when he was their prisoner, so that he did not become weak.

In my seven-year-old patient's fantasy about the lion we had a bare indication of the working over of the ambivalent attitude toward the father. The circus fantasy goes considerably further in this respect. By the same process of reversal the dreaded father of reality is transformed into the protective beasts of the fantasy, but the dangerous father object himself reappears in the figure of the thief. In the story about the lion it was uncertain against whom the father substitute was going to protect the child, whose ownership of the lion merely raised him in a general way in the estimation of other people. But in the circus fantasy it is quite clear that the father's strength, embodied in the wild beasts, served as a protection against the father himself. Once more, the stress laid on the former savageness of the animals indicates that in the past they were objects of anxiety. Their strength and adroitness, their trunks and the uplifted finger obviously were really associated with the father. The child attached great importance to these attributes: in his fantasy he took them from the father whom he envied and, having assumed them himself, got the better of him. Thus the roles of the two were reversed. The father was warned "not to do it again" and had to ask for pardon. One remarkable point is that the promise of safety which the animals finally forced him to make to the boy depended on the latter's continued ownership of them. In the "postscript" about the feeding of the thief the other side of the ambivalent relation to the father finally triumphed. Evidently the daydreamer felt obliged to reassure himself that, in spite of all the aggressive acts, there was no need to fear for his father's life.[17]

The daydream has remained a rarely used means of learning about unconscious processes, although it is, so to speak, palpably at the surface. The reason may be that daydreams are generally experienced as a relief, and daydreamers are considered to be people who withdraw from reality. The positive psychic function of daydreams has very rarely been emphasized. We would therefore like to add another brief example which Anna Freud interpreted with the aid of well-known literature for younger readers.

For instance, a seven-year-old boy whom I analyzed used to amuse himself with the following fantasy. He owned a tame lion, which terrified everyone else and loved nobody but him. It came when he called it and followed him like a little dog, wherever he went. He looked after the lion, saw to its food and its comfort in general, and in the evening made a bed for it in his own room. As is usual in daydreams carried on from day to day, the main fantasy became the basis of a number of agreeable episodes. For example, there was a particular daydream in which he went to a fancy-dress ball and told all the people that the lion, which he brought with him, was only a friend in disguise. This was untrue, for the "disguised friend" was really his lion. He delighted in imagining how terrified the people would be if they guessed his secret. At the same time he felt that there was no real reason for their anxiety, for the lion was harmless so long as he kept it under control.

From the litle boy's analysis it was easy to see that the lion was a substitute for the father, whom he, like Little Hans, hated and feared as a real rival in relation to his mother. In both children aggressiveness was transformed into anxiety and the affect was displaced from the father onto an animal.[18]

We find in children's literature a counterpart to the above-described lion fantasy:

> In many books for children—perhaps the most striking instances are the stories of *Little Lord Fauntleroy* and *The Little Colonel*—there is a small boy or girl who, contrary to all expectations, succeeds in "taming" a bad-tempered old man, who is powerful or rich and of whom everybody is afraid. The child alone can touch his heart and manages to win his love, although he hates everyone else. Finally, the old man, whom no one else can control and who cannot control himself, submits to the influence and control of the little child and is even induced to do all sorts of good deeds for other people.[19]

The subject of the first children's story is the American novel *Little Lord Fauntleroy* by Frances Hodgson Burnett,[20] filmed several times and still a favorite of children. Strangely enough, Anna Freud committed a *lapsus calami*—a slip of the pen—in writing Alice instead of Frances as the author's first name. Despite the pleasure of "catching" the psychoanalyst in an error, an adequate interpretation is regretfully impossible.

The effect of Anna Freud's book was astonishing. It very soon became a classic of psychoanalysis and remains—at least among German readers—Anna Freud's best-known book: a bestseller of psychoanalytic literature. The *Internationale Zeitschrift für Psychoanalyse* immediately published several reviews, and we quote below a few excerpts from one by Ernest Jones:

> . . . above all the unusual and refreshing clarity. Not only is the meaning of each sentence unmistakable, but, like her father, Anna Freud is capable of really clarifying matters and of shedding light on the various subjects she touches on. . . .
>
> The reserve noticeable in this book is another striking feature. In many cases the author could have pursued arguments and analyses, but she prefers not to exceed what in her view can be safely ascertained. . . .
>
> A third outstanding quality of her work is its agreeable style. It is a sheer pleasure to encounter such masterful language, in which each sentence is clear and certain in its simplicity. One doesn't quite know whether to admire Anna Freud's style more in her explication of difficult theoretical points or in her fascinating description of clinical material. Undoubtedly this book will take its place among the classical works of psychoanalytic literature.[21]

Jones's praise is directed mainly at form and description. In regard to the content, he expressed reservations he had previously voiced fairly often, and which should not be passed over in silence. The review contains statements such as: "I consider this a highly disputable claim, and it is quite possible that the final truth lies in the opposite direction." Jones's critique here is, as on many other occasions, double-tongued. Subsequent developments have confirmed only his approvals, and none of even his impartial objections was of much significance later.

Other reviews, such as a very long one by Otto Fenichel, are even more noteworthy. Fenichel, who had moved from Berlin to Oslo in 1933, wrote a very detailed review while still in Prague, where he settled for some time before he was forced to escape to the United States in 1938. He ranked the book with classical psychoanalytical literature:

> It seems to us that the significance of this book lies in the manner in which it clarifies and makes comprehensible to the reader complicated and obscure connections, by demonstrating—in a style comparable to that of Freud's classic works—empirical data, verifiable by analysts, in a new way. The "theory of the mechanisms of defense" then gives the impression of being merely a synopsis of factual phenomena, whose interconnections have thus far not been understood, but which can now be used to clarify and systematize further factual phenomena, primarily the formation of the defense functions.[22]

Among the Vienna circle, it was above all Ernst Kris who expressed unreserved concurrence in his detailed review.

Puberty, or the Search for Extremes

With statements that have received relatively little attention, Anna Freud exceeded her self-imposed limits at the end of *The Ego and the Mechanisms of Defense*. There she offered a psychoanalysis of puberty she later returned to again and again. In its conception it was a completely new psychoanalysis, one well suited to explain current alarming juvenile problems such as extremism and terrorism.

One of the two sections, "The Ego and Id at Puberty," had already been published as a single essay in 1935 in the *Zeitschrift für Psychoanalytische Pädagogik*.[1] It is actually odd that psychoanalysis, which attributes so much significance to the development of sexuality, should neglect puberty—precisely the stage when, according to the general understanding, sexuality bursts so violently into one's life. Anna Freud had a plausible explanation for this: Psychoanalysis had focused its attention mostly on pregenital sexuality, whose significance for both normal and abnormal emotional life became the theory's central theme, because, according to psychoanalytic knowledge, no major breakthrough occurs in puberty.

Rather, it signifies simply "one of the phases in the development of human life."[2] Anna Freud also introduced the notion of the "ego's primary antagonism to instinct."[3] This notion was already present to some extent in Freud's demarcation of boundaries between the id and the ego, one of the ego's essential tasks being the denial or transformation of instinctual desires. But if instinctual demands increase enormously during puberty, the ego must react accordingly. Special forms of instinctual processing in adolescents, such as asceticism, idealization, and hunger for identification, can explain phenomena characteristic of puberty. Anna Freud provided a very apposite description of the pubescent psyche:

> Adolescents are excessively egoistic, regarding themselves as the center of the universe and the sole object of interest, and yet at no time in later life are they capable of so much self-sacrifice and devotion. They form the most passionate love relations, only to break them off as abruptly as they began them. On the one hand, they throw themselves enthusiastically into the life of the community and, on the other, they have an overpowering longing for solitude. They oscillate between blind submission to some self-chosen leader and defiant rebellion against any and every authority. They are selfish and materially minded and at the same time full of lofty idealism. They are ascetic but will suddenly plunge into instinctual indulgence of the most primitive character. At times their behavior to other people is rough and inconsiderate, yet they themselves are extremely touchy. Their moods veer between light-hearted optimism and the blackest pessimism. Sometimes they will work with indefatigable enthusiasm and at other times they are sluggish and apathetic.[4]

She augmented this in another passage:

> The changeableness of young people is a commonplace. In their handwriting, mode of speech, way of doing their hair, their dress, and all sorts of habits they are far more adaptable than at any other period of life. Often a single glance at an adolescent will tell us who is the older friend whom he admires. But their capacity for change goes even further. Their philosophy of life, their religion and politics alter, as they exchange one model for another, and, however often they change, they are always just as firmly and passionately convinced of the rightness of the views which they have so eagerly adopted.[5]

Finally, Anna Freud also accepted Siegfried Bernfeld's concept of prolonged adolescence. According to Bernfeld, these adolescents especially have an unquenchable thirst for brooding, musing, and talking about abstract subjects.

Although adolescents are granted the greatest possible freedom today and their behavior meets with the utmost understanding, one is often suddenly disconcerted by their peculiar and at times brutal behavior. We wonder how this could have come about. In such cases, Anna Freud's insights and reflections on juvenile behavior deserve special attention.

In 1968, journalists asked Anna Freud how she explained that so many adolescents not only do not seek but even reject the help of psychoanalysis. She replied: "Young people now are not interested in man's struggle against himself, but in man's struggle against society. They see that what psychoanalysis may lead to is adaptation to society. That is the last thing they have in mind."[6]

Added Organizational Duties

The new duties Anna Freud had to take over after she completed *The Ego and the Mechanisms of Defense* were a result of Helene Deutsch's emigration. Life separated the paths of these two famous psychoanalysts as early as 1934, but their mutual attachment persisted over great distances. There have been quite a few attempts to describe them as competing for Freud's favor, especially since the motif of the "three sisters" resurfaces here. But there is no evidence to bear out such speculations. Helene Deutsch wrote in this regard:

> We worked together in the Vienna Institute, and there were never any serious elements of controversy between us. Like me, Anna was the youngest of three sisters and her father's chosen heir, the one sharing her father's interests and strivings. This might have been a reason for the ease with which I often identified with her. We had first met in the Wagner-Jauregg Clinic when I was a staff member and Anna was attending Freud's lectures there; I still remember how she looked entering the lecture hall on the arm of her father. When we reminisce about our first meeting Anna can visualize my white doctor's coat, and I recall that she wore a green suit on that occasion. From the beginning I felt a kind of tenderness toward her that never left me, notwithstanding her eventual fame and importance in the psychoanalytic movement.[1]

It was because of her position as Wagner-Jauregg's assistant at that time (1912–18) that Helene Deutsch had on a white doctor's coat. The contact between the two women was at first distant and superficial. Deutsch, who was working in another section of the Wagner-Jauregg Clinic at the time of Anna Freud's ward rounds there, may not have even known about them, and hence was not mentioned by Anna Freud in this context.

The motif of the three sisters emerged again in Deutsch's life on another occasion, and it is interesting that she patently omitted Anna Freud. Obviously, she did not feel she and Anna Freud were rivals.

Three of Freud's women pupils achieved a certain degree of prominence as "pioneers in feminine psychology" (that was the phrase Freud used in his writings). These were Ruth Mack-Brunswick, Jeanne Lampl-de Groot, and myself. I experienced this linking of my name with two other women's as a kind of trauma. It seemed to be a repetition of my childhood, when I was one of three sisters—though in the later trio I was not the youngest. But now I was a mature woman and had the opportunity to deal with this problem in analysis. Whether it was because of my analysis with Freud or my knowledge of his respect for me, I eventually lost my feelings of competition and jealousy. These feelings never recurred during my later career. I was too fascinated with the work and too aware of my increasingly secure place in the psychoanalytic movement to become involved in rivalries.[2]

Helene Deutsch's emigration virtually forced Anna Freud to take over her Vienna posts. First, problems regarding training persisted. Anna Freud took over the chairmanship of the Vienna Training Institute. It should be mentioned that, in addition to child analysis, she soon began to conduct training analyses, in part with a substantial number of future leading psychoanalysts. She also led many of the seminars, and it became clear that the directorship of the Training Institute was hers; furthermore, she was responsible for questions of training within international committees. Since she was also vice president, she held the two chairmanships available in Vienna. This entailed not only extensive organizational work, but further training duties. In the summer of 1936, she took over the leadership of three training classes: Advanced Technique of Child Analysis; Problems of Technique, with Eduard Bibring; and Seminar for Working Educators, with Annie Angel-Katan, Berta Bornstein, Dorothy Burlingham, Edith Buxbaum, and Editha Sterba.

Despite unremitting housekeeping problems at 7 Berggasse, it was possible to acquire new rooms for the Training Institute. The German Psychoanalytic Societies and the publishing house, and above all the confiscation on March 24, 1936, of books stored in Leipzig, were other sources of great concern. What had been feared all along was beginning to befall the German Society. Despite the emigration of all Jewish psychoanalysts and despite the obliteration of Freud's name and writings, the new president, Felix Böhm, was unable to preserve the society in its original format. No longer permitted to be an independent organization, it was now a branch of the "International General Medical Society for Psychotherapy," whose president had become Matthias Heinrich Göring, a distant cousin of Hermann Göring. On March 8, Anna Freud traveled to Brno in Czechoslovakia—then still neutral territory—where she had a long conference with Böhm. These events notwithstanding, on the eve of Freud's birthday on May 5, new rooms were dedicated to psychoanalysis in Vienna at 7 Berggasse. The International Psychoanalytic Association, the Vienna Psychoanalytic Institute, and the Ambulatorium were also accommodated there and remained active until March 1938.

At that time Czechoslovakia was still an island of freedom in Europe, and the University of Prague again flourished briefly. A number of Gestalt psychologists and some psychoanalysts, such as Annie Reich and Otto Fenichel, had retreated to Prague, and Roman Jacobson and other Russian emigrants taught there. Hence the choice of Marienbad, a popular resort town, as the location for the Fourteenth International Psychoanalytic Congress, held on August 2–8, 1936. The proximity of Vienna also played a role, since Anna Freud now wanted to be easily accessible to her father, in whom cancer had again been diagnosed. One hundred ninety-eight participants convened in Marienbad, a large number indeed. Even Helene Deutsch, who had just emigrated to the United States, attended as a member of the Boston Psychoanalytic Society. The focal point of the congress again lay not so much in scientific discussions—Anna Freud gave no lecture—as in deliberations on organizational issues.

The Internationaler Psychoanalytischer Verlag experienced some relief when the Leipzig book stocks were returned on July 8, 1936, following the diplomatic intervention of England, France, and the United States, with the cooperation of the Austrian government. Jones had these immediately brought to 7 Berggasse in Vienna, where the publishing house was then managed by Martin Freud. Of course, the lost markets could not be recovered. As president of the International Psychoanalytic Association, Jones proposed establishing within the publishing house an international center for psychoanalytic biography, which would distribute for a fee information that had thus far been given without charge. Further, each member was to make a minimal annual contribution of $5.00.

> In the discussion of this proposal, Anna Freud emphasized that to be dependent on occasional contributions and the good will of single individuals is unworthy of an institution so closely affiliated with the International Psychoanalytic Association as the publishing house is. It is therefore a matter of extreme importance to better secure the financial basis of the publishing house by creating this new institution, which the IPA itself urgently needs.[3]

The center was established, but after only two years it had to be transferred to London.

Anna Freud's membership on the journal committee was approved in various elections. She was further elected vice president of both the International Psychoanalytic Association's central executive committee and the International Training Commission. Except for the question of whether to include postanalysis in the official training curriculum, now raised for the first time, the same issues that were of concern at earlier congresses were again debated at Marienbad. The reports mention Anna Freud as a participant in every discussion. This was also the first time that she reported on the work of the Vienna Society.

Sigmund and Martha
Bernays Freud.

The house at 19
Berggasse, Vienna.

3

Family portrait, about
1898. Left to right, first
row: Sophie, Anna,
Ernst; second row:
Oliver, Martha Freud,
Aunt Minna Bernays;
third row: Martin,
Sigmund Freud.

Anna with her
parents, about
1898.

4

(*Above*) Anna with her sisters and brothers in Berchtesgaden, 1899.

(*Below*) Martha and Sigmund Freud's silver wedding anniversary, September 13, 1911. Clockwise from left: Oliver, Ernst, Anna, Sigmund and Martha Freud, Mathilde, Minna Bernays, Martin, Sophie.

5

6

7

8

(*Above*) Anna's two sisters, Mathilde Freud Hollitscher and Sophie Freud Halberstadt.

(*Below*) Ernst and Martin Freud, on furlough in 1916, with their father in Salzburg.

9

10

11

(*Above left*) Sigmund Freud and sixteen-year-old Anna on vacation
in the Dolomites, 1912.

(*Above right*) The Goethe Prize, 1930.

(*Below*) Anna and Sigmund Freud in Berlin, August 1928.

12

13

(*Above*) **The Goethe Prize ceremonies. Left to right: Alfons Paquet, Mrs. Landmann, Director Beutler, Anna Freud, Mr. von Weinberg, Lord Mayor Landmann.**

(*Left*) **The house at 19 Berggasse, 1938, with a swastika over the door.**

(*Below*) **The laconic entry in the Gestapo report that Freud had "announced his departure" for London in June 1938.**

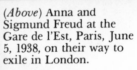

15

(*Above*) Anna and Sigmund Freud at the Gare de l'Est, Paris, June 5, 1938, on their way to exile in London.

(*Left*) Sigmund and Martha Freud in the garden at 20 Maresfield Gardens, London.

16

The house at 20
Maresfield Gardens.

17

One of the last photographs of
Sigmund Freud.

The Anna–Antigone medal, quoting
Freud's phrase, SUPPORTED BY MY
DEVOTED ANNA–ANTIGONE. The
obverse reads WITH GRATITUDE TO
ANNA FREUD ON HER RETURN TO
VIENNA 1971 A 27.

Leo Rangell presents
the medal to Anna
Freud in Vienna, 1971.

20

Anna Freud, about
1914.

21

22

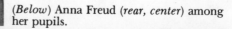

(*Above*) The elementary school of the Cottage Lyceum, where Anna Freud attended school and later taught.

(*Left*) At the Sixth International Psychoanalytic Congress in The Hague, 1920. Freud's student Otto Rank is at the right.

23

(*Below*) Anna Freud (*rear, center*) among her pupils.

24

25

Anna Freud's consultation room, across from her father's at 19 Berggasse.

The title page of *Introduction to the Technique of Child Analysis*, published in 1927.

EINFUHRUNG IN DIE
TECHNIK DER
KINDERANALYSE

VON

ANNA FREUD

INTERNATIONALER
PSYCHOANALYTISCHER VERLAG
WIEN

26

The Eleventh International Psychoanalytic Congress, Oxford, 1929. Left to right, at intervals: first row: Otto Fenichel (3), Hanns Sachs (5), Rudolph Loewenstein (6), Hermann Nunberg (9); second row: Sándor Ferenczi (1), Abraham Arden Brill (2), Karen Horney (4), Marie Bonaparte (5), Max Eitingon (6), Anna Freud (7), Ernest Jones (8); third row: Sándor Radó (6); fourth row: Franz Alexander (1), Karl Lewin (10), René Spitz (15), Ella Sharpe (17).

27

The home of the Hampstead Child Therapy
Course and Clinic, London.

The Montessori "Children's House" (left) on Vienna's
Rudolphsplatz. In 1937, Anna Freud and Dorothy
Burlingham rented part of the building for the
Jackson Nursery.

30

Anna Freud and a friend in 1967.

Paula Fichtl, the Freuds'
housekeeper in Vienna and
London.

31

Dorothy Burlingham and
Anna Freud.

32

Four stills of Laura, the
subject of James
Robertson's film "A Two-
Year-Old Goes to the
Hospital."

(*Opposite above*)
Anna Freud and
August Aichhorn in
Lausanne, 1949.

(*Opposite below*) Dorothy
Burlingham and
Anna Freud.

34

35

Julius Wagner-Jauregg

Paul Schilder

Heinz Hartmann

Max Eitingon

Lou Andreas-Salomé

Siegfried Bernfeld

Maria Montessori

Melanie Klein

Wilhelm Reich

Ernest Jones

Max Schur

Otto Rank

Marie Bonaparte

Helene Deutsch

Margaret Mead

John Bowlby

Robert Waelder

René Spitz

Anna Freud, with Dr.
H. Donaldson Jordan
and Howard B.
Jefferson, receiving
an honorary doctorate
from Clark
University, Worcester,
Massachusetts, in
April 1950.

Anna Freud at the
Austin Riggs
Foundation in
Stockbridge,
Massachusetts, 1950.

Participants in the Austin Riggs Foundation's symposium. Left to right, at intervals: first row: Dorothy Burlingham (4), Elisabeth Gellerd (5), Beata Rank (7), Helene Deutsch (8), Anna Freud (9), Annie Katan (12), Editha Sterba (13); second row: Berta Bornstein (3), Dora Hartmann (5), Mary O'Neil Hawkins (6), Jenny Waelder Hall (8), Grete Bibring (9), Margaret Mahler (12), Hanna Fenichel (15); third row: Heinz Hartmann (1), René Spitz (2), Marianne Kris (3), Ernst Kris (4), Robert Waelder (20), Rudolph Loewenstein (22), Erik Erikson (23), Richard Sterba (26).

38

39

Anna Freud at Western Reserve University, Cleveland, Ohio, 1956. In the background is Maurits Katan.

40

At the Hanna Pavilion in Cleveland, September 22, 1956. Anna Freud is in the first row, holding a bouquet.

With Rudolph Loewenstein, Worcester, Massachusetts, 1957.

41

42

With Heinz Kohut at the
Menninger Foundation,
Topeka, Kansas, April
1966.

Samuel Lipten and
Anna Freud at the
Chicago Institute for
Psychoanalysis,
December 21, 1966.

43

Receiving an honorary
doctorate from the University
of Chicago, 1966.

Receiving an honorary
doctorate from Columbia
University, New York,
in 1978, at the age of
eighty-two.

44

Anna Freud, with Dorothy Burlingham, strolls through the old
section of Vienna in 1971, on her first return to the city since her
exile in 1938.

47

Participants at the Twenty-seventh International Psychoanalytic
Congress, Vienna, 1971. Left to right: Serge Lebovici, Samuel
Ritvo, Peter van der Leeuw, Jeanne Lampl-de Groot, Anna Freud,
Leo Rangell.

A dinner in Vienna, 1971. Left to right: Frances Gitelson, Leo
Rangell, Gertrude Sandner Fröhlich, Anna Freud.

48

Ceremonies at the
award of an
honorary doctorate
by the Medical
School of the
University of
Vienna, May 26,
1972.

50

With Dorothy Burlingham and Richard F. Sterba
after giving the Freud Anniversary Lecture in
Vienna, 1978.

The Last Year in Vienna

Nineteen thirty-seven began sadly: Lou Andreas-Salomé, almost seventy-six years old, died on February 5 at "Loufried" in Göttingen. In her, Anna Freud lost a friend and an untiring correspondent. Andreas-Salomé's richly faceted personality will become better known with the publication of her collected correspondence.

On April 30, the members of the Freud family who remained in Vienna moved to the Grinzing house, where Freud spent his eighty-first birthday. A flood of letters, more voluminous than ever, arrived. The second four-country psycho-analytic conference was held on May 15–17, during the Pentecost season, attended by 144 listeners. On Whitsunday, Anna Freud was moderator of the first symposium, "Early Developmental Stages of the Ego: The Primary-Object Love." At the second symposium, "Review of Psychoanalytic Education," moderated by Edoardo Weiss (who had emigrated to New York), she gave the first report. Anna Freud was thus granted a prominent position—no longer as the daughter of the founder of psychoanalysis, but as a reflection of her own scientific significance and her rank in psychoanalytic organizations. In her lecture, she explained some of the disagreements within psychoanalytic pedagogy on the basis of its historical development.

It was widely expected at that time that National Socialism would become firmly established in Austria, since Nazis were already participating in the government. While this threat was becoming more and more imminent, Anna Freud and Dorothy Burlingham devoted themselves to a new task: the care of a group of young children at the Montessori Kindergarten, The Children's House, on Rudolphsplatz. This was actually an expanded and improved successor to the first Montessori Kindergarten in Vienna (see p. 65 above). It had been built by the municipality under the supervision of Emma Plank, and its administration and supervision were then handed over to the Vienna Montessori Society. Anna Freud and Burlingham took over a group of twelve children between the ages of one and two with—as we would say today—serious environmental damages,[1] i.e., "socially disadvantaged children from among the most indigent population."[2] The teacher was Herta Wertheim. In a letter to his son Martin, Freud expressed his opinion on his daughter's commitment with both affection and irony: "Anna is enjoying her so-called vacation—i.e., she is playing with the little babies instead of the big ones."[3]

Anna Freud's relationship to Montessori educational theory and her appreciation of Maria Montessori's work and the Montessori Children's House occasioned misunderstandings, particularly since Freud himself had written to Montessori (see p. 65 above) that his daughter counted herself among Montessori's supporters. Anna Freud therefore saw the need to clarify the relationship:

> I have always valued the Montessori method, but was far from being an "enthusiastic supporter." Montessori was entirely unpsychological and completely unanalytical. I have never worked in the Montessori Kindergarten nor supervised one of its departments. The facts were entirely different. The Montessori Kindergarten was in financial difficulties during that time and forced to rent out a third of the beautiful Children's House. My own creation, the Jackson Day Nursery, was the tenant, but otherwise fully independent of the Montessori people. The nursery was financed by Dr. Edith Jackson of America and also supported by Dorothy Burlingham, and our plan was to study the prekindergarten age group (1–3). The children we admitted belonged to the poorest in Vienna, children of the unemployed who had exhausted all the welfare assistance they were entitled to. Unlike the Montessori Kindergarten, this was an analytical–educational experiment.[4]

The day nursery lasted only two years; the Nazis closed it as soon as they marched into Austria. The Montessori movement had long since succumbed to the pressure of political circumstances. Maria Montessori left Italy in 1934 and went to Spain. Lilli Roubiczek-Peller left Vienna with her husband in 1934, and worked first in Jerusalem and later in the United States, where she was active as a psychoanalyst until her death in 1966. Wherever one turned—emigration and flight.

Anschluss and Emigration

In the spring of 1938, the Nazis took over Austria, Hitler's home. National Socialist riots broke out on March 1 in Graz and elsewhere. On March 13, Austria's annexation to the German Reich was declared. German troops marched into Vienna, cheered on by a blinded population who had longed for the Anschluss even before Hitler's rise. The persecution of political opponents set in, and for Jews there was no mercy. The members of the Freud family still living in Vienna could no longer ignore the question of emigration. (Ernst Freud had been living in England since 1933, where he was busy with his architectural work.) The only question left was how to carry out the move.

The weeks preceding the Freuds' emigration—in particular Anna Freud's role during that time—have been described movingly and in detail by Ernest Jones and Max Schur. To be sure, both dwelt in their accounts on the repeated efforts to rescue Freud. Jones here displayed an energy, circumspection, and generosity that eclipse all of his ambivalence, assuring him merely through these efforts a place in history and in the history of German culture in particular. Edmund Engelman systematically photographed the Berggasse apartment and its residents during those days,[1] making it one of the few well-documented stages in Sigmund and Anna Freud's lives.

But we must not forget the fate that awaited the ostracized who were condemned to wait for their slaughterers because they—the obscure—were helped by no one and had no possibility of leaving the country.

Freud was now almost eighty-three years old, having lived nearly eighty of those years in Vienna. Psychoanalysis as a new epistemological and therapeutic method had become a worldwide movement that lent this century its unique stamp, even if it was and will probably remain controversial. Everything subsumed under the name psychoanalysis will remain linked with the name of Freud. During the days preceding the emigration he was rather passive. He could not desist from thinking and writing, but the problems that had so radically changed daily life affected him very little. His life was approaching its end, not only because of his age but because his cancer had broken out again. Anna Freud had lived in Vienna for forty-three years, a time during which her fate had become so intimately knotted with the fate of psychoanalysis and of her father that she was unable to act outside them. Although Jones had to make great efforts to persuade Freud to emigrate, there was in fact—excepting suicide—no other option.

This was the course of events: On March 13, the day Austria's annexation to the German Reich was declared, the Vienna Society advised all its members to emigrate, using whatever means they had available. Only two days later, Jones came to Vienna. Anna Freud met him at once and asked him to exert his influence as a foreigner in the already occupied rooms of the publishing house at 7 Berggasse. After the Leipzig experience, there was hardly a doubt that destruction threatened the book stocks of the publishing house. In Freud's apartment, Anna Freud had to hand over the petty cash from the safe to the Nazis. Jones provided the Freud family with the entrance permit for England, neither an easy nor an automatic matter in times when refugees from Germany and Austria were flooding the world. But it was far more difficult to obtain the exit permit from Austria. William C. Bullitt, Freud's coauthor who had become the American ambassador in Paris, was able, through President Roosevelt, to induce his colleague in Vienna, the American chargé D'affaires Wiley, to intervene on behalf of the Freuds' emigration. Mussolini was also interpellated—such were the efforts merely to obtain a travel permit from one country to another for Freud and his family. And Germany was not yet even in a state of war. On March 17, Princess Bonaparte, whose diplomatic status was also of invaluable help, arrived from Paris. On March 20, 1938, only eight days after the Anschluss, the Nazis dissolved the Vienna Psychoanalytic Society.

A select circle met that day at 3:00 P.M. in the small meeting room of the Vienna Psychoanalytic Society at 7 Berggasse, but it was powerless in the face of the police inspector, Dr. Sauerwald, who was appointed by the Nazis. Participants were Ernest Jones as president of the International Psychoanalytic Association, Marie Bonaparte and Anna Freud as vice presidents, and Carl Müller-Braunschweig as secretary of the German Society for Psychotherapy. Paul Federn and Anna Freud represented the Vienna Psychoanalytic Society (that is, Anna Freud attended in a double capacity), as well as Eduard Hitschmann, Eduard Bibring, Heinz Hartmann, Ernst Kris, Robert Waelder, Willie Hoffer, Herta Steiner, and Martin Freud. Sigmund Freud himself was absent. The outcome of the meeting was that the Vienna Psychoanalytic Society had to surrender fiduciary rights and duties to the German Society for Psychotherapy.

The results of this ruling bring some cheerfulness into this grim chapter. The Vienna Society indeed had to surrender its rights and duties, but only the trusteeship—that is, legally it still existed. The Nazis were so meticulous in their formal bureaucratic operations that a petition for dissolution had to be filed in Vienna on August 25, 1938—five months later—with the Deputy Police Inspector for the Disbanding of Clubs, Organizations, and Leagues. The injunction for dissolution had to be served in compliance with regulations. All members of the executive committee had meanwhile been forced to emigrate. Hence the later attempts to serve Freud and other committee members with the injunction, without which the Society could not be dissolved. The Society thus continued to exist—to be sure in name only—as a functionless structure. After World War II, this simply spared the reestablished Vienna Society the need to request admission to the International Psychoanalytic Association.

Two days later, on March 22, Anna Freud was interrogated by the Gestapo for an entire day and returned home only late that evening. Those were anxious hours for those expecting her at home, since so many people had vanished without a trace after such a summons. There were real grounds for the worst fears. The will Freud had made indicated that he had deposited Dutch gulden in Zurich. Since the Nazis already urgently needed foreign currency, they imposed severe penalties on foreign-currency holders and used every means to bring back and confiscate money deposited abroad. It seemed highly probable that a copy of the will had fallen into the hands of Police Inspector Sauerwald during the liquidation of the publishing house. This assumption was later confirmed. Yet Sauerwald had decently kept silent about the find, which no one could then have known about. After the war, Anna Freud signed a certificate that considerably facilitated Dr. Sauerwald's denazification. When Freud was already in London, the Nazis attempted to extort the Dutch gulden through Freud's lawyer in Vienna, Dr. Alfred Indra. Freud replied that before he would give up the gulden, all his Vienna possessions would have to be returned to him.[2]

Anna Freud had taken along Veronal to the interrogation, because she was afraid she would be tortured. The American chargé d'affaires was evidently able to intercede successfully prior to the interrogation. At any event, following a call from the American Embassy, Anna Freud was offered a chair in a room; before, she had had to wait in the hall. Only that evening was she able to return home unharmed, to the relief of the entire family.

The chicanery, however, had still not ended. The family was left waiting. The tension was tormenting. Despite all the diplomatic interventions, it took several weeks before the exit permits were issued. Schur reports on an interesting incident from this period:

> It was not until quite recently that Anna Freud told me the following story and authorized me to publish it. When things were at their worst and escape seemed hopeless, Anna asked Freud: "Wouldn't it be better if we all killed ourselves?" To which Freud replied with his characteristic mixture of irony and indignation: "Why? Because they would like us to?"[3]

Even if suicide as a last alternative befitted the character of neither Freud nor his daughter, it was still Sigmund Freud who had once remarked he would rather let himself be slain than emigrate.

Freud's bank accounts in Austria were confiscated; beyond that, he was required to pay the "Reich emigration tax," one of the usual impudences of that time. Anna Freud passed the waiting period by sorting out, with the help of Marie Bonaparte, papers to be burned and selecting from the book stocks those to be taken along. To be sure, one could not safely reckon on taking along one's possessions. The remaining books were later sold in New York and are now the proud possession of the Psychiatric Institute. Nonetheless, the bulk of the library was transferred to London. During these last weeks in Vienna, Anna Freud was also able to complete the translation of Marie Bonaparte's *Topsy*,[4] which she had begun in 1936. She also translated *The Unconscious* by Israel Levine.[5] The exit permit was finally issued, but not for all family members at once. Astonishingly, they were allowed to take along their household possessions.

Dorothy Burlingham, who had come to be considered a member of the family, was the first to leave. As an American, she had no difficulties with her exit. On May 5, Martha Freud's sister Minna Bernays (Aunt Minna) was able to emigrate. On May 16, Martin Freud, whose wife and children had met him in Paris, arrived in London. On May 24, Mathilde Hollitscher and her husband Robert left Vienna. On Whit Saturday 1938, scarcely three months after the Anschluss, the last group—consisting of Freud and his wife Martha, Anna Freud, and two household employees (one of whom, Paula Fichtl, remained in charge of Anna Freud's household all her life)—left Vienna. Anna Freud was accompanied by the pediatrician Josephine Stross, who also assumed the care of Freud during the journey; he needed, among other things, nitroglycerin and, as a heart remedy, strychnine.

Upon his arrival in Paris, Freud found the numbers of journalists and photographers who had come to meet him annoying. Of the photographs that were taken then, had been most active in facilitating his emigration. Other photographs show Anna Freud in a knit hat at the train window behind her father. Ernst Freud, who had flown in especially from London, was waiting in Paris and then made the trip to London with the rest of the family. Freud's nephew Harry was also with them.

After a twelve-hour rest at Marie Bonaparte's residence in Paris, they resumed the journey by train to Calais, then by ferry to Dover, and finally to London, where the group arrived on the morning of June 6. After the Parisian experience, the train came in on a special track to avoid photographers, journalists, and onlookers. The English knew how to honor the event. In London, the family was met by the family members who had already arrived and by a series of analysts, some of whom were living there in exile. But Jones led Freud so quickly to his car that he could greet no one, and even his son Martin saw him only briefly from the customs line. They drove slowly from Victoria Station—with a brief stop at Regent's Park—on to North London, where the house at 39 Elsworthy Road became their first London residence. There, journalists had the opportunity to ask questions and take photographs. Martin, and particularly Anna Freud, who spoke English well, found it easy to give an account to journalists. Anna Freud said, "Please tell the world that everyone has been very friendly to us, the police in Vienna, the authorities in England, all of them. My father hopes to find here the possibility of resuming his work. He left Vienna to find peace. He was glad to return to England [Freud had been in England as a student sixty years before] and is happy to be here. We are happy for everything that has been done for us and grateful that we are allowed to live here."[6]

The journalists asked whether it was true that Freud had been badly treated in Vienna. Anna Freud replied, "In Vienna we belonged to the few Jews who were politely treated. It is not true that we were under house arrest. My father had indeed not left the apartment for weeks, but that was because of his bad health. We could all come and go undisturbed. Even when we crossed the [German-French] border we were not disturbed and could sleep through."[7] One is reminded here of a report from Jones that Freud suggested adding the following statement to his signature on a police document certifying the "decent treatment": "I can heartily recommend the Gestapo to anyone."[8]

To be sure, in her description Anna Freud meant to protect those left behind, among them four old aunts, Freud's sisters, who later perished under Nazi persecution. That Freud and his family belonged to the few Jews in Vienna who had been decently treated should have been sufficiently convincing testimony. Did not those in power expose their brutal character clearly enough when they arbitrarily robbed scientists like Freud of what had been their life and work? It is odd how rapidly the world is ready to believe that torturers are not really torturers if those who ask for asylum are indeed rescued.

Thus ends the first half of Anna Freud's life, and thus ends an epoch in German intellectual history. Anna Freud's fate was certainly tolerable: without being further threatened, she was able to live, write, and work, perhaps even more effectively than she would have under normal circumstances in Vienna. For her terminally ill father, exile became the tragic conclusion of his life.

After Sigmund and Anna Freud's emigration, virtually nothing remained of psychoanalysis in Austria, since the last analysts who had stayed behind followed Freud's example at the first opportunity. Of the one hundred twenty members of the Vienna Society, only four were in Vienna at the end of 1938. The German Group continued to exist for some time after all its Jewish members had emigrated. It became a division of the Institute for Mental Psychology and Psychotherapy, founded in 1936. As such, it was able to train candidates and admit new members but had to pretend it had nothing to do with psychoanalysis. Freud's name—and of course Anna Freud's as well—could no longer be mentioned. Books on psychoanalysis were removed from public bookstores, and archival indexes were destroyed.

It is certainly no sheer accident that prohibited writings were preserved. We must bear in mind that only seven years passed from 1938 until the end of World War II—a truly brief span in historical time—and that most psychoanalysts were still in possession of their creative powers. But it was not easy to reknot the cut threads. In German-speaking countries, years went by before economic conditions permitted republication of the lost literature, and some works have still not been published. Nor was literature in foreign languages available for a long period. Personal contacts were lacking. After the suffering inflicted on them, many emigrants could bring themselves to visit Germany and Austria only many years after the war. And how much had changed! Meanwhile, developments had not stalled outside German-speaking countries but had proceeded rapidly, whereas Germany could only slowly keep abreast of them.

It is understandable, then, that decades were necessary to redress even slightly the few years of standstill in psychoanalysis. Even today, this has not been completely achieved. After the war, Anna Freud never sought out Germany again and only after decades did she visit Vienna.

London

When she arrived in London, Anna Freud announced to the journalists her hope of receiving a work permit. But finding a new home for the family was obviously the most pressing issue. The furnished house on Elsworthy Road was meant only as a temporary residence. It was still uncertain whether the books, the art collection, and the furniture would all survive the trip, or whether only a part would arrive. On September 3, Freud, his wife, and Anna moved to the Esplanade Hotel. The other children looked for other accommodations. Minna Bernays had to be put in a nursing home. While Martin Freud had no prospects of finding work as an attorney, Ernst, as an architect, could be more hopeful. Finally, on September 16, Martha Freud and Paula Fichtl were the first to move into the new house in Hampstead. Freud and his daughter joined them on September 27. All their belongings even arrived from Vienna, and Ernst Freud deftly adapted them to the new rooms. This house at 20 Maresfield Gardens, located in the genteel residential district of Hampstead, near the northern limits of London, was thenceforth destined to assume the role of the house at 19 Berggasse.

By contemporary standards it was a very large and beautiful house, on whose first floor a spacious study facing the garden could be set up for Freud. The rest of the house offered ample space for the living and working needs of the other residents. Altogether it was far more spacious and pleasant than the apartment in Vienna, where the family had also enjoyed a good deal of room. All this was enhanced by the beautiful surroundings—a street lined with trees and similar-looking villas—so that 20 Maresfield Gardens came to replace both Berggasse and Grinzing in one.

Jones knew that Freud would not enjoy the house for much longer, even if the growth of his cancer could once again be halted. While Freud was staying at the Esplanade Hotel, he had had to undergo surgery of several hours. The house would therefore soon fall to the share of his heirs, first of all to Anna Freud, whose exceptional significance needed no further discussion. She was acknowledged everywhere, even after her child psychoanalysis had been so virulently criticized under Jones's aegis in the very same London.

We know that at 20 Maresfield Gardens Freud resumed the pattern of his previous life as soon as his strength permitted. He saw patients and worked on the third part of *Moses and Monotheism*, a lucid and mature work. The house survived the bombings without damage and remained an intellectual center where Anna Freud and Dorothy Burlingham lived until their deaths (in 1982 and 1979, respectively) with Paula Fichtl.

The Fifteenth International Psychoanalytic Congress

Surprisingly enough, it was possible to hold a psychoanalytic congress on August 1–5, 1938, despite the political turbulence. This was the first congress to be convened on French territory, in Paris, headed of course by Jones, who was still president. Freud's lecture, "The Progress of Intellectuality," was probably read by Anna Freud; the minutes mention nothing to that effect. Anna Freud did not read her own paper but moderated the session "Ego Strength and Ego Weakness" with Paul Federn, who had been able to emigrate to New York and came to Paris to attend the congress. The list of lecturers for this topic reflects the changed situation: Otto Fenichel (Los Angeles), Edward Glover (London), René Laforgue (Paris), Hermann Nunberg (New York). If the language of psychoanalysis had thus far been German, and if the mother tongue of more than half the psychoanalysts had been German, thenceforth this was no longer to be the case.

It was the international status the psychoanalytic organization had attained that made this congress possible so soon after the explusion of most of the analysts from German-speaking countries. Leading psychoanalysts were multilingual; Freud himself spoke English, French, and Italian well, and Anna Freud was comfortable in English. Other psychoanalysts, however, had great difficulty learning a new language, English in this case. Usually they finally mastered English exceedingly well but retained a strong foreign accent, which occasioned many jokes, as in the case of Franz Alexander. The Viennese accent finally became something akin to the distinguishing mark of a good analyst.

Today, students of psychoanalysis or psychiatry must know English, since the professional literature is written predominantly in English and usually translations are available only much later.

During sessions of the congress, the deplorable situation was discussed: the psychoanalytic institutes of Berlin and Vienna and even of Rome had already been dissolved. The Prague Union, an offshoot of the Vienna Society, had ceased to exist. The American Psychoanalytic Association proposed reorganizing the International Psychoanalytic Association so that it would continue to exist, though the American organization would be independent—i.e., only loosely attached to it and under no obligation of friendly cooperation. This would have annulled all decisions reached at previous congresses on the continuing membership of refugees from German-speaking countries. As usual, Anna Freud actively participated in discussions and together with others blocked the acceptance of a motion by Laforgue that would have vehemently reprimanded the American group for this proposal. Had this motion been accepted, it would have probably meant a schism. The issue was thus adjourned and referred to the committees for deliberation.

At the end of the plenary session of the International Training Commission, Anna Freud again broached the subject of postanalysis. In her usual way she pitted difficulties and advantages against each other:

> One of the advantages is that the analyst is not merely dependent on the analysand's obviously one-sided self-description, but forms his own impressions of the latter's behavior and effect on others. The difficulties lie not only in the reality of much of the relationship between the analysand in postanalysis and his analyst, but in the fact that the analyzed analyst's knowledge of analysis often does not weaken the ego resistances, but rather strengthens and obfuscates them. [1]

The elections ratified the positions Anna Freud had been holding thus far.

It may astonish us that Anna Freud was able to perform her functions and duties at a congress so soon after the dramatic political events—as if nothing had happened in the interim, as if she had not lost her home and become an exile. It is noteworthy that psychoanalysis as an intellectual movement had suffered no greater losses than those mentioned; it is even more pleasing that, through the international cohesiveness of the International Psychoanalytic Association, it was frequently able to offer protection and a new sense of home to those bereft of their original associations, since the exiles were surrounded by familiar faces they had debated, argued, and worked with for many years.

Thus, it was precisely through its international structure that the psychoanalytic organization preserved its unity and the continuity of research. The plight of emigrants from other professions—psychology, sociology, or clinical psychiatry—was quite different. It is more than understandable, then, that Anna Freud was able to defend the common cause of psychoanalysis at the Paris congress despite problematic external circumstances, including her father's relapse. She remained loyal thereafter to the International Psychoanalytic Association, in which she played a leading role, mainly in the capacity of vice president.

At the Paris congress, the Paris Society nominated Sigmund Freud, Anna Freud, and Ernest Jones as honorary members. Sigmund Freud became an honorary member of the British Psychoanalytic Society, while Anna Freud was admitted as a member.

As early as 1938, Anna Freud gave three public lectures in England, in German, which have not been published. In a letter to Marie Bonaparte, Freud stressed that his daughter's language especially had been highly praised. Unlike other exiles, Anna Freud had delivered a number of lectures in English long before her emigration. She owed her unflagging practice foremost to her American friend Dorothy Burlingham, because she often spoke English—or rather, American English—with her and her children in Vienna. She therefore quickly adapted to the new language and was soon able to speak and write English as fluently as German. Later she said that she hardly noticed whether she was using English or German when dictating.[2] Unlike the language of other emigrants, her German was not permeated with English idioms. What she was to write later in English not only retained the unique clarity of her style but also benefitted from the structure characteristic of English.

Freud's Death and the Beginning of World War II

Nothing auspicious marked the beginning of 1939. Renewed attempts to treat Freud's cancer with radiation therapy led instead to a deterioration in his condition, giving rise to fears of his imminent death. The signs of war proliferated, and news pointing to war constantly alternated with optimistic reports. At any event, the subject of war was on everyone's lips. Under such circumstances, Anna Freud no longer dared leave her father. She temporarily suspended her own plans and considerations to devote herself entirely to his care. Now, even more than before, it was she who carried the full burden.

That Sigmund Freud completed *Moses and Monotheism* in March 1939 was a sign of his intellect's unflagging energy despite his advanced age and illness. For the first time in their lives, Freud gave his daughter a copy with a personal dedication— almost a gesture of farewell. During this critical period, Freud's physician and friend Max Schur had to leave for New York for more than ten weeks. Ill with appendicitis, he had not even been able to accompany the Freud family on the journey from Vienna to London, where he would have been extremely useful. Under such circumstances, psychoanalysts do not always tend to perceive only objective constraints.

Anna Freud remained with her father, reporting regularly to Schur. She did not even attend the 1939 congress of French-speaking psychoanalysts in Paris. Sigmund Freud wrote to Marie Bonaparte: "You know that Anna won't be coming to the meeting in Paris because she cannot leave me; I am growing increasingly incapable of looking after myself, and more dependent on her."[1]

World War II broke out, and Freud still had to witness the efforts made to protect his most valuable possessions, manuscripts, and antiques from the threat of destruction. During his last weeks, Anna Freud got up several times during each night to treat the open cancer tumor with orthoform. The end finally came. Freud reminded Schur of his promise to offer assistance in case of death, asking him at the same time to inform Anna of everything. Schur has movingly described these last days and hours in his biography of Freud. On September 23, 1939, shortly before midnight, Freud died.

One would think that after the painful separation was overcome, Anna Freud would then have been able to turn all her energies to her analytical work, whether theoretical or practical. Unlike other emigrants, she enjoyed many advantages. She had her own house, was living with her mother and siblings, and even the familiar service personnel was still with her. She owned Freud's library and had become very well known in the professional world. Still, it is important to realize that Anna Freud had no work permit, although she was obviously allowed to practice training analysis. But would it even be possible to continue to afford the house? Moreover, there was the fear that the Germans would invade England. Would it become necessary to escape from here too? And where to? For Anna Freud the lay analyst, America was not easily accessible. She could not count on a work permit in the United States. Perhaps she now had the chance to disengage herself from Freud's shadow. Yet neither then nor later did she have such intentions, though she did discover her own path. World War II determined every consideration anyway. At the time of Freud's death, the blitzkrieg in Poland was almost over. That Anna Freud published no new works between 1938 and 1941 may also bespeak the immense difficulties she faced.

First, her assistance to refugees from the Continent was taxing for her. But even the British Psychoanalytic Society, to which Anna Freud belonged, was in a grim predicament. In the spring of 1938, Anna Freud continued the seminars begun in Vienna, but those scheduled for the summer had to be cancelled. Jones had ruled the British Psychoanalytic Society with patriarchal benevolence. Melanie Klein, evidently convinced of the correctness of her ideas, knew how to profit from the freedom he granted her.

However, M. Nina Searl, of whom Freud did not think very highly—she had visited him once in Austria during a vacation—withdrew from the organization following disagreements with Klein, whom she had loyally supported over a long period. Without mentioning the reasons, Jones announced her withdrawal at the last prewar congress in Paris in 1938: "Miss Searl felt it necessary to step out of the organization on theoretical grounds. All of us deplore the loss of such an esteemed member."[2] Melitta Schmideberg was the next analyst who refused to follow her mother unconditionally. At the beginning of the war, Jones and Klein retreated to the country, while the other analysts continued their discussions in London. It thus became evident how far their ideas had moved under Klein's influence from what had been said and done in the psychoanalytic organizations of Vienna and Berlin. Despite the impressive number of his publications, Jones was quite uninterested in theoretical debates; his books were predominantly explications of Freud's work. In his capacity as Jones's representative, Edward Glover would have been competent to maintain the theoretical standard, but he usually kept a certain distance. He did not measure up to his prematurely deceased brother James, and was considered somewhat eccentric. He had a mongoloid daughter he decided to treat as if she were completely normal—they were frequently seen together—while his wife devoted herself almost exclusively to her care.

Actually there should have been ample room for Anna Freud's talent and initiative. A small number of psychoanalysts from Vienna had settled in London: K. Friedländer, H. Maas, Barbara Lantos, and Ernst Kris, who was an important support for Anna Freud in London. Robert Waelder had also intended to move to London, but received no entry permit.[3] The increasingly preconceived debates had come to such a deadlock that any innovation would have ended in a schism between the followers of Melanie Klein and those of Anna Freud. The newcomers' reserve, their gratitude for the extraordinary help they received, the burdens imposed by the war, as well as Anna Freud's attempts to prevent a schism at all costs demanded that London's hospitality not be encumbered by a spectacular schism in the British Psychoanalytic Society. Freud himself had dropped a word in London to avoid any conflicts that would undermine the right to hospitality.

Despite the shining reputation the British Psychoanalytic Society enjoyed— attributable above all to Jones's long relationship with Freud—its predicament made it impossible to immediately resume the work begun in Vienna. Anna Freud of course made herself available for any work the organization needed. In June 1939, she introduced herself with the lecture "Sublimation and Sexualization." In addition to the seminar on child analysis she had already given in the summer of 1939 and continued in the spring of 1940, from October 1941 to July 1942 she set up a weekly technical seminar, as she had previously done in Vienna. Moreover, she practiced training analysis; the number of candidates, however, had dropped drastically as a result of the war. Finally, succeeding her father in this task, Anna Freud edited the last issue of the *Internationale Zeitschrift für Psychoanalyse* in 1940.

In keeping with her functions in Vienna, Anna Freud was also admitted to the training committee of the British Psychoanalytic Society. Consisting of Ernest Jones, Edward Glover, Melanie Klein, and Ella Sharpe, it did not offer her many chances of finding an ear for her own ideas. Nor did this change when Grete Bibring from Vienna joined the committee in the course of the year and immediately began to hold seminars. As Hermann Nunberg's student, she enjoyed Anna Freud's full confidence. She later rose to the position of vice president of the International Psychoanalytic Association.

For Anna Freud, this was the situation in 1939: Her immense creative power was not being put to full use, and she had no opportunity to acquire new experience in the field of child analysis. After the war began, she therefore faced the difficult task of professional and private, linguistic and cultural reorientation. The task that finally became hers has since become world-renowned under the name of the Hampstead Nurseries.

The Wartime Hampstead Nurseries

The wartime children's nursery was opened in October 1940, during the first phase of the German bombing raids. As these became more frequent, finally destroying large parts of London and other large English cities, they also affected the children. Many lost not only their homes but also their parents. It was the cause of such children that Anna Freud embraced.

At first she received money from private sources to alleviate the children's most immediate needs. A house at 13 Wedderburn Road in Hampstead was made available on a loan basis, a Swedish organization provided furniture, and Anna Freud was able to have a relatively safe semisubterranean air-raid shelter built. It was thus possible to begin to admit children. In March 1941, when the money had been exhausted, other financial support enabled the work to be carried on for several more months. Finally, following the intervention of Eric G. Muggeridge, an American organization, the Foster Parents' Plan for War Children, assumed the total costs until several months after the war, during which time an interruption in support threatened the home only once. Two more homes were opened with this money, the young children's nursery at 5 Netherhall Gardens in London (Hampstead) for children who could not be sent to the country without their mothers, and New Barn, a country home in Essex.

The initially small number of children gradually rose to 90. A total of 190 children found shelter at the Hampstead Nurseries over the span of several years. Prompted by the American donors, Anna Freud submitted monthly reports which were also valued for their description of daily life in the wartime children's nurseries. Though Anna Freud wrote that she sometimes found those obligations irksome, she did have sufficient time for them during the long nights of air raids. The collected reports published after the war convey, precisely through their regularity, a continuous picture of both the events and Anna Freud's everyday life during the war.[1] Anna Freud's gift for exact observation and for objective yet sympathetic description has made this one of the most interesting books on war ever published. Strangely, it has thus far been withheld from German readers. Michael Schroeder translated it only for the collected works, now under preparation. The reader of Anna Freud's reports experiences the war from the perspective of a children's nursery in a hailstorm of bombs. Anna Freud always speaks of "we," referring to the assistants—usually too few—and to the children.

For Anna Freud, the wartime nurseries were multiply significant, because they absorbed all her abilities and desires. Thus, she was finally in a position to prove her gratitude to her host country for having given her refuge. At the same time she was able to render a kind of war service and mitigate some of the miseries caused by the war. Finally, she pursued what had already intensely interested her at the Jackson Nursery in Vienna during the last period before the emigration: caring for groups of children. Just as she and Dorothy Burlingham had raised the latter's children together, she was now able to raise a large group of children with her friend. And, although this large family viewed her as the mother, the concept of "mother" had to be consciously avoided. Though Anna Freud never writes about herself in these reports, we can hardly know her better personally than through this ostensibly objective book. But these would not be Anna Freud's reports if they did not at the same time convey her always clear observations and considerations on child analysis. Toward the end of the war, the latter even constituted the bulk of the reports, and her experiences with the children widely influenced and determined her later thought. The enduring realization is that children can bear a great deal, be it nights in shelters, deprivation, and much more, but they are immensely sensitive to separation from their parents, particularly from the mother.

In her first report, Anna Freud conveyed an impression of the premises and staff at the house on Wedderburn Road:

Out of the numerous applications that came in, 25 children were chosen. The result of our endeavors is the following:

1. We now have a house containing one large nursery equipped as a complete Montessori nursery school; one toddlers' room with plenty of space to run around in; one very large room with straw matting equipped as [a] dressing room and a room for afternoon naps; one babies room fitted out with cribs; one doctor's office with a sunray lamp; one hospital room for children who are ill with noninfectious diseases; one parents' clubroom which is used especially on Saturdays and Sundays; one work and staff room for meetings, sewing purposes, unpacking of gifts, etc.; four staff bedrooms. In addition, the basement of the house contains [the] kitchen and dining room and, last but not least, two shelters, one with 18 beds, the other with 6 beds and 3 baby cribs. This shelter belongs to the type of indoor, half-basement shelter which is strengthened with heavy wooden beams, calculated to carry the weight of the whole upper house in case it collapses. Shelters of this kind are no protection against direct hits by a high explosive bomb, but they are supposed to withstand the blast and all other emergencies, even if the high explosive bomb should drop only a few yards away. The beds are not the usual type of shelter bed but the ordinary type

of bed with spring mattresses used in peacetime, built in tiers of twos or threes. They are so big that one child can be placed at each end without their feet touching in the middle. . . .

2. Our staff at the moment consists of: a pediatrician, Josephine Stross, M.D., who is in attendance two or three hours every day; a head nursery school teacher, Miss Hedy Schwarz, with two assistants and two trainees; a baby nurse; a cook, Miss Sofie Wutsch; a social worker, Mr. James Robertson; a bookkeeper, Miss Jula Weiss; various help for laundry, cleaning, etc. This seems a large number, but they are all kept busy owing to the helplessness of the infants we are dealing with. Four members of the staff are British: the rest are refugees from Austria, Germany, Czechoslovakia, and Holland. Four important members of the staff are volunteer workers.[2]

The children admitted to the home came largely from destroyed or heavily damaged houses and from dissolved families, but there were also two other groups:

Tube Sleepers, i.e., children who have been taken by their mothers to the deep Tube [subway] shelters at night since the *blitzkrieg* in September. They slept on the platform with the trains running in and out until 1 A.M. Some of them in this way lost their ability to sleep, cried out continually, and had to be hushed and quieted by their mothers with various methods so as not to disturb the adult population around them, a state of affairs not favorable either to mother or to child.

Children Sent Back from Evacuation, (a) because they could not stand the sudden separation from their mothers and developed conditions that their foster parents were unable to deal with; (b) because the mothers were dissatisfied with the billets or wanted the children where they could at least keep an eye on them; (c) infants who had been evacuated with their mothers now come back because their mothers had to return home to look after an ill husband.[3]

In her third monthly report, Anna Freud described a major air raid:

An outstanding event during this month was the big air attack on London in the night of Wednesday, April 16th. Even for people who had gone through the period of the so-called blitz in September and October, the events of this night were rather surprising and alarming. There was more gunfire than ever before, the sound of falling bombs was continuous, the crackling of fires which had been started could be heard in the distance, and again all these sounds were drowned by the incessant droning of airplanes which flew over London, not in successive waves as in former raids, but in one uninterrupted stream from 9 o'clock in the evening until 5 in the morning.

The neighborhood of the Children's Center was lucky enough to escape all damage since the raid was concentrated on various other parts of London. Not even incendiaries were dropped on our district, and the nearest landmine fell at the safe distance of half a mile from Wedderburn Road.

The older members of the staff were, of course, awake and patrolled the house; the younger members went down from their attic bedrooms and joined the children in the shelter. The children themselves, to our astonishment, slept peacefully as usual and never noticed what was going on above them. Whether it was due to the fact that the heavy wooden beams of the shelter ceiling lessen all noise or whether the quiet atmosphere in which they had fallen asleep carried them through the restlessness of the night outside, the facts are that no one took notice except Billie, who sat up suddenly and said, "Gunfire." His mother, who was on shelter duty, answered: "Yes, but gunfire does not hurt anybody," whereupon Billie lay down and slept again.

Janet woke as usual and asked to be put on the pot, but remained completely oblivious of the bombing. The two babies, Jeffrey and Ralph, woke once and cried for a while, but since that happens nearly every night, it is difficult to determine whether it had any connection with the outside noises.[4]

Anna Freud's detailed description of single cases brings into relief the conditions with unusual vividness. The story of Billie, for example, reveals the fundamental problem of separation from the mother, showing at the same time how such a separation could be accomplished without causing severe reactions:

Billie, a boy of 3 years and 2 months, of pleasing appearance, well built and rather big for his age, was sent to us after one unsuccessful attempt at evacuation to the country. In the billet where he had been placed, he had, as the report stated, "fretted" so much for his mother that he was sent back to her after a very few days. Unluckily, their reunion was of short duration. He contracted measles and had to suffer another enforced separation from his mother. After dismissal from the hospital she brought him directly to us since she had been warned not to take him after illness to the Tube station where she herself was sleeping regularly with her husband. She admonished him to be "a good boy," and promised to visit him if he would promise not to cry for her.

The state of affairs that developed after she left was a most unhappy one. Billie tried to keep his promise and was not seen crying. Instead, he would nod his head whenever anyone looked at him, and assured himself and anyone who cared to listen with the greatest show of confidence that his mother would come for him, she would put on his overcoat and would take him home with her again. Whenever a listener seemed to believe him, he was satisfied; whenever anybody contradicted him, his self-control left him and he would burst into violent tears.

This same state of affairs continued through the next two or three days with several additions. The nodding took on a more compulsive and automatic character and to the sentence "My mother will put on my overcoat and take me home again" was added an ever-growing list of clothes that his mother was supposed to put on him. "She will put on my overcoat and my leggings, she will zip up the zipper, she will put on my pixie hat." When the repetitions of this formula became monotonous and endless, someone asked him whether he could not stop saying it all over again.

Again Billie tried to be the good boy his mother wanted him to be. He stopped repeating the formula aloud, but his moving lips showed that he was saying it over and over to himself. At the same time he substituted for the spoken words gestures that showed the position of his pixie hat, the putting on of an imaginary coat, the zipping of the zipper, etc. What showed as an expressive movement one day was reduced to a more abortive flicker of his fingers the next day. While the other children were mostly busy with their toys, playing games, making music, etc., Billie, totally uninterested, would stand somewhere in a corner, moving his hands and lips with an absolutely tragic expression on his face. These movements did not stop even when he was dressing or eating, going up or downstairs. He refused most kinds of foods, but he faithfully drank milk.

We were shocked to see an apparently healthy child develop a compulsive tic under our very eyes. All attempts to get in contact with him were unsatisfactory. Not that it was impossible to break in on his compulsive behavior with understanding words, affection, and sympathy. But in such moments, instead of reiterating his false assurances, he would break through to the truth, burst into tears, and develop an excess of grief that one felt at a loss how to meet.

From the second day on we had made attempts to reach his mother and induce her to visit him regularly. Unluckily again, she had fallen ill with a bad influenza and was lying in a hospital. A Sunday afternoon visit from his father did not bring the slightest comfort. It took more than a week before his mother was dismissed from the hospital. Then she came immediately to us. We discussed the situation with her and persuaded her to stay in our house for a while.

Billie's state changed immediately. He dropped his symptom and instead clung to his mother with the utmost tenacity. For several days and nights he hardly left her side. Whenever she went upstairs or downstairs, Billie was trailing after her. Whenever she disappeared for a minute, we could hear his anxious questioning through the house or see him open the door of every room and look searchingly into every corner. No one was allowed to touch him; his mother bathed him, put him to sleep, and had her shelter bed next to his.

A few days were sufficient to do away with this abnormal state of affairs. Slowly Billie lost his excessive clinging and turned at times to other children to join in their play. His mother was first allowed to go home for an hour to cook a meal for his father. Billie waited anxiously for her reappearance and signs of his former anxiety appeared in his expression. But after a further week or two these symptoms too disappeared. Billie's mother was allowed to come and go freely and Billie became a member of the nursery like any other child. At the present time he is one of the most active children in the playroom, his former rather girlish appearance has changed to definitely boyish behavior, he jumps and climbs, he is very good at building and keeps himself busy from morning till night. He is a very good eater, satisfied only after repeated helpings.

After some consideration we offered the mother, who is a specially nice woman and had previously been employed as charwoman in a day nursery, the post of emergency night nurse in our two shelters. That means that she still spends five nights weekly in the same house with Billie, the other two at home or in the Tube station with her husband. But it does not seem to affect Billie now whether she sleeps in or out.

The interesting point about this story is that it does not seem to be the fact of separation from the mother to which the child reacts in this abnormal manner; rather, he seems to react primarily to the traumatic way in which this separation took place. Billie can dissociate himself from his mother when he is given three or four weeks to accomplish this task. If he has to do it all in one day, it is a shock to which he responds with the production of symptoms. This means that even children with neurotic potentialities such as Billie's could be spared much unnecessary suffering and symptom formation by more careful handling.[5]

A later report informs the reader of Billie's fate and includes another case of separation reaction:

While daily all over England more and more children are separated from their mothers and evacuated for the sake of safety, we are still concerned with the various possible effects of such separations. Billie, the boy described in Report 2, is still doing excellently. In his present life, where he is at times with his mother, and on other days and nights without her, he is completely undisturbed. He has made a remarkable development toward manliness. He has shed all remaining soft girlish ways, which were apparent when we first saw him; he likes only boyish pursuits, is respected in the nursery as the leader of games, and is extremely active in the garden. It remains to be seen whether he is also able to stand a more complete separation from his mother. An opportunity to make that experiment may occur when we ourselves open a country house for children.

We had another opportunity of observing the worst effects of sudden separation in Dell, a little girl of 2½ years, whose admittance was mentioned in Report 2. In accepting Dell we gave in to the urging of her mother, who was frightened that the child would be infected either with tuberculosis by the grandmother with whom she shared the room or with some kind of shelter disease in the very primitive place where they all spent the nights. The mother seemed rather desperate and worn out with anxiety. She begged us to let Dell benefit from the favorable conditions in our house, at least for the few weeks which she would need to find a billet in the country for herself and the child. Dell was a beautiful little girl, marvelously developed, sparkling with life and gaiety, and seemed extremely independent for her age. It was this very independence of the child, together with her evident interest in the toys, the other children, and the new surroundings which induced us to fall in with the mother's wishes. Dell was taken to the nursery where she was deep in play after a few minutes. She said good-bye to her mother in a friendly way, but hardly noticed when her mother left her. Only half an hour after her mother had left the house, Dell suddenly realized what had happened. She interrupted her play, rushed out of the nursery, and opened every single door in the house to look for her mother in the room behind it. In her running around she behaved exactly like a stray dog who has lost his master. This lasted a few minutes and then she rejoined the play group.

These attacks of frantic search repeated themselves with even greater frequency. Dell's expression changed, her brightness disappeared, her smiles gave way to an unusually sullen frown which changed the whole aspect of the child. It is difficult to say, of course, whether this sullenness of Dell's was completely new or whether this was the way in which she had previously reacted to difficulties in her life.

The hope that Dell, with her outgoing manner, would soon attach herself exclusively to some adult person in the house was not fulfilled. Her interest seemed to turn first to one of the workers in the nursery itself, but before a real attachment was formed she suddenly developed a great liking for our nurse and clung to her with unexpected affection. But this attachment too had no time to ripen. Dell suddenly showed a decided preference for men, turned to all male visitors, claimed other children's daddies loudly as her own, and would on evenings or Sundays afternoons sit for hours on a visitor's or fire watcher's lap, much to the men's embarrassment. Her attitude was little influenced by visits from her mother, who came at times and took her out for walks. Her preference for men would indicate that her affection had turned from her mother to her father; but when during her stay with us her father suddenly appeared on army leave, she did not appear to treat him differently from other visitors.

Something had evidently gone completely wrong in her relations with the adult world. Her outstanding symptom was the continual abandoning of people she was attached to at the moment for the sake of others who were new to her. Whereas in Billie's case separation from the mother had brought on a compulsive clinging to her memory, in Dell's case the result was outwardly the opposite. She lost the stable relationship to her parents which had so far governed her life, was unable to form lasting attachments, and lived continually in search and expectation accompanied by feelings of deep discontent. We know this symptom of flight from one object to the other in adult neurotics as one of the results of early disturbances in their mother relationship.

Although Dell's symptoms quieted down and were less apparent after a few weeks, especially after a prolonged stay in the sickroom where she was surrounded by a quiet homelike atmosphere, she never regained the high spirits and bright appearance which had been her main characteristics when she came.

Dell's mother found a billet in the country and took her off according to arrangement after she had been with us for eight weeks. In her case, the physical advantages of being saved from shelter life were outweighed by the shock the separation from her mother meant for her. She was given no time for psychic preparation: on the one hand, separation was too complete; on the other hand, her stay under the new conditions was too short to make up for all the misery of adaptation.[6]

Once again aerial warfare over London changed its form. After the blitz and the endless bomb waves came the V-1's and V-2's, the much less predictable automatic missiles. Despite the variety of dangers, all three houses of the Hampstead Nurseries remained undamaged. Meanwhile, Anna Freud had internally reorganized the homes. At the beginning, the entire nursing staff was responsible for all the children. Certain children, however, soon developed a special preference for some persons while rejecting others. To prevent inequity toward some children, others had to be denied affection. Familylike groups were therefore formed which brought about substantial relief and improvement. Anna Freud's war experiences do not lend support to those theories hostile to the concept of family as developed by some modern theoreticians; rather, they prove how meaningful—for children, at any rate—life within a family is.

Anna Freud followed many of Montessori's educational principles, as well as the fundamental considerations that had been decisive for Siegfried Bernfeld in the Baumgarten Nursery. The children were not to be turned into civilized individuals by means of control, fear of punishment, or other stringent disciplinary measures; rather, they were to discover their own way to order and culture through carefully guided freedom. This concept concurred with English educational tradition. Unlike various contemporary theoreticians, Anna Freud saw the goal of youngsters as their adaptation to the civilized world, a process that required a certain amount of renunciation of their instincts.

The following is one of Anna Freud's daily reports:

New Barn [one of the houses of the Hampstead Nurseries] had a narrow escape when an American fighter plane, the pilot of which had bailed out, cleared the roof of the main house, the adjoining staff house, and the treetops of the garden, crashed into the next field, and burned up. There was great excitement in the neighborhood with police, soldiers, and airmen coming to the rescue. The children were very upset, especially the big ones, who had heard the noise across the field in school. The general opinion was that the crash had been on New Barn. Since it was near school closing time, they all came rushing home to see whether the house was still standing. Their next concern was the pilot, who was for a while believed to have perished with the plane. Each child felt certain that it had been his particular airman, the one who had entertained them at the Christmas party at the American airdrome. There was great relief when the pilot was reported to have landed safely.

Netherhall Gardens and New Barn hear fairly equal numbers of V-2s and occasional V-1s. So far both houses have escaped all damage, but many of the London parents of our children were less fortunate during the past months and reports about their flats or rooms being bombed or blasted again are coming in continually. On Parents' Sunday in New Barn, though it was otherwise as pleasant a parents' day as ever, it was painfully clear that some of the mothers were in low spirits due to fear of the rocket bombs and anxiety for relations in the Forces who are involved in the battles now being fought in Europe and in the Japanese war.[7]

We close this chapter with a report on Tony, which distinctly illustrates the affectionate objectivity, if we may say so, with which Anna Freud knew and guided each of the children under her care. Again, we find here the problem of separation:

In Report 12 we cite[d] Tony as an outstanding example of those cases where children pass through too many hands, receive one shock of separation after the other, and in the end withdraw into themselves and completely lose their emotional contact with the outer world. We also describe[d] there how in our house Tony first regained some of his feelings in contact with a nurse who held him in her arms while she was taking his temperature. In Report 13 we mentioned how much Tony missed his mother's visit on the day when, after the scarlet fever quarantine, the first official visitors' bus brought all the parents out to New Barn. Up to that time we were in correspondence with the mother, sent her several letters and reports about Tony's progress, and heard from the father, who visited twice while he was on leave, that she received them with great pleasure. Her answers stopped when she was not allowed anymore to write. We heard nothing more until the information came that she had died.

Tony, who is completely ignorant of all these happenings, has in the meantime formed a violent attachment to our sicknurse. His liking for the first nurse who had, as he called it, "given" him his temperature passed and he gave no visible signs of upset when she left us. But in December he came down with scarlet fever and spent weeks in the sickroom under the care of our Sister Mary Simon. He began to like her very much and this attachment deepened when again a few weeks later he returned to the sickroom with some minor illness. At the same time he began to lose his impersonal behavior, and all sorts of very vivid and passionate character traits started to appear.

The first period of his love for Sister Mary was by no means a happy one. He treated her as his possession, but his early experience had already taught him how easily possessions can be lost. This tinged his affection for her with a continual fear and insecurity. He would cling to her desperately, would be violently jealous whenever he saw her handle other children, and would demand her sole attention which he could not get. Once, on a walk, when other children took her hand, he called out excitedly: "That is my hand!" Curiously enough, he restricted this demand to the left hand only. Sister Mary was allowed to give her right hand to the other children, but he himself would then not touch that hand anymore. He wavered continually between expression of his devotion for her and of anger and resentment. When she gave him his evening bath, he would throw his toys and his teddy bear into the tub and then accuse her that she had done it. In the middle of the night he would wake up and scream for her. But, in spite of all this violent display of emotion, he was at that time not yet able to run toward Sister Mary when he saw her. He would only look up at her and smile shyly. Only when she lifted him up would he throw his arms around her neck and then look suddenly completely happy for a moment.

The most conflictful time for him was always bedtime. From the moment of undressing on he would cry quietly. Whatever he was asked, he would answer: "No. I do not like my Teddy; my car and I do not like you." He would order Sister Mary out of the room when she stayed with him, and he cried for her return when she was gone. She usually had to take him out of his bed once more, and only after he had cried quietly to himself for a few minutes in the bathroom would he, suddenly peaceful, allow her to tuck him into his bed.

He was no bed wetter at this time. The symptom had completely disappeared the moment he entered our house.

This period was certainly not easy, either for him or for the Sister, who at times had serious doubts whether the attachment to her was not more harmful than helpful to the child. Onlookers were especially worried by the disappearance of all the superficial adaptation which he had previously shown. His obedience was gone. The "good" little boy who was ready to fit in with every routine had changed to a violently demanding child, quite able to upset a whole bedroom full of children.

The Sister's own patience and interest and some encouragement offered from our side helped her to see the situation through. She met Tony's stormy outbreaks with unfailing kindness and affection. The result was that his reactions changed after a surprisingly short time. He now became very intimate with her. He performed all sorts of small tasks for her and he even told her something about his very few scraps of memory: "You know, Mary, my daddy carried my mummy in his arms." He can now feel more sure about her even when he is separated from her in the house. He plays in the nursery while she is busy in the sickroom. He only has to know where she is and to be given complete freedom to run and look for her at any moment.

When he has been dressed in his nursery in the morning, he now rushes over to her part of the house, throws his arms around her to say good morning, and then, like lightning, rushes off again to get his breakfast. Instead of accusing her of committing all his misdeeds, as he did before, he now shares with her the glory of his actions. Once, when he was helping her in the sickroom, a young nurse played with him and he, in fun, pretended to be strong enough to knock her over. He shouted with delight and, after she had left the room, turned to the Sister and said: "Didn't we kick her, Mary, didn't we?" Whenever she passes him in the house, he will just quietly look up and then say: "That was my own Mary."

There are interesting signs to show that with growing security his attachment has a tendency to become unselfish. When she told him one day that she was leaving the house to post a letter in the village, he just nodded without complaining and said to the other children: "My Mary has her [day] off today." When she went to London for a few days on leave, she prepared him carefully for the separation and found him eager to help her pack her bag. He stood quietly on the steps of the house to wave good-bye to her. And when the car which was supposed to take her moved forward a few yards to another position, he suddenly screamed out in great excitement: "Mary, Mary, you must get in or they will go without you." At that moment he had quite forgotten his own longing for her in the desire to see her plans fulfilled.

This progress in his return to normal emotions and affections cannot be expected to run along smoothly and uninterruptedly. He still returns to more difficult moods. He then is restless in his sleep and suddenly wakes up weeping: "My Mary has not said good night to me." He is more clinging on these days and less ready to remain with the other children. Bed wetting now reappears at times, usually when he has experienced some disappointment during the day. But even on these more troubled days he remains open, affectionate, and in good contact with his surroundings.

He was extremely shaken one day when another soldier father came on leave. He saw a man, very much his father's height and in the same uniform, come up the drive and rushed out to meet him. When he realized that the face he looked up to was that of a stranger, he stopped in his tracks and began to scream. He was carried back to Sister Mary to be comforted, but he sobbed for hours, and then, rather compulsively, repeated to himself over and over again a sentence which she had used to quiet him: "All soldier daddies look alike in their uniforms."

We only need to compare the extreme violence and liveliness of his emotions with the complete lack of emotional response which he had previously shown to realize what forces of repression had been at work in him.

He is an unusually beautiful child and he looks healthy. But to our concern he does not gain weight or loses shortly whatever he has gained. His examination for tuberculosis was negative before he came to us. But we intend to have him X-rayed again in the near future.

Tony has so far not been informed of his mother's death. When his father is on his next army leave, he will have to tell him. Consciously the news may mean little to him by now. He has not seen his mother for 18 months and he did not recognize a photo of her shown to him the other day.

On our urging his father now sends him postcards with messages which Tony enjoys greatly and carries about with him.[8]

In 1945 the war came to an end. After five years of existence, the Hampstead Nurseries were no longer needed. The children could return to their families. With the dismantling of the nurseries on November 1, 1945, Anna Freud completed her task.

The monthly reports on Anna Freud's days at the Hampstead Nurseries were not the only writings published during this time. During the war it had become necessary to publish the insights gained from recent experiences, which could be efficiently applied to the manifold problems of children who had lost their families. In 1942, Anna Freud and Dorothy Burlingham therefore wrote a report *Young Children in War-Time: A Year's Work in a Residential War Nursery*. A second publication by Anna Freud and Burlingham, *Infants Without Families: The Case For and Against Residential Nurseries*, appeared in 1944. The complete reports on the Hampstead Nurseries were published in English in Volume III of Anna Freud's writings. Later there were further publications. In her book on twins, Burlingham also reported in detail on Mary and Madge, the identical twins she took care of in the Hampstead Nurseries.[9] Others have reported on the later developments of various children who had been accommodated in the nurseries.[10]

While active in the Hampstead Nurseries during the war, Anna Freud also devoted steadfast attention to adult analysis,[11] but she had little time for organizational tasks within psychoanalytic associations during that period. Nonetheless, debates on the correct theoretical and practical paths of psychoanalysis obviously did not flag, according to Melitta Schmideberg,[12] and continued even during the London blitz. But neither Anna Freud nor Ernest Jones was able to summon the strength to raise cardinal theoretical problems during those times. In May 1943, however, Anna Freud gave a lecture based on her activities at the Hampstead Nurseries entitled "On the Early Social Behavior of Children: An Introductory Report on Several Observations." Following conflicts within the British Psychoanalytic Society, whose details we shall not dwell on here, Edward Glover resigned in 1944 as general secretary of the International Psychoanalytic Association. Anna Freud again assumed those duties until Grete Bibring relieved her following the elections of 1949.

Six Children from a Concentration Camp

The new tasks Anna Freud turned to after the war involved victims of German concentration camps. These were six children, survivors of Theresienstadt, on whom she did not report in more detail until 1951, using Sophie Dann's notes.[1] The Nazis had committed a "select group" of Jews to Theresienstadt and temporarily allowed them to survive. Like the children in the Vienna Baumgarten Nursery, these too had lost their parents. About their parents, victims of National Socialist persecution, only scanty biographical information was available.

These children had been taken from shelter to shelter as babies, and when they were 6–12 months old they finally arrived at Theresienstadt, where other inmates took care of them under extremely poor conditions. After the war, in 1945, the six survivors arrived with the first transport of one thousand children to England, where it was decided to keep these very young children together, and not put them in a large children's community for at least a year. Mrs. Ralph Clarke, who had already intervened on behalf of the Hampstead Nurseries, put a country house at the nurseries' disposal, Bulldogs Bank in West Hoathly, Sussex, south of London. The American Foster Parents' Plan for War Children, which had made the Hampstead Nurseries financially possible, also assumed the expenses for these six children. The new nursery was managed by the sisters Sophie and Gertrud Dann, who had already fulfilled important functions at the Hampstead Nurseries. This group thus constituted, though under different curcumstances, a sequel to the Hampstead Nurseries, the regrettable difference being the absence of monthly reports.

It was revelatory for psychoanalysis that these little victims of the Nazi regime had been deprived of the vital early relationship with a mother or a corresponding surrogate. On the other hand, they had developed deeply intimate group relationships among themselves very early on. The absence of an individual "history" at the beginning and during the observations is so pervasive that Anna Freud did not feel competent to discuss each particular case, but describes all the children from varied perspectives. Again, Anna Freud showed her eminent skill in observing small children and in describing their behavior. The theoretical psychoanalytical frame of reference protected her against sentimentality, although the children's tragic history would have offered ample opportunity for maudlin accounts which a wide public would have certainly welcomed. As always, Anna Freud was concerned not only with humane principles but also with psychoanalytic knowledge.

When the children arrived, it was immediately noticeable that they knew none of the emotions many parents are often distressed by. That is, they showed neither sibling envy, jealousy, rivalry, nor competition among themselves. On the contrary, they were very attached to each other—were, one could say, closely huddled together—and showed signs of anxiety and alarm when one of the children was temporarily absent from the group. The explanation is simple: Since there was no person for whose love it was worthwhile to compete, no forms of competition had developed. The observations were astonishing and impressive. For example, one child received a present, certainly an exciting event. The other children helped unpack it, held whatever they were told to hold, and were grateful for what they received, but showed no envy when the recipient kept most of the present for himself. That is, they also acknowledged private property without envy and did not insist, as might have been expected, on collective property.

Unusual also was the children's anxious behavior, which was based on traumatic memories. Above all, they were terribly afraid of dogs. The only animal in Theresienstadt was a watchdog, and it is not even certain whether they actually saw the dog or only heard terrifying stories about it. At any event, the children screamed whenever a dog came in sight, turned pale, and clung to the adults. This fear was gradually overcome through contact with "friendly" dogs, that is, by means of a currently known technique of behavior therapy called desensitization. Even so, the old fright reaction recurred once when the children unexpectedly saw a dog while on a walk. As Sophie Dann later reported, the children screamed when they suddenly saw a dog on the deserted path.[2] The dog was standing very quietly. One of the children, however, turned pale, bit his lip, and claimed the dog had bitten it. One boy remained completely agitated for hours. Anna Freud added that one of those children moved to America as an adult and for a long time did not lose his dog phobia. But one day he sent a photograph of himself with an enormous dog at his side, a remarkable proof that he had overcome his phobia, revealing at the same time how deep and threatening this fear must have been.

Yet Anna Freud was also able to draw attention to positive aspects: the children were able to develop psychic defenses, to master their fears, and to learn social behavior. They were indeed overly sensitive, restless, aggressive, and difficult, but neither degenerate nor psychotic. Anna Freud lent her support to these children later as well, and above all tried to guide them safely through the difficult period of puberty.[3] Whenever it was possible, she maintained contact with them.

Teaching—And No Return

After the war, the psychoanalytic movement had to seek a new beginning, not only in practical work with children but also in its theoretical and even organizational aspects. A return to Vienna, Berlin, or the other cities would have seemed appropriate for Anna Freud and all those psychoanalysts who had emigrated from Vienna, indeed for all German-speaking psychiatrists and psychoanalysts. For many of them, only a few years separated their persecution and the end of the war. Still, hardly anyone took this ostensibly obvious path. Hans Hoff, who had taken over the teaching chair of the Vienna Clinic for Nervous Disorders shortly after the war, belonged to the few exceptions. Economic considerations may have also played a role during the first postwar years. For a long time the ruins left behind by total war offered no fertile soil for psychoanalysis. Most emigrants, including Anna Freud, were so deeply wounded that they were reluctant even to contemplate returning home. No government of the German Federal Republic found it necessary to invite back those it had expelled and robbed of their citizenship—neither intellectuals nor scientists, politicians nor artists. This was and will remain disgraceful.

During the war, the psychoanalytic movement had developed in different ways. In France, it was strongly suppressed after the German troops marched in. The German-speaking members Heinz Hartmann and René Spitz were able to escape in time to the United States. Marie Bonaparte was already in Athens. Still, a small psychoanalytic group continued to work at St. Anne's Hospital. The British Society was able to train analysts and to hold seminars and courses throughout the entire war, but suffered a great deal under the stress imposed by the war.

In non-European countries, conditions seemed more auspicious. No fewer than twenty new psychoanalytic organizations were founded, for instance in Argentina in 1943. Psychoanalysis received fresh momentum particularly in the United States, partly from the influx of European emigrants, but also because of the enormous need for training not only in civilian institutions but in the military establishment as well. The developments in the United States led to a complete shift in emphasis. If the language of psychoanalysis had been German before the war and nine-tenths of the psychoanalytic literature had been published in German, the language of psychoanalysis was now English. This shift was so encompassing that the psychoanalytic literature written in German is even now hardly read in non-German-speaking countries. The number of members of psychoanalytic organizations worldwide rose to 800, of whom about 450 were now living in the United States. Moreover, psychoanalysts in the United States have asserted themselves in psychiatry as well, where—unlike in the past—they even became predominant. At the same time, American psychiatry—significantly abetted by psychoanalysis!—became and remained the international leader in the field.

A new journal, *The Psychoanalytic Study of the Child*, first published in 1945 in yearbook format, also reflected the changed circumstances. A group of former Viennese psychoanalysts, Anna Freud, Heinz Hartmann, and Ernst Kris, were responsible for its publication, but it was nevertheless oriented toward America and England. Among the editors in the United States were two other emigrants, Otto Fenichel and René Spitz, but familiar American names already predominated: Phyllis Greenacre, Edith B. Jackson, Lawrence S. Kubie, Bertram D. Lewin, Marian C. Putnam. In England, Willie Hoffer and Edward Glover contributed to the journal. It thus reflected relatively well the changes in the power constellations. Unlike the *Zeitschrift für Psychoanalytische Pädagogik*, which had meanwhile been discontinued, the goal of the new journal was no longer to underscore general psychoanalytic experiences in the area of education, but to focus for the first time on child psychoanalysis. Through Anna Freud's and (beginning in 1949) Ruth Eissler's initiative in particular, the journal rapidly reached the leading position it has since maintained. Marianne Kris joined the editorial staff in 1957. Anna Freud repeatedly used *The Psychoanalytic Study of the Child* as a favorite organ of publication. For the first issue she wrote an essay, "Indications for Child Analysis,"[1] in which she reformulated the essential ideas of *Introduction to the Technique of Child Analysis*. The second issue, published in 1946, contained another contribution by Anna Freud on disturbances in children's eating habits.[2] As in the case of many other scientific journals, a monograph series was added to the yearbook beginning in 1965. The yearbook was first published by International Universities Press, and later by Yale University Press, since a second focal point of training analysis for child psychoanalysts had developed at Yale University.

In the British Psychoanalytic Society, circumstances remained complicated even after Edward Glover's resignation. (After twenty-nine years as president, Jones had resigned in 1942. His successors were first Sylvia Payne, then John Rickman.) That Melanie Klein's disciples remained a circumscribed group within the organization did not prevent Anna Freud from putting her energies at the organization's disposal. In 1946–47, she again belonged to its training committee. She also taught courses, among them the seminar "Principles of Psychoanalysis" in 1947. It must have been around that time that Ishak Ramzy, later president of the Psychoanalytic Society of Topeka and whose houseguest Anna Freud was in 1962, wanted to attend one of her evening seminars; he himself no longer knew exactly when:

> It was one wintry, dreary evening when my steps led me to the old address of the London Institute of Psycho-Analysis, that I looked at the board on the

ground floor to see where I was supposed to go, saw the location of the room, but found on the board another announcement, that Miss Freud was not conducting the class that evening and that someone else, whose name I cannot remember, was taking her place. Though I was under no obligation yet to be counted, I was too weary to turn around and leave, so I went up two or three flights of steps and entered the room, took a seat, and looked at the first group of analysts I had ever seen gathered together. You can just imagine what fantasies and anxieties and curiosity they aroused in me when I looked at each of them from the corner of my eye, unable to stare at them as I imagined they were staring at me.

At the side, facing the door, sat quietly a lady, the lady whom I supposed to have been substituting for Miss Freud. Quietly she continued the seminar after my obtrusive appearance, and I started to look and listen. The more I looked the more I became nonplussed. The lady's presence and serenity, the clarity of her presentation and the confidence that emanated from her gentle voice caught my attention. Her being one-of-a-kind in voice, in attire, arrested my ability to locate even her accent. Under the pressue of this first encounter with analysts and my frustrated curiosity, I began to discuss with the lecturer, and to discuss strongly and tenaciously. I did not know it then, but I must have felt that I was at the crossroads, in front of a challenge that might change my career. My mind had been filled during the day with figures, averages, percentiles, coefficients, and controversies between my teacher Cyril Burt and his counterpart on this side of the ocean, Thurstone of Chicago. And here was this quiet teacher in this humble room, talking about *the* way to understand human psychology through the understanding of only one single individual.

I recall I did not overtly give up that night my belief in the importance of large numbers, but the more I heard, the more I became convinced that there was another way. The seminar ended, everyone moved toward the door, and on the doorstep I whispered to the only person there with whom I had some acquaintance, "When is Miss Freud going to teach this class?" He said, "But that was Miss Freud who was teaching this evening!" You can imagine my reaction.[3]

Ramzy was wrong in assuming that Anna Freud would derive psychological principles from a single example. Naturally, psychoanalytic research, like any other science, derives systems and their constituent rules empirically. It would otherwise be impossible to apply the acquired experience to new cases. Ramzy's vivid report nonetheless shows how someone using the old—though in psychology still predominant—statistical method of obtaining knowledge had to be "converted" to another type of research—in this case through the influence of Anna Freud's personality and her activities in the British Psychoanalytic Society. Still, Anna Freud was never able to identify as well with the London Society as she had once with the Vienna one. She was thus all the more able to serve the interests of the

International Psychoanalytic Association, whose vice president she would soon become. Next to child psychoanalysis, international relations increasingly became her field of work.

A New Institute

Jones opened the first international postwar congress in 1949 with the jocular remark that it had been the habit of psychoanalysts to convene in Holland after world wars, Zurich being an exception now. Indeed, the first postwar international psychoanalytic convention in 1947 had again been held on Dutch territory, in Amsterdam, where Anna Freud gave the lecture "Transformation of Instinct in Early Childhood," in which she drew on her war experiences in Hampstead.

Another lecture she gave that same year before the Psychiatric Section of the Royal Society of Medicine addressed the problem of aggression.[1] The world was concerned with this subject then as it is today. After the belief that culture could bridle and channel aggression into civilized paths had crumbled, there was a desire to probe the roots of war and the enormous collective aggression it released among nations. The relationship between individual and collective aggression stirred particular interest. Anna Freud pointed out that of course human aggression had pervaded every historical period, and World War II had in fact revealed nothing new. Only the ways of looking at and evaluating aggression had changed. Again, we see Anna Freud at many conventions. For example, on May 27, 1947, she spoke in London on "The Sleeping Difficulties of the Young Child," a subject she returned to in 1949 and 1950.[2]

The most important event of 1947 was no doubt the establishment of the Hampstead Child Therapy Course, courses in child psychoanalysis made possible by the assistance of Kate Friedländer and the cooperation of several members of the British Psychoanalytic Society. These training courses were started when former colleagues from the Hampstead Nurseries insisted on a more comprehensive training program that would include training analysis. Moreover, the creation of these courses also meant the founding of an "Anna Freud school," although neither Anna Freud nor any of her closer colleagues ever used the term. On the basis of the courses' content the name "Hampstead Method" was adopted.[3] Child psychoanalysis thereby became organizationally independent of general psychoanalysis, surely more in practice than in theory, without however being at variance with the "other" psychoanalysis. Rather, it was a matter of adequately applying psychoanalysis to children, that is, of using Anna Freud's theoretical and practical innovations.

The task of the courses in child psychoanalysis did not consist merely in the direct training of the analyst. Since child psychoanalysis varies from adult psychoanalysis only in the age of patients and their inability to free-associate, the institution Anna Freud created was at the same time a place where Freudian psychoanalysis was taught and further developed.

Since 1947, four to eight candidates have been trained yearly at Hampstead. The basic pattern was identical to the model developed in Vienna: training analysis, supervised analysis, participation in seminars on actual case histories, and, finally, theoretical and practical studies in seminars and lectures. On Wednesdays, Anna Freud still held her legendary "Wednesday Seminar," in which individual case histories and general subjects were discussed. Since 1978, various seminar reports have also been published. Today, more than one hundred child analysts have been trained at Hampstead. The older among them have reached important positions at universities and other training centers. Their geographical distribution too reveals the shift from the past: at the time of this writing, forty-four Hampstead analysts work in England, almost as many in the United States, and only five in other parts of the world. Not even once does the home of psychoanalysis, the German-speaking cultural milieu, figure in statistics—such are the lasting consequences of Hitler's barbarism.

Despite her extensive teaching duties at Hampstead, Anna Freud remained active on the teaching committees of the British Psychoanalytic Society and in seminars and lectures until 1955.

We have seen that before World War II the question of lay analysis threatened to undermine the cooperation between the International and the American Psychoanalytic Associations, while only the repeated postponement of decisions and the formation of committees were able to prevent a schism. The American Psychoanalytic Association had meanwhile developed into an organization with full legislative power over local psychoanalytic societies, and now negotiated with the International Psychoanalytic Association. In the summer of 1948, an American delegation of psychoanalysts came to London to seek an agreement with the Europeans. Delegates were the Bibrings, whom Anna Freud knew well from Vienna and London days, and several Americans: Carl Binger, Sophie Dunn, Sándor Lorand (an emigré Hungarian psychoanalyst), John Millet, John Murray, and Parker. The European party was represented by Anna Freud, Ernest Jones, W. H. Gillespie, Sylvia Payne, John Rickman, and Usher. The far-reaching agreement that was achieved necessitated a change in the statutes of the International Psychoanalytic Association, and at the next congress Jones described the agreement as satisfactory without going into its details.

In August 1948, Anna Freud delivered a lecture at the World Congress for Psychohygiene in London. The various national psychohygienic societies had just merged into the World Federation for Mental Health (WFMH). It was believed that psychohygienic measures would be able to prevent a new war, and that it was there-fore necessary to expose the psychological roots of war. Heinrich Meng, who had once worked with Anna Freud on the *Zeitschrift für Psychoanalytische Pädagogik* and had maintained a steady correspondence with her from Basel, where he had settled, devoted increasing attention to psychohygiene and received a teaching chair in psychoanalysis and psychohygiene in Basel. At the congress on psychohygiene, Anna Freud again spoke on aggression, addressing the problem from a psychoanalytical perspective, yet without attempting to draw psycho-cultural conclusions.

In the summer of the same year, through the intervention of Marie Bonaparte, who had meanwhile returned to Paris, UNESCO invited Anna Freud to lecture on "Educational and Psychological Techniques for Changing Mental Attitudes Affect-ing International Understanding."[4] This special organization of the U.N., commit-ted to the well-being of children throughout the world, had been established in Paris in 1945. Here too the question was asked what education could do to prevent future wars. In her lecture, Anna Freud moved from the subject of aggression to the war experiences in the Hampstead Nurseries, where she had learned so much about the life of orphans, and then drew the following conclusions:

> By inquiring into the modern educational and psychological techniques for changing mental attitudes, UNESCO is avoiding one of the gravest errors of past eras: the setting up of new ideological aims for mankind, without questioning whether such aims are compatible or incompatible with human nature.
>
> Better human understanding between nations as a new ideological aim presupposes in a whole generation of children the development of qualities such as tolerance, love of peace, freedom from fear and prejudice, the ability to identify with fellow beings and to evaluate their individual or national characteristics in an objective manner.[5]

The First Postwar Psychoanalytic Congress

After eleven years of standstill, an international psychoanalytic congress could finally be convened in Zurich on August 15–19, 1949. The first to be held after the war as well as the first after Freud's death and the last under Jones's presidency, it amply documented the altered situation.

The congress may have seemed to symbolize the return of psychoanalysis to a German-speaking country where, incidentally, C. G. Jung was still living. But the choice of the location certainly did not mean a renaissance of psychoanalysis. A meeting with Jung, which could have lent wings to the historian's imagination, had evidently not even been considered. Not only were the theoretical and practical therapeutic discrepancies between Freudian psychoanalysis and the Jungian school felt to be too profound to allow a meaningful discussion; even more damaging were the unforgotten political invectives Jung had voiced at the beginning of Hitler's dictatorship.

Anna Freud did not hesitate to participate actively at the congress held in this small European, German-speaking area—German Switzerland—that had remained unscathed by Hitler. She won a personal triumph. Her lecture, "Some Clinical Remarks Concerning the Treatment of Cases of Male Homosexuality,"[1] a new subject she would be concerned with in the following years, brought her long standing ovations. Ishak Ramzy, who reported this event, had gone up to her at the podium and heard her say with her typical mixture of irony and objectivity to Jones, who was congratulating her for her lecture: "I hardly believe that everything was meant for me."[2] Indeed, the effect of the ovation was that she was being treated as if she were Freud's representative.

At the Zurich congress, Willie Hoffer showed a film made at the Hampstead Nurseries on the eating habits of younger and older children. It was the first time Anna Freud commented on behavior observed on the screen, and she would often do so again. Her gift for precise observation and clear description was thus excellently brought into relief.

For the first time an American, Leo Bartemeier of Detroit, was elected president at the Zurich congress. Although Jones must have had tactical goals in mind by recommending him, the election indicated the new reality. Bartemeier, only a few months older than Anna Freud, was trained at the Psychoanalytic Institute of Chicago between 1930 and 1935, and had just been elected president of the American Psychiatric Association for the 1951–52 term. This is an influential association, whose presidency carries great significance. Various lines thus converged in Bartemeier: he was the first psychoanalyst to become president of the American Psychiatric Association *and* both the first clinical psychiatrist and the first American to become president of the International Psychoanalytic Association. Thus far, presidents of the International Association had been persons close to Freud.

American psychoanalysts were thus beginning to feel a stronger obligation to the International Psychoanalytic Association. The latter had always made efforts toward the establishment of new psychoanalytic societies, and in Latin America several new ones had been set up at that time. While a large number of respected American psychoanalysts were still absent from the Zurich congress, South Americans were more widely represented.

In Zurich, Anna Freud transferred the office of general secretary to Grete Bibring, knowing it would be in good hands. It became noticeable at this congress how many psychoanalysts who had stood close to Anna Freud had died during the last decades in the countries where they had sought refuge: Max Eitingon in Palestine; Hanns Sachs, Ernst Simmel, and Otto Fenichel in the United States. And A. A. Brill, the pioneer of American psychoanalysis, was no longer alive. Paul Schilder, from Vienna's clinical period; Ruth Mack Brunswick; Karl Landauer, who became a victim of Nazi persecution in Holland—they too were gone. And Alice Balint had passed away in England. Two months after this congress, on October 17, 1949, August Aichhorn would die in Vienna.

Jones's resignation after more than twenty-two years as president was followed by standing ovations from the attending members and gave Anna Freud the opportunity to honor him with spirited words. It was thanks to Jones that so few analysts became victims of Nazi persecution—in particular that her father did not move to Holland, where he would have suffered Landauer's horrible end, but instead was admitted to England, where he was able to live his last year in peace. Anna Freud then made mention of the workload Jones had taken on during the difficult years, which she was able to gauge from her close position as general secretary. Anna Freud's convincing and cordial words, followed by persistent ovations, bespoke her enduring sense of gratitude, obligation, and loyalty not only toward England as her host country, but also toward Jones, whose disagreements with her on certain issues were surely familiar to congress participants.

In 1949, Anna Freud for the first time wrote and published again in German, although English had become and remained her scientific language. The essay "On Certain Difficulties in the Preadolescent's Relation to His Parents" was published in the volume *Psychotherapy*, edited by Maria Pfister-Amende.[3] Anna Freud had always been considered an analyst of young children, since that was indeed her first field of work. In this and later essays, she showed that she was equally conversant with problems of puberty, which she masterfully described. We will return to this topic later.

August Aichhorn

August Aichhorn—we have already spoken of him extensively—had decisively marked Anna Freud's ideas and her mode of interacting with children and adolescents. She quoted him in many of her works, always with the highest esteem and even admiration. When Aichhorn died, she wrote a most warm-hearted and personal memorial.[1]

Aichhorn is frequently cited in modern psychoanalytic educational literature, and his pioneering achievements with juvenile delinquents are highly praised. Thus far his biography has not been written, and only those who have known him personally are truly knowledgeable about his personality and work.[2] Born on July 27, 1878, into a well-to-do family, Aichhorn was seventeen years Anna Freud's senior. Until nearly the middle of his life, nothing seemed to intimate the new thoughts and projects he would be capable of developing. After the death of his twin brother he became, at the age of twenty, an elementary-school teacher, exactly as Anna Freud did later, and fulfilled his teaching tasks dutifully for ten years. *

Aichhorn was averse to continual teaching and to waiting decades for his retirement. He thus took over the direction of a municipal office that had established educational advisory centers and supervised homes for adolescents. Today we would say that Aichhorn was an official working with juveniles. Before World War I, however, when Montessori's theories were spreading through Europe, such tasks demanded much more enthusiasm than they do today.

Aichhorn was already forty years old when he found his life's task. Immediately after World War I, he and several inspired colleagues took over a home for delinquent juveniles in Oberhollabrunn in Lower Austria, about fifty kilometers northwest of Vienna. This activity came to an end in 1920, but was then resumed for two years in Sankt Andreä. Only now did Aichhorn turn to psychoanalysis, and in 1922 he became a member of the Vienna Psychoanalytic Society, at about the same time as Anna Freud.

The work Aichhorn reported on in his famous book *Wayward Youth* (1925) thus already lay behind him when he became a psychoanalyst. He was first of all a practitioner, and less a theoretician; it was in his interaction with juveniles that he discovered how they could be helped. But it is insufficient to describe this gift as "intuitive," because Aichhorn was always thoughtful in his actions. What he lacked, however, was the theoretical frame of reference to describe and communicate his knowledge.

Aichhorn was at first inconspicuous in the Vienna psychoanalytic group, since he mostly listened, scarcely participating in discussions. He spoke only when he himself had something to present. Perhaps he felt uneasy with the free-floating intellectual manner of the debates in which participants often displayed their self-complacency along with their rich imagination. Yet Sigmund Freud evinced warm interest for his work from the very beginning and viewed it as a new, practical application of psychoanalysis. Paul Federn became Aichhorn's training analyst, and the like-minded Willie Hoffer and Anna Freud offered him friendship. Aichhorn

---

*Interestingly, the Swiss representative of psychoanalytical education and child analysis, Hans Zulliger (1893–1965), had also taught in the canton of Bern since 1912. At the teachers' seminar, Ernst Schneider, the seminar leader, had drawn his attention to psychoanalysis. In Switzerland, Jacques Berna (b. 1911) today practices in Zurich the child analysis developed by Zulliger and represented by Oskar Pfister. But Zulliger, in contrast to Aichhorn, has always remained active as a teacher.

was among the few people in connection with whom Anna Freud spoke, even publicly, of "friendship."

It was his involvement with psychoanalysis that prompted Aichhorn to impart his experiences in *Wayward Youth*, first published in 1925. Aichhorn was forty-seven years old when his first work became available. He did not write very much later—a very instructive example that even relatively late in life one can, under unusual circumstances such as contact with Freud and psychoanalysis, write a book on one's extraordinary observations and experiences that otherwise would have been lost. At the same time, Aichhorn's case shows that it is possible to achieve fame with a single book. It seems that Aichhorn was not entirely aware of what he had embarked on while writing the book. Actually, he had planned only an introduction to psychoanalysis for those who, like him, were professionally working with juvenile delinquents. At the same time he intended to present to psychoanalysts the special problems of such juveniles. Indirectly, however, he accomplished something entirely different: he alloyed his vivid descriptions and his humane, teacher's understanding of juveniles with psychoanalytical theories. According to Aichhorn, criminality can be explained as an interruption in the development of the personality. To be sure, other significant and current factors are necessary for delinquency to become manifest. Aichhorn viewed disturbances in the parental home or a rupture in the early parent–child relationship as responsible for the later misbehavior of juveniles. It follows from this unequivocal psychoanalytic model that it is absurd to treat only the symptoms. Rather, the lag caused by the arrested personality development requires compensatory action. At that time, when the hereditary aspect of criminality was widely believed in, Aichhorn's ideas had a revolutionary effect and his insights necessarily led to a more humane attitude toward juveniles. It seems that Aichhorn himself had stood on the threshold of degeneracy during his youth, but had nevertheless been able to choose the side of society—or rather, both sides. To the juvenile delinquent, he did not represent the attitudes of a society that obviously had to condemn and punish a delinquent's behavior. Nor did Aichhorn attempt to justify the juvenile's criminality before society. In each case he strove to grasp the juvenile's personality and to gradually steer him into a noncriminal life. Aichhorn's highly praised gift was to speak with juveniles so that they felt entirely understood, though he did not seek to become their friend. This is borne out by many impressive examples from his experiences that vividly lay bare his procedures even to a contemporary audience. Unintentionally, Aichhorn thus also laid the foundations of the therapy of criminals.

The book nevertheless caused limited reverberations at first. Success came only with the English translation in 1935, and the book was subsequently translated into many languages.

At the age of fifty-four, Aichhorn resigned from his position with the city of Vienna and devoted himself to psychoanalytical educational counseling, while also holding seminars on the subject at the Vienna Psychoanalytic Institute. He remained in Vienna during the war, where a small circle of people interested in his work gathered around him and met regularly in the evenings in his apartment at 110 Schönbrunnerstrasse. Scorned and banished as psychoanalysis was, he remained loyal to it. Aichhorn and his family survived the war in "inner emigration" while one of his sons was temporarily sent to a concentration camp. It was Aichhorn's misfortune that his apartment was bombed, though the war's destruction was not as great in Vienna as in German cities. Aichhorn found a refuge in Frankenfels in Lower Austria, where he was able to wait out the war.

Soon after the war, Anna Freud resumed contact with Aichhorn from London. She also made efforts to have the Berlin Psychoanalytic Society rebuilt. W. Solms-Rödelheim quotes a letter Anna Freud wrote to Aichhorn on February 21, 1946:

> The National Socialists' destruction of the old institute and of the books, the closing of the Ambulatorium, and the dismantling of the psychoanalytic publishing house in 1938 seemed to mean the end of psychoanalysis in Austria. This affected all the members of the International Psychoanalytic Association all the more, since Vienna was more than just the birthplace of psychoanalysis. From its inception to its destruction, the Vienna Psychoanalytic Institute had incessantly stimulated and fertilized psychoanalytic research and work in the entire world.[3]

The Institute was reopened on April 10, 1946, and Aichhorn became president of the Vienna Society. In 1947, Anna Freud and Aichhorn were able to meet again in Switzerland at the conference of the Union Internationale de Protection de l'Enfance. On his seventieth birthday on July 27, 1948, International Universities Press of New York dedicated to Aichhorn a volume it had published, *Searchlights on Delinquency*,[4] at that time probably the most exceptional honor bestowed on someone who had remained in his home country during the Nazi period. The volume was edited by K. R. Eissler, one of Aichhorn's students who had emigrated to New York. Paul Federn wrote the dedication, and Anna Freud contributed the essay "Certain Types and Stages of Social Maladjustment,"[5] in which she discussed educational principles relevant to early childhood. The volume contains numerous significant contributions and by 1975 had gone through seven printings—indeed a rarity for a dedication volume.

Anna Freud not only wrote an obituary on the occasion of Aichhorn's death in 1949, but later used every opportunity to mention him. To illustrate that in children the famine period of 1914–18 was followed by eating disturbances rather than by recuperative eating binges, she recounted the following episode:

> I can remember a parents' meeting—quite a new idea at that time—at which Aichhorn asked the parents to tell him what was the difficulty in handling their children that came to their minds first. The audience, not used to a discussion, felt shy and embarrassed; after a pause a father got up and said, "The most difficult thing is to make our little daughter eat her breakfast." Then a storm

broke among the parents and they all described the methods which they used to make their children eat, such as paying a penny for each piece of bread eaten, or promising an outing for each cup of milk drunk.[6]

In 1959, when a memorial volume was under preparation for the tenth anniversary of August Aichhorn's death, Anna Freud immediately contributed an essay "On Certain Phases and Types of Asocial Behavior and Degeneracy"[7] based on Aichhorn's fundamental theses, which she elaborated. According to this article, not all types of asocial behavior and degeneracy are a "result of disturbances during the first year or of damages the object love has suffered during that period." She distinguished three phases and types of asocial behavior, the third of which "is based on the complete repression of phallic masturbation, which inundates the ego with instinctual material. This sexualization of ego activities provokes certain widely known forms of psychopathic behavior." Even in the seventh decade of her life, Anna Freud was guided by Aichhorn's thoughts.

America, 1950

In April 1950, Anna Freud took her first trip to America. Many others would follow in the next years. The attention and enthusiasm that welcomed her there exceeded by far what she had experienced in England, at international psychoanalytical congresses, or even on the Continent. To be sure, the growing esteem for her during the next decades had various aspects: not everywhere was it meant chiefly for her, but often for Sigmund Freud's daughter. She represented her father's work clearly and objectively, with great persuasive power and, moreover, in her personal, very winning manner. At the age of fifty-five, she was more self-confident, and her personality had become even more radiant. Since the spread of psychoanalysis was one of her most important aims in life, she willingly assumed this task despite her aversion to being in the public eye. Again the danger arose that her own work would not receive the recognition it deserved. The agenda of lectures, trips, meetings, and personal encounters she followed on her eighteen-day trip to the United States equaled the achievement of a modern company executive.

On April 17, 1950, Anna Freud delivered her first lecture to the New York Psychoanalytic Society, the largest in the world by then, comprising a quarter of the world's psychoanalysts. To check the influx of listeners, each member received only one admission ticket, but a large crowd assembled nonetheless. Only slightly changed, the title of her lecture matches her lecture at the Zurich congress: "Clinical Observations on the Treatment of Manifest Male Homosexuality."[1] In very detailed psychoanalytic studies, she described the therapeutic progress of four of the men she had treated. The question of prognosis played an important role. Anna Freud concluded that neither open motivation for treatment nor the type of homosexual behavior can predict success, but that the determinant factor lay rather in early development preceding the phallic stage. In the cases she treated, development had proceeded rather undisturbed until the phallic stage. Only later did the abnormal inability to identify with the father, subsequently followed by the choice of a homosexual object, develop. During the discussion part of the lecture, Anna Freud's old acquaintances from Vienna who were then working in New York spoke: Hermann Nunberg, Heinz Hartmann, Ludwig Eidelberg, Edmund Bergler, and Grete Bibring. During Anna Freud's visits to America, it became customary for her friends from Vienna to gather around her.

Several days later, on April 20, Anna Freud's attendance at the festivities for the sixtieth anniversary of the founding of Clark University in Worcester, Massachusetts, was even more clearly a symbolic act. Before World War I, on the university's twentieth anniversary in 1910, Freud gave his lectures on psychoanalysis there, which acquainted a large circle in America with him and with psychoanalysis.

Freud's first step on the American continent had acquired a symbolic meaning, which was then deepened by Anna Freud's first visit to America. Clark University celebrated its jubilee with a symposium on genetic psychology, in which Anna Freud represented psychoanalysis with the lecture "The Contribution of Psychoanalysis to Genetic Psychology."[2] Fully aware of the symbolic and historical function of her lecture, she first discussed the development of psychoanalysis in America and then told of her father's surprise at finding some knowledge of psychoanalysis in the United States as early as 1920.

In one of her few historical presentations, Anna Freud then used the theme of the symposium to shed light on the relationships between psychoanalysis and academic psychology. Contrary to the current, widely spread belief reflected in magazines, literature, and public opinion, which hardly distinguishes between psychology and psychoanalysis, the relationship between psychoanalysis and academic psychology evolved with even greater difficulties than that between psychoanalysis and medicine, out of which the former has, after all, developed. We cannot actually claim that the relationship has fundamentally changed since. Academic psychology is largely oriented toward the relatively undynamic scientific ideal of the natural sciences, to which psychoanalytic theories cannot adjust. Even behavior therapy, which has grown out of academic psychology, has come into being mostly out of an antipsychoanalytic sentiment, revealing, if one wishes to see it thus, the significance attributed to this "dangerous" discipline called psychoanalysis and the honor it is granted. That, however, does not imply that there are not some excellent psychoanalysts among psychologists.

On the same occasion, Clark University awarded the title Doctor *honoris causa* to Anna Freud who, having never earned an academic title, was now Dr. Anna Freud, member of—oddly—a faculty of law. This honor was indubitably meant at least as much for her father as for her, hence it too carried a symbolic character. Such awards were always a double-edged matter. While always very great, the honor was usually conferred on scientists when their work was essentially completed; it was nearly always bound with the feeling that they now belonged to the rubbish heap. Nevertheless, Anna Freud accomplished essential portions of her work after receiving this mark of distinction.

In the two aforementioned lectures, Anna Freud repeatedly mentioned her experiences in child psychoanalysis, but she concentrated more on general psychoanalytic questions. A symposium on developmental problems, organized by the Austin Riggs Foundation in her honor on April 23 and 24, 1950, in Stockbridge, Massachusetts, now redressed the neglect of child psychoanalysis. Austin Fox Riggs in 1923 was the first to establish a complete organization for the treatment of psychiatric disturbances in university students. This branch of psychiatry has always been viewed as more or less belonging to child and juvenile psychiatry, because university students, even though they are counted as adults, suffer from special problems arising precisely from their as yet undefined social status. The Austin Riggs Foundation had invited an impressive series of psychoanalysts and child analysts who had emigrated to the United States, and Anna Freud was again among old Viennese acquaintances. The list of outstanding participants in the discussion is noteworthy: Grete Bibring, Berta Bornstein, Helene Deutsch, Erik H. Erikson, Elisabeth Gellerd, Phyllis Greenacre, Heinz Hartmann, Mary O'Neil Hawkins, Bertram Lewin, Rudolph M. Loewenstein, Margaret Mahler, Marian Putnam, Beate Rank, Melitta Sperling, René Spitz, Emmy Sylvester, Robert Waelder. The discussion was led by Robert Palmer Knight, medical director of the Austin Riggs Foundation since 1947 and professor of psychiatry at Yale University. Unfortunately, the tapes recording the entire discussion were technically defective, so nothing survived from the two-day talk.[3]

This gathering was not the last at which Anna Freud spoke during her eighteen-day trip. She gave a speech before students of Harvard and Radcliffe colleges; she stirred enthusiasm with a lecture at Western Reserve University in Cleveland, Ohio; and concluded her trip by attending the annual convention of the American Psychoanalytic Association in Detroit, where she spoke before a large nonprofessional audience. On this occasion she was elected an honorary member of the American Psychoanalytic Association, an honor no doubt different in import from honorary membership in the Palestinian Psychoanalytic Association, which Eitingon had proposed to her immediately upon its establishment. Honorary membership in the American association reflected, rather, the characteristic tendency in America to acknowledge her tasks as those of Freud's daughter. Still, it was astonishing how Anna Freud was able, at the age of fifty-five, to become and remain a viable member of American intellectual life—contrary to her position in Germany and Austria.

In 1950, Anna Freud also attended the meeting of European psychoanalysts in Paris. Now began for her the continuous archival work on Freud's estate, claiming a considerable part of her energies in the years to come. After his resignation from the presidency of the International Psychoanalytic Association, Jones began to work on a biography of Freud. The three-volume edition, the first of which was published in 1953, was to become Jones's most significant and best-known work. Several biographies of Freud had already been written, for the interest in his life and work was always very great, but they were, each in its own way, incomplete and today are largely forgotten, even though they temporarily fulfilled their function. Anna Freud not only allowed Jones access to many still unpublished letters and documents, but, as it was in her nature to serve what she deemed good, she generously put her own very precise knowledge at his disposal. With her assistance, Jones was able to create his monumental work, still unsurpassed by far, despite some weaknesses that have surfaced in the course of years. It transpires from Jones's text that Anna Freud did not attempt—as one might have assumed—to influence the content. She would surely have written certain things differently.

Erik Erikson

In Stockbridge, Anna Freud also met an intimate friend from Vienna who had become perhaps the most fashionable psychoanalyst in the United States during the seventeen years since she had seen him, and who was about to provide a new explanation of American culture: Erik Erikson.

Erikson was born on June 15, 1902, near Frankfurt. Both his parents were Danish; they had separated before his birth. He grew up with his mother, Karla Abrahamsen, in Karlsruhe and became acquainted with his "fatherland" only as an adult, mainly because his mother had concealed his "identity" from him. In Karlsruhe, his mother married the Jewish pediatrician Dr. Theodor Homburger, who adopted Erik (later he carried the names of both fathers, Erik Homburger Erikson), but was not pleased with the artistically inclined boy. He would have preferred to see him become a typical physician. After he graduated from high school, Erik hiked through Europe for several years, then enrolled in the Baden Landscaping School until he was finally able to study at the Munich Academy of Arts.

His destiny took a decisive turn in 1927 when he came to Vienna, where he was in the immediate proximity of Anna Freud. After her arrival in Vienna in 1925, Dorothy Burlingham established a small private school, where not only her own four children studied but also those of other Americans who were in Vienna primarily to be analyzed by Freud. Peter Blos, who had taken over the directorship of this school, was Erikson's most intimate friend. They had known each other from Karlsruhe and together had explored the beauty of Florence. It was Peter Blos who had drawn his friend Erikson to Vienna.

Erikson's only duty at the school was to teach art. He thus made contact with children whose parents were undergoing psychoanalysis and some of whom (for example, Burlingham's children; see p. 119 above) were being analyzed by Anna Freud. Very great resistance would have been required not to be drawn into psychoanalysis. The concerted efforts of both women soon resulted in drawing the two teachers from the private school into psychoanalysis. Blos became an analyst. Erikson, too, went into training analysis with Anna Freud. Although he joined his training analyst on her longer trips to Berlin to maintain the continuity of analysis, his resistance to psychoanalysis remained firm for a long time; it finally disappeared completely, according to psychoanalytic rules. In 1975, Erikson described how he had again and again told his analyst during analysis that he saw in psychoanalysis no arena for his artistic inclinations. He felt he was an artist, not a therapist. Anna Freud replied quietly: "You might help to make them see."[4] The resistance gave way completely only after Erikson met his future wife, Joan Serson, at a carnival ball in Luxemburg in 1929. She also belonged to the group of Americans in Vienna, and she was also in analysis (with Ludwig Jekels). After the wedding she too became a teacher at the private psychoanalytic school.

Erikson wrote his first psychoanalytic work, "The Future of Enlightenment and Psychoanalysis," in 1930.[5] In 1933, he completed his training and emigrated to Denmark. But he was a foreigner in his homeland. America, his wife's country, admitted him.

The six years in Vienna left a decisive mark on Erikson. Those were years when ego psychology was being discussed in Vienna, not only by Anna Freud. Erikson has repeatedly referred to her book *The Ego and the Mechanisms of Defense*, published after his departure. To ego psychology Erikson added the problem of identity—his own problem which had presumably been the main subject in his analysis with Anna Freud. Since about 1940, Erikson has spoken of ego identity, striking a chord of paramount significance in American culture. The variety of cultural roots in its population, the enormous size of the country, and the absence of locally entrenched traditions make it extraordinarily difficult for Americans growing up to find their identity.

Erikson has also shown lifelong loyalty to the problems of children and juveniles he had learned about in Anna Freud's child seminar. To be sure, as many another analyst, he did not merely render what he had learned, but expressed his own creativity. An entire generation would welcome and approve of Erikson's descriptions of the eight developmental stages and of the difficult years of adolescence. To each life stage, Erikson assigned its own—even if failing—identity. Thus came into being a closed system, by no means in contradiction with Freudian psychoanalysis, but essentially expanding the latter toward socio-cultural aspects, a system American culture assimilated with enormous rapidity.

The year 1950, when Erikson and Anna Freud again stood face to face, was another fateful one for Erikson. His first major work, *Childhood and Society*, was published.[6] The most fertile decade of his life also began with that year, during which the stimulation and generosity of the Austin Riggs Foundation enabled him to write his other main works.

Neither Anna Freud nor Erikson ever showed any need to compare and contrast their works, which revolved around themes central for both, namely, youth and the ego. They always quoted each other respectfully.

The International Psychoanalytic Congress in Amsterdam

In the summer of 1951, the Seventeenth International Psychoanalytic Congress, the second postwar congress, was held in Amsterdam on August 5–9, with 450 participants. An international congress had also been held in Holland, in The Hague, in 1920.

Anna Freud again fulfilled a variety of functions, as vice president as well as lecturer. In "Negativism and Emotional Surrender,"[1] she discussed again her experiences with former homosexuals. Negativism here meant "refusal to establish relationships with other people," or, in psychoanalytic terms, "absence of object relationships"—i.e., the opposite of emotional surrender or total dependence on a single person. Anna Freud participated in "The Mutual Influences in the Development of Ego and Id,"[2] a memorable panel discussion. Princess Marie Bonaparte was responsible for this symposium; Heinz Hartmann and Willie Hoffer, Anna Freud's two old friends, introduced it. Anna Freud opened the discussion with a preparatory essay. Other participants were Melanie Klein, Sacha Nacht (Paris), Clifford M. Scott (London), Hermann Nunberg (now in New York), H. G. van der Waals (Amsterdam), and Jacques Lacan (Paris). One of the rare events both Klein and Anna Freud attended, it was also the only occasion when Lacan engaged in a discussion with the two women.

It is difficult to imagine contrasts within psychoanalysis greater than those revealed in this discussion. This was the last international congress Lacan attended as a member. He and his group were expelled before the next congress.

Several years after he withdrew from official psychoanalysis, Lacan expressed his views on the aforementioned subject in a seminar held on February 17, 1954, entitled "Discourse Analysis and Ego Analysis."[3] Subtitled "Anna Freud or Melanie Klein," it reflected the theoretical conflicts and alluded to the bitterness of the schism in which Anna Freud played a lively part. Lacan said, "It is not fortuitous that these two ladies [Anna Freud and Melanie Klein], not without analogy to each other, have set themselves in regal rivalry against each other." Of Anna Freud's best-known work, *The Ego and the Mechanisms of Defense*, Lacan said caustically that it was "on the level of a truly well-transmitted legacy of Freud's last work on the ego," that is, there was nothing original in it. To articulate the contrast between Anna Freud's and his own position, Lacan labeled Anna Freud a rationalist. One need not necessarily refute this interpretation, but it becomes interesting only within the contrast.

Lacan stood, oddly, within the tradition of German idealism. With its implicit depth of insights, darkness was for him at once spiritual need and surrealistic gesticulation. No wonder, then, that Melanie Klein was much closer to him. There are, in psychoanalysis too, rationalistic and idealistic traditions.

Lacan applied his thinking to ego psychology as well, explaining that two split egos must be radically distinguished from each other. Otherwise, Lacan said in one of his profound yet opaque statements, the ego could not be master of errors, the seat of illusions, and the site of passion while also possessing the function of *méconnaissance* [misconstruction] in analysis.

In Amsterdam, Anna Freud was intent on describing her ideas on the ego's structure and development, which matured during the war. This again indicates that she pursued older ideas in the light of new experiences.

The business sessions of this congress carried as much weight as the scientific discussions. As always, Anna Freud took a lively interest in problems that now included the admission of the German Psychoanalytic Societies. After the war, as soon as travel abroad was permitted, the first emissaries from Berlin arrived in London in 1946 to seek advice from Anna Freud. After the war there were economic reasons to leave the various psychotherapeutic movements in their existing format of a joint organization, while in Vienna, thanks to Aichhorn's efforts, psychoanalysts again formed an alliance in April 1946. In Berlin the situation remained unpredictable. Finally, the group around Harald Schultz-Hencke, today included among neoanalytic schools, split off. This group gained great recognition in Germany but remained largely unknown outside German-speaking territories. Although unequivocally leaning on Freud's theories, Schultz-Hencke had nonetheless deviated from psychoanalytic theory on several points. During the Hitler period, he was therefore able to teach and to train depth-psychologists—the concept of psychoanalysis was scornfully dismissed as a "Jewish invention"—within the framework of a mandatory organization in which various therapeutic schools taught the "science of the soul," as psychotherapy was then called.

In Zurich it had come to an open dispute. Carl Müller-Braunschweig had meanwhile formed a new organization without Schultz-Hencke and his supporters: the German Psychoanalytic Association, which was acknowledged by the International Association. Felix Böhm felt deeply insulted by this decision, since he had attempted to salvage whatever could possibly be salvaged after the Nazi takeover. Anna Freud remembered well the talks they once had in Bohemia. Böhm asked for two years until the next congress to guide the old German Psychoanalytic Society onto a favorable path of progress, that is, to isolate the group around Schultz-Hencke. At that point, Anna Freud entered the debate, showing that neither were Böhm's merits called into question nor was the decision directed against him. Even so, her final remark was sarcastic: "I see no reason why the [old] Society, if it should happen to work out as Dr. Böhm suggests, could not reapply for recognition in the future."[4] It did not reapply.

The question of lay analysis again became the subject of the international congress, though now the matter was finally settled formally. During all these years, the American Psychoanalytic Association had been reluctant to acknowledge non-physicians. They were indeed granted admission to the local branch societies; some were even honorary members. But membership in the national association, an exclusively American addition to the organizational structure, remained restricted to medical doctors. As a result, nonphysicians could not become members of the International Psychoanalytic Association either. This affected first of all psychoanalysts who had emigrated from German-speaking countries before World War II and who, for the most part, were working as training analysts in the United States. The American Psychoanalytic Association now made available to those psychoanalysts immediate membership in the international association. The Americans had always rejected such a proposal, and now it was surprisingly made precisely by the American Psychoanalytic Association, which, however, did not have to relinquish its fundamental rejection of nonmedical psychoanalysts who wanted to practice in the United States. In this discussion, which took place at the congress, Anna Freud said:

> I should like to support this proposal very warmly, and I think we in Europe should be grateful for it. I well remember the time when we hesitated to make these lay analysts Members-at-Large because we felt that thereby we might offend our American colleagues by sending them members of our own making before asking them to acknowledge this status. It is very fine indeed that the proposal to make them Members-at-Large now comes from our American colleagues. I think it a great step forward in the collaboration between the American and European Societies, and I think it very fair that the situation will be eased by an initiative from the American side, where these colleagues live and work.[5]

No one spoke after Anna Freud, and the proposal was unanimously accepted. When Anna Freud asked to speak at the end of the congress—without any inducement and contrary to her habit of expressing her opinion only on certain questions—she obliquely revealed her relief at the resolution of this tiresome question:

> I only want to add one sentence to what Dr. Jones has said before, namely that Dr. Bartemeier and his secretary, Dr. Grete Bibring, as President and

Secretary of the Association, have accomplished in the last two years a thing which we thought hardly possible and which contributed today to our choice of the next president [Heinz Hartmann, now considered an American]. They have given us the feeling that the International Psychoanalytical Association has taken good care of all things, whether they came from the American or the European side. I hope that in the future local considerations as to the place from where our president comes may be totally dropped, and that we may become a truly international society again.[6]

Through her decisive expressions of opinion, Anna Freud grew to be the arbiter of controversies she unsuccessfully tried to shun. Her words had become so effective that her voice—even her silence—often brought about decisions. Kurt Eissler, for example, reported at this congress on the Sigmund Freud Archives, compiled through private initiative and containing taped interviews with leading figures on the history of psychoanalysis. Regarding this matter, Jones said that he had always given historical material to Anna Freud for the Freud Museum that was later established in Vienna, asking her whether the Freud archives did not belong there as well. Marie Bonaparte also challenged Anna Freud to express her opinion. The latter, however, chose silence and continued to actively support both establishments concerned with the history of psychoanalysis.

Several weeks after this congress, on November 2, 1951, Anna Freud's mother, Martha Freud, died in London at the age of ninety. She had lived for thirteen years after her emigration, twelve—throughout World War II and the postwar period—with her daughter at 20 Maresfield Gardens. Jones dedicated a brief obituary to her in the *International Journal of Psychoanalysis*. It is deplorable that no effort has thus far been made to study Martha Freud's role in her family and her attitude toward psychoanalysis. It is improbable that the wife of the founder of psychoanalysis and the mother of the founder of child psychoanalysis did not possess estimable virtues that impressed themselves on psychoanalysis, though they have yet to become manifest.

The Hampstead Child Therapy Course and Clinic

In 1952, a children's clinic for psychoanalytic therapy was annexed to the training institute for child therapy that was founded in 1947. Thus, the institution created by Anna Freud and Dorothy Burlingham, and which claimed a large part of their energies, attained its final format—The Hampstead Child Therapy Course and Clinic. The establishment of the clinic was made possible by a grant that provided the money to purchase the building. Anna Freud was initially the only director and Liselotte Frankl the chief psychiatrist, while A. Bonnard, Josephine Stross, and Willie Hoffer worked as consulting physicians.

As a charitable institution, the Hampstead Clinic obviously remained further dependent on donations for its sustenance. Every year several hundred thousand pounds sterling had to be raised. The money came from the Psychoanalytic Research and Development Fund, the Grant Foundation, and the Taconomic Foundation, all in New York; from the Field Foundation; and from several other, predominantly American, sources. In 1956, the purchase of a new house made a broader range of activities possible. Another house was added in 1967.

Two codirectors now worked with Anna Freud at the clinic: Clifford Yorke and Hansi Kennedy. Work at the Hampstead Clinic was divided into four principal areas:

1. *The clinic as center of the organization.* This was under the medical directorship of Clifford Yorke. Its main function consisted in the psychoanalytic treatment of children, with usually fifty to seventy children being treated at any one time. This included complete analyses of five hours per week, with the staff's full awareness of the long duration therapy requires. This work could be accomplished only because a large number of psychoanalysts were available and because trainee analysts—depending on their level of competence—also assumed the treatment of some of the children. The clinic distinguished between the following groups of children: a) children with typical infantile neuroses, suitable for treatment by supervised trainees; b) children with disturbances in progress, with whom it was attempted to prevent more severe stages; c) severely disturbed children who had been referred by other clinics; d) children particularly interesting for research, for ex-

ample, pubescent juveniles, handicapped or blind children, orphans, "child heroes," and mother–child couples. Adult analyses were conducted if required as part of the child's therapy.

2. *Medical-psychological counseling for young children.* The counseling center for mothers was headed by the pediatrician Josephine Stross, a friend of Anna Freud's, who came to London from Vienna in 1938. Dr. Stross guided the sixty mothers she regularly counseled through the difficulties of their children's first two years.

3. *The educational unit.* Included here was first of all the kindergarten, led by Mrs. M. F. Friedmann, which admitted children between three and five years old. The staff attempted to influence the everyday problems of the children, using educational measures derived from psychoanalysis, a task that from the very beginning had been especially close to Anna Freud's heart.

The educational division was also responsible for the continued education of children who had been treated at the clinic, as well as for an individual educational child-care system for highly disturbed children suitable for neither group nor analytic therapy.

A special unit, under the directorship of Dorothy Burlingham and A. Curzon, was in charge of blind children and the counseling of mothers of blind infants. This department was established following the analysis of a series of blind children who not only had to endure their blindness, but were exposed to further, avoidable burdens: emotional rejection by the mother, the mother's depressive reactions to these emotions, the child's reaction to both, repeated periods of hospitalizaton and the accompanying separation from the mother, checkups and treatment by physicians who were usually insensitive to both the child's and the mother's feelings and fears.

4. *Research.* It is well known that psychoanalysis has again and again borne the reproach of not providing hypotheses that can be empirically verified or refuted. In the early 1950's in particular, when a neopositivist scientific ideal was worshiped, psychoanalysis too faced the demand to adjust its methods to this scientific-theoretical approach, which psychoanalysts have indeed largely come to accept. When Anna Freud was awarded her honorary doctorate by the University of Vienna in 1972, Hans Strotzka, a prominent psychoanalyst, stressed in his encomium as particularly praiseworthy that Anna Freud "supported a sober and realistic verification of our psychoanalytic science," and that she made efforts toward a "careful scientific verification or refutation of postulates."[1] In one of his few laudatory writings about Anna Freud, S. L. Lustman made very similar statements.[2]

It thus seems as if after World War II Anna Freud was drawn into the vortex of neopositivism as it was most vigorously represented by Karl Popper—another Viennese who had emigrated to London—and his school.[3] In London, under Popper's influence, Hans Eysenck became a contentious foe of psychoanalysis. He was a psychologist who had emigrated from Berlin to London and had made it his life's task to attack psychoanalysis with arguments belonging to a science foreign to psychoanalysis.[4] Even if Popperism has now been largely refuted,[5] its influence has still not been undermined. On the other hand, rigorous theoretical studies have meanwhile been done—indeed stimulated by so-called Popperism—that disclose the nature of psychoanalytic insight.[6]

It is unquestionably true that neither Sigmund Freud nor Anna Freud developed a scientific-theoretical methodology. Most psychoanalysts believe in the existence of the id-ego-superego system in the objective world without realizing its theoretical nature. Now, this theory was built according to the same logical—I say *logical*—principles that constitute theories in the natural sciences. There has never been thus far, apart from psychoanalysis, a theory of the psyche with a similarly logical structure.

Philanthropists too succumb to certain ideas of scientific standards and want to donate money only if scientific success can be expected. Anna Freud was dependent on financial donors, whom she always gratefully mentioned in her scientific reports. At any rate, the Hampstead staff attempted to broaden the scope of knowledge growing out of psychoanalysis and to adapt it to needs in other disciplines. Anna Freud frequently expressed her views on this matter, yet in her theories and development as a psychoanalyst she remained largely unaffected by it.

If one examines the publications of the Hampstead Clinic, one discovers that practice fared better than theory. Experiments were not followed through, and statistical studies were sparse and usually limited to simple comparisons. As long as those who processed the material for statistical comparisons belonged to the psychoanalytic school and used psychoanalytic principles when collecting their data, the results could not challenge the theory. The work therefore consisted essentially in pooling the experiences of analysts in the same group and thus creating a regular exchange of insights among analysts treating similar cases.[7] Children with the same problems could also be conceived of as a group and observed as such.

Somewhat more problematic were the so-called natural experiments, i.e., children in whom "either nature or fate has caused either the elimination or the exaggeration of one specific innate or environmental factor."[8] For example, motherless and congenitally blind children were examined and compared. To be sure, only an analogy is involved here. Nature cannot set up experiments, but occasionally presents special cases. These experiences lend themselves to generalization, though obviously with considerable limitations.

The research of the Hampstead group was not spared criticism even among psychoanalysts. Most of all, it bore the reproach of having retained a strictly individual concept of theory and therapy while entirely overlooking new developments in psychoanalysis, such as group analysis and family therapy. The reproach of conservatism came from psychoanalysts themselves, since they too viewed later developments as progress beyond earlier achievements.

The Hampstead Clinic developed a method called indexing,[9] which Dorothy Burlingham introduced as a study project as early as in 1953. Material culled from analyses was separated into various single areas (categories) and compiled in a register, the so-called Hampstead Index. To provide a relatively balanced perspective, a small group of older analysts supervised the project. Among the subjects, for example, were: instinctual content, ego activity, object relationships, fantasies, anxieties, defense mechanisms, compromise formations, traumatic experiences. Thus, if one wanted information on discoveries in the area of defense mechanisms, one would look up this term in the register and find there many more observations than a single analyst could have provided. Even this was not a strictly scientific procedure, but a systematic exchange of experiences that was valuable particularly in a homogeneous school. Another study that made use of the Hampstead Index addressed "psychic lines of development." In a preface to Bolland and Sandler, *The Hampstead Psychoanalytic Index*, Anna Freud wrote:

> What we hope to construct by this laborious method is something of a "collective analytic memory," i.e., a storehouse of analytic material which places at the disposal of the single thinker and author an abundance of facts gathered by many, thereby transcending the narrow confines of individual experience and extending the possibilities for insightful study, for constructive comparisons between cases, for deductions and generalizations, and finally for extrapolations of theory from clinical therapeutic work.[10]

The Hampstead Clinic consciously cultivated contacts with other sciences. Its "natural" neighbors were not only educators—always present, so to speak, at deliberations—but pediatricians, whose training did not, as a rule, provide psychological or even psychoanalytic approaches to children. We will later see how Anna Freud, in a conversation with pediatricians, effectively applied her experiences with children and pediatricians.

Clifford Yorke, the medical director of the Hampstead Clinic, described Anna Freud's life in Hampstead in a radio interview in 1974:

> Her day is filled with work. It begins at 8 A.M. She has a number of patients—adults and children—and keeps herself fully informed about what happens in the clinic. She not only reads all the reports, she not only studies the minutes of the various research groups and meetings, but in many of the latter also participates personally. She attends to the clinic's finances, to the frequent inquiries of people interested in meeting her, and I am again and again surprised not only that she does all this, but also at how effectively she does it. Even if her health is not as good as I would like it to be, she nonetheless has an extraordinary amount of energy and her mental capacity is absolutely unequaled. Her manner of working has often surprised me, particularly when she was working on something she was very interested in. For example, I was discussing a problem with her: "Miss Freud," I said, "today I saw a patient and the symptoms were such-and-such and he said such-and-such. What do you think of it?" and she stopped, and thought for a while. For a moment she

completely withdrew her attention from me and was deeply engrossed in the problem. And then one could see how she resumed the contact, saying: "We need to think about it." Then she would develop a fruitful thought. One could follow her suggestion, perhaps raise small objections, or agree, or work at it. It is quite extraordinary. And I see it as a sign of her greatness as a scientist that she is sometimes able to emerge from her reserve and say: "I don't think that we will be able to answer this question for quite some time."

Those who have seen her in group discussions know about her extraordinary ability to connect the right ends, to bring into relief the core of a problem and its essential characteristics, in a manner of which only few people are capable. I know no one in the psychoanalytic world capable of it. She infuses the most difficult and tense discussions with life when she sheds light on something in her own way, at times more in detail, sometimes with a simple appropriate remark with which she summarizes the entire situation. "Well," she might say at the end of a long discussion, "it seems as if the parents say that on one hand there is something wrong with the child, but on the other hand that the child is all right." And then she would go on and tell a story that would shed light precisely on this situation. "I remember someone taking his Rolls-Royce to Spain and the Rolls-Royce broke down. He had to notify the factory in England to repair the Rolls-Royce. The factory flew in mechanics and parts, the car was rebuilt and was again on its way in good health. But a bill never came, so the owner wrote to Rolls-Royce: I received no bill for the repairs you did on my Rolls-Royce when it broke down in Spain. And the factory replied: A Rolls-Royce never breaks down." This is a typical Anna Freud story.

Like her father, Anna Freud had the talent to speak fluently and to write her speech down almost verbatim later.

Travels and Lectures, 1952–55

Two years after her first trip to America, Anna Freud returned. This trip was not as turbulent nor fraught with as many pressures as the first one. In addition to other activities, she lectured before medical students at Western Reserve University in Cleveland, Ohio, on Lake Erie. This university had just opened a medical school and the students were in their first year. As an innovation, the university revived a very old custom: each student was assigned a pregnant women, assisted at checkups throughout the pregnancy and at delivery, and then remained with the mother and child for a further period.

Anna Freud endeavored to prepare students as yet entirely unexperienced in medicine for the coming events, while cautiously avoiding psychoanalytic concepts; she correctly assumed that the students were still unfamiliar with psychoanalysis, or even with general psychology. One may feel that she was wasting her efforts on such an inexperienced audience. But the circumstances conformed entirely to her wishes. She was convinced of the importance precisely of the child's first developmental steps, and again defended the view that medical students should from the very beginning be made familiar with human psychology. After receiving training in the natural sciences, it is often too late for the student to gain true familiarity with psychology.[1]

The London Congress, 1953

The Eighteenth International Psychoanalytic Congress was held from July 26 to July 30, 1953, at Bedford College, Regent's Park, London, in Anna Freud's immediate neighborhood. As at the previous congress, she prepared a lecture and agreed to chair a symposium. The revised lecture was published simultaneously in English and German in 1966 under the title "About Losing and Being Lost."[2] Anna Freud studied here all the ramifications of the phenomenon of losing, a topic already redeemed from its apparent meaninglessness by Freud in *The Psychopathology of Everyday Life*: from the child who constantly loses objects to the "lost souls" of fairy tales that restlessly roam about at night as spirits of the dead searching for the people they once loved and for whom they have become lost objects on which feelings of longing can be projected. It is one of the few lectures into which Anna Freud wove a personal recollection dating back to a period she had spent in the Austrian mountains during her youth and showing how long she had been concerned with the theme of losing. She recalled a young girl, an enthusiastic mountain climber who had climbed high up in the Alps, where she sat down by a waterfall. There she lost her hat, in itself an insignificant event which she easily accepted. At night, however, she was unable to sleep and persistently imagined her lost hat in the desolation and solitude of the mountain.

The symposium Anna Freud chaired focused on "Defense Mechanisms and their Significance for Psychoanalytic Technique." Rudolph Loewenstein from New York, Sylvia Payne and Willie Hoffer from London, and Raymond de Saussure from Switzerland participated. The congress again displayed an altered picture. In his opening speech, Heinz Hartmann remarked that the end of the pioneering period in psychoanalytic history involved a concomitant change in the nature of those drawn to psychoanalysis. Later, Anna Freud would often discuss this remark. Psychoanalysis had no doubt reached a stage of full bloom. The widely respected

International Association numbered a thousand members, and Hartmann therefore had to enjoin modesty. Two years before, Bartemeier also warned psychoanalysts against adopting their patients' view of them as omnipotent and omniscient. The special role Anna Freud played during this time becomes apparent in an anecdote Martin Grotjahn tells.

At the congress, Grotjahn lectured on "Contemporary Trends in Psychoanalytic Training." He had already begun his lecture when the door opened and Anna Freud came in, escorted by Ernest Jones on one side and Dorothy Burlingham on the other. Since Jones was walking with a cane, all three advanced very slowly through the reverentially silent crowd. Grotjahn interrupted his lecture until they had sat down in the first row. Grotjahn then resumed his lecture. The three latecomers began to whisper among themselves, pointing to the program. Grotjahn became insecure, thinking he said something "officially" offensive. Finally, Anna Freud and her escorts rose and left the room. Later it turned out that they had wanted to listen to another lecture and had mistaken the door.

Grotjahn's fear that he may have said something wrong reflected the general atmosphere of the congress. During business sessions, debates revolved chiefly around tendencies toward schism, a malady that has afflicted individual psychoanalytic associations to this day, constituting part of the history of psychoanalysis. The early period was marked by separations initiated by Jung, Adler, Stekel, and Rank, and this was later continued in America by Sándor Radó, Karen Horney, and others. Were these schisms inevitable? Anna Freud frequently took part in discussions intent on preserving the unity of the International Psychoanalytic Association.

Laura

In 1953, Anna Freud reviewed a film for the first time.[3] The film, whose subject Anna Freud and others had often addressed, even led to improvements in certain areas. The subject was the psychological effects of medical intervention and of the concomitant daily procedures on a hospitalized child. James Robertson, who made the film, followed a two-and-a-half-year-old girl with his camera during her eight days of hospitalization for umbilical hernia surgery, a banal matter, neither upsetting for the parents nor a matter of great import for the physicians. Nothing particular occurred during these eight days—no complications, hardly appreciable postsurgical pains, nothing even remotely terrifying.

The child received exceptional medical and nursing care, and the parents were allowed to visit her every two days. Nonetheless—as Anna Freud made clear—the child went through a severe psychological crisis during these eight days. Edited so that the essential events seem to be almost concealed, the film shows the child at home before hospitalization and then twice daily during hospitalization at defined times—that is, not on the basis of special events. The purpose of this ostensible objectivity was to refute the argument that the film had been edited with preconceptions. That is also why Laura was not a special child. She had been randomly selected from the waiting list of the National Health Service.

Anna Freud underscored that, despite excellent care, Laura nonetheless suffered severely from the shock of separation from her parents, a point she had always stressed, as in the case of the Hampstead children. Implied here was also a criticism of modern hospital procedures, although the adult is far less sensitive to the discomfort of a sterile hospital atmosphere than a child. But Anna Freud's evidence was in consonance with an opinion that has meanwhile become pervasive: the more refined the technical medical and hygienic perfection, the greater the patient's fears.

The film shows, for example, how the station nurse quickly and dexterously removed the surgical stitches, assisted by another nurse. Anna Freud explained that, on the level of inner reality, this event could nevertheless have been experienced as a severe intrusion into the body's integrity: beings with a ghostlike appearance (because of their clothes) moved toward the child with a serious expression and inflicted pain on her without warning. Events such as these multiply fantasies that would tend to torment a naturally weak child in need of protection. The child becomes afraid of being attacked, injured, and destroyed, fears entirely sensible in themselves in that they motivate the child to seek the proximity of the protective parent. But here the parents are not available. Anna Freud's commentary reveals how, on the basis of her experience, she drew conclusions from apparently paltry signs. For example, Laura did not want the nurse to remove a chair that was near her bed. Explanation: This was the chair the mother had sat on. Disappointment in the strangers who had taken her mother away therefore flared up in this small scene. To remove the chair would have meant inflicting further grief on Laura. Laura was bathed upon her admission to the hospital (all hospitals apparently believe that parents bring only dirty children) and could not suppress her panicky fear. Explanation: Laura felt that her body had been delivered into the hands of strangers. She received rectal anesthesia and reacted with fear of being attacked.

What is most frightening about this film is actually not immediately visible, but was clarified by Anna Freud. Throughout her entire hospitalization, Laura did not play. She was allowed to bring along a teddy bear she then held in her arms, pressing it to herself as she would have liked to be held and pressed, but she did not play with it.

One may certainly expect—as did Anna Freud—that, following release from the hospital and some convalescence time, a healthy child would regain both an inner and an outer balance, with the assistance of the parents. But what happens if such experiences recur? What happens when illness and medical intervention are more serious and require longer hospitalization? Finally, it remains true that even the smallest intervention can inflict heavy damages.

Since these observations were made, knowledge of the possibly damaging results of hospitalization has been widely disseminated. Mothers often refuse— rightly or not—to put their small children in a hospital. In West Germany there is an Action Committee for Hospitalized Children in charge of some useful and some less useful functions. There is, for example, a system whereby the mother is allowed to stay in the hospital with her child. But endless difficulties arise with the hospital administration, and we are still far from taking care of children psychologically as well as we do medically.

America and the Geneva Congress

In 1954, Anna Freud was again in America, seeming to have gradually established a two-year pattern for trips to the United States. The occasion was an invitation to the lectures celebrating Freud's birthday, held at the New York Academy of Medicine. The academy owns lecture halls and seminar rooms, and houses a very large general medical library in its building. The invitation to the Freud Anniversary Lectures was itself a great honor. Since Anna Freud's lecture was held on a Wednesday, it became known historically as the "Wednesday Lecture." She gave it on May 5, on the eve of Freud's ninety-eighth birthday. The subject, "Psychoanalysis and Education," sounds rather general. Yet Anna Freud referred here to education in the widest sense, discussing primarily very early childhood.[4]

The concept of the "rejecting mother," particularly in its overly simplistic form, had meanwhile achieved great popularity. On the one hand, the mother as the first object the child relates to was held responsible for all the child's neuroses and psychoses; on the other hand, excessively anxious mothers made unrelenting efforts not to frustrate their beloved baby in the least, thus tormenting both themselves and the family. Both attitudes falsely invoked psychoanalysis, which, in fact, had never developed such a concept, despite its emphasis on the extraordinary significance of object relationships during the first stages of life. Anna Freud showed, however, that during the earliest stages of development it is mostly a matter of the child's physical needs—feeding, cleanliness, et cetera—and of their satisfaction and frustration. No mother, no matter how devoted, can fully respond to the infant's or young child's every need. Here, too, Anna Freud repudiated all extremes.

On the following Saturday, May 8, the New York Psychoanalytic Society and Institute organized a convention on infantile neuroses at Arden House, a country house near New York, where a large number of Anna Freud's old acquaintances again met with American psychoanalysts. We find familiar names among the speakers: Ernst Kris, the chairman; Phyllis Greenacre, whose accomplishments Anna Freud discussed in a long, impromptu commentary; Heinz Hartmann, Bertram D. Lewin, Rudolph M. Loewenstein, Edith Jacobson, René Spitz, Robert Waelder, Marianne Kris, Grace McLean Abbate, Mary O'Neil Hawkins, Anita Bell, Bela Mittelmann, Margaret Mahler, Gustav Bychowski. Time and again, Anna Freud patiently discussed the questions and ideas of the speakers, the symposium becoming, quite unintentionally, an Anna Freud symposium.[5]

On May 13, Anna Freud attended the dinner of the Child Welfare League of America in Atlantic City, New Jersey, where her lecture, "The Concept of the Rejecting Mother," carefully examined the reasons that can motivate a mother to reject her child temporarily or permanently. But, as she said, the child may experience rejection even if rejection has not occurred, for example in the case of separation due to external circumstances or to the mother's death. On this trip Anna Freud also accepted an invitation to lecture before the Philadelphia Association for Psychoanalysis.[6]

During the same year, Anna Freud became an honorary member of the New York Psychoanalytic Society and Institute (not identical with the American Psychoanalytic Association, of which she was already an honorary member). Gradually, honors piled up for Anna Freud to such an extent that we shall now mention only those of a special nature. She also became an honorary member of the Netherlands Society for Psychiatry and Neurology and thus for the first time honorary member of a nonpsychoanalytic professional association. Does this augur a change in Europe, such as that earlier seen in America, where the traditionally polar positions of psychoanalysis and academic psychiatry have gradually vanished?

The Nineteenth International Psychoanalytic Congress, held on July 24–28, 1955, in Geneva, was a routine meeting with long scientific programs and a great many receptions and comprehensive business sessions dealing with complicated problems of membership, but without special zeniths or nadirs. Anna Freud neither lectured nor chaired a symposium. In the business sessions, she asked to speak only once, to decline a proposal by Otto Fleischmann of Vienna that she be elected president of the International Psychoanalytic Association. Three people—that was new—were candidates for election: Heinz Hartmann, W. H. Gillespie, and Raymond de Saussure. Hartmann was reelected.

Sigmund Freud's Centennial

In 1956, celebrations took place throughout the world on Sigmund Freud's hundredth birthday. The number of these events and the variety of themes discussed at conferences and symposia again showed how rapidly the psychoanalytic movement had left behind it pioneering stage during the postwar period. At Freud's last residence, 20 Maresfield Gardens, the London County Council's commemorative plaque was unveiled. On Freud's hundredth birthday, Anna Freud herself inaugurated the new house for her Hampstead Clinic, since the old one had become too small. In honor of the birthday, she invited all the psychoanalysts present in London to her house on May 6. She agreed to lecture on "Diagnosis and Assessment of Childhood Disturbances"[1] on the occasion of the University of Amsterdam's centennial celebration for Freud. But she decided against participating in the many other celebrations held in various parts of the world.

In September 1956, Anna Freud again traveled to America, faithfully keeping to the two-year pattern, explicable in part by the time required to raise new funds. Every two years, new efforts had to be made to insure her work's financial foundation. She first went again to Cleveland, where she lectured at Western Reserve University Medical School on "Emotional Factors in Education," later published under the title "Psychoanalytic Knowledge Applied to the Rearing of Children."[2] This lecture is noteworthy because it renders, in her characteristically clear and detailed way, her view on questions that only today have come to be widely acknowledged as problematic. She discussed attitudinal changes in a world altered by psychoanalysis, in particular in the area of education. Psychoanalysis—or, rather, the knowledge of the significance of educational influences during the first years of life—perforce raised expectations that better and happier people would grow up if only this knowledge were well applied. Eschatological healing capacities, as are now professed by various trends, were expected of psychoanalysis. Anna Freud said: "What the public expected of us was no less than a revolutionary, but systematic, well-integrated guide to the rearing of a new, healthier, and happier generation."[3]

Not only did Anna Freud repudiate this expectation; she also probed its motives. The discovery that sexual impulses do not awaken first during puberty, but exist from birth, led to the early sexual enlightenment of children as well as to an unprecedented tolerance toward sexual activity. Indeed, this contributed to a freer relationship between parents and children. The very great disappointment, however, was that neither this tolerance nor the current, by far less strict toilet training prevented neuroses.

Parents relinquished entirely or partially their parental authority to protect their child from the deleterious results of an identification process whereby the child internalizes parental permissions and prohibitions, that is, assimilates them into the superego. This certainly brought about a fortunate relaxation in the relationship between generations, but for children "the change left an unfilled gap in the place from which help, guidance, and direction had emanated before."[4] Where fear came into play, the error was especially grave. Surely, in the center of authoritarian education stood the fear of one's parents, and "every infringement [of internalized prohibitions] leads to anxiety feelings—i.e., guilt, which plays a major part in instigating neurotic character formation or symptomatology."[5] But now, the absence of authority entailed the absence of its protection and assistance and, above all, of the possibility of finding one's identity. This then led to the

> most devastating anxiety of all, a fear of the loss of his own integrity and identity. . . . This may solve the riddle why children who are brought up with

extreme leniency and permissiveness are not happier than others; why, on the contrary, they are only too frequently restless, irritable, given to extreme temper tantrums, and under the domination of a nondirected, more or less free-floating anxiety.[6]

It is noteworthy that as early as 1956 Anna Freud expressed views that could easily be incorporated into an explanation of contemporary terrorism in Europe. The terrorists, young men and women, come largely from extremely lenient families, and only rarely from authoritarian ones. These young people find their identity, as well as extensive freedom from fear, in the group—a group that purportedly struggles for the lofty goal of progress and socialism, but which authorizes brutality without the slightest visible remorse. Anna Freud therefore never raised her voice to defend such unsuccessfully developed juveniles. Rather, it was a matter here of the consequences of misunderstanding the conclusions of psychoanalytic theories.

Finally, Anna Freud discussed "freedom for aggression," attributable to the recognition of the aggressive instinct by psychoanalysis as "a determining force in the development of the human personality,"[7] on a par with sexuality. Pursued to its extreme, the argument would thus demand that the instinct of aggression be acted out as unconditionally as sexuality. "Children with their aggression and destructiveness let loose were less lovable as human beings than they had been before and they taxed the parents' forbearance to the utmost."[8]

Listening to these words, one feels transported to antiauthoritarian children's centers and to deliberately undisciplined schools. The unchaining of all aggression had never been Anna Freud's aim. "Here, the true task of applying new knowledge is to find a way of instituting controls of the drive without rendering it more dangerous by condemnation."[9]

One can easily see why it was precisely Anna Freud who warned at such an early stage against false expectations regarding psychoanalytical education: the inevitable disappointment inevitably led to the complete repudiation of a psychoanalytically oriented education. Yet it seems that the middle road between extremes Anna Freud persistently recommended is followed only reluctantly, whereas the tendency to one or the other extreme is more common.

On September 22, 1956, Anna Freud spoke at the Hanna Pavillion in Cleveland on "The Assessment of Borderline Cases" of children, by which she meant not the boundary region between neurosis and psychosis, but borderline cases between neurosis on the one hand and mental retardation, criminality, and perversion on the other.[10]

Margaret Mead in London • The Paris Congress

The year 1957 began with a public encounter between two women who had already reached legendary stature during their lifetime: Margaret Mead and Anna Freud. On January 30, 1957, Margaret Mead came to London as president of the World Federation for Psychohygiene to give an Ernest Jones Lecture. Anna Freud's task was to follow the lecture with words of appreciation. Mead chose the subject "Changes in Parent–Child Relationships in an Urbanized World" and showed a film on a "primitive" mother–child couple during the hours and days following birth. It was a subject that had deeply concerned Anna Freud, and in her address she also alluded to her disagreement with some of Mead's ideas. But the time and the festive occasion were unsuited to a more extensive discussion.

The Twentieth International Psychoanalytic Congress, held from July 28 to August 1, 1957, in Paris, stirred sad and distressing memories about the last congress held in the same city in 1938. There were no sensational events now. Anna Freud participated in a panel discussion on "The Contribution of Direct Child Observation to Psychoanalysis," a subject she also addressed in her lecture.[1] E. C. M. Frijling-Schreuder, Lieselotte Frankl, Melanie Klein, and D. W. Winnicott were among those who took part in the discussion.

The business sessions focused on the participation of associate members at these very sessions. Anna Freud had proposed that they participate without the right to vote. Melanie Klein objected and wanted to know how they could be prevented from voting. Anna Freud believed that, having been trained in institutes and entrusted with the care of patients, these colleagues deserved the trust that they would abstain from voting if they did not have the right to do so. Jones suggested a compromise that Anna Freud accepted: associate members could participate, but, to allow for "supervision," they had to sit apart. We see that serious problems were no longer of concern here. Finally, Anna Freud proposed that a telegram be sent to Nunberg thanking him for his establishment of a foundation serving exclusively psychoanalytic aims.

At the Paris congress, Heinz Hartmann, the president, resigned, as did Ruth Eissler, who had been general secretary for six years. W. H. Gillespie, defeated in the elections two years ago, became the new president.

Soon after the congress, Anna Freud traveled to the United States for the fifth time. She interrupted her two-year pattern to participate at a memorial session in honor of Ernst Kris organized by the New York Psychoanalytic Society. Preceding this session, on September 18, she expressed her views on "Adolescence"[2] at the thirty-fifth–anniversary celebration of the establishment of educational counseling for juveniles in Worcester, Massachusetts. The event went on for two more days and closed with another lecture by Anna Freud, "Termination of Treatment,"[3] published only years later. Again, many old acquaintances as well as American psychoanalysts gathered around Anna Freud and came forward to speak: Grete Bibring (Boston), Annie Katan (Cleveland), Marianne Kris (New York), Berta Bornstein (New York), and many others. The difficult problem of the termination of analysis had often been discussed; the termination of child analysis had thus far not been addressed.

On September 24, 1957, the commemoration for Ernst Kris took place at the New York Academy of Medicine, where Anna Freud had already spoken. Various participants spoke throughout the day, which ended in the evening with the main commemorative lecture, given by Anna Freud.[4] The friendship between Anna Freud and Ernst Kris and his wife Marianne dated back to the Vienna days. Marianne Kris, the daughter of Freud's friend Oskar Rie, had been Anna Freud's friend in Vienna, and through her had come to meet Freud, who analyzed her free of charge. Her sister Margarete was married to Hermann Nunberg. Ernst Kris was one of the most significant psychoanalysts who had been in training analysis with Anna Freud. In Vienna he had belonged to the circle of outstanding men around Freud, and in the United States he contributed widely to the dissemination of psychoanalysis. Marianne and Ernst Kris had a daughter they had named Anna. They were active in the Child Study Center at Yale University, directed first by Ernst Kris and, after his death, by Marianne Kris.

Nevertheless, Anna Freud did not use the occasion to dwell on memories of Ernst Kris, but in her detailed lecture she raised only scientific questions drawn from his work, such as the question of the predictability of a person's future life on the basis of insights gained from this person's childhood analysis. If, during extended therapy, the child's psyche is opened to the analyst, revealing the child's relationship to people and life, then it should be possible to predict, at least approximately, the child's future development. In his research projects at Yale, Ernst Kris seemed to have steered precisely toward this goal. His approach, however, characteristic of the natural sciences, was based on the premise that the same rules are valid for the future as for the past, thus ensuring the predictability of events.

In her detailed essay, Anna Freud not only refuted this method with careful examples, but also showed why future developments are fundamentally unpredictable. As an illustration, I would like to use an image here Anna Freud herself did not use: In a newly begun game of chess, not only general rules remain valid, but in its course thus far that particular game has also taken a certain direction that precludes some possibilities, leaving room, however, for many others that are subject to the rules that have thus far been pertinent, though perhaps only to that game. The course of the single game thus remains unpredictable. Anna Freud offered several felicitous examples, of which we shall quote one:

> Example 3 is of a different nature. I quote it from the longitudinal observation of a small boy, undertaken by his father, himself a well-known educator [J. C. Hill, *Dreams and Education*, 1926]. According to the father's notes, this boy first showed interest in *water* at the age of twelve months, when he began to do without diapers during [the] daytime; he was occasionally found patting a pool of water he had made on the floor. "Little pools of rain-water also interested him, and he thoroughly enjoyed smacking the water in the bath or wash-hand basin. At fourteen months he was very interested in turning water-taps on and off. When taken to the water-closet he watched the rush of water with great interest. At two years of age he spent hours controlling water supplies, filling and emptying buckets, tins, jars, tea-pots, hot-water bottles. He wanted to know where the water came from to the water-closet bowl. When he was taken to a gentleman's lavatory outside, he always insisted on seeing the hole down which the water went, and the cistern which supplied the water. At two and a half years he was tracing every pipe he could see; water-supply pipes, drain pipes, rain-pipes, gas pipes. Hours were spent lighting and turning out gas jets." Before he was three, the father had to take the cover off the water-closet cistern to satisfy his curiosity. "He spent about half an hour every day for a fortnight, standing on a ledge up at the cistern. . . . He filled the cistern to the overflow, and wanted to know the function of every detail of the mechanism." The father goes on to show how the child's interest spread from here to fireplugs, fire engines, water pumps, the gas works, and the sewage works. In nursery school, at the age of four and a half years, when told the story of Moses in the Bulrushes and asked to draw a picture of Moses in his cradle, he supplied the cradle with a long line, representing a "drain pipe" leading away from it.
>
> For the direct observer of children, a behavioral picture of this kind gives rise to a number of important questions. He will have no difficulty in diagnosing the underlying presence of powerful pregenital interests with [a] special preponderance of curiosity directed toward the urinary function and . . . the inside of the human body. He will feel less certain about the degree of desexualization of curiosity (i.e., neutralization) achieved by the child. Accordingly, he will be unsure whether what he sees should be assessed as the beginning of a true sublimation which will enrich the ego, or as the beginning of a fixation to a primitive pregenital level which will restrict it and sooner or later lead to pathology. Is it the correct procedure to assist the boy in his researches (as his father has done) or should he be helped to detach himself from his overriding interest in the subject and develop toward further levels, as treatment would do in all probability?
>
> In the case in question the answer has been supplied by the further life

history of the boy. In the thirty years since the observation was made, he has developed into a physicist of unusual ability and standing, the recorded incidents evidently representing the first steps in the direction of this lasting sublimation. This, to my mind, does not signify that other, almost identical pictures, seen for diagnosis, could not lead to opposite results. In spite of all theoretical advances concerning the subject of sublimation, we are still—with Ernst Kris— impressed by the fluidity and uncertainty of these developmental processes. Perhaps we shall learn that it is not the sublimatory process itself from which we can take our cue, identical states or forms of sublimation possibly leading to different results; rather, we have to look for our evidence to accompanying circumstances and conditions in that total picture of the personality. For example, persistent water play of the kind described above may acquire a different and less favorable aspect when it is accompanied by bed wetting.

However that may be, correct assessment of sublimation in the very young remains a difficult matter; so does the prognosis for the future and the appropriate handling of the child based on our judgments. As matters stand now, we are still apt to do little for those children in whom fixations and pathological development are in the making. On the other hand, there is also the danger that we may interfere too much or too soon and thereby (as somebody expressed it jokingly in discussion) "nip future physicists in the bud."[5]

One cannot therefore conclude whether an early and unusual interest in water and tubes will later become a neurotic fascination that interferes with the personality's unencumbered development or even thwarts it entirely, or whether, on the contrary, it will lend the mature personality the enduring strength to engage in very similar activities. Still, one thing becomes clear from this impressive example: the boy's intense and abnormal interests are neither inconsequential nor marginal, but extremely significant and determinant for his entire life. Only the direction of this determinant factor remains for a long time uncertain.

Fiftieth Anniversary of the Vienna Psychoanalytic Institute

On April 14 and 15, 1958, the Vienna Psychoanalytic Institute celebrated its fiftieth anniversary. After World War II, it had to contend with considerable difficulties and, despite Aichhorn's efforts to promote psychoanalysis, it could not regain its old rank. It even lost more analysts, who were urgently needed there. Despite the official support the authorities had meanwhile extended, Vienna was not a congenial place for psychoanalysis after the war. The attendance of outside guests at the anniversary celebration was rather meager. Indeed, Fritz Morgenthaler, Paul Parin, and Raymond de Saussure came from nearby Switzerland; Ulrich Ehebald and W. D. Groschitzky from the Federal Republic of Germany; P. J. van der Leeuw from Holland. But of the many emigrated Viennese psychoanalysts, only the untiring Willie Hoffer—as Anna Freud's emissary, so to speak—made the trip to Vienna. Anna Freud made do with a congratulatory letter in which she equated the beginning of the psychoanalytic movement with the founding of the Vienna Institute. By that she probably meant that psychoanalysis, abetted by the organization it had chosen for itself, was able to establish itself in the world as a movement even its opponents have imitated. Actually, the Berlin Institute had been established earlier and had served as the model for all other countries. Furthermore, the psychoanalytic movement had already been in existence prior to the establishment of this organizational form. In her retrospective on the fifty years that had passed, Anna Freud found it almost incredible that psychoanalysis should have traveled around the world during this period, so deeply marking our century's thought. She also congratulated Alfred von Winterstein, the celebration's honorary chairman who had been a member of the Institute for fifty years, indeed a rare jubilee. When Anna Freud admitted that she envied Winterstein, she revealed that she would have remained in Vienna had circumstances permitted. There was thus reason for strong feelings on all sides.[1]

The discussions of the Vienna Society did occasionally focus on child psychoanalysis.[2] However, hardly anything penetrated to the outside, in particular because the Vienna Society had not yet acquired another independent newsletter. Only in 1961 was the Child Therapy Division of the Vienna Society established. It grew out of the private practice of two psychologists, Hedda Eppel and Erika Danneberg, and was later supported by the two women, a psychoanalytically oriented physician, and a psychoanalytically trained social worker.[3]

John Bowlby

On November 5, 1958, Anna Freud and John Bowlby engaged in a discussion at the British Psychoanalytic Society. The occasion was Bowlby's well-known lecture on "Separation Anxiety."[1] It was one of the very rare cases when Anna Freud entered a confrontation on her own accord. She explained her motives in the introduction:

> I should not have asked for speaking time tonight if John Bowlby in his paper had not referred repeatedly to the work on separation carried out in the Hampstead Nurseries during the war, work for which Dorothy Burlingham and I were responsible. On the one hand, Bowlby gave credit to our findings; on the other hand, he discounted or discredited our interpretations of the facts. I feel that these two attitudes, taken together, create a misleading impression of our work which I am anxious to correct. [2]

Despite the unusually caustic language of her introduction, here too Anna Freud eschewed an open polemic. John Bowlby, who was born in London in 1907, indeed quoted Freud frequently in his works, but on the basis of his thinking he cannot be considered a psychoanalyst, as he often is. His most important roots go back on the one hand to ethology; on the other, to the Melanie Klein school.

The concept of ethology stems from the Greek words *ethos* (habit, custom, habitat) and *logos* (theory) and was originally a branch of zoology that studied the habits and behavior of animals. Konrad Lorenz added new observations and theories to this science; further, he knew how to present this so-called behavioral research in accessible form to a wide audience. Only in the last decades have efforts been made to benefit from observations on animals in research on the human psyche. To be sure, only analogical inferences are possible, since animals are of course incapable of conveying their intrapsychic processes linguistically.

The fundamental assumptions of Bowlby's theories are unequivocally drawn from ethology. There are, according to him, five *innate* reactions that determine the infant's behavior and remain determinant throughout one's entire life: sucking, grasping, following, crying, and smiling. The animal analogy goes so far that—according to Bowlby—crying and smiling serve mainly to activate maternal behavior and are therefore "social triggers on maternal instinctual triggers." [3]

Clearly, "instinct" is not meant here in the psychoanalytic sense. Hence the contrast between the psychoanalytic and ethological theories of instincts was not what prompted Anna Freud to a rectification. Bowlby's premise was rather an observation that had also concerned Anna Freud time and again: namely, the reactions of children between the ages of six months and three years to separation from the mother when, say, surgery or placement in a home was necessary. Bowlby had elaborated explanatory theories on the subject at the Tavistock Clinic and the Tavistock Institute for Human Relations.

Despite the brief presentation of Bowlby's thoughts here, those conversant with Anna Freud's mode of thinking will be able to distinguish between the different approaches. Anna Freud had indeed often stressed the likelihood of far-reaching consequences for even a short separation between mother and child. Unlike Bowlby, she did not see here a type of reflex or two innate synchronized instincts, but only the child's particular experience of the separation. That is why one cannot understand the psychological meaning of a separation on the basis of external events. We will again quote Anna Freud on the subject of separation:

> Referring back to Bowlby's earlier papers on "Separation Anxiety" (1960) and "The Nature of the Child's Tie to His Mother" (1958), it becomes possible to point to a basic difference in orientation between his and our theoretical approach. Bowlby is concerned on the one hand with a biological theory which assumes the existence of an inborn urge tying an infant to the mother, on the other hand with the behavior resulting from this tie ("attachment behavior") or from the untimely disruption of the tie (separation anxiety, grief, mourning). For him, the gap between biological urge and manifest affect and behavior is bridged by certain actions and events occurring in the external world which activate inherited responses.
>
> If this description of Bowlby's position can be accepted as correct, it may serve to explain some of our dissatisfaction in following his line of argumentation. Not that, as analysts, we do not share Bowlby's regard for biological and behavioral considerations; but taken by themselves, not in conjunction with metapsychological thinking, these two types of data do not fulfill the analyst's requirements. As analysts we deal not with drive activity as such but with the mental representations of the drives. In the case of the biological tie of infant to mother, this representation has to be recognized, I believe, in the infant's inborn readiness to cathect objects with libido. Equally, we deal not with the happenings in the external world as such but with their repercussions in the mind, i.e., with the form in which they are registered by the child.[4]

Since she sensed Bowlby's lecture as a provocation, Anna Freud felt compelled to tersely outline again the essence of her theory. It is evident that despite Bowlby's reference to Freud's works, it was not an easy matter to bridge the gap between the two theories.

Anna Freud Speaks with Pediatricians

We have repeatedly seen that Anna Freud developed her thoughts most clearly when in front of an audience. She also always adjusted her lectures so that her explanations suited her audiences' capacity to understand them. To be sure, developments in her life and the positions she occupied in psychoanalysis led, in the course of years, to situations in which she spoke to psychoanalysts who themselves had had decades of experience and did not need an explanation of theories the noninitiated found complicated. In May 1959, however, Anna Freud engaged in an unprepared discussion with pediatricians. In front of her was an audience that had only a vague idea about psychoanalysis and no better one about general psychology. Only their interest in children was common to both audience and speaker, provoking a discussion of generally significant subjects.

Anna Freud's answers very succinctly summed up the most essential thoughts of her life. We shall therefore quote longer excerpts from her discussion with the pediatricians.[1]

> When I came here this afternoon I came quite unprepared—or you might say, prepared for the worst—namely, ready to answer questions that will be difficult to answer as such. Each question which will be asked here would probably be quite easy to answer in a wider context. Therefore, I thought that it might be useful for me to have an idea in my own mind how to deal with your inquiries.
>
> There will, I hope, be a future time when all medicine will have a double orientation—namely, an orientation directed simultaneously toward the body and the mind. This will then presuppose that all people who practice medicine will also receive a double training: that they will learn approximately the same amount about the body and the mind. In this future, distant and improbable as it now seems to us, people will handle questions of this kind in a specific way. They will call on their own double knowledge, and they will weigh the claims of the body and the mind against each other; knowing all sides of the human personality well enough, they will be able to do so.
>
> Until then one has to use one's imagination, and I shall, therefore, try to give my answers as this perfect medical practitioner or consultant of the future might do; in his thoughts, he would weigh whatever he does to the child's body against its repercussions on the mind; and whenever he interferes with the child's mind, he would think of the body at the same time.[2]

The introductory words reveal that the issues here were not just psychoanalysis or the theory of child therapy, but that Anna Freud was developing a concept that, contrary to the still reigning theory, divided the entire medical profession into two equally legitimate poles: medicine dealing with the body and medicine dealing with the psyche. In Anna Freud's view, both areas ought to merge into one discipline. The first question referred to an apparently rather marginal problem of pediatrics.

> *Question:* Do you feel that the use of suppositories is justifiable as a medical procedure, e.g., suppositories of aminophylline at the very beginning of an asthmatic attack; or the giving of medicines by rectum, as is frequently done in France? Is there a difference in the cultural pattern in France which enables this to be tolerated, and does it do any harm or not?
>
> *Answer:* I would like to apply the point of view outlined above to this

particular question. What about suppositories, and why is the question asked at all? Suppositories and enemas have been given and temperatures taken in the child's anus for countless years without any such question being asked.

Then came the discoveries of the people who worked with the child's mind and who found that this particular body opening has a number of functions. One is a purely bodily function, namely, that of elimination. But there is also a secondary function, which is to provide excitation for the child and, especially at certain ages and stages of development (approximately between two and four years), excitation of a very strong and pleasurable kind. Thus, whenever doctor, nurse or mother, for purely medical reasons, interferes with that part of the child's body, a secondary effect is set in train. The child feels excited; this is pleasurable until he learns that this is not a very nice kind of pleasure. After that he feels violently upset by such interference with his body. This reaction has in time become rather widely known and has made people wary of interfering with that body opening.

Then an additional piece of information was added. These actions not only provide bodily excitation at the moment, but the accumulated bodily excitation in the anal region may set up certain trends of development which will be unwelcome later on. They strengthen the importance of these anal sensations and keep them going at a time when the child should have outgrown them and substituted other, for example, genital, excitations for them. This is, I would say, how knowledge stands at the moment.

I return now to the physician who keeps body and mind in his thoughts simultaneously. He will have to ask himself in each case: is it imperative that I carry out this particular action? If it is imperative, then I have to risk whatever side effects may develop. Can I instead use a medical procedure of some kind which has no such side effects? If so, I would prefer to do that.

Thus, the question will have to be answered in a different manner on different occasions. If temperatures can be taken under the arm, there is no need to excite the child anally. If suppositories have to be given for some important reason, then it has to be, and one has to risk the side effects.[3]

Anna Freud teaches here that it is always important not to give simple instructions for a procedure that would be appropriate for any number of slightly varying cases, but that each case has its own applicable viewpoints, which are, however, derived from empirically developed psychoanalytic theories. The following question, then, of whether a suppository or an injection should be preferred can be answered only with complicated considerations in mind.

Q: Supposing one is faced with a child with asthma, do you think it is less harmful to insert a suppository against resistance than to inject a vein against resistance? Is it perhaps alternatively any more harmful to give a suppository without resistance than to give an injection into a vein without resistance? I will give you one particular example of a small girl cyanosed with asthma. In the next room was her mother with a day-old baby; this girl was absolutely livid about this situation. I popped a suppository into her bottom and went away and told the general practitioner to let me know if she was not better, and I heard no more. Would it have been better under those circumstances if I had struggled with her—and it would have been a struggle—to give her an injection of aminophylline into a vein?

A: I am here to ask questions as well as to answer them, and there is room here for an intermediate question, asking what kind of side effect we see after injections. When that has been answered, all we have to do is to weigh the effect of injections against the effect of suppositories. We find children who will take an injection without much upset and fight violently against the insertion of a suppository, but we also find children who will take a suppository without fighting and scream violently when given injections. We know that there are big guardsmen who will faint when they are given an injection.

Let us compare the two events. We know now that suppositories have an unexpected effect on the child's mind, representing to the child, [though] not to the adult who is carrying out the action, interference with a body opening, therefore an attack of a certain kind. To other people injections represent an attack, but of a different kind—not on a body opening, but an attack with a sharp, long, pointed instrument. Both happenings have a symbolic meaning: the one represents an anal attack, the other represents a sexual attack of another kind, namely, a phallic one. As I said before, there are individuals impervious to the one and highly susceptible to the other, and the other way round. Still, we know injections have to be given; but I think doctors who know the possible meaning of injections for the child will know better how to prepare, how to quiet the child, and how to diminish the possible shock.

By the way, it is an interesting experiment, for anybody who wants to make it, to observe how different children of the same age react to routine injections, their behavior ranging from complete panic to heroic indifference. These reactions, when we learn to compare them, give us valuable information about the personality of the particular child.

My answer to the above question is thus as follows: in some moment of stress, when action is immediately necessary, it may not be possible to weigh the side effects against each other; afterward the pediatrician will have the opportunity to see whether the child is upset or not, to think again, and to come either to the same or a different conclusion with regard to the next patient.

Q: The point has been stressed in France that the use of suppositories would be more harmful in boys than in girls because it would favor some latent trends toward homosexuality. I would like to have your opinion about it.

A: This is perfectly true. The aftereffects are more dangerous for boys than for girls.[4]

The next question referred to cuddling and tenderness with children, something magazines and television programs discuss from time to time, though there is hardly any scientific literature on the subject.

Q: I have very rarely heard cuddling discussed, and it seems to me to play a big part in human relations between parents and children in the first few years of life. One notices that when one asks mothers or fathers whether their children are cuddly, what a tremendous variability there is. One notices this with one's own children. Some children like to be cuddled in a very nice babyish way, at least for some time in the day, up to about five, six or seven years; others, often perhaps little boys, never like it. Mother will say he is a nice little boy, she has never had any trouble with him, but no, he has never, even as a baby, liked cuddling. It obviously gives immense satisfaction to many parents to have a child who likes being cuddled. Would you care to discuss the question of cuddling?

A: In psychological discussions that have gone on in recent years, cuddling has come into its own again—I would say with a vengeance. There was a period in the upbringing of children here in England, the Truby King period, in which cuddling was discouraged, in which it was not thought necessary to give the young child extra satisfactions and bodily attention apart from those actions which were necessary for bodily health and growth.

Recent developments in psychology and in psychoanalysis have shown a very different picture, namely, that as the infants grow and develop, the needs for contact with the people in their environment become as imperative as the needs for food, sleep, and warmth (i.e., the basic bodily needs), and that children whose basic physical needs are fulfilled do not thrive well if the corresponding emotional needs are not fulfilled at the same time. It is perfectly true that the need for cuddling, that is, for pleasurable close contact with the parents, especially the mother in the earliest years, is not expressed to the same degree by all children.

I think it makes the mother so happy to have a cuddly child because she can feel quite certain that this child is in very good contact with her. With the child who refuses cuddling, the mother feels that this is not only a refusal of a certain form of skin contact, bodily warmth, and nearness, but that it may be a failure to have good emotional contact with her altogether. If it were that, then it would mean a serious lack in the personality development of that particular child. Actually, if you follow the early histories of highly abnormal children, the so-called atypical or autistic ones, you will invariably hear that they have never been cuddly, that they have not achieved the normal nearness to the mother in their first and second years of life, and this points to a deeper defect.

This does not mean that all children who are not cuddly are abnormal. When the mother complains, for instance, that her child is not very cuddly, I think I would ask further questions. I would inquire whether that child looks for contact with the mother in other ways, always wants to see the mother and follow her with his eyes, or always wants to listen to the mother and is frightened if the mother is not heard at least walking around in the next room. It means the child may express his desire for nearness to the mother in various forms. Cuddling is one way, a normal way certainly for the first two years of life. And I think it would not harm pediatricians to inquire, at least with every difficult child, how matters stand in this particular respect.[5]

The question of what to do with a child who cries constantly concerns physicians and parents, in particular when the crying provokes commiseration in other people.

Q: I would like to raise the ever-present problem of the crying infant. Most of us are faced with this from time to time; we find various causes— feeding, colic, overanxious parents, and so on—but many of us are finally reduced to the regular administration of barbiturates. I recently had a patient who has, I think, moved about ten times because the neighbors complain. One need not emphasize the importance of that effect upon the child. How can we as pediatricians investigate this problem at our level? Or should this problem be referred for a more careful psychoanalytic study, and at what stage?

A: The crying infant is a problem equally to you and to us, and the referral for investigation at a psychoanalytic level is less promising because it is not so easy to investigate infants psychoanalytically. You will find, therefore, that our reasoning when such a mother and child come to us is very much like yours. Namely, our first thought is of a physical reason. Is there any physical disturbance which the mother has not found, which the pediatrician has not found, which makes it impossible for the child to be comforted? Let us see then that all these possibilities are excluded by experimenting with the feeding, by instructing the mother, and so on.

Then there is a further question which we ask ourselves: is this mother unable to give the child the comfort that other mothers are able to give? We all know that it is not unusual for children to have times of crying and discomfort, but the normal situation is that if there is no physical reason, the mother will be able to bring comfort and quiet to the child. Here, I believe, we arrive at the stage when we look for the reason either in the mother or in the child, and the less serious case would be if it is in the mother.

I have very recently had occasion to go through the files of our pediatrician at the Clinic concerning contacts with children in the first year. When I sorted out the crying infants who were finally in need of sleeping pills, I thought in one or two cases that the child was in need of this physical method because of a failure in the mother; another mother might have been able to supply what the drug has to supply here—a quieting, soporific effect—but something in the mother, a restlessness, an anxiety, an inability to relate to the child, may have prevented her from doing so.

I think it would be interesting to pool resources here. I am very much against the easy solution that wherever there is something wrong with the infant, there is something wrong with the mother—I do not think that is true at all. Infants have a right to their own disturbances—they are people. But with the crying infant, I believe, we have one of the many instances where one has to go into the situation very carefully, and compare the methods of comforting of one mother with those of other mothers.

I saw an instance of a crying infant, really a wildly shrieking one, the other day in a shop. This was a perfect baby of about eleven months. The mother had taken him in a pram into a big store where she was about to buy him a beautiful pale blue spring coat—a big day for the baby. But she put the pram with the baby at one end of the store and went to the counter at the other end, where she had to wait for her turn. The baby felt deserted and began to shriek. One would not have known that she was the mother of the shrieking baby. She never turned her head. In the end, the people in the shop got so disturbed that she went and picked the baby up and he was quiet. Then the whole thing started all over again, about trying on the spring coat; every time the mother did the right thing, the baby was quiet; every time she failed to do it, the baby shrieked. It was evidently a battle between the two, the mother thinking, "I'll see who wins," and the baby thinking, "*I'll* see who wins."

This is a crude illustration and does not fit our case completely, except that I believe that the inability of a mother to stop a crying baby may have causes of which she is not aware at all, and then the two enter into a battle with each other which can increase many times over. This diagnosis would be the less serious one; besides, I think there are infants who cannot be comforted for psychological reasons, just as others cannot be comforted because of an organic disturbance, because there is something wrong in them. There is something wrong in their development, they are oversensitive, they get more anxious, more excited, more frightened, more upset by events than a normal child. Therefore, this kind of early screaming can really point to serious abnormalities. Again, in the history of the very abnormal children, we often hear about unmanageable crying in the first year. That is as far as we have gone in our explanations. I know it is not very far.[6]

Inevitably, one comes to the poor eater, a problem that today concerns more and more parents all over the world.

Q: I would appreciate some guidance on the child who refuses to eat. We tend to work on a rule of thumb, trying to induce indifference in the parents, trying to get them to give up the struggle or to send the child to live with his grandmother. But we do meet those who persistently go wrong. We meet those who get into states of severe malnutrition. I have seen a child in a state of anorexia nervosa that was indistinguishable from that found in older children;

and I do not think we deal with this situation very well. I am sure we would all be very grateful for a word or two of guidance.

A: I wish a word or two of guidance would do away with the feeding disturbances. It is indeed a big chapter, at least it is a big chapter in *our* books, and I think it should be a big chapter in *your* books too.

It is a comparatively straightforward matter if one is able to organize the feeding of the child from the beginning, and to guide the mother through the various phases of breast or bottle feeding, drinking from a cup or spoon, introduction of solids, variety of foods, and following the child's preferences or avoidances. If the pediatrician or psychologist guides a mother through these phases, he will probably nip many feeding disturbances in the bud. The situations that come to him when a child absolutely refuses food for no organic reason are already end results, usually of years of battle between mother and child. There are many people who have written about feeding disturbances and I am one of them.[7] It is not an easy subject, and also not easy to summarize.

But perhaps it is good to keep in mind that, again, for the child, food is not only a material matter. In the first year of life, food and mother are more or less one and the same. The child cannot feed himself without the mother, and hunger, the sight of the mother, and the experiences of satisfaction become for the child one whole. The mother herself feels this. She feels that when the child refuses food he refuses her, and takes it as a personal offense, very often quite rightly, since this close unity between mother and food endows the feeding process with all the difficulties of the mother relationship. It is the mother who gives the food, who refuses the food and who is refused by the child. Very many children know that control of the mother is possible for them by eating or not eating.

I think, therefore, that one type of feeding disturbance is to be viewed from the aspect of the child's relationship to the mother. In modern feeding methods one tries to combat this unity between food and the mother by urging the child, as early as possible, to feed himself. At least we establish for the child a direct way to the food, bypassing the mother, in the second year, but still it will be the mother who gives the food or refuses it. I was greatly impressed when I read in the Platt Report, in the discussion of the feeding of children in hospitals, that while many children will refuse to eat in hospitals when they are separated from their mothers, there will be an equal number of children who will eat in the hospital even though they do not eat well with their own mothers. This is perfectly true; there are many children who will eat in the absence of their mothers but not in their presence. This, I think, is the diagnostic sign which you can use if you want to determine whether the type of feeding disturbance you are dealing with is the one closely connected with the mother.

There are of course other types. There is a feeding disturbance that comes roughly between two and four years, at the time when the child first becomes overinterested in anal products and then turns against the whole subject; much of the child's disgust of feces is apt to go over to food and to exclude certain forms, consistencies, and colors in food. These are the children who suddenly refuse to eat spinach or chocolate sauce or sauces of any kind, who are very suspicious of brown things and of certain shapes. I remember a little three- or four-year-old boy coming to the table in the nursery and finding on his plate some small sausages and mustard. He looked at the plate with horror and gently picked up the small sausage, and with an expression of disgust put it on the ground, where he thought it belonged. He felt this was not edible and should hardly be touched. The disturbances in this group are not serious, since children outgrow the phase of disgust, usually when their toilet training is fully established.

At a somewhat later stage we may encounter another type of eating disturbance which is connected with the child's ideas of impregnation, pregnancy, and birth. On a certain level of sexual development children believe that babies grow in the stomach as the result of the mother having eaten something specific (as in some well-known fairy tales), and such fantasies, when warded off, may lead to an avoidance of food and a fear of getting fat. Other children again may feel that eating is an aggressive act which destroys the food, and they may restrict their diet to a vegetarian one for fear of being "murderers." With other children, the aggressive and destructive tendencies are turned against their own bodies. In the well-known anorexia nervosa, the refusal of food is placed in the service of self-destructive suicidal impulses which often enough succeed in reaching their aim. There is a long path from the early, common feeding troubles based on the relationship to the mother to these later, very complex pathological structures.

As you see, it is as impossible to give general prescriptions for the handling of feeding disturbances as it would be to prescribe in general for stomach upsets or fever; their treatment depends not on their surface appearances but on the underlying meaning which is expressed by them.[8]

Anna Freud not only answered questions but on her own initiative came to speak of generally interesting topics. In earlier lectures she had already discussed the changes psychoanalysis had effected in the world, in particular changes in the psychological situation of mothers. She broached this problem within a further complex of questions:

Q: I am bothered these days by a great many mothers who seem to suffer from psychological misinformation. There is the mother who is so anxious to breast-feed, because she is told it is the right thing psychologically, that she fails. She then feels guilty for ever after that she has destroyed a very important relationship with her baby. Then there is the mother who fails to pick up the early cues of toilet training in her child, because she has read somewhere that early and coercive toilet training is a bad thing. Or the mother who has a child in the hospital and can never treat that child naturally afterward, because she is terrified that "separation" has occurred. Now the poor pediatrician, in trying to reassure this mother, is immediately told, "Well, I have heard it on the television," or "I read it in a certain paper or book," and that printed word carries much more value than anything he could tell her anyway. I wonder, do you recognize this danger, and what can we do to protect mothers from it?[9]

Finally, Anna Freud returned to the fundamental views she had stated at the outset:

I now have a question to ask the pediatricians here, and it is probably not a question that you will find easy to answer. When we went through the program for this particular study group, I was very struck by your growing interest in the psychosomatic disorders; this means that you are becoming very interested in the reaction of the body to the mind. Not all the disturbances that manifest themselves as physical, you now say, have physical causes; some of them seem to have their origins in the mind. Certain things going on in the mind have certain repercussions in the body, and you would like to know more about that.

I always wonder why you are not equally interested in the other side of the picture, namely, what repercussions the truly organic disturbances which you treat have on the mind of the child. I often regret that pediatricians care more for the psychosomatic side and are less interested in the psychological after-effects of physical illness.

There are questions such as the following: take, for example, a digestive disturbance in the first year of life, with a great deal of pain and discomfort, one that cuts out the pleasure in nourishment which belongs to that age. Will this have a lasting effect on the child's personality? There has been pain at a time when there should have been pleasure; there has been an overemphasis on the digestive tract; there have been times of revulsion against food or unsatisfied hunger.

I think whenever you handle a physical disturbance of this kind, you should ask at the same time what it means in psychological terms, just as you have asked today what rectal manipulation means in psychological terms. Whenever you interfere with the body of a child in some massive way, you should ask yourself: what will the child make of this? Perhaps some day there will be another study group dealing exclusively with the other side of the subject, namely, with the question of what illness and medical interference mean in terms of the child's psychological development.[10]

■
The Copenhagen and Edinburgh Congresses

Nineteen fifty-nine was another congress year. For the first time, the location was Copenhagen. Changes had again occurred. The European societies had regained their strength, enabling no less than 920 psychoanalysts to attend the congress. Many young European psychoanalysts came to see those great personalities familiar to them from the psychoanalytic literature, to hear them speak and perhaps meet them personally. With patience and understanding for such desires, Anna Freud made herself available for an open discussion. She actively participated—how could she not?—and led a symposium in German on "Developments in the Therapeutic Application of Psychoanalysis." Participants recall her ability to disentangle the obscure questions of inhibited or nervous speakers. The esteem Anna Freud enjoyed was reflected in the 172 secret votes—far above everyone else's—ratifying her position as vice president.

The Twenty-second International Congress, held in Edinburgh from July 30 to August 3, 1961, showed Anna Freud in the same situation. She was now sixty-five years old and her work had long been beyond dispute. Since the number of those who experienced and shaped the earliest beginnings of psychoanalysis had gradually been waning, Anna Freud held in every respect an exceptional position as both a connective link and a guardian of tradition. At this congress she opened a roundtable discussion on parent–child relations,[1] carefully criticizing previously published lectures by Phyllis Greenacre and D. W. Winnicott, well-known analysts from New York and England respectively.

With the Menningers in Topeka

After a five-year interlude, Anna Freud traveled to the United States in 1962 to be a guest of the Menninger Foundation in Topeka, Kansas, for ten days—a triumphant sojourn for her, yet bound up with an unusual workload verging on exploitation. Karl Menninger and Topeka are relatively unknown in Europe; many know no more about Topeka than that its location is somewhere in the American Midwest. We will therefore briefly dwell on the significance of this place.

The Menninger Clinic, today known as the Menninger Foundation, was founded in 1919 by Charles Frederick Menninger, who had emigrated from Switzerland. For a long time it served as a traditional psychiatric hospital. But at the age of eighty, Charles Frederick was suddenly fascinated by psychoanalysis and insisted on being analyzed, a wish he could be dissuaded from only with great effort. It is also told that, although this old gentleman always welcomed progress, his wife was hardly able to adjust to her new life in America and could not even carry on a conversation in English.

The actual ascent of the Menninger Clinic was initiated by the two sons, who were born in Topeka. Karl August, the better known of the two, was born in 1893—a contemporary of Anna Freud. *The Vital Balance*[1] contains his psychiatric "philosophy." He wrote numerous other books—in particular he insisted on more humane criminal courts. William Claire Menninger was born in 1899. Both brothers were trained in psychoanalysis in Chicago.[2] Karl Menninger had already visited Freud in Vienna, where he was analyzed by Ruth Mack Brunswick. At the 1930 congress on psychohygiene, he showed great enthusiasm for psychoanalysis and became friends with Leo H. Bartemeier, later president of the American Psychiatric Association. From 1922 on, the Menninger brothers determined the fate of the clinic, which is managed today in its third generation by Roy Wright Menninger (b. 1926).

The First World Congress for Psychohygiene, held in Washington in 1930 and organized by Clifford Beers, founder of the movement, had already signaled a historical shift—even in American psychoanalysis. Here, under William Alanson White's chairmanship, powerful European currents affected American trends for the first time. In the Europe of the early 1930's, clairvoyant minds could already sense the approach of National Socialism and all its terrible consequences. Sándor

Radó, one of those clairvoyants, very early foresaw the imminence of World War II and was convinced that a war's catastrophes would entail crucial setbacks for the psychoanalytic movement. Radó belonged to a group of respected analysts of the Berlin Institute who had been invited to Washington for the congress. Franz Alexander, Karen Horney, Hanns Sachs, and Otto Fenichel also accepted the invitation and were welcomed with special cordiality in Washington. The lecture by these Berliners, who were viewed as representatives of European psychoanalysis, met with enthusiastic interest. From a current perspective, it is interesting that all those invited from Berlin were later admitted to the United States as immigrants, each of them later pursuing his own path. At this congress, Alexander was invited for a visit by Robert Hutchins, president of the University of Chicago. Soon thereafter, he received a professorship in psychoanalysis at Chicago, which has come to be considered the first professorial chair in psychoanalysis ever. (This is incorrect, since Sándor Ferenczi had already held such a chair in Budapest in 1919, which, given the precarious political circumstances, did not enjoy a long existence.)

In the early 1930's, the stream of European—primarily German—emigrants began to flow into the United States. The Menningers made efforts to direct as many as possible to Topeka, and for many of them provided the highly sought-after "affidavit." The immigration of psychoanalysts to Topeka reached such proportions that the local airport was referred to in jest as the "International Psychoanalytic Airport."

This influx was highly significant for the region around Topeka, since no higher level of qualified psychiatry existed at that time in the Midwest—neither good training institutes nor satisfactory psychiatric treatment for patients. As a result, the population yielded with relative equanimity to checkups and treatment by these foreigners who had hardly mastered English, and willingly revealed to them their most intimate thoughts and feelings. Of the German psychoanalysts who came to Topeka, many never remedied their awkward English.

For Europeans, the situation was as follows: Those from Vienna and Berlin found in Topeka that side of America presented mostly in jokes. New York and New England, with their intellectual traditions, could have been attractive, as might the great industrial city of Chicago, and certainly California with its intelligentsia always ready for novelty. But Kansas? This was tantamount to exile.

The Menningers perhaps did not act exclusively out of magnanimity, since they created a system of mutual give and take, successful for all its participants—European analysts, patients, and the Menningers. A certain unjust criticism therefore refers to one of Karl Menninger's remarks to Laura Fermi: "We didn't know whether we were lending a helpful hand or whether we were taking advantage of a given situation."[3] Karl Menninger underestimated or even deprecated the significance Topeka had for emigré psychoanalysts. They received security, ample possibilities for interacting with like-minded professionals, recognition—even admiration—and a secure income from practicing their profession. Such auspicious conditions were rarely offered to immigrants, even in the United States. That

Topeka became, through the Menningers, a unique center for psychoanalysis such as had never existed before is indisputable.

Despite Anna Freud's five previous visits to the United States, as a representative of psychoanalysis, this trip was long overdue. The official occasion included lectures, a memorial reading for C. F. Menninger, two readings within the framework of a Sloan professorship—all scheduled for her two-week trip. Moreover, the Psychoanalytic Institute of Topeka was celebrating its twentieth anniversary. This alone meant an official celebration and three lectures she had agreed in advance to deliver from the manuscripts she had prepared for the occasion. [4]

Anna Freud's Menninger reading and her other lectures were preliminary sketches of the book she was writing, *Normality and Pathology in Childhood,*[5] in which, for example, the Menninger lecture was included in the third chapter under the title "Regression as a Principle in Normal Development." She therefore developed the thoughts for this book before an expert audience that assisted her in the final draft of the manuscript by asking questions. Finally, a symposium, "Progress in Child Psychoanalysis," was arranged, in which Marianne Kris, Margaret Mahler, and Helen Ross, her old acquaintances, as well as moderator Ishak Ramzy from Topeka, participated.

The Menninger Foundation remained therefore entirely within its tradition when it lavished honors upon Anna Freud, making her presence into a psychoanalytic triumph for the entire region, but also expecting of her a volume of work under which even a younger person could have collapsed. As soon as Anna Freud arrived on September 16, accompanied by Helen Ross, her schedule was considerably expanded. She spoke at clinic conferences, debated with small groups, visited training classes at the psychoanalytic institute and case conferences at the C. F. Menninger Memorial Hospital, participated in various case conferences in child psychiatry, spoke at the patients' club and with training teachers of the psychoanalytic training institute, and discussed various research projects during other meetings. This list is hardly complete.

Despite her comprehensive schedule, Anna Freud did not let the Midwestern landscape slip by; Ishak Ramzy remarks admiringly that the day after her arrival, loyal to her old Austrian habits, she took a long walk through the surrounding area before the others even got up. When Marianne Kris and Margaret Mahler arrived on Saturday from New York, she was thus able to show them Topeka's sights as if she had long since been living there—very much to the pride of Topekans.[6] Since no honorary doctorate nor any similar honor was to be awarded, Anna Freud was made an honorary member of the Psychoanalytic Institute of Topeka. She was the first to be awarded this distinction.

While Anna Freud was in Topeka, the sad news of Princess Marie Bonaparte's death arrived from Paris. Both Sigmund and Anna Freud were much indebted to her. At the 1959 Copenhagen congress, Marie Bonaparte had gathered together two hundred analysts at her Danish country house. Anna Freud did not attend the memorial sessions at the psychoanalytic congress in Paris in 1963, but wrote instead a brief obituary which was translated into French.[7] In it she discussed chiefly Marie Bonaparte's autobiography, which she had been permitted to read and which, except for the first volume, was not yet available to the public.

The Stockholm Congress

At the Twenty-third Psychoanalytic Congress in Stockholm, held from July 28 to August 1, 1963, Anna Freud participated as usual in the scientific discussions. At the business sessions, she and Jeanne Lampl-de Groot, having conferred beforehand, proposed to reserve speaking time at the next congress for young analysts, and not to allow only international celebrities to speak. Here Anna Freud expressed not only her fairness toward young analysts but also her concern for the continuation and further development of psychoanalysis. She was the first to voice such a concern.

By 1963, psychoanalysis had reached the summit in terms of international recognition, having virtually become a fad in the United States through the influence of the media. As a whole, psychoanalysis was standing on firm ground at that time; here and there a few cracks were visible in the brickwork, but few tendencies to schism were evident. This was a situation that should have highly pleased Anna Freud. She justified her proposal by underscoring her concern that innovations be furthered and interest stimulated through the participation of young analysts.

America, 1964

In 1964, Anna Freud surpassed her previous activities in the United States. She made her seventh visit there in April. She participated at a New York symposium on infantile trauma on April 3–5. Cospeakers now included new acquaintances among the old: Sidney S. Fürst, Leo Rangell, Peter B. Neubauer, Phyllis Greenacre, Marianne Kris, Joseph Sandler, Albert J. Solnit, and Robert Waelder. Anna Freud used the occasion to present and clarify her own thoughts on infantile trauma, one of the key concepts in psychoanalysis, partly by replying to the questions of participants.[1]

The symposium was organized by the Psychoanalytic Research and Development Fund, whose president was Hermann Nunberg. On April 13, a celebration took place at the New York Academy of Medicine in honor of Nunberg's eightieth birthday and was later continued as the Herman Nunberg Lectures. Karl Menninger and Anna Freud gave encomia.[2] Anna Freud's long relationship with Nunberg was many-faceted, but neither intimate nor even personal.

Born on January 23, 1884, in Bedzin, Poland, Nunberg was eleven years Anna Freud's senior and already known as an analyst when she was taking her first steps in the field. He was married to Margarete Rie, the daughter of Freud's friend Oskar Rie and, like her sister Marianne Rie Kris, a friend of Anna Freud's. Like Anna Freud, Nunberg admired Siegfried Bernfeld, whose book on the Baumgarten Nursery he praised as a valuable possession even in his old age. In Vienna, Nunberg had been Willie Hoffer's training analyst; Hoffer became Anna Freud's loyal colleague in London for many years.

But beyond these connections, there was not much that the two held in common. Nunberg himself mentioned Anna Freud only peripherally in his memoirs.[3] On her part, Anna Freud stressed her respect for the former member of the Vienna Psychoanalytic Society and limited herself to an outline of Nunberg's work.

Nunberg is considered the founder of training analysis, which he first proposed at the 1918 Budapest Congress, at Freud's instigation (see p. 34 above). His name was even more familiar as the editor of the *Minutes of the Vienna Psychoanalytic Society*.[4] He saw to the first English publication of the four volumes, while only two volumes had appeared in the German original. Nunberg moved to the United States as early as September 1932, where he began first to build a psychoanalytic association in Philadelphia. His motive for leaving Austria was not political, but it is said that in 1932 he was already attempting to convince Freud to emigrate to the United States. His training manual, *Fundamentals of Psychoanalysis in Relation to the Neurosis*,[5] rendered his own understanding of psychoanalytic theory. Anna Freud considered the book impeccable among the few psychoanalytic manuals. Nunberg, who was already forty-seven years old when he moved to the United States, did not abandon his extremely active way of life. He remained, as Anna Freud stressed, the same on both sides of the ocean. Nunberg died in New York on May 20, 1970, at the age of eighty-six.

On the twentieth anniversary of the Citizens' Committee for Children, celebrated in April 1964 at the Cosmopolitan Club in New York, Anna Freud gave a third lecture on the application of psychoanalytic knowledge in children's hospitals.[6] Again she underscored that psychosomatic ideas have found a relatively easy entrance into the theory of child therapy, and that today it is almost a truism to attribute many infantile illnesses to psychic causes. But the reverse—that physical illness and the medical intervention it requires inevitably lead to far-reaching influences on the child's psyche—has still not received the attention it deserves.

On June 12, 1964, Anna Freud received another honorary doctorate. Jefferson Medical College in Philadelphia, Pennsylvania, awarded her the title of Doctor of Science (Dr. *rer. nat.*). Prior to the festive award ceremony in the afternoon, a small incident occurred at the Barclay Hotel, located in the heart of the city at the corner of Rittenhouse Square and 18th Street, which had been chosen as Anna Freud's residence and the location of the banquet. That morning Anna Freud was sitting in the lobby talking with Grete Bibring and Mrs. Guttmann[7] when Floyd S. Cornelison, who had been in charge of all the arrangements but did not know Anna Freud personally, wanted to go over to them. At the same moment he saw the president of the college, Dr. Bodine, walking toward the ladies to greet them. Cornelison, who felt socially obligated to introduce the honorary guest to the president, mistook Grete Bibring for Anna Freud and tried to introduce *her*. But the president paid him no attention because he had just turned toward Mrs. Guttmann, greeting her with the words: "How do you do, Miss Freud?" Cornelison tried to correct the blunder, saying cautiously: "No, no." The president turned away from the three ladies and, with the words "Then where is she?" looked for her through the entire lobby. This amusing situation, certainly unpleasant for the gentlemen, again sheds light on how reserved Anna Freud appeared and how little fuss she made about herself. The other two—certainly not unknown—women must have conveyed an impression of greater importance.[8]

That evening, the psychiatric division of the college gave a dinner at the Barclay in honor of Anna Freud. Besides Cornelison, Robert Waelder, an old friend and student from Vienna who had been in analysis with Anna Freud, also spoke. Then professor of psychoanalysis at Jefferson, he had evidently urged that this distinction be awarded. Waelder recalled their common days in Vienna and added:

> If anyone in those days had predicted to Anna Freud and to me that we would meet here tonight, on this particular occasion, we would have dismissed it as pure fantasy. On the other hand, if anybody had predicted at that time that we would both have to flee from the city in which we were born and had grown up, we would have thought that, too, to be utterly incredible.[9]

For Robert Waelder, who died not long thereafter, Anna Freud's honorary promotion was both climax and farewell.

This was the second American honorary doctorate conferred on Anna Freud; it would be followed by others. Her award address contained the "Curriculum Vitae of a Lay Analyst," as she explicitly described herself.[10] In this curriculum vitae, from which excerpts have frequently been quoted, Anna Freud broadly described her development as an analyst. She then spoke about the period before psychoanalysis was organized, a time no doubt more difficult than the present. Now institutes offered courses and seminars in which students could study psychoanalytical theories from the professional literature, and then through training analysis be prepared for analytical practice. On the other hand, Anna Freud believed that the earlier period had an advantage over the present in that students first learned the classical technique before attempting to develop their own variations. She went on to say that no one was expected, back then, to write theoretical essays on psychoanalysis before having completed training, whereas today some young analysts prematurely felt obligated to be original—a dig at modern psychoanalysis, which tends toward abstract theorizing and often toward merely purported changes in technique. By no means concerned with orthodox rigidity, Anna Freud underscored that each analyst creates for himself in the course of time the kind of work he deserves.

It is interesting that the statement "he deserves" stems from one of Anna Freud's recollections of her youth in Vienna, which she retained incompletely and which she has somewhat distorted:

> One more personal addition: When I was a young girl and dissatisfied with my appearance—as girls often are—I felt comforted by a saying then popular in Vienna: "After a certain age every woman gets the face that she deserves," i.e., the face she creates for herself.[11]

The "popular saying" was in fact a quotation used here in modified form. The statement was first made by Karl Emil Franzos (1848–1904), who wrote in 1875, "Each country has the Jews it deserves," and was described by Franzos himself as "the key to the modern history of the Jews."[12] In Anna Freud's version, the words seem harmless: The girl who thinks she is ugly turns into a self-confident woman. The original quotation, however—well applicable to Anna Freud—implies an altogether different matter: a young Jewish woman in a country that no longer wants her and a mature Jewish woman in a country worthy of her.

In the autumn of 1964, Anna Freud again found herself in the United States. On November 4, she lectured at the New York Academy of Medicine, where she had often been a guest, on the occasion of Heinz Hartmann's seventieth birthday (see pp. 31–32 above). She expounded her concept of ego psychology, trying to distinguish it from Heinz Hartmann's ego psychology, which enjoyed wide recognition at that time.

▬
Cindy

In 1965, the complete adoption records of a girl born on January 9, 1960, were published. The welfare department of the state of California made available the entire file of the case, which has become known as *Cindy* in psychoanalytic literature. The descriptions show that, notwithstanding the efforts the American authorities made in taking care of this child, crucial errors were committed. In her detailed commentary on this case, Anna Freud stated in full clarity her fundamental insights and convictions.[1]

After her birth, Cindy was brought first to a couple who wanted to adopt her. But the authorities were asked to intervene when it became known that the couple was in the process of divorce. Moreover, when the social worker visited the couple in their apartment, she discovered that Mrs. Andrews was not taking good care of Cindy. Cindy is described as a very beautiful baby with long eyelashes, large blue eyes, long blond hair, and regular facial features. But Mrs. Andrews did not really know how to handle her. In one instance, the child would have fallen out of her cradle while being rocked if the social worker had not been present. Cindy also displayed a serious developmental lag. She was always very quiet, almost motionless; she had no toys and showed no interest in her environment. She took no note of the social worker's presence. Being in the process of divorce and forced to go back to work as a secretary, Mrs. Andrews was unable to always take care of the child, and left her with various people during the day. On the basis of the report of the welfare bureau, the court revoked Mrs. Andrews' custody. Anna Freud expressly viewed this step as positive. She also indicated that Cindy never lacked physical care:

> There is no time in Cindy's life when her basic needs are not fulfilled, that is, when she is lacking for proper nourishment, appropriate clothing, hygienic housing, or when she is treated harshly. She does not suffer the fate of institutionalized children whose individuality is submerged in enforced community life at an age when the normal infant yearns for personal relationships.[2]

But Anna Freud was concerned not with the self-evident physical care, but with the development of the emotional and intellectual life. That is why she approved of the court's decision.

It is in accordance with the Court's findings that Cindy, at the age of ten months, presented the typical picture of an infant who has been born normal, but who has been allowed to remain insufficiently stimulated and underdeveloped so far as emotional attachment and sensory and motor potentialities are concerned. As such infants do—unless they are grossly neglected or unduly frightened—Cindy smiled indiscriminately at everybody, but her expression remained bland and blank and nothing in the environment aroused sufficient interest in her to protest against it or to induce her to reach out for it.[3]

Cindy was then brought to foster parents who, as was later proved, had been carefully chosen. Mrs. Johnson, the mother, had already adopted two girls, aged eleven and five when Cindy arrived. In previous years she had also taken excellent care of other children. Mrs. Johnson was first given the opportunity to meet Cindy. When the social worker brought her, the five-year-old adopted daughter was present. Cindy smiled indiscriminately at everyone and did not protest when Mrs. Johnson took her in her arms. The report says: "She has apparently been with a large variety of people and acknowledges every person indiscriminately." Despite this behavior, Mrs. Johnson was moved by the child and found her pretty. A farewell was then arranged between Cindy and Mrs. Andrews and her son from a previous marriage. But Cindy remained completely impassive and, despite her eleven months, showed nothing to indicate that she recognized Mrs. Andrews or that the separation meant anything to her.

Cindy began to run only at the age of fourteen months, was still very unsure on her feet after a month, and still showed no interest in her environment. At the age of sixteen months, she knew a few words but no sentences. It was only at the age of seventeen months that the social worker got the impression that Cindy could distinguish her from Mrs. Johnson. It soon became obvious that Mrs. Johnson had a lucky touch in dealing with Cindy, because the latter began clinging to her very closely. Cindy had meanwhile grown into a pretty little girl who at first sight looked like a big doll with her large blue eyes, blond hair, and delicate, pale face. She had developed a passionate relationship to Mrs. Johnson, sat in her lap whenever she could, and did not want to leave her. Mrs. Johnson was very considerate in this respect and almost never left her alone. But when she had to be briefly absent, Cindy always ran a fever. Toward strangers, including the visiting social worker, Cindy now remained extremely reserved; she thawed a little after half an hour, but was still anxious to have her foster mother close by. No doubt she continued to experience a great separation anxiety. In her intimate relationship with her foster mother, however, she developed very rapidly, reached the verbal level appropriate for her age, began to show her feelings, and protested loudly when a toy was taken from her. While playing with her six-year-old foster sister, she defended her rights very energetically. In short, it was agreed that, at the age of twenty-one months, Cindy had recovered from her developmental lag and developed an intimate relationship with her foster mother.

Anna Freud viewed the steps taken and Mrs. Johnson's behavior as clearly positive, justifying her evaluation with several theoretical reflections. When she was brought to Mrs. Johnson, Cindy needed particularly intensive motherly care:

> What she had missed and what was sorely needed for her development was a stable central figure whom she could recognize as the invariable dispenser of food, comfort, and affection and to whom, in return, her own awakening emotions could attach themselves firmly. Such a tie is necessary for the infant's learning to discriminate between the familiar and unfamiliar, the known and unknown in the environment. It is only in the interaction with such a loved figure that the infant develops intelligent interest and directs attention to the material objects and happenings in his surroundings. The mother's pleasure in his successes in reaching, touching, grasping, recognizing, and moving stimulates his own satisfaction and spurs him on to make new efforts and advances. Where this exchange is missing, the child remains dull, uninterested, and lacking in responses as Cindy did.
>
> At the time when Mrs. Johnson took over, more was expected of her than the usual developmental stimulation, which is the duty of the ordinary mother; the task before her was more of a remedial, therapeutic nature. Responses had to be elicited belatedly since much valuable time had remained unused in the first year of life. Luckily, Cindy was young enough still to have them elicited, and thereby to escape the fate of many other children about whom less trouble is taken with the result that they are branded as dull, retarded, of substandard mentality at some later date in their lives, usually at school entry.
>
> However this may be, it needed all of Mrs. Johnson's resources of maternal affection, ambition, understanding, perseverance, time, bodily and mental effort to effect changes, and it is greatly to her and the agency's credit that these were brought about.[4]

But now comes the decisive point at which Anna Freud's views and those of the authorities acutely diverged. It was found that precisely the normalization of Cindy's development now made her adoption by a new family possible. The welfare department made great efforts to find the right family and to arrange the transition. After the situation was carefully investigated and long reports were drawn up, authorities found Fred Sims, a thirty-seven-year-old German, and his wife, Hanna, a thirty-one-year-old woman of Scotch-Irish descent. Both had been married before and from the breakup of their marriages had learned to build a particularly exemplary marriage. They had already adopted a girl, whom they had successfully guided through her first hardships. But they did not want to raise her as an only child. This, then, seemed an ideal situation for Cindy. The transition was made particularly easy for her. The adoptive parents listened to Cindy's history for an entire morning. The social worker came more and more often to visit Mrs. Johnson, and took Cindy for walks. The transition was effected one step at a time. Cindy was allowed to visit the Simses until they finally took her in.

So much thoughtfulness, so much psychological acumen and consideration toward the child seemed almost ideal, even exaggerated. It is here, however, that Anna Freud's criticism comes in. She condemned the separation, convinced that a child cannot transfer his feelings toward a maternal figure from one person to another as one transfers a dress from one hanger to another. This is not easily noticed in children, though the effects are later very powerful. Anna Freud explained these reactions and, in keeping with her psychoanalytic experiences, compared the separation to a child's bereavement of his mother:

> Owing to the very urgency of their needs, their dependent helplessness, and their complete inability to look after themselves, young children cannot spend much time on mourning and are forced instead to accept substitute care and to all external intents and purposes to adapt to altered circumstances. This does not mean that their unhappinesses are less severe than they will be in later life. But it obscures the recognition by the adult world that a serious blow has been dealt to [them]. . . . Separated by fate from their first love object, most children establish their further emotional attachments on a more tentative, less satisfying or trusting and—as future life will show—on a more shallow basis.[5]

This is why Anna Freud condemned the procedures of the authorities with unusually harsh words:

> Seen against the background of experience with individuals who have undergone such and similar fates, the agency's action to seek further placement for Cindy seems to me an unenlightened, dangerous, and unwarranted step. . . . Nor does all the careful work which is spent on preparation help since you cannot prevent emotional upset in a two-and-a-half-year-old by approaching him through intellect and reason. So far as Cindy and her own understanding of the event are concerned, she loses the only effective mother whom she ever had in her life and, moreover, one whom she had acquired after delay, hardship, and emotional neglect. It is difficult to conceive how she can weather the experience without being harmed, even if harm remains under the surface for the present, and becomes visible only at a later date.[6]

The welfare authorities reacted to Anna Freud's criticism as early as June 1964. They expressed gratitude for her explanations and, in a carefully formulated reply, showed that they had given much thought to this case. Nevertheless, they upheld the decision, justifying it essentially on the grounds of legal and institutional constraints. Cindy's natural parents were temporarily inaccessible, they would not have given Cindy up for adoption, the authorities could act only within legal regulations, et cetera. Anna Freud did not reply, but there can be hardly a doubt that these arguments did not impress her, since her considerations were always determined by the child's well-being and not by compliance with legal regulations or adjustment to institutional constraints. Laws and institutions are made by people; they should be improved to fulfill their goal of serving the child's well-being.

Cindy is only the most impressive example of a comprehensive work by Anna Freud in which she engaged in a juridical discussion on the changing legal status of the child. From total legal dependence on his parents, the child has increasingly become a legally independent person in this century. This change did not evolve unproblematically. In 1963 and 1964, Anna Freud was visiting professor at the law school of Yale University, where she discussed these issues with Joseph Goldstein and Jay Katz in a seminar on "The Family and the Law."[7] Later she worked with Joseph Goldstein and Albert J. Solnit (of the Child Study Center of Yale University). All three wrote a small book, *Beyond the Best Interests of the Child*,[8] which grew out of laborious discussions in New Haven, Rathmore (Ireland), and finally Maresfield Gardens. All participants had the feeling, known to other coauthors as well, that it would have been easier to write a book alone. The common text has become such that even Anna Freud's style is no longer discernible. The book was soon translated into other languages (Anna Freud herself saw to the German translation of the first three chapters) and affected developments in legislation.

Anna Freud, CBE, LL.D., Sc.D.

The Twenty-fourth International Psychoanalytic Congress took place in Amsterdam on July 25–30, 1965. It was the first congress to accept Anna Freud's proposal to allow the younger generation ampler space for lectures—fifty-two lectures were given altogether—which older members followed with prepared commentaries. It was also the first congress dedicated to a single subject: compulsion neuroses. Finally, another innovation was added: Anna Freud closed the congress with a summary of all the lectures. A rather difficult task, it was nonetheless of particular concern to her, and, as always, she was able to separate the central from the peripheral, the fertile from the unfertile thought.[1]

On December 3, 1965, Anna Freud reached the age of seventy. It was her wish not to receive honors on this day. The president of the International Psychoanalytic Association sent her a congratulatory telegram; otherwise, the event was observed in strict privacy. Still, Anna Freud could not avoid some official honors. On England's honors list, issued every new year, her name appeared as Commander of the Order of the British Empire. For the first time she also received an honorary doctorate from a European university rife with tradition: Sheffield University awarded her the title of Doctor of Law. The University of Chicago honored her with the distinction Doctor of Science. Thus we sometimes find, according to English custom, the abbreviations LL.D., Sc.D. after her name, though these do not exhaust her honors.

With the publication that year of *Normality and Pathology in Childhood*, Anna Freud gave to herself and her professional world an important birthday gift. For her father's seventieth birthday, she had completed her first book, *Introduction to the Technique of Child Analysis*. The new book, her most comprehensive independent work, contained her views on normal and abnormal child development. We have already seen that she read parts of the book in Topeka before its final revisions. Other parts had previously been published separately. Yet, unlike her earlier books, this one did not derive only from lectures, but was conceived as a whole. It was a precise summary of Anna Freud's thought on child psychology and psychopathology, taken from her entire life, especially the last two decades. The title conveys the balanced focus, so important to her, on the normal and abnormal in child psychology.

Although the text moves essentially on the metapsychological level, Anna Freud never failed to give guiding hints on the techniques of child therapy. The psychological "developmental lines" are even more clearly articulated than in previous works; through them, she sought to depict realistically the child's development and achievements.

> There are similar lines of development which can be shown to be valid for almost every other area of the individual's personality. . . . Such lines . . . lead, for example, from the infant's suckling and weaning experiences to the adult's rational rather than emotional attitude to food intake; from cleanliness training enforced on the child by environmental pressure to the adult's more or less ingrained and unshakable bladder and bowel control; from the child's sharing possession of his body with his mother to the adolescent's claim for independence and self-determination in body management; from the young child's egocentric view of the world and his fellow beings to empathy, mutuality, and companionship with his contemporaries; from the first erotic play on his own and his mother's body by way of the transitional objects . . . to the toys, games, hobbies, and finally to work, etc.[2]

In another passage, Anna Freud emphasized the parents' influence—negative and positive—more energetically than ever before: "The possibilities for beneficial intervention in the developmental realm are almost as unlimited as those for harmful interference with development."[3]

The book was written in English and by 1974 had seen five printings. Anna Freud did not have it translated into German, but instead herself adapted a German edition that was first published in 1968. A comparison between the two editions shows that these are not two different books, but that Anna Freud allowed herself more freedom in translating than a translator would have been permitted, to bring it closer to the German-speaking reader.

Critics received the book enthusiastically, not very astonishing in one such as Heinz Hartmann, her clinical teacher from former days, who dedicated to the book a long and detailed discussion in the *International Journal of Psychoanalysis.*[4] But Margaret Mead also used the occasion to requite Anna Freud's friendly words, making at the same time a personal confession:

> Miss Freud's ideas have been such an integral part of my own thinking for so many years that I find in this book a vivid illustration of her theoretical path since she presented a "picture of childhood" as seen by a psychoanalyst in the first *Handbook of Child Psychology*, through *The Ego and the Mechanisms of Defense* which reached me in the midst of my field work in Bali and helped to organize my comparative observations on character formation in different cultures, to the inclusive sweep of the present work.[5]

As Anna Freud was not uncritical of Margaret Mead's work, the latter, despite her acknowledgment, made several fundamentally critical remarks. She underscored, for example, that Anna Freud remained within the theoretical and conceptual frame of "orthodox Freudian theory," and that she accepted only those innovations that expanded already accepted concepts. This reproach of orthodoxy is occasionally heard from other sources as well, though surreptitiously. The mere mention of the word—with its implications of rigidity and repudiation of the new—implies reproach. Yet such arguments always display the same logical error. Since psychoanalytic theory consists of reciprocally related single parts or rules, the removal of one of these of necessity alters the entire theory. In other words, if the phenomena of psychoanalytic theory were to prove inadequate to explain observable psychic phenomena, either the theory would have to be revised or an entirely new one designed. Insofar as Anna Freud succeeded in convincingly explaining the many complicated processes she reported on by merely expanding psychoanalytic theory, she invalidated the reproach of orthodoxy, though, predictably, it was not to be silenced. The idea of orthodoxy here possibly thrives on the absence of epistemological reflections in Anna Freud's work and on her frequent adherence to the psychoanalytic definition of what constitutes a fact. But this fundamentally scientific–theoretical argument changes nothing in the practical application of psychoanalytic theory.

René Spitz

January 1966 saw Anna Freud again in Zurich, where the Swiss Psychoanalytic Society had arranged a celebration in honor of René Spitz's seventy-ninth birthday, with Anna Freud as the main speaker.[1] For her, this was an occasion to argue with a work bearing an extreme affinity to hers, but on which she had thus far not expressed her views in detail.

René Spitz was a psychoanalyst famous for his works on developmental psychology and psychopathology. He was an exile from Vienna. Born in Vienna on January 29, 1887, he was already a physician in 1910 when he became acquainted with psychoanalysis. During the 1920's and 1930's he was a member of the Vienna Psychoanalytic Society. He emigrated first to France, then in the late '30's to the United States, where he was active as a training analyst at the New York Psychoanalytic Institute from 1940 until 1957. His reputation, based on his direct observation of children—especially motherless (or, in analytical terms, objectless) children—was established rather late in the United States. The concept that brought him world fame was "anaclitic depression" (dependence depression).

In 1946, Spitz reported on a thus far unknown behavior of infants who had been living in hospitals for some time, separated from their mothers, hence deprived of emotional relationships and affective interactions. After an approximately three-month stay in the hospital, the whining and crying ceases; the children sit up in their beds with blank stares and an impassive expression, hardly taking notice of what is happening around them. It is difficult if not impossible to make contact with the children in such circumstances. The effects of the absence of an object, which can even lead to the child's death, can be rectified if the object relationship is resumed within three months.[2] A complete series of films on early child development has meanwhile become well known.

At the age of retirement, Spitz returned to Europe, settling in Geneva, where he wrote other important books. He died on September 14, 1974, in Denver, Colorado, during his last visit to the United States. He was eighty-seven years old.

In her birthday lecture for Spitz, given in German, Anna Freud referred in particular to his first book, *The First Year of Life*, published in 1965. The apparent similarity between their work interests vanishes on further probing. While Spitz's interest was focused almost exclusively on the child's first year, Anna Freud's interest started at the end of that stage, or, in analytical terms, at the transition from primary to secondary processes and from the pleasure to the reality principle. Though a psychoanalyst, Spitz drew his theoretical principles not from analytic therapy, as did Anna Freud, nor from memory, associations, and dreams, but from observations in the psychological laboratory, assisted by a trained staff, films, and test sheets.

Despite these methodological differences and diverging interests, both concurred in their evaluation of the child's dependence on the mother during this early developmental stage, viewing it as the most cardinal human realtionship. Neither failed to insist on the deleterious consequences of the severance of such a bond. Anna Freud described the mother as the first legislator in the child's life, who regulates its satisfactions, pleasures and pains, wish fulfillments and denials.

■

Anna Freud in American Intellectual Life

We cannot exactly determine when Anna Freud became a figure in American intellectual life. The 1970 survey of psychiatrists and psychoanalysts in the Preface to this book no doubt pertains to the most recent period. At the time of her trips to America in 1966 and 1968, Anna Freud was already well known beyond professional circles.

In April 1966, Anna Freud again traveled to Topeka, where she spoke on April 2 on the significance of psychoanalysis for the further training of the clinical psychiatrist.[1] Topeka had become exemplary among the many other institutions of its kind. During the training of young psychiatrists, psychoanalysis was not only cited as one of many types of psychotherapy, but the prospective experts also familiarized themselves with the fundamental principles of psychoanalytic theory, a procedure Anna Freud obviously welcomed. That is why she addressed this subject in Topeka in its fundamental aspects, showing again how few illusions she entertained about the practical realism of most training situations.

Several days later, on April 9, Anna Freud introduced the first scientific congress of the American Association for Child Psychoanalysis, held in Topeka, with a paper on the history of child analysis.[2] Presumably, she could have used this occasion to bring into relief both herself and her merits, as she indeed deserved. Instead she brought up scarcely known names and events whose references have hardly been checked, since this lecture has frequently served as a historical source even for her critics, such as Paul Roazen, to whom it obviously did not occur that Anna Freud could unjustly dismiss the merits of others. But we have already discussed this problem.

Next on the schedule was again New Haven, Connecticut, where the Child Study Center of Yale University and the Children's Bureau held a joint session. Anna Freud's task was only to summarize the results. In the summary, however, she raised fundamental questions of whether an orphan would be better off in an institution or with a foster family. Again, she regretted that various institutions such as kindergartens, schools, and children's hospitals influence the child's development without having any knowledge in areas other than their own speciality.[3]

In the summer of 1966, the Sixth International Congress for Child Psychiatry took place in Edinburgh, where on July 25 Anna Freud gave a lecture on puberty, an old subject for her, on which she was able to offer new points of view.[4] The 1966 lecture series did not end here. Anna Freud went again to the United States—it was her tenth trip to America—where, on December 21, she spoke on "The Ideal Psychoanalytic Institute: A Utopia"[5] at the Chicago Institute for Psychoanalysis. It was Heinz Kohut who had prompted the trip and the subject. They had long ago developed an amicable professional relationship within the International Psychoanalytic Association that lasted over many years. His works on narcissistic neuroses, relatively remote from her own interests, always met with her recognition.

The Twenty-fifth International Psychoanalytic Congress took place in Copenhagen from July 23 to July 28, 1967. Its subject was "acting out"—the "living out" of infantile wishes and feelings—and it has entered history as the acting-out congress. It is again symptomatic of the period that even in Germany the English equivalent of the term is now better understood than the Freudian term "agieren." As usual, Anna Freud was an active participant. She opened the congress with a lecture in accordance with the program, "Acting Out"[6]—an exemplary lecture if we view Anna Freud as the executor of an unspoiled psychoanalytic theory. She discussed all the aspects of acting versus speaking in therapy. Yet undertones of concern could be detected, because some analysts increasingly dismissed free association and dream interpretation as the route to the unconscious in favor of the repetition and reexperiencing of old emotional situations. A few years earlier, Anna Freud had already noticed that analysts who had set too high psychotherapeutic goals had sobered up somewhat. At the same time she alluded to the many faddish psychotherapies, such as primal scream or Gestalt therapy, psychoanalysts often turned to out of disappointment.

Anna Freud also participated in two roundtable discussions at the congress. The business sessions addressed membership fees, which increased slightly every two years. Anna Freud gave a rather long speech in favor of a single drastic hike in fees that would cover all expenses. Her proposal was accepted and the fee, set at $20, did not have to be raised for several years.[7]

In April 1968, Anna Freud again went on an American lecture tour. On Freud's one hundred twelfth birthday, she gave the eighteenth Freud Anniversary Lecture at the New York Psychoanalytic Institute.[8]

Nineteen sixty-eight was the year of student unrest which, insofar as it was directed against parents, always met with Anna Freud's understanding. But for its forms—in particular its violence—she had no word of pardon.

In what may be one of her most significant lectures, Anna Freud used the opportunity to share her thoughts on the future of psychoanalysis with a large audience. At the last two international congresses, had already alluded to her concern about the future. One can see that the concerns she showed at seventy-three, developed on the basis of her experience of life, embraced psychoanalysis in general and child psychoanalysis in particular.

Oddly enough, some wanted to detect "orthodoxy" in Anna Freud precisely on the basis of this lecture. If orthodoxy is tantamount to intellectual rigidity, this lecture is exactly the opposite, since she criticized certain tendencies within psycho-analysis with unusual frankness. Then she again discussed changes within psycho-analysis, by now far beyond its pioneering stage. Desirable contacts with psychiatry, medicine, education, psychology, ethology, sociology, and law had developed and had enticed many an analyst away from his original profession. The ever-increasing number of dynamic psychotherapies derived from psychoanalysis not only suggested to the patient that the same results could be achieved with less energy and in a shorter period, but also fostered a belief in analysts that they no longer needed the patience, perseverance, and asceticism that were once expected of them.

Anna Freud perceived dangers for psychoanalysis precisely in its international success, which she should have, after all, been proud of. She believed that both the infusion of classical academic social sciences with psychoanalytic theories and the more recent dynamic therapies that had strongly enhanced the popularity of psy-choanalysis entailed in crucial areas the risks of dilution on the one hand and of orthodoxy on the other.

Anna Freud pointed to the potential problems resulting from the difference between those drawn to psychoanalysis today and those who had responded to it in the past. During the pioneering period of psychoanalysis, mainly unconventional types and skeptics dissatisfied with official science—but also eccentrics, dreamers, and even neurotics—were attracted to psychoanalysis. Now it was the passionless, industrious type inclined to objectivity, but also to abstraction, who volunteered to be a training candidate. Rebellious adolescents no longer found an outlet in psycho-analysis, which, being in the hands of their parents' generation, was already sus-pect. Psychoanalysis was no longer an adventure, nor could it be a means of social protest, sanctioned as it was by society. Because psychoanalysis encouraged the individual to conform to social conditions, young people sensed in it a threat to their originality and revolutionary spirit. Psychoanalysis thus lost an essentially vitalizing element. In 1970, Anna Freud very severely censured the "rigidity, conservatism, and bureaucracy" of psychoanalytic organizations,[9] which denied access to many valuable candidates interested in psychoanalysis. Finally, she criticized a theoretical point of view concerning the developmental significance of the first year of life which had recently gained a large number of followers:

> Departing from this position [Freud's remarks on the prehistory of the Oedipus complex], a considerable cross-section of the psychoanalytic community today pins their faith on the analysis of the first year of life, with the purpose of therapeutically modifying the impact of the earliest happenings. Freud's discovery that every neurosis of the adult is preceded by an infantile neurosis and that the latter has to be analyzed before the former can be reached, is paraphrased by them as follows: every infantile neurosis in the oedipal period is preceded by fateful interactions between infant and mother in the very first days and months of life, and it is this archaic, preverbal phase which has to be revived in the transference and analyzed before later infantile neurosis can be approached effectively. This view is held today by many analysts of otherwise widely divergent opinions.[10]

The reader will easily recognize here some of Melanie Klein's thoughts, which Anna Freud had already contended with in her first book. Along with Klein, she also mentioned René Spitz, D. W. Winnicott, and Herbert Rosenfeld. More clearly than ever, Anna Freud pointed to the difficulties, problems, and dangers the analysis of the preverbal stage raises. She warned against the "almost magical" idea that the analysand is able to revert to the "prepsychological, undifferentiated, and unstructured state, in which no divisions exist between body and mind or self and object."[11] In such ideas—inaccessible to scientific and rational methods, yet adamantly held—Anna Freud correctly perceived a problem for the future of psychoanalysis.

Anna Freud spent most of this trip in New Haven. She spoke at a seminar on family law[12] and received another honorary doctorate in law from Yale, one of the most venerated universities of the world.[13] Finally, on April 21, at the third congress of the American Association for Child Psychoanalysis in New Haven, she spoke on "Indications and Contraindications for Child Analysis."[14]

During Anna Freud's sojourn in the United States, James Strachey died in England in April 1967. Anna Freud dedicated a brief obituary to him, in which she concentrated on his merits as the translator of Freud's works into English, a task to which he devoted twelve years of his life.[15]

The Twenty-sixth International Psychoanalytic Congress was held in Rome from July 27 to August 1, 1969. It was the first such congress since Anna Freud's youth that she did not attend. With her approval, it was decided at this congress to hold the next meeting in Vienna. Anna Freud had not set foot in her homeland since her emigration—still, a psychoanalytic congress in Vienna without her would have been unthinkable.

In April 1970, Anna Freud came to the United States for the twelfth time, again to New Haven. [16] On June 27, she lectured in Geneva before the European Psychoanalytic Federation, again raising issues that would not be resolved in her lifetime. [17] What would become of child psychoanalysis? She decried the general situation in this area—not without an undertone of resignation. The assumption had once been that adult analysts would be eager not only to reconstruct these developmental stages in adult analysis but also to expand their knowledge through indirect observation of the various developmental stages and their disturbances in children. Just as child analysts have to familiarize themselves with the problems of adults, every adult analyst needs the knowledge provided by child analysis. This procedure has not been followed, however. Adult analysts have shown hardly any interest in child analysis, and—in England at least—the time that child analysts devote to child analysis is not even counted as a training period in psychoanalysis.

Too much in child analysis is bound up in the person of Anna Freud! Despite the aforementioned difficulties, there were also positive aspects to report. Anna Freud was able to point to half a dozen training sites: there was Tavistock, with its own training institute, in London; training courses had been established in Leiden and Amsterdam; child therapists could be trained in Cleveland, Ohio; and in New York City there was the Child Development Center. As a multiregional organization, the American Association for Child Analysis represented important interests. Furthermore, Serge Lebovici and René Diatkine were working as child therapists in Paris. D. W. Winnicott, however, who achieved recognition with Kleinian analysis, withdrew from organized training (he died in 1971).

Return to Vienna

For the first time in the history of psychoanalysis, an International Psychoanalytic Congress, the twenty-seventh, took place in Vienna, on July 25–30, 1971. Oddly, this historically significant meeting owes its renown to the frivolous bestseller *Fear of Flying*, by Erica Jong, [1] which begins on the Pan Am flight that brought 117 American psychoanalysts to Vienna. Though much could be said on this subject, neither the novel nor its first-person narrator will be interpreted analytically here. But the novel's success can be viewed as a symbol for the gold that literature has so often washed out of the sand of psychoanalysis.

After thirty-two years of exile, Anna Freud, now almost seventy-five, again set foot on Austrian soil. She did not reveal what feelings the return home stirred in her; what she said in the business sessions and the closing lecture spoke for itself.

On the occasion of this congress, an exhibit, including photography, was opened in Freud's old apartment at 19 Berggasse, transforming it into a museum. Not too long before, there had still been a desolate air about the apartment; nevertheless, psychoanalysts from all over the world had visited it again and again. Henri Ellenberger reported on his visit there on August 24, 1957.[2] A sullen young woman, smoking a cigarette, reluctantly answered the bell and showed him through a partitioned apartment where nothing reminiscent of the past remained. Now, at last, the city of Vienna saw the necessity of doing something for its banished son and his equally banished daughter.

In the business sessions, Anna Freud spoke in detail about the apartment at 19 Berggasse, suggesting appropriate uses for the rooms. In what was perhaps the longest speech she had ever given in a business session, she disclosed her concern for the continued existence of psychoanalysis beyond her own lifetime. She asked for donations, because the stair hall was in a deplorable state, even though the apartment itself had been renovated. She encouraged making the exhibit permanent and enlarging it, given the available bare walls. Her chief request: She wanted to see a comprehensive psychoanalytic library established, with a reading room and a loan program for students. Toward this aim, she proposed that all writers of psychoanalytic books and articles donate a signed copy of their work to the library; it was the same proposal she had once made in the Berggasse apartment before her emigration. Finally, she suggested that the museum be used as an international meeting place for psychoanalysts, anticipating at the same time that the rooms that were once spacious enough for the entire psychoanalytic world could now accommodate only a negligible part of it.

At her suggestion, the Freud family donated to the museum the furniture from Freud's waiting room, where the Wednesday Society once convened. The family later bequeathed all dispensable psychoanalytic books to the Vienna library. It is noteworthy that at the same congress K. R. Eissler, in his capacity as secretary of the Sigmund Freud Archives in New York, announced that the Freud family, at Anna Freud's behest, had donated over twenty-five hundred of Freud's letters to the archives, among them the "engagement letters" and the "travel letters," and that these had been placed in the Library of Congress in Washington. Here, too, we see that the center of gravity of psychoanalysis had shifted to the United States.

Anna Freud closed the Vienna congress with a detailed paper on its main topic, aggression.[3] We may assume that this subject had been deliberately chosen because the Freud family had been forced to escape Nazi aggression in 1938. Yet perhaps no one among those engaged daily with the psyche's hidden symbolism thought of such superficial symbolism. At any event, Anna Freud did not discuss thoughts and feelings about aggression related to her own life. Still, in the opening sentences of her lecture, spoken in German, she alluded to the deeply personal significance of her return home:

Since I arrived in Vienna, many have asked me what such a return feels like. Personal feelings are not appropriate at a public occasion, but thoughts on analysis are relevant. And so I only want to say briefly that my return to Vienna has reawakened my thoughts about my work here: the building of our clinical and theoretical institute, work for the city of Vienna under the kindergarten and elementary-school inspector Tesarek, my work with Aichhorn for the city of Vienna at the Juvenile Counseling Center. One thing is difficult to imagine: if we hadn't been interrupted by the political events, if we had continued building on the same beginnings, where would psychoanalysis be in Vienna today?[4]

She delivered her paper in English. After a rigorous analysis of all facets of the problematic concept of aggression, she turned to the subject of death and dying. A manuscript by K. R. Eissler, "Death Drive, Ambivalence, and Narcissism," had inspired her. She quoted Eissler's remark based on Schopenhauer and Freud that death is one of the most important events in a person's life and that every psychological system worthy of the name must therefore allocate to death an important place in its theoretical edifice.[5] She herself recalled R. M. Rilke, the poet of her youth and friend of her friend Lou Andreas-Salomé. Rilke, she said, saw the evolution toward death as the meaning of life. Without quoting him literally, she found the meaning of Rilke's statements embedded in *The Notebooks of Malte Laurids Brigge*[6] and in "The Book on Poverty and Death," Book III of *The Book of Hours.*[7]

In this hour of recollections, then, she revealed her deep familiarity with the poet of her youth and with his views on death. As she spoke, examples from child psychoanalysis came to mind. She remembered children with a neurotic fear of death who, experiencing the process of growing up and getting older as steps toward death, were reluctant to grow up. In the next sentences she compared the libido, as the life- and self-preservation instinct, with aggression, which is most powerfully expressed in the death instinct. She found that both instincts are always fused, and for the purpose of study their respective actions have to be disentangled. Anna Freud closed the lecture and the congress with the statement that, on this higher plane, death could not be attained except by way of the vicissitudes of life.

Anna Freud's return to her home at the age of seventy-five closed a circle of her life, though many tasks still lay ahead of her.

The next year, Anna Freud visited Vienna again. This time, on May 26, she was awarded her first honorary doctorate in medicine, by the medical faculty of the University of Vienna, where her father had once been a member. Here more than ever before, Sigmund Freud's inclusion in the award was indubitable; the Viennese psychoanalyst Hans Strotzka, who had promoted the award, spoke in his encomium of a "symbolic act."

Anna Freud herself showed full awareness of the situation. After the melody of "Gaudeamus Igitur" had faded away, she said:

Academic honors and distinctions cannot be inherited in this world. Yet this rule notwithstanding, I feel—and I am not the only one—that today I have inherited my father's share in the University of Vienna: his promotion to doctor of general medicine in 1881, to university lecturer in 1885, his nomination as Professor Emeritus in 1902. I am entering upon a legacy which I feel has become ever larger in the course of years. What I promise today to the University of Vienna, besides my deep gratitude, is that I will never use the title M.D. without the *honoris causa*, not only to prevent misunderstandings, but also to remember always the honor granted to me today.[8]

The medical faculty questioned whether Anna Freud was ready for this symbolic act and as a precaution had asked her whether she would accept the award. After all, she was to be honored officially by a city that had imposed the most humiliating exile on both her and her family. Surely one could not forget how many Jewish citizens were never able to see their native Vienna again because they had been gassed in death camps. It was thus no pompous statement, common on such occasions, when Hans Strotzka emphasized that the medical faculty also felt honored by the permission to award the honor to Anna Freud.

At the end of the award ceremonies, a long line of congratulators formed in front of Anna Freud, eager to shake hands and exchange a few words with her. In the crowd also stood Gertrud Hollstein, Anna Freud's friend from her schooldays and three years her senior.

While waiting, the friend reminisced: From 1909 to 1912 they had both been students at the Cottage Lyceum, inseparable friends who shared and discussed everything. Either Gertrud—or, as Anna used to call her, Trude—came daily to Berggasse, or Anna went to her house on Gymnasiumgasse. Trude proved herself above all as a listener. When they sat at the desk in Anna's room, Anna reading aloud from her large notebook the continuation of the endless family story, external reality vanished for both girls. And even if Trude was sometimes slightly bored, she always admired her friend's spellbinding imagination. Professor Freud also came in frequently during his "academic quarter"—the ten minutes between sessions—and quietly exchanged a few words with the girls. Trude remembered that the Freuds spoke so softly at home that they almost whispered.

Gertrud Hollstein then recalled the days preceding the outbreak of World War I, when Anna was about to take her first trip to England. For many days the girls were not only busy meticulously arranging everything; they also drew up an exact inventory of every personal belonging—each pencil, each trifle—as if the thought had already occurred to Anna that she might have to remain in England forever.

In 1912, after they graduated from high school, their relationship slowly became less close, because life had begun to separate them. While Trude went on to study social work at a special school, Anna became a teacher.

Immediately after World War II, new contact was made between the two through August Aichhorn, which later turned out to be infelicitous for Gertrud.

She had gone with Aichhorn to Oberhollabrunn to investigate whether the evacuated barracks could be useful. Aichhorn very naturally took her arm—even today, half a century later, she could feel his hand under her naked arm. She, who had always shunned men, gladly accepted Aichhorn's gesture and became his closest colleague in Oberhollabrunn. Later she also helped him write his book *Wayward Youth*, since he was not used to writing and at the beginning found it difficult to formulate his thoughts on paper. It was she who told Aichhorn about psychoanalysis and who tried to persuade Anna Freud to check on the conditions in St. Andrä. Anna Freud finally came, was excited about the work, and formed a close professional and personal relationship with Aichhorn. Later, Gertrud Hollstein's relationship to Aichhorn and Anna Freud became less and less close. Gertrud finally married and had to take care of her own family. After she became a widow in 1944, she and Aichhorn resumed their old friendship. When she heard that Anna Freud had mentioned Aichhorn in the first sentences of her lecture at the International Psychoanalytic Congress in Vienna a year earlier, she remembered something else: After World War II, she had written a long letter to her friend, in which she had revealed all her affectionate feelings and memories. She had let Aichhorn read the letter before he traveled to Switzerland to meet Anna Freud and to deliver the letter. Since she received no answer, she wondered whether the letter ever reached her. At any event, she had not sought contact with her school friend since. Now, however, since the newspapers were full of Anna Freud's arrival in Vienna, she came to the celebration with a small nosegay in early Victorian style. When Anna Freud entered the hall, surrounded by university and state dignitaries, Gertrud Hollstein tried in vain to discover something in her features that would remind her of her old friend. It was—in the first moment—a complete stranger who was being honored here. But while Anna Freud was speaking, Gertrud Hollstein noticed a feature of the chin, a certain movement, which she—and probably no one else present—was able to recall. For her, Anna Freud's entire person regained its earlier nature. As she now stood close to her and heard her speak, Anna Freud was, oddly, both strange and familiar. Finally, she was able to hand her the flowers and exchange a few words of greeting. Outside, she thought she remembered that Anna Freud had said, "Why didn't you let me hear from you?" and "Write to me." But already she no longer knew whether it had been wishful thinking or reality, whether she had indeed heard the words or only imagined them. It also became clear to her how much the decades had separated her from this woman who was now honored by the entire world. Thus, she decided against writing. Past and present had met only for a brief moment.[9]

In the old lecture hall of the psychiatric clinic that she had once entered on the arm of her father, Anna Freud used the occasion of the award to speak before medical students and to argue with them. During the discussion, one of the students, probably still under the influence of the student movement of the late 1960's which had insisted foremost on the realization of social ideals, asked about the direct connection between neuroses and economics. Even today attempts are being made to demonstrate from various perspectives that the capitalist economic system necessarily causes illness, hence also neurotic behavior. Such thoughts were alien to Anna Freud, and that is why her reply unexpectedly focused on the economic aspects of the psychic apparatus, a much more significant point of view in psychoanalytic theory.[10]

Conclusion

With Anna Freud's return to Vienna, the two parts of her life and work met again, and her thoughts on this occasion ventured into both past and future. She now well deserves to be integrated into the intellectual history of the twentieth century. How important is she?

There is first the question of Anna Freud's tradition and her handling of it. Was she a traditionalist? Was she an "idealist"? Was she a great female figure? An imitator? Her father's obedient daughter?

I think Anna Freud herself gave us the key to understand her. We have already mentioned the lecture she gave at the Chicago Institute for Psychoanalysis on December 21, 1966, entitled "The Ideal Psychoanalytic Institute: A Utopia." In her introduction, she remarked that Heinz Kohut was in fact responsible for the title. Had it been her choice, the title would have been: "My Own View of What a Psychoanalytic Institute Ought to Be." To explain this apparently trifling distinction, she returned to her own childhood:

> At the age before independent reading, when children are read to or told stories, my interest was restricted to those which "might be true." This did not mean that they had to be true stories in the ordinary sense of the word, but that they were supposed not to contain elements which precluded their happening in reality. As soon as animals began to talk, or fairies and witches, or ghosts to appear—in short, in the face of any unrealistic or supernatural element—my attention flagged and disappeared. To my own surprise, I have not altered much in this respect.[1]

Despite this explanation, Anna Freud allowed the word "utopia" to remain in the title although it was no doubt in her power to change it. This shows how well Heinz Kohut knew Anna Freud, since he was able to win her over to the lecture, its title, and its explanation. Realism and utopia *both* remained determinant concepts for Anna Freud, the former visibly, the latter in the background.

Anna Freud can easily be labeled a realist, since she always made an effort to provide rational explanations and to elevate everything to the level of consciousness and speech. The irrational, the vague, and the obscure—of necessity connected with interest in preverbal developmental stages—were not only entirely alien to her theory, but her innermost being was equally averse to them. Her concern had always been to illuminate the dark, to explain the apparently abstruse, to comprehend the incomprehensible. Others, particularly some of her opponents, found precisely the obscure attractive and lost interest in the irrational as soon as reason penetrated it. Even more, they often wanted to muddle what was already clear. This "clarté" has always been viewed as a trait of the gallic spirit, and some have even claimed that Anna Freud cannot be included in the German cultural tradition. But this description is pertinent only to the last century and in particular to Hitler's gloomy mystical ideology. Today the opposite is true. One finds in the German tradition more clarity than in the French, where currently the obscure (for example, structuralism) exerts an increasing power of attraction, even in psychoanalysis. Note, for example, the almost untranslatable, intentionally obscure writings of Lacan, with whom Anna Freud once argued. Those who label Anna Freud a realist are, as she herself would have agreed, correct.

But it is noteworthy that rationality is attributed to a human being who as a woman dedicated the major part of her life to the welfare of children. It is precisely such women that our culture does not expect to be primarily rational. In this sense, Anna Freud represents something feminists strive for: independent in her thinking, independent of men, she was respected and esteemed by men and women alike. Yet no feminist can invoke her as an example, for she was far from their aspirations. She never attempted to compete with men, but never lost their respect. And her intimate contact with children notwithstanding, she refused to be honored as the "great mother." She remained "Miss Freud."

But can the rational alone be responsible for the strength and perseverance with which she maintained an incredibly high standard of achievement into very old age? It is never reason that moves mountains. Indeed, such strength can flow only from the irrational. Throughout her entire life, Anna Freud worked on a utopia: the realization and perfection of a comprehensive theory capable of explaining the psyche. A utopia, because Anna Freud never claimed it was attainable, and because experience informs us that we can at best make efforts toward it. But how can one approximate an unfamiliar phenomenon? Our efforts can spawn only a concise explanation of *familiar* psychic symptoms by means of a theory—in this case psychoanalysis—that determines what is to be viewed as a symptom. The theory's strength thus aims at the explanation of the inexplicable. That is why the idealist in Anna Freud is probably more important than the realist in her. Yet she professed ideals only to the extent that these are attainable.

That Anna Freud's ideals were bound up with psychoanalysis has never been doubted. For a long time psychoanalysis has also operated as an ideology; as such, it won enthusiastic followers and bitter enemies, results that are actually related. Anna Freud was the first to recognize and admit that the waning powers of psychoanalysis were responsible for the decrease in the number of its enemies.

Within psychoanalysis, however, she did not merely expand her father's work or continue it as a follower. Her own creation was a psychoanalysis for children. Despite her own objections, there was neither before her nor contemporaneous with her a comparable system. Of course, there were a few observations, a few remarks. But we mean something else here. Next to the already extant adult psychoanalysis, Anna Freud provided a self-sufficient theory of the child's normal and disturbed psyche. Were one to disagree with Anna Freud, only a theory offering more satisfactory explanations of observed phenomena could compete with hers.

From Anna Freud's psychoanalytic theory of the child, a distinct therapy—a psychotherapeutic technique—is logically derived, which can be learned and successfully applied. Such a congruence between the theory and therapy of the child's psyche can be found nowhere—not in Sigmund Freud and not even in Piaget, with whom Anna Freud cannot be compared for various reasons.

Finally, Anna Freud created, even if late in life, the organizational instrument that ensured the persistence of theory and therapy, of research and action beyond her lifetime. This purpose is served by the Hampstead Child Therapy Course and Clinic, as well as by the *Bulletin of the Hampstead Clinic*, which has appeared since 1978 as a journal alongside *The Psychoanalytic Study of the Child*.

The International Psychoanalytic Association, whose honorary president Anna Freud was for decades, also deserves mention. Anna Freud resembled her father in a quality that was not very conspicuous in her. Far from making superficial and vacuous comparisons, we refer here to her organizational gift, which for many decades enabled her very delicately to guide an international organization whose members are known to be difficult and self-willed, and whose cohesion she still symbolizes, much like her father. Only her organizational gift she put entirely (or almost entirely) in the service of the paternal legacy, interfering perhaps with the dissemination of her own ideas. She was, in this sense, entirely a daughter, not a son. It is very instructive in this situation to visualize the daily life that Anna Freud imposed upon herself when she was over eighty years old, an age in which almost every other person would prefer to lead a life of leisure. She continued to live in 20 Maresfield Gardens, the only house Freud ever purchased but which gained significance only through his daughter, a significance comparable to that of Berggasse 19.

Anna Freud continued to dedicate several hours of the day to single analyses, between which she had small meals, always under the care of Paula Fichtl. Between and even during her meals, she made various telephone calls. Visitors from all over the world came—not always well-wishers—who invariably met with a friendly reception. In the evening, and sometimes during the day, she sat at her typewriter answering letters, often on the history of psychoanalysis, and seldom did she let people wait very long for an answer.

Freud's literary estate had to be managed. Accused of deliberately withholding one thing or another, it was here she encountered the sharpest animosities. Nevertheless, many of those who tried to profit financially from the high publicity value of psychoanalysis attest to having enjoyed her support. At times she misplaced her trust. Throughout the world, there was no end to the honors she continued to receive, nor to the lectures she was invited to give. In 1975, the Austrian ambassador in London awarded her the Merit Insignia of the Republic of Austria; in 1978 she was awarded an honorary doctorate by Columbia University in New York. In May 1978, Anna Freud traveled to Vienna for the third time, to deliver the Freud Anniversary Lecture on Freud's one hundred twenty-second birthday.

Eventually, in 1981, when she could no longer travel because of her health—she suffered frequently from dilatation of the bronches which led to pneumonic ailments—she was awarded an honorary doctorate by the University of Frankfurt. In her last years, Anna Freud developed a fundamentally new concept of child psychoanalysis which she, however, could no longer apply herself. The future of psychoanalysis, so she imagined, would focus not so much on the child's developmental stages and their failures or premature arrest, as on each separate developmental path leading the child into adulthood—that is, on the child's evolution from total dependence on the mother to independent adulthood, the development of infantile anxiety into adult control of anxiety and of bodily functions, the unfolding of health consciousness and of the care of one's own body, and the development of the capacity for camaraderie and friendship. Here Anna Freud separated herself from Aichhorn; and at the end of her life she also moved beyond Freud's Darwinistic stage approach to sexuality, without, however, intending to challenge it in principle.[2]

In the end, we are allowed to ask what would have happened had Anna Freud stayed in Vienna, had her life evolved according to her original plan, within the context of German culture and language. We see at once that this question is inseparable from another question: What course would the larger developments have taken had Anna Freud and the other psychoanalysts been able to remain in Germany and Austria? One thing is certain: Problems and schisms within the psychoanalytic movement would have arisen anyway. Ultimately, however, the question cannot be answered without surmising what would have happened if Hitler and the National Socialists had not come to power. Here such a question clearly becomes absurd: History is irreversible and cannot be transformed into a "What if?"

Actually, a strange paradox developed. Although Anna Freud, who lived in London, was only a few minutes' flying time from the German cultural sphere, she became so unreachable in a kind of mystical distance from the German consciousness that no one dared to confer honor and acclaim on her. For the reader who only spoke German, the major part of her work remained inaccessible for a long time. The situation was the other way around for the English reader: the second phase of Anna Freud's life became very familiar to him. Her work was accessible, she was always visible, and the media frequently reported about her. Her fluency in the English language made her German background appear insignificant and remote. In short, she appeared close, real, and English, with a distant Austrian background.

Anna Freud is a clear example, as are so many others, that Hitler not only brought immense suffering on Europe, but that he damaged Germany most of all. Although Anna Freud was honored like almost no other emigrant, she remains a symbol of a hard fate that is at once Austrian, German, psychoanalytic, and Jewish.

Notes

Common abbreviations have been used for familiar texts from the Freud literature.

Sigmund Freud, *The Complete Psychological Works: Standard Edition*, 24 vols., ed. and trans. James Strachey in collaboration with Anna Freud, assisted by Alix Strachey and Alan Tysson (New York: W. W. Norton, 1976). Cited: *Standard Edition*.
Ernest Jones, *The Life and Work of Sigmund Freud*, 3 vols. (New York: Basic Books, 1953–57). Cited: *Jones*.
Max Schur, *Living and Dying* (New York: International Universities Press, 1972). Cited: *Schur*.
Anna Freud, *The Writings of Anna Freud*, 8 vols. (New York: International Universities Press, 1965–81). Cited: *Writings*.

Freud's published correspondence is quoted from the following texts:

Sigmund Freud, *Briefe 1873–1939* ["Letters 1873–1939"] (2d ed.; Frankfurt: S. Fischer, 1968). Cited: *Briefe*.
Sigmund Freud, *The Letters of Sigmund Freud*, ed. Ernst L. Freud, trans. Tania and James Stern (New York: Basic Books, 1966). Cited: *Letters*.
The Letters of Sigmund Freud and Arnold Zweig, ed. Ernst L. Freud, trans. Elaine and William Robson-Scott (New York: Harcourt Brace Jovanovich, 1970). Cited: *Zweig*.
The Sigmund Freud and Lou Andreas-Salomé Letters, ed. Ernst Pfeiffer, trans. William and Elaine Robson-Scott (New York: Harcourt Brace Jovanovich, 1972). Cited: *Andreas-Salomé*.
Sigmund Freud, *The Origins of Psycho-Analysis: Letters to Wilhelm Fliess, Drafts and Notes, 1887–1902*, ed. Marie Bonaparte, Anna Freud, and Ernst Kris, trans. Eric Mosbacher and James Strachey (New York: Basic Books, 1954). Cited: *Fliess*.
A Psycho-Analytic Dialogue: The Letters of Sigmund Freud and Karl Abraham, 1907–1926, ed. Hilda C. Abraham and Ernst L. Freud, trans. Bernard Marsch and Hilda C. Abraham (New York: Basic Books, 1966). Cited: *Abraham*.
The Freud/Jung Letters, ed. William McGuire, trans. Ralph Manheim and R. F. C. Hull (Princeton: Princeton University Press, 1974). Cited *Freud/Jung*.
Psychoanalysis and Faith: The Letters of Sigmund Freud and Oskar Pfister, ed. Heinrich Meng and Ernst L. Freud, trans. Eric Mosbacher (New York: Basic Books, 1963). Cited *Pfister*.

For many of the references, I am grateful to my colleagues in the research seminar on the history of the emigration movement of German-speaking psychiatrists, 1933–38, which I held in Mainz from 1971 to 1978. This seminar inspired a large number of dissertations. For numerous references I am especially grateful to Roland Besser and his dissertation, "Leben and Werk von Anna Freud" ["The Life and Work of Anna Freud"] (Mainz, 1976).

Preface to the English-language Edition

1. Raymond Dyer, *Her Father's Daughter: The Work of Anna Freud* (New York: Aronson, 1983).
2. *The Freud Journal of Lou Andreas-Salomé*, trans. Stanley A. Leavy (New York: Basic Books, 1964).

Preface

1. Arnold Rogow, *The Psychiatrists* (New York: G. P. Putnam's Sons, 1970), p. 109.
2. Freud to Roy Winn, cited in *Jones*, III, 179.

1895, The Year of Anna Freud's Birth

1. *Standard Edition*, vol. II.
2. *Standard Edition*, vols. IV–V.
3. Anna Freud refutes this: "Sophie was never my father's 'favorite daughter.' In the beginning it was rather my sister Mathilde who had the closest relationship to him." (Communication to the author.) Freud's relationship to his eldest daughter has in fact never been investigated closely enough. She had hardly anything to do with psychoanalysis. But she had an extraordinary practical sense and was socially adept, and hence a valuable member of the psychoanalytic organization. With each of his daughters, Freud had a totally different relationship.
4. *Fliess*, December 3, 1895, p. 136.
5. Communication to the author.
6. Lucy Freeman, *The Story of Anna O.* (New York: Walker, 1972).
7. *Standard Edition*, vols. VIII, VI.

Vienna, 1895

1. E. Stransky, "Aus einem Gelehrtenleben um die Jahrhundertwende: Rückschau, Ausblick, Gedanken" ["A Pundit's Life around the Turn of the Century: Review, Outlook, Reflections"]. The manuscript is in the archives of the Institute for the History of Medicine of the University of Vienna, catalogue number 2065.
2. *Ibid.*
3. Jonathan Miller, ed., *Freud: The Man, His World, His Influence* (Boston: Little, Brown, 1972).
4. Hermann Bahr, *Ver Sacrum*, No. 1, January 1898.
5. Cf. Christian M. Nebenhay, *Gustav Klimt. Sein Leben nach zeitgenössischen Berichten und Quellen* ["Gustav Klimt: His Life from Contemporary Reports and Sources"] (Munich: Deutscher Taschenbuch Verlag, 1976).
6. "Psychoanalysis and Libido Theory," *Standard Edition*, XVIII, 242. Cf. also Martin Grotjahn, *The Language of the Symbol* (Los Angeles: Mara Books, 1971).
7. Cf. Johanne Peters, ed., *Alexander Blok* (Mainz: Hase und Koehler, 1972), and *Symbole der sinnlichen Wahrnehmung im lyrischen Werk A. A. Bloks* ["Symbols of Sensuous Perception in the Lyrical Work of A. A. Blok"] (Kiehl: Diss, 1968).

Childhood and Youth

1. The German includes two words for "strawberry," one of them the dialectical *Hochbeere*.
2. "Dreams as Wish Fulfillments," *Standard Edition*, IV, 130.
3. *Standard Edition*, V, 643–44.
4. *Ibid.*, XV, 132.
5. *Letters*, August 20, 1898, p. 238.
6. *Fliess*, August 1, 1899, p. 289.
7. *Ibid.*, January 16, 1899, p. 274.
8. *Ibid.*, June 27, 1899, p. 284.
9. *Ibid.*, July 3, 1899, p. 284.
10. Anna Freud: "I never attended an upper elementary school for the middle class, only elementary school." (Communication to the author.) The statements made here about her school attendance are based on written information from the Austrian Federal Ministry for Education and Art, on the basis of available information. It must therefore remain moot whether the documents of the Ministry for Education are incorrect or whether Anna Freud's memory failed her.
11. Communication to the author.
12. *Writings*, VI, 102. "Regression as a Principle in Mental Development," *Bulletin of the Menninger Clinic*, XXVII (1963), 126–39; a variation appears in *Writings*, VI, 93–107.
13. *Jones*, II, 55.

14. Communication to the author from Anna Freud.
15. *Letters*, November 28, 1912, pp. 293–94.
16. *Ibid.*, December 13, 1912, pp. 294–95.
17. Hugo Heller's son, Thomas Heller, now owns a bookstore in New York.
18. *Standard Edition*, vol. XII.
19. *Pfister*, March 11, 1913, p. 61.
20. Quoted in *Jones*, II, p. 93. In a letter Freud wrote on the same day to his daughter Sophie, he also mentions the engagement (*Letters*, p. 289).
21. *Letters*, July 9, 1913, p. 301.

Cordelia and Antigone

1. *Standard Edition*, XII, 301.
2. "Lear carries Cordelia's dead body on to the stage. Cordelia is Death. If we reverse the situation it becomes intelligible and familiar to us.—She is the Death-goddess who, like the Valkyrie in German mythology, carries away the dead hero from the battlefield." *Ibid.*
3. I. Grubrich-Simitis, ed., *Sigmund Freud. Das Motiv der Kästchenwahl* ["Sigmund Freud: The Theme of the Three Caskets"]. Facsimile edition, with an afterword by Heinz Politzer (Frankfurt: S. Fischer, 1977), p. 62.
4. See the letter to Ferenczi of October 12, 1928: "Many cordial greetings to you as well as to Frau Gisella, also from my faithful Antigone—Anna." *Letters*, p. 382. To Arnold Zweig, May 2, 1935: "Even supported by my devoted Anna–Antigone I could not embark on a journey." *Letters*, p. 224.
5. Communication from Mrs. Gertrud Hollstein, February 7, 1979.
6. Henrich Heine, *Poetry and Prose*, ed. Jost Herman and Robert C. Holub, trans. Louis Untermeyer (New York: Continuum, 1982). When I first wrote this book, I did not know that the song's text was by Heine. The source in which I found it did not name Heine as the lyricist. Several letters have since made me aware of the fact. This information was also taken up by some reviews, which did not skimp on caustic remarks and even flourished into suspicions of anit-Semitic malevolence. With deep regret I acknowledge the gaps in my classical education. But I am somewhat exonerated in that neither Anna Freud nor Gertrud Baderle knew that Heine was the poet in question, and even some of my philologist friends—mostly students of German philology—to whom I had shown the text did not draw my attention to the error. The reason must obviously be sought in the fact that one does not expect, or refuses to acknowledge, patriotic—even martial—tones in Heine's work.
7. This statement was made by Gertrud Baderle Hollstein. She recalls that the "professional talks" were held during the school year and at Lake Garda. According to Jones, the Freud family stayed at Lake Garda in 1909 while Freud was lecturing in America. It is possible that Freud did in fact visit his family at Lake Garda for several days after returning from America at the end of September 1909. Another possible date is the summer of 1912, which the entire family spent at Lake Carezza (Karer), after Anna Freud had graduated from high school, but this is less likely.
8. "A Form of Altruism," *Writings*, II, 123–27.
9. *Jones*, II, 99.
10. *Jones*, II, 173; *Schur*, p. 290.

The Beginning of World War I

1. *Jones*, II, 173.
2. *Letters*, p. 305.
3. Excerpt from a letter to the author from Heinrich Otte of Vienna, July 16, 1979.
4. Communication to the author from Dr. Gerda Schöler Borotha, February 6, 1979.
5. Communication to the author.
6. This photograph was kindly made available by Mrs. Etta Neumann.
7. The entry of June 16, 1922, in Schnitzler's diary points to this. I am grateful to Dr. Bernd Urban for showing me this entry and to Dr. Heinrich Schnitzler of Vienna for permission to cite it.
8. "The Role of the Teacher," *Harvard Educational Review*, XXII (1952), 229–34; "Answering Teachers' Questions," *Writings*, IV, 560–68.
9. *Writings*, V, 512.

10. *Andreas-Salomé,* p. 28.
11. Helene Deutsch, *Confrontations with Myself: An Epilogue* (New York: W. W. Norton, 1973), p. 142.
12. *Briefe,* s. 324–326.
13. *Writings,* V, 511.
14. "I . . . have never given up my academic post, but have continued with it for thirty-two years, and finally gave up my voluntary lectures in 1918." *Pfister,* p. 95.

Ward Rounds at the Vienna Psychiatric Clinic

1. "Doctoral Award Address" (1967), *Writings,* V, 507–16. The speech was given on June 12, 1964, but not published until later.
2. K. L. Kahlbaum, *Die Gruppierung der psychischen Krankheiten und die Einteilung der Seelenstörungen* ["The Classification of Psychic Illnesses and Emotional Disturbances"] (Danzig: Kafemann, 1863).
3. Anna Freud confirmed this in a detailed talk with the author and repeated her position in a letter.
4. Frank J. Sulloway, *Freud, Biologist of the Mind: Beyond the Psychoanalytic Legend* (New York: Basic Books, 1979).
5. *Standard Edition,* XIX, 215.
6. *Ibid.*
7. *Writings,* V, 512.
8. Paul Schilder, *Introduction to a Psychoanalytic Psychiatry,* trans. Bernard Glueck (1928; New York: International Universities Press, 1951).
9. Communication to the author.
10. Heinz Hartmann, *Ego Psychology and the Problem of Adaptation* (1939; New York: International Universities Press, 1958).
11. "Links Between Hartmann's Ego Psychology and the Child Analyst's Thinking," in R. M. Loewenstein, L. M. Newman, M. Schur, and A. J. Solnit, eds., *Psychoanalysis—A General Psychology: Essays in Honor of Heinz Hartmann* (New York: International Universities Press, 1966), pp. 16–27; *Writings,* V, 204–20.
12. Anna Freud, *The Ego and the Mechanisms of Defense* (1936; rev. ed. 1966), *Writings,* II.
13. For the biography of Heinz Hartmann, see Rudolph M. Loewenstein, "Heinz Hartmann, Psychology of the Ego," in F. Alexander, S. Eisenstein, and M. Grotjahn, eds. *Psychoanalytic Pioneers* (New York: Basic Books, 1966), p. 469; R. M. Loewenstein *et al.,* eds., *op. cit;* Anna Freud, "Heinz Hartmann, A Tribute," *Writings,* V, 499–501; R. Schafer, "An Overview of Heinz Hartmann's Contributions to Psychoanalysis," *International Journal of Psychoanalysis,* LI (1970), 425; S. Lebovici, "Heinz Hartmann. Nécrologie," *Revue Française de Psychanalyse,* XXXV (1971), 191–95.

Training Analysis and the Postwar Period

1. Paul Roazen, *Freud and His Followers* (New York: Alfred A. Knopf, 1971).
2. *Jones,* II, 32.
3. Herman Nunberg, *Memoirs, Recollections, Ideas, Reflections* (New York: The Psychoanalytic Research and Development Fund, 1970), p. 35.
4. Edoardo Weiss, *Sigmund Freud as a Consultant: Recollections of a Pioneer in Psychoanalysis* (New York: Intercontinental Medical Book Corp., 1970), November 1, 1935, p. 81.
5. "The Problem of Training Analysis," *Writings,* IV, 421.
6. Cf. also Wolf von Eckardt and Sander L. Gilman, *Bertolt Brecht's Berlin: A Scrapbook of the Twenties* (Garden City, N.Y.: Doubleday/Anchor, 1975).
7. Unpublished letter to Max Eitingon of October 12, 1919.
8. *Letters,* December 2, 1919, p. 325.
9. *Briefe,* May 16, 1920.
10. *Letters,* February 4, 1920, p. 328.
11. Communication to the author from Anna Freud.
12. *Jones,* III, 27.

First Independent Works

1. Julien Varendonck, *The Psychology of Daydreams* (New York: Macmillan, 1921). Anna Freud's translation: *Über das vorbewusste phantasierende Denken* ["On Preconscious Fantasy Thought"] (Leipzig: Internationaler Psychoanalytischer Verlag, 1922).
2. "Beating Fantasies and Daydreams" (1922), *International Journal of Psychoanalysis*, IV (1923), 89–102; *Writings*, I, 137–57.

Lou Andreas-Salomé

1. *Andreas-Salomé*, August 28, 1917, p. 62.
2. *Ibid.*, August 2, 1920, p. 105.
3. *Ibid.*, September 6, 1920.
4. *Ibid.*, September 13, 1921, p. 108.
5. *Ibid.*, October 20, 1921, p. 109.
6. The description is based on the account of the visit in Andreas-Salomé's diary (see below). Anna Freud wrote to the author that there never was a servant called Fräulein Betti.
7. Cf. Rudolph Binyon, *Frau Lou, Neitzsche's Wayward Disciple* (Princeton: Princeton University Press, 1968). The richest source for such frequently pertinent remarks is the works of Lou Andreas-Salomé herself, particularly *The Freud Journal of Lou Andreas-Salomé*, trans. Stanley A. Leavy (New York: Basic Books, 1964), and *Lebensrückblick* ["Retrospect"] (Frankfurt: Insel Verlag, 1968). Cf. also H. F. Peters, *My Sister, My Spouse: A Biography of Lou Andreas-Salomé* (New York: W. W. Norton, 1974).
8. Lou Andreas-Salomé, *Friedrich Nietzsche in seinen Werken* ["Friedrich Nietzsche in His Works"] (Vienna, 1894).
9. Lou Andreas-Salomé, *Mein Dank an Freud* ["My Gratitude to Freud"] (Vienna: Internationaler Psychoanalytischer Verlag, 1931) and *The Freud Journal of Lou Andreas-Salomé*.
10. Edith Weigert told the author that Lou Andreas-Salomé introduced a peculiar variation of the psychoanalytic technique. She herself lay down on the couch and had her analysand sit in the chair behind her. Others who knew her well confirm that this technique is consistent with her nature.
11. We find the following entries in Schnitzler's diary: "December 7, 1921: Dress rehearsal. . . . Lou Salomé and Miss Freud were also present." "December 15, 1921: Dinner with Frau Lou Salomé and Miss Freud." I am grateful to Dr. Bernd Urban for showing me these entries and to Dr. Heinrich Schnitzler for permission to quote them.
12. *Standard Edition*, XVII, 175–204.
13. *Andreas-Salomé*, July 20, 1920, p. 103.
14. *The Freud Journal of Lou Andreas-Salomé*.
15. "Schlagephantasie und Tagtraum," *Imago*, VIII (1922), 317.
16. *Berggasse 19: Sigmund Freud's Home and Offices, Vienna 1938. The Photographs of Edmund Engelman* (New York: Basic Books, 1976).
17. Communication to the author from Anna Freud.
18. Rudolph Binion writes about this: "Freud worried over this youngest child of his because of her father fixation, the more since he on his side was as much stuck on her as on his cigars. He looked to Lou hopefully to help him, tear him loose. Lou would not: she deemed Anna's incestuous setup more blissful than any alternative within normalcy." Binion, *op. cit.*, pp. 372–73n.
19. Freud to Ernst and Lucie Freud, *Letters*, p. 336.
20. Letter of December 10, 1973, to the author from Hans Lobner.
21. Freud to Andreas-Salomé, *Andreas-Salomé*, September 8, 1922, p. 118, and her undated letter, probably several days later, p. 119.
22. Andreas-Salomé to Freud, *Andreas-Salomé*, September 3, 1924, p. 138.
23. Abraham Kardiner, *My Analysis with Freud: Reminiscences* (New York: W. W. Norton, 1977).

Lecture at the Society

1. *Writings*, I, 149.
2. A. Lorenzer, *Sprachzerstörung und Rekonstrucktion* ["The Destruction and Reconstruction of Language"] (Frankfurt: Suhrkamp, 1970).
3. *Andreas-Salomé*, p. 122.

4. *Ibid.*, June 26, 1922, p. 115.
5. *Ibid.*, July 3, 1922, p. 117.
6. *Jones*, III, 86.

Beginning an Independent Practice

1. *Writings*, V, 513–14.
2. *Schur*, p. 89. The quotation is from *Jones*, III, 91.
3. *Jones*, III, 93.
4. *Andreas-Salomé*, p. 233, n. 160.
5. *Ibid.*, September 4, 1923, p. 126.
6. Freud to Eitingon, September 26, 1923, in *Jones*, III, 94.
7. Quoted with the generous permission of Dr. Heinrich Schnitzler. I am again grateful to Dr. Bernd Urban for showing me this entry.
8. *Imago*, IX (1923), 264–65; *Writings*, I, 158–61.

The Beginnings of Child Psychoanalysis

1. *Pfister*, p. 91.
2. *Jones*, III, 96.
3. R. Fülöp-Miller and F. Eckstein, eds., *The Diary of Dostoyevsky's Wife*, trans. Madge Pemberton (1925; New York: Macmillan, 1928).
4. J. Lavrin, *Lev Tolstoj* ["Leo Tolstoy"] (Hamburg: Rowohlt, 1961).
5. Robert Byck, ed., *The Cocaine Papers of Sigmund Freud*, Notes by Anna Freud (New York: New American Library, 1974).
6. "A Short History of Child Analysis" (1964), *The Psychoanalytic Study of the Child*, XXI (1966), 7; *Writings*, VII, 49.
7. "Child Analysis as a Subspecialty of Psychoanalysis," *Writings*, VII, 209.
8. *International Journal of Psychoanalysis*, VI (1925), 106.
9. Hermine Hug-Hellmuth, ed., *A Young Girl's Diary*, Prefaced with a letter by Sigmund Freud, trans. Eden and Cedar Paul (1919; New York: T. Seltzer, 1921).
10. Cyril Burt, in his review of the English edition of *A Young Girl's Diary*, *British Journal of Psychology*, II (1921), 353–57. Hermine Hug-Hellmuth replied with a letter (*ibid.*, p. 257) in which she guaranteed that the book was authentic (i.e., unrevised) but did not touch on the imputation of authorship. In his reply to this letter, Burt reported on further correspondence (*ibid.*, pp. 255–58) in which Hug-Hellmuth had made matters rather more suspect by claiming that the diary's original was lost, that only her own copy of it was available, and that the author of the "diary" was inaccessible.
11. Hermine Hug-Hellmuth, "Vom wahren Wesen der Kinderseele. Das Kind und seine Vorstellung vom Tode" ["On the True Nature of the Child's Soul: The Child and His Idea of Death"], *Imago*, I (1912), 268–98; "Über erste Kindheitserinnerungen" ["On First Childhood Recollections"], *ibid.*, II (1913), 78–89, 513–36; "Inderbriefe" ["Indian Letters"], *ibid.*, III (1914), 462–76; "Vom frühen Lieben und Hassen" ["Early Love and Hate"], *ibid.*, V (1917), 121–22; "Vom 'mittleren' Kinde" ["The 'Middle' Child"], *ibid.*, VII (1921), 84–94.
12. Accounts can be found in the *Neue Freie Presse*, September 9 and 10, 1924; the *Illustrierte Kronen-Zeitung*, September 11, 12, and 14, 1924; the *Deutschösterreichische Tages-Zeitung*, September 10, 1924.
13. First and foremost in the lecture "Zur Technik der Kinderanalyse" ["The Technique of Child Analysis"], *Internationale Zeitschrift für Psychoanalyse*, VII (1920), 179–97; also in *A Study of the Mental Life of the Child*, trans. James J. Putnam and Mabel Stevens (1913; New York: Johnson Reprint, 1970). In other writings, she described the child's psyche primarily from the psychoanalytic point of view or gave reports on child psychology: *Neue Wege zum Verständnis der Jugend. Psychoanalytische Vorlesungen für Eltern, Lehrer, Erzieher, Kindergärtnerinnen* ["New Paths to Understanding Adolescents: Psychoanalytical Lectures for Parents, Teachers, Educators, Kindergarten Teachers"] (Leipzig and Vienna: F. Deuticke, 1924); Hug-Hellmuth's working methods are clearly described here.
14. *Deutsch, op. cit.*, p. 161.
15. *Die neue Jugend und die Frauen* (Vienna: Kamönenverlag, 1914); "Die Psychoanalyse in der Jugendbewegung," *Imago*, V (1919), 283–89.

16. Bernfeld reported on the work of the kindergarten under his direction: *Kinderheim Baumgarten. Bericht über einen ernsthaften Versuch mit neuer Erziehung* ["The Baumgarten Nursery: Report on a Serious Attempt at a New Education"] (Berlin: Jüdischer Verlag, 1921).

17. *Ibid.*

18. "Willie Hoffer, M.D., Ph.D.," *The Psychoanalytic Study of the Child*, XXIII (1968), 7–9.

19. Bernfeld's most important publications on the adolescent question: "Das Archiv für Jugendkultur" ["The Archive for Youth Culture"], *Der Anfang*, 1913, pp. 51–54; "Ein Archiv für Jugendkultur" ["An Archive for Youth Culture"], *Zeitschrift für angewandte Psychologie*, 1914, pp. 373–76; "Ein Institut für Psychologie und Soziologie der Jugend" ["An Institute for Adolescent Psychology and Sociology"], *Annalen der Naturphilosophie*, XIII (1920), 217–51; *Kinderheim Baumgarten, op. cit.*; *Die neue Jugend und die Frauen, op. cit.*; "Die Psychoanalyse in der Jugendbewegung," *op. cit.*; "Über Schülervereine" ["Student Associations"], *Zeitschrift für angewandte Psychologie*, XI (1916), 167–213.

20. Ada Müller-Braunschweig, "Ein Fall von Schattenangst und Fragezwang (bei einem dreijährigen Knaben)" ["A Case of Fear of Shadows and Compulsive Question-asking (on the Part of a Three-Year-Old Child)"], *Zeitschrift für Psychoanalytische Pädagogik*, IV (1930), 134–45; "Zur Psychoanalyse des stotternden Kindes" ["The Psychoanalysis of Children Who Stammer"], *Neue Erziehung*, 1928, pp. 10 f.

21. Brief obituary by Willie Hoffer in the *Internationale Zeitschrift für ärztliche Psychoanalyse*, XXV (1940), 102–3. Cf. also Alice Balint, *La mère et l'enfant* ["Mother and Child"] (Budapest: Pantheon, 1941); "Die mexicanische Kriegshieroglyphe atl-Tlachinolli" ["The Mexican War Hieroglyphs at Tlanchinol"], *Imago*, IX (1923), 401–36.

22. *Freud/Jung*, March 5, 1908, p. 130.

23. "Ein Fall von multipler Perversion mit hysterischen Absenzen" ["A Case of Multiple Perversion with Fits"], in *Jahrbuch für psychopathologische und psychoanalytische Forschungen* (Leipzig and Vienna: F. Deuticke, 1919), II, 1st half, 59; "Über Urethralerotik" ["Urethral Eroticism"], *ibid.*, 2d half, p. 409.

24. *Freud/Jung*, February 2, 1910, p. 291.

25. Isidor Sadger, "Über Prüfungen und Prüfungsträume" ["Tests and Test Dreams"], *Internationale Zeitschrift für Psychoanalyse*, VI (1920), 140–50; *Über Schülerselbstmord (Diskussion des Wiener Psychoanalytischen Vereins)* ["Student Suicide (Discussion of the Vienna Psychoanalytic Society)"] (Wiesbaden: Bergmann, 1910); "Aus den Sexualleben eines Jungen vom vierten bis achtzehnten Lebensmonat" ["From the Sexual Life of a Boy Between Four and Eighteen Months Old"], *Zeitschrift für Psychoanalytische Pädagogik*, III (1929), 127–30; "Vom ungeliebten Kinde" ["The Unloved Child"], *Fortschritte der Medezin*, 1916, p. 34; "Zum Verständniss infantiler Angstzustände" ["Understanding Infantile States of Anxiety"], *Internationale Zeitschrift für Psychoanalyse*, III (1915), 101–5; "Verstehen wir die Liebe unserer Kinder?" ["Do We Understand the Love of Our Children?"], *Zeitschrift für Psychoanalytische Pädagogik*, III (1928), 318–22.

26. On Berta Bornstein and her work, cf. *The Psychoanalytic Study of the Child*, XXIX (1974), 1–40. A bibliography of her works is included there. The significant contribution, "The Analysis of a Phobic Child: Some Problems of Theory and Technique in Child Analysis," was published in *ibid.*, III/IV (1949), 181–226.

27. The main work of Maria Montessori (1870–1952) was published under the title *The Montessori Method* (1909; rev. ed. New York: Schocken Books, 1964). Interest in the Montessori method is again on the rise. Cf. also J. E. Standing, *Maria Montessori, Leben und Werk* ["Maria Montessori: Her Life and Work"] (Stuttgart, 1959); E. M. Standing, *The Montessori Revolution in Education* (New York: Schocken Books, 1966); Paula Lillard, *Montessori: A Modern Approach* (New York: Schocken Books, 1972); Mario M. Montessori, *Education for Human Development: Understanding Montessori*, ed. Paula Lillard (New York: Schocken Books, 1976).

28. Translated from the Italian by Anne E. George (New York: Schocken Books, 1964).

29. *Letters*, December 20, 1917, pp. 319–20.

30. Anna Freud, introduction to Rita Kramer, *Maria Montessori, Leben und Werk einer grossen Frau* ["Maria Montessori: The Life and Work of a Great Woman"] (Munich: Kindler Verlag, 1977).

31. "Psychoanalysis and the Upbringing of the Young Child" (1934), *Writings*, I, 180.

1925

1. *Internationale Zeitschrift für Psychoanalyse*, XI (1925), 522.

2. *Ibid.*, p. 254.

3. *Andreas-Salomé*, September 2, 1925, p. 160. Anna Freud refuted this statement, which was based on Andreas-Salomé's letter: "This paragraph is entirely incomprehensible to me; I don't know where this information comes from. Neither Robert Hollitscher nor Eva Rosenfeld had anything to do with Munich, nor did Siegfried Bernfeld. I think the entire thing is a misunderstanding" (communication to the author).

Yet Andreas-Salomé's letter from Munich and Hanover, dated September 2, 1925, in which she described the events, is explicit: "This is just a first quick word from here. I arrived in Munich two hours ago, but in my thoughts I was really still with you among your mountains, my heart full of gratitude for these long-anticipated weeks. As we left the station—in our princely first-class compartment—the big moon, now almost full, looked at us in all its magic beauty, which you for your part cannot have seen as we did on your way home—a perception which in view of my own defective bump of locality I owed solely to Anna's regretful assurance that this was the case; just as to my great pleasure she kept pointing out the Schüler Villa or the Südbahn Hotel, although this seemed to me to be a sort of magic trick, giving the whole countryside a familiar look, as if it would accompany me all the way to Germany and as far as Göttingen.

"So we still had two happy hours together, and arrived three-quarters of an hour late in [Munich], in an indescribable mêlée due to school excursion trains filled with sick children. Despite all this your son-in-law managed to fish us out with the skill of a boy scout, and took us to Frau Eva R[osenfeld]'s, where we were joined by Dr. Bernfeld and had a very pleasant time. After this, cruel fate separated Anna and me at the station" (*Andreas-Salomé*, p. 160).

4. *Standard Edition*, XIX, 248–58.
5. Freud to Karl Abraham, *Abraham*, September 11, 1925, p. 395.
6. *Ibid.*, September 8, 1925, p. 394.
7. "Karl Abraham," *Standard Edition*, XX, 277–78.

Freud at Seventy

1. *Letters*, May 10, 1926, p. 369.
2. *Andreas-Salomé*, May 13, 1926, p. 162.
3. *Abraham*, July 21, 1925, p. 390.
4. Freud to Andreas-Salomé, *Letters*, May 13, 1926, p. 163.

Introduction to the Technique of Child Analysis

1. *Einführung in die Technik der Kinderanalyse* (Vienna: Kindler Verlag, 1927); included in *Writings*, I, as "Four Lectures on Child Analysis."
2. Cf. Martin Grotjahn, "Freuds klassische Fälle" ["Freud's Classic Cases"], in *Psychologie des 20. Jahrhunderts* ["Psychology of the Twentieth Century"], ed. D. Eicke, vol. II: *Freud und die Folgen* ["Freud and the Consequences"] (Zurich: Kindler Verlag, 1976), 147.
3. *Writings*, V, 514.
4. Communication to the author.
5. *Writings*, I, 8–9, 27, 28–29, 33–34, 41–43, 61–65, 167–69.

Anna Freud's Theory of Child Analysis

1. "Child Analysis as a Subspeciality of Psychoanalysis," *Writings*, VII, 213–14.
2. *Writings*, I, 11.
3. *Ibid.*, pp. 12–13.
4. *Ibid.*, p. 13.
5. *Ibid.*, p. 30.
6. *Ibid.*, p. 44.
7. *Ibid.*
8. *Ibid.*, p. 46.
9. *Ibid.*
10. *Ibid.*, p. 65.
11. Anna Freud did not make a sharp distinction between superego and ego ideal in this context.
12. *Writings*, I, 172.

13. *Ibid.*, p. 61.
14. *Zeitschrift für Psychoanalytische Pädagogik*, I (1927), 279.
15. *Internationale Zeitschrift für Psychoanalyse*, XIV (1928), 540–46. It is interesting for the historian that Radó inserted in his review his own comments concerning the problem of narcissistic personality disturbances, which was to become topical only several decades later: "In the material on patients from the Technical Colloquium led by the lecturer at the Berlin Psychoanalytic Polyclinic, cases whose nature was difficult to determine (character disturbances, schizoidism, etc.) and whose common trait was severe infantile helplessness and social dependence came to the foreground at the expense of the increasingly rare transference neuroses." Since about 1970, this finding has become a frequent scientific commonplace which has finally acquired what was felt to be a valid scientific dimension in the work of Heinz Kohut: *The Analysis of Self: A Systematic Approach to the Psychoanalytic Treatment of Narcissistic Personality Disorders* (New York: International Universities Press, 1971); *The Restoration of the Self* (New York: International Universities Press, 1977).

Melanie Klein

1. I have used the following sources: A. J. Lindon, "Melanie Klein, 1882–1960: Her View of the Unconscious," in F. Alexander, S. Eisenstein, and M. Grotjahn, *Psychoanalytic Pioneers* (New York: Basic Books, 1960), pp. 360–72; Elisabeth R. Zetzel, "Melanie Klein" (obituary), *Psychoanalytic Quarterly*, 1961, pp. 420–25; W. R. Bion, H. Rosenfeld, and H. Segal, "Melanie Klein" (obituary), *International Journal of Psychoanalysis*, XXXXII (1961), 4–8; Willie Hoffer, "Melanie Klein" (obituary), *ibid.*, pp. 1–3; "Melanie Klein," in *International Encyclopedia of the Social Sciences*, ed. David L. Sills (New York: Macmillan, 1968); "Mrs. Melanie Klein: Exploring the Child's Mind," obituary in *The Times* (London), September 23, 1960. I am grateful to Mr. Eric Clyne of London for further information.
2. Birth certificate issued by the Jewish Bureau for Cultural Affairs, Vienna, 2709 [1882].
3. Melitta Schmideberg, "A Contribution to the History of the Psychoanalytic Movement in Britain," *British Journal of Psychiatry*, CXVIII (1971), 61–68.
4. Information to the author from Eric Clyne.
5. "Der Familienroman in statu nascendi," *Internationale Zeitschrift für Psychoanalyse*, VI (1920), 151–55. Willie Hoffer is therefore mistaken in his obituary when he refers to "The Development of a Child" (1921; *International Journal of Psychoanalysis*, IV [1923]) as Klein's first publication.
6. In *New Directions in Psycho-Analysis*, edited by Melanie Klein, Paul Heimann, and R. Money-Kyrle (London: Tavistock, 1955), p. 4.
7. *Ibid.*, p. 6.
8. See note 3, above.
9. "Zur Genese des Tics," *Internationale Zeitschrift für Psychoanalyse*, XI (1925).
10. "The Psychological Principles of Infant Analysis" (*International Journal of Psychoanalysis*, VIII [1928]) was expanded to become "The Psychological Foundations of Child Analysis," Chapter 1 of *The Psychoanalysis of Children*, trans. Alix Strachey (1932; rev. ed. New York: Dell/Delacorte, 1975).
11. *Ibid.*, p. 55, n. 1.
12. A note in Klein, Heimann, and Money-Kyrle, *op. cit.*, p. 3, n. 3, states: "A description of this early approach [play technique] is given in Anna Freud's book *Einführung in die Technik der Kinderanalyse.*"
13. *Writings*, I, 37.
14. *Ibid.*, pp. 37–38.
15. *Ibid.*, pp. 38–39.
16. *The Psychoanalysis of Children*, pp. 37, 38.
17. *International Journal of Psychoanalysis*, VII (1926), 31–63; Klein, *Contributions to Psychoanalysis 1921–1945* (1948; New York: McGraw-Hill, 1964), pp. 87–116.
18. *International Journal of Psychoanalysis*, VII (1926), 62.

The London Anti–Anna Freud Symposium

1. Communication to the author.
2. "Symposium on Child Analysis: Melanie Klein," *International Journal of Psychoanalysis*, VIII (1927), 370.
3. Ella Sharpe in *ibid.*, p. 374: "The problem of child analysis seems more subtly implicated with the

analyst's own deepest unexplored repressions than adult analyses. Rationalizations that the child is too young, that the weakness of the child's super-ego makes an admixture of pedagogy with analysis indispensable, and so on, are built upon the alarms of that very same infantile super-ego in the analyst that he has to deal with in the child before him. That infantile 'super-ego' in the last resort becomes the dictator in the situation between analyst, child and parent, and only so far as that deepest level is analyzed in the analyst can we look for scientific accuracy in the matter of child analysis."

4. Cited by Otto Fenichel, *Internationale Zeitschrift für Psychoanalyse*, XIV (1928), 559.

5. In the correspondence between Freud and Jung, it is more often Jung who depicts Jones's character with caustic words. But Freud also alludes to this in his sparse comments on Jones. Freud writes on May 3, 1908: "Jones is undoubtedly a very interesting and worthy man, but he gives me a feeling of, I was almost going to say racial strangeness. He is a fanatic and doesn't eat enough. . . . How, with your moderation, were you able to get on with him?" (*Freud/Jung*, p. 145).

Jung on July 12, 1908: "Jones is an enigma to me. He is so incomprehensible that it's quite uncanny. Is there more in him than meets the eye, or nothing at all? At any rate he is far from simple; an intellectual liar (no moral judgment intended!) hammered by the vicissitudes of fate and circumstance into too many facets. But the result? Too much adulation on one side, too much opportunism on the other?" (*ibid.*, p. 164).

Finally, Jung on March 7, 1909: "By nature [Jones] is not a prophet, nor a herald of the truth, but a compromiser with occasional bendings of conscience that can put off his friends. Whether he is any worse than that I don't know but hardly think so, though the interior of Africa is better known to me than his sexuality" (*ibid.*, p. 208).

On the basis of later historical developments, one tends perhaps to believe Jung less. But Freud too writes on February 24, 1909: "From Jones and about him I have received very strange news and I am in very much the same situation as you when he was with [Emil] Kraepelin" (*ibid.*, p. 206). Kraepelin only scorned and ridiculed Freud's works. On May 17, 1910, Freud writes: "Jones himself is making up for last year's ambiguities with indefatigable zeal, great skill and, I was going to say, humility" (*ibid.*, p. 317).

6. Klein developed these ideas only in 1928 in "Early Stages of the Oedipus Conflict," *International Journal of Psychoanalysis*, IX (1928), 167–80. But the London discussion already contained an unequivocal indication; cf. *ibid.*, VIII (1927), 352: "The analysis of very young children has shown me that even a three-year-old child has left behind him the most important part of the development of the Oedipus complex. Consequently he is already far removed, through repression and feelings of guilt, from the objects whom he originally desired. His relations to them have undergone distortion so that the present love objects are now *imagos* of the original objects."

Ernest Jones's Role in Child Psychoanalysis

1. *Jones*, III, 197.
2. Communication to the author from Melitta Schmideberg.
3. *Jones*, III, 197.
4. *Ibid.*, p. 137.
5. *Writings*, VIII, 349–50.
6. *Ibid.*, p. 351.
7. *Ibid.*, pp. 352–53.

Psychoanalysis and Education

1. *Zeitschrift für Psychoanalytische Pädagogik*, 1st year, 1927, Information for Readers.
2. *Ibid.*, I (1926/27), 1.
3. Heinrich Meng, *Leben als Begegnung* ["Life as Encounter"] (Stuttgart: Hippokrates Verlag, 1971).
4. *Psyche*, XXV (1971), 728.
5. 1931; New York: Emerson Books, 1935; *Writings*, I, Part II.
6. *Writings*, IV, 260–79.
7. *Ibid.*, I, 110.
8. *Ibid.*, pp. 94–95.
9. *Ibid.*, p. 94.
10. *Ibid.*, p. 125.
11. *Ibid.*, p. 126.

12. Aichhorn, *Wayward Youth* (1925; New York: Viking, 1935).
13. *Writings*, I, 128.
14. *Ibid.*

Lay Analysis and the Scope of Psychoanalysis

1. *Standard Edition*, XXI, 161–66.
2. *Writings*, I, 162–75.
3. The government of West Germany has been preparing a Psychotherapy Law for years, which will legally regulate the field of lay therapy.
4. *Standard Edition*, XX, 183–251.
5. Alexander and Margarete Mitscherlich, *The Inability to Mourn: Principles of Collective Behavior*, trans. Beverley R. Placzek (New York: Grove Press, 1975).
6. *Standard Edition*, XX, 230.
7. Jones, "Diskussion der Laienanalyse" ["Discussion of Lay Analysis"], *Internationale Zeitschrift für Psychoanalyse*, XIII (1927), 169–92.
8. *Standard Edition*, XX, 246.
9. Jones, "Besprechung von Freuds Buch *Die Frage der Laienanalyse*. Unterredungen mit einem Unparteiischen" ["Review of Freud's *The Question of Lay Analysis*: Discussions with an Impartial Person"], *Internationale Zeitschrift für Psychoanalyse*, XIII (1927), 101–7. The *International Journal of Psychoanalysis*, VIII (1927), 174 ff., contains a comprehensive discussion by twenty-eight leading psychoanalysts in which all the arguments are repeated.
10. *Jones*, III, 201.
11. *Ibid.*, pp. 288–90.
12. *Ibid.*, p. 295.
13. Max Eitingon, "Bericht über die Berliner Psychoanalytische Poliklinik" ["Report on the Berlin Psychoanalytic Polyclinic"], *Internationale Zeitschrift für Psychoanalyse*, X (1924), 229–40.
14. Eitingon, "Sitzung der internationalen Unterrichtskommission" ["Session of the International Training Commission"], *ibid.*, XIII (1927), 480–81.
15. "Laienanalyse" ["Lay Analysis"], *ibid.*, pp. 324 f.
16. *Jones*, III, 295–96.

A Calm Year

1. *Jones*, III, 139.
2. To Ernest Simmel, *Letters*, November 11, 1928, pp. 382–83:
"Dear Dr. Simmel,
"You are right. Once upon a time these rings were a privilege and a mark distinguishing a group of men who were united in their devotion to psychoanalysis, who had promised to watch its development as a 'secret committee,' and to practice among themselves a kind of analytical brotherhood. Rank then broke the magic spell; his secession and Abraham's death dissolved the Committee.
"When on leaving Tegel I expressed the desire to acknowledge by a token the quite extraordinary kindness with which you managed to transform for me a time of personal difficulty into a time of comfort, my daughter suggested that I renew the old custom with you. And indeed, apart from my personal indebtedness to you, I don't know anyone in Berlin who, by the purity and intensity of his allegiance, would be more worthy of inclusion in that circle—if it still existed.
"Forms may pass away, but their meaning can survive them and seek to express themselves in other forms. So please don't be disturbed by the fact that this ring signifies a regression to something that no longer exists, and wear it for many years as a memory of your cordially devoted
"Freud"
3. *Internationale Zeitschrift für Psychoanalyse*, XV (1929), 366.

The Frankfurt Psychoanalytic Institute

1. *Pfister*, p. 128.
2. Nelly Wolfheim, "Aus den Anfängen der Kinderanalyse und der psychoanalytischen Pädagogik" ["The Beginnings of Child Analysis and Psychoanalytical Education"], *Psyche*, V (1951/52), 310–15.

3. It seems doubtful whether Erich Fromm should be numbered among the founders of the Frankfurt Psychoanalytic Institute, as Rainer Funk claims, since his name is nowhere mentioned in Karl Landauer's reports. Cf. Funk, *Erich Fromm: The Courage to Be Human* (New York: Continuum, 1982).

4. For a history of the Institute for Social Research, see Martin Jay, *The Dialectical Imagination: A History of the Frankfurt School and the Institute for Social Research, 1923–1950* (Boston: Little, Brown, 1973).

5. *International Journal of Psychoanalysis*, XI (1930), 246 ff.

6. Quoted in Eva Laible, "Anna Freud und die Entwicklung der Psychoanalyse" ["Anna Freud and the Development of Psychoanalysis"], in *Jahrbuch der Psychoanalyse* ["Yearbook of Psychoanalysis"] (Bern: H. Huber, 1978), X, 41–62.

7. *Frankfurter Zeitung*, 1929; *Abendblatt*, February 25, 1929; *Für Hochschule und Jugend*, No. 150, p. 5.

8. *Frankfurter Zeitung*, November 3, 1929, p. 6.

9. Jones reports (III, 145) that, in addition to Eitingon, Lou Andreas-Salomé visited Freud in Vienna for his birthday. But this is an error, due perhaps to a linguistic misunderstanding. Two days prior to Freud's birthday, Andreas-Salomé spoke of "a little *letter-visit* for the day after tomorrow." Five days later, Freud began his reply, "Many thanks for your birthday *visit*," and then explained that he could thus—in writing—converse much better with her than verbally, as during the Tegel visit (*Andreas-Salomé*, p. 179).

10. *Andreas-Salomé*, May 4, 1929, pp. 177–79.

11. Freud to Andreas-Salomé, *ibid.*, May 9, 1929, p. 145.

12. Anna Freud's report on her own lecture, in *Internationale Zeitschrift für Psychoanalyse*, XV (1929), 518.

13. *The Freud Journal of Lou Andreas-Salomé*, July 28, 1929.

14. During her vacation in July, Anna Freud wrote to Andreas-Salomé, "Papa is writing something" (*Andreas-Salomé*, p. 181).

15. Max Schur reported on his treatment in *Schur*.

The Goethe Prize for Sigmund Freud

1. Jones also writes that the idea was Paquet's, but adds that Alfred Döblin was also of assistance, obviously without being sure that this was the writer Alfred Döblin, since he describes him as an "analytically oriented psychiatrist" (*Jones*, II, 151). This is actually not true. Döblin spent his early medical career in a country hospital as a physician for internal and nervous diseases—a neurologist showing distinctly German influences. But on Freud's seventieth birthday, Döblin gave one of the main lectures before the German Psychoanalytic Society in Berlin; altogether, he had a positive attitude toward Freud. In 1956, when he informed the German translator of the Jones biography how the Goethe Prize came about, Döblin himself was already suffering from Parkinson's Disease (he was then staying at the Quisisana Sanatorium in Baden-Baden), to which he succumbed in 1957.

2. A report on the granting of the prize, including the addresses, can be found in the *Frankfurter Zeitung*, August 29, 1930, morning edition, pp. 1–2. "Träger der Goethepreises der Stadt Frankfurt am Main im Speigel der Zeit von 1927–1932," *Berichte der Stadt Frankfurt* (Frankfurt: Verlag August Osterreith, 1963) also draws essentially on the *Frankfurter Zeitung* report. The most detailed account can be found in Heinrich Meng, *op. cit.*, pp. 78 ff.

3. *Standard Edition*, XX, 73.

4. *Jones*, September 15, 1930, III, 152.

5. The reference here is obviously to euthanasia (*Andreas-Salomé*, p. 189).

Dorothy Burlingham

1. Ludwig Binswanger, *Sigmund Freud: Reminiscences of a Friendship*, trans. Norbert Guterman (New York: Grune & Stratton, 1957), p. 88.

2. *Andreas-Salomé*, p. 238, n. 218.

3. *Letters*, p. 411.

4. Helene Deutsch, *op. cit.*, p. 142.

5. Dorothy Burlingham made numerous contributions to the psychoanalytical literature, the following in collaboration with Anna Freud: *Young Children in Wartime: A Year's Work in a Residential War*

Nursery (1942), Writings, III, Part I, and Infants Without Families: The Case For and Against Residential Nurseries (1944), Writings, III, Part II.

6. For example, father and daughter had each written a letter to Andreas-Salomé on October 22, 1930.

The Shadows of the Future

1. Max Eitingon and Anna Freud, "Kongress" ["Congress"], Internationale Zeitschrift für Psychoanalyse, XVII (1931), 419.

2. Anna Freud, "Berich über den XII. Internationalen Psychoanalytischen Kongress" ["Report on the Twelfth International Psychoanalytic Congress"], ibid., XIX (1933), 246.

3. C. P. Oberndorf, A History of Psychoanalysis in America (New York: Grune & Stratton, 1953).

4. Internationale Zeitschrift für Psychoanalyse, XIX (1933), 256.

5. "The Psychoanalysis of the Child," in C. Murchison, ed., A Handbook of Child Psychology (Worcester, Mass.: Clark University Press, 1931), pp. 555–67.

6. "Erzieher und Neurosis," Zeitschrift für Psychoanalytische Pädagogik, VI (1932), 393–402.

7. Ibid., p. 398.

8. Ibid., p. 399.

9. Die Psychoanalyse des Kindes (Vienna: Internationaler Psychoanalytischer Verlag, 1932); The Psychoanalysis of Children, op. cit.

10. Franz Alexander's review of Klein's book in Internationale Zeitschrift für Psychoanalyse, XIX (1933), 219–26.

1933, Germany's Fateful Year

1. On the centennial of Paul Federn's birth, his son Ernst Federn tried to put his father in the correct historical perspective, since the latter's merits had not received their due honor: Ernst Federn, "Fünfunddreissig Jahre mit Freud" ["Thirty-five Years with Freud"], Psyche, XXV (1971), 721–37. Yet Federn's great worth lay in areas other than organization.

2. Jones, III, 175.

3. Thomas Mann, Tagebücher 1933–1934 ["Diaries, 1933–1934"] (Frankfurt: S. Fischer, 1977).

4. Jones, III, 182. June 10, 1933.

The Lucerne Congress

1. Jones, III, 191.

2. This description essentially follows David Boadella, Wilhelm Reich: The Evolution of His Work (Chicago: H. Regnery, 1974).

3. M. Higgins and C. M. Raphael, eds., Reich Speaks of Freud (New York: Noonday Press, 1967). The German version, evidently a verbatim transcription of a taped interview conducted in German and later translated by Therese Pol into English, was published in 1969 under the title Wilhelm Reich über Sigmund Freud ["Wilhelm Reich on Sigmund Freud"] as a pirated edition without indicating publisher or place.

4. Writings, I, 176–88.

The Ego and the Mechanisms of Defense

1. Chapter 2 of The Ego and the Mechanisms of Defense, Writings, II, 11–27.

2. Zweig, February 13, 1935, p. 102.

3. Andreas-Salomé, January 6, 1935, p. 204.

4. Jones, III, 208.

5. Ludwig Eidelberg, Take Off Your Mask (New York: International Universities Press, 1948); Eidelberg, ed., The Encyclopedia of Psychoanalysis (New York: Free Press, 1968).

6. Jones, III, 199.

7. Eidelberg, "Zum Studium des Versprechens," Imago, XXII (1936), 196–202; "A Contribution to the Study of Slips of the Tongue," International Journal of Psychoanalysis, XVII (1936), 462–70. The

subject became so significant for Eidelberg that he returned to it again and again: "A Further Contribution to the Study of Slips of the Tongue," *ibid.*, XLI (1960), 596–603.

8. *Standard Edition*, XX, 45–61.

9. On the historical development of the concept of defense, see P. J. van der Leeuv, "On the Development of the Concept of Defense," *International Journal of Psychoanalysis*, LII (1971), 51–57; J. D. Lichtenberg, "On the Defensive Organization," *ibid.*, p. 451; Robert S. Wallerstein, "Development and Metapsychology of the Defense Organization of the Ego," *Journal of the American Psychoanalytic Association*, XV (1967), 130–49; E. Pumpian-Mindlin, "Defense Organization of the Ego and the Pscychoanalytic Technique," *ibid.*, pp. 150–65.

10. *Standard Edition*, XX, 87–172.

11. *Writings*, II, 28.

12. *Ibid.*, p. 132.

13. *Ibid.*, pp. 132–33.

14. *Ibid.*, p. 116.

15. *Ibid.*, pp. 88, 94–95, 111–12.

16. *Ibid.*, pp. 112–13.

17. *Ibid.*, pp. 75–77.

18. *Ibid.*, p. 74.

19. *Ibid.*, p. 79.

20. Frances Hodgson Burnett, *Little Lord Fauntleroy* (New York: The Century Co., 1886).

21. *Internationale Zeitschrift für Psychoanalyse*, XXII (1936), 595–96.

22. *Ibid.*, p. 609.

Puberty, or the Search for Extremes

1. *Zeitschrift für Psychoanalytische Pädagogik*, IX (1935), 319–28; *Writings*, II, 137–51.

2. *Writings*, I, 139.

3. *Ibid.*, p. 157.

4. *Ibid.*, II, 137–38.

5. *Ibid.*, p. 168.

6. *The New York Times*, April 17, 1968, quoted in Rogow, *op. cit.*, p. 195.

Added Organizational Duties

1. *Op. cit.*, p. 142.

2. *Ibid.*, pp. 137–38.

3. *Internationale Zeitschrift für Psychoanalyse*, XXIII (1937), 190.

The Last Year in Vienna

1. According to statements to the author by Emma N. Plank, Cleveland, Ohio. Professor Plank was director of the Vienna Montessori elementary school between 1931 and 1938, and therefore no longer directly involved in the work at the Children's House.

2. Communication to the author from Anna Freud.

3. Freud to Martin Freud, *Letters*, August 16, 1937, p. 438.

4. Communication to the author.

Anschluss and Emigration

1. Engelman, *op. cit.*

2. *Letters*, July 20, 1938, pp. 449–50.

3. *Schur*, p. 499.

4. Marie Bonaparte, *Topsy: Die Geschichte eines goldhaarigen Chows*, trans. Anna and Sigmund Freud (1938; Frankfurt: S. Fischer, 1981) [*Topsy: The Story of a Golden-Haired Chow*, trans. Princess Eugenie of Greece (London: Pushkin Press, 1975)]. Anna Freud's Foreword to the 1981 edition appears in *Writings*, VIII, 358–61.

5. Israel Levine, *The Unconscious: An Introduction to Freudian Psychology* (New York: Macmillan, 1923).
6. *Manchester Guardian,* June 7, 1938, p. 10.
7. *Ibid.*
8. *Jones,* III, 226.

The Fifteenth International Psychoanalytic Congress

1. Report on the plenary session of the International Training Commission in *Internationale Zeitschrift für Psychoanalyse,* XXIV (1939), 484.
2. Communication to the author.

Freud's Death and the Beginning of World War II

1. *Letters,* April 28, 1939, p. 458.
2. *Imago,* XXIV (1939), 366.
3. Communciation to the author from Anna Freud.

The Wartime Hampstead Nurseries

1. *Infants Without Families: Reports on the Hampstead Nurseries, 1939–1945; Writings,* Vol. III.
2. *Writings,* III, 3–5.
3. *Ibid.,* p. 6.
4. *Ibid.,* pp. 24–25.
5. *Ibid.,* pp. 19–22.
6. *Ibid.,* pp. 36–38.
7. *Ibid.,* pp. 466–67.
8. *Ibid.,* pp. 241–46.
9. *Twins: A Study of Three Pairs of Identical Twins* (New York: International Universities Press, 1952).
10. J. Bennet and I. Hellman, "Psychoanalytic Material Related to Observations in Early Development," *The Psychoanalytic Study of the Child,* VI (1951), 307–24; H. W. Kennedy, "Cover Memories in Formation," *ibid.,* V (1950), 275–84; I. Hellman, "Hampstead Nursery Follow-up Studies, I: Sudden Separation," *ibid.,* XVII (1962), 159–74.
11. Communication to the author from Anna Freud.
12. "My Experience of Psychotherapy," *Journal of Contemporary Psychotherapy,* VI (1974), 121–27.

Six Children from a Concentration Camp

1. Published originally under the unassuming title "An Experiment in Group Upbringing," by Anna Freud in collaboration with Sophie Dann, *The Psychoanalytical Study of the Child,* VI (1951), 127–68; *Writings,* IV, 163–229.
2. Anna Freud, "Special Experiences of Young Children, Particularly in Times of Social Disturbance," in Kenneth Soddy, ed., *Mental Health and Infant Development* (New York: Basic Books, 1956), I, 141–60.
3. *Ibid.*

Teaching—And No Return

1. *The Psychoanalytic Study of the Child,* I (1945), 127–49; *Writings,* IV, 3–38.
2. "The Psychoanalytic Study of Infantile Feeding Disturbances," *The Psychoanalytic Study of the Child,* II (1946), 119–32; *Writings,* IV, 39–59.
3. Ishak Ramzy, "Introduction of Anna Freud," *Bulletin of the Menninger Clinic,* XXVII, No. 3 (1963), 123–24.

A New Institute

1. "Aggression in Relation to Emotional Development: Normal and Pathological," *Writings,* IV, 489–97.

2. *Ibid.*, pp. 605–9.

3. J. Bolland and J. Sandler, *The Hampstead Psychoanalytic Index: A Study of the Psychoanalytic Case Material of a Two-and-a-Half-Year-Old Child*, The Monograph Series of the Psychoanalytic Study of the Child, ed. Ruth Eissler, Anna Freud, Heinz Hartmann, and Marianne Kris (New York: International Universities Press, 1965).

4. The lecture was not published in its first version. A version written shortly afterward was published under the title "The Bearing of the Psychoanalytic Theory of Instinctual Drives on Certain Aspects of Human Behavior," in Rudolph M. Loewenstein, *Drives, Affects, Behavior* (New York: International Universities Press, 1948), I, 259–77; "Instinctual Drives and Their Bearing on Human Behavior," *Writings*, IV, 498–527.

5. *Writings*, IV, 524.

The First Postwar Psychoanalytic Congress

1. See "Studies in Passivity," Part I, *Writings*, IV, 245–56.

2. Ramzy, *op. cit.*, p. 125. The event possibly belongs at the Amsterdam Congress of 1951; Ramzy could not remember exactly.

3. *Die Psychohygiene* (Bern: H. Huber, 1949), pp. 10–16; *Writings*, IV, 95–106.

August Aichhorn

1. "Obituary of August Aichhorn," *International Journal of Psychoanalysis*, XXXII (1951), 51–56; *Writings*, IV, 625–38.

2. Cf. "August Aichhorn" (1974), *Writings*, VIII, 344–45.

3. W. Solms-Rödelheim, "Psychoanalyse in Österreich" ["Psychoanalysis in Austria"], in D. Eicke, ed., *op. cit.*, II, 1182.

4. K. R. Eissler, ed., *Searchlights on Delinquency* (1949; 7th ed. New York: International Universities Press, 1975).

5. *Writings*, IV, 75–94.

6. *Ibid.*, p. 447 n.

7. L. Bolterauer, ed. *Aus der Werkstatt des Erziehhungsberaters. Gedenkschrift zur 10. Wiederkehr des Todestages von August Aichhorn* ["From the Workshop of the Education Counselor: Writings for the Tenth Anniversary of August Aichhorn's Death"] (Vienna: Verlag für Jugend und Volk, 1960). The contribution by Anna Freud is on pp. 195–206.

America, 1950

1. Report by Herbert Waldborn in *Psychoanalytic Quarterly* XX (1951), 337–38.

2. *Writings*, IV, 107–42.

3. "Problems of Child Development," *The Psychoanalytic Study of the Child*, VI (1951).

4. Erik H. Erikson, *Life History and the Historical Moment* (New York: W. W. Norton, 1975), p. 30.

5. "Psychoanalysis and the Future of Education," *Psychoanalytic Quarterly*, IV (1935), 50–68.

6. Erikson, *Childhood and Society* (New York: W. W. Norton, 1950). Cf. also E. Pumpian-Mindlin, "Anna Freud and Erik Erikson," in F. Alexander *et al.*, eds., *op. cit.*, pp. 519–33.

The International Psychoanalytic Congress in Amsterdam

1. In the program, the lecture is announced under the title "Negativism and Emotional Surrender." In Anna Freud's own report, the title is expanded to "Notes on a Connection between the States of Negativism and of Emotional Surrender," *International Journal of Psychoanalysis*, XXXIII (1952), 265; see "Studies in Passivity," Part II, *Writings*, IV, 256–59.

2. "The Mutual Influences in the Development of Ego and Id: Introduction to the Discussion," *Writings*, IV, 230–44.

3. Jacques Lacan, *Das Seminar. Buch I, 1953–1954. Freuds technische Schriften* ["The Seminar, Book I, 1953–1954: Freud's Technical Writings"], ed. Norbert Haas (Olten and Freidburg/Br.: Walter Verlag, 1978), pp. 83–85. The following quotations are also from Seminar VI.

4. *International Journal of Psychoanalysis*, XXXIII (1952), 259.

5. *International Journal of Psychoanalysis,* XXXIII (1952), 256.
6. *Ibid.,* p. 259.

The Hampstead Child Therapy Course and Clinic

1. H. Strotzka, "Laudatio anlässlich der Verleihung des Ehrendoktorates der Medizinischen Fakultät in Wien für Frau Doktor h.c. mult. Anna Freud, am 26. Mai 1972" ["Encomium at the Award of the Honorary Doctorate of the Medical School of Vienna to Anna Freud, May 26, 1972"] (manuscript).
2. "The Scientific Leadership of Anna Freud," *Journal of the American Psychoanalytic Association,* XV (1967), 810–27.
3. Karl R. Popper, *The Logic of Scientific Discovery* (New York: Basic Books, 1959).
4. Cf. H. J. Eysenck, *Wege und Abwege der Psychologie* ["Paths and Digressions in Psychology"] (Reinbeck bei Hamburg: Rowohlt, 1956); Eysenck and Glenn D. Wilson, *The Experimental Studies of Freudian Theories* (London: Methuen, 1973); Eysenck, *Psychoanalyse—Wissenschaft oder Ideologie?* ["Psychoanalysis—Science or Ideology?"], Mannheimer Forum 74/75, pp. 9–42; A. Mitscherlich and L. Rosenkötter, *Hans Jürgen Eysenck oder die Fiktion der reinen Wissenschaft* ["Hans Jürgen Eysenck, or The Fiction of Pure Science"], Mannheimer Forum, 74/75, pp. 54–67.
5. Cf. K. Hübner, *Kritik der wissenschaftlicher Vernunft* ["Critique of Scientific Reason"] (Freiburg/ Munich: Alber-Broschur Philosophie, 1978).
6. A. Lorenzer, *Die Wahrheit der psychoanalytischen Erkenntnis. Ein historisch-materialistischer Entwurf* ["The Truth about Psychoanalytic Insight: A Historical-Materialistic Sketch"] (Frankfurt: Suhrkamp, 1974).
7. "Research Projects of the Hampstead Child-Therapy Clinic," *Writings,* V, 9–25.
8. *Ibid.,* pp. 14–15.
9. Bolland and Sandler, *op. cit.,* illustrate this by means of a single case.
10. *Ibid.; Writings,* IV, 484–85.

Travels and Lectures, 1952–55

1. The lecture was published under the title "Some Remarks on Infant Observation" in *The Psychoanalytic Study of the Child,* VIII (1953), 9–19.
2. *Writings,* IV, 302–16.
3. Laura is described in "James Robertson's A Two-Year-Old Goes to the Hospital: Film Review," by Anna Freud, *Writings,* IV, 280–92. She also discusses the subject in "Children in the Hospital," *ibid.,* V, 419–35.
4. "Psychoanalysis and Education," *Writings,* IV, 317–26. Anna Freud gives here only a detailed summary of her lecture, but takes the subject up again in a lecture she gave several days later, "The Concept of the Rejecting Mother," *ibid.,* 586–602.
5. The complete discussion was published from a tape transcription: "Problems of Infantile Neurosis: Contribution to the Discussion," *Writings,* IV, 327–55.
6. "Problems of Technique in Adult Analysis," *Writings,* IV, 377–406.

Sigmund Freud's Centennial

1. *Writings,* VIII, 34–56.
2. *Writings,* V, 265–80.
3. *Ibid.,* p. 267.
4. *Ibid.,* p. 272.
5. *Ibid.*
6. *Ibid.,* p. 273.
7. *Ibid.*
8. *Ibid.,* p. 274.
9. *Ibid.,* p. 275.
10. *Ibid.,* pp. 301–14.

Margaret Mead in London • The Paris Congress

1. *Writings*, V, 95–101.
2. *Ibid.*, pp. 136–66.
3. "Problems of Termination in Child Analysis," *Writings*, VII, 3–21.
4. "Child Observation and Prediction of Development," *Writings*, V, 102–35.
5. *Ibid.*, pp. 128–30.

Fiftieth Anniversary of the Vienna Psychoanalytic Institute

1. *International Journal of Psychoanalysis*, XL (1959), 79.
2. W. Huber, *Psychoanalyse in Österreich seit 1933* ["Psychoanalysis in Austria since 1933"] (Vienna: Geyer-Edition, 1977), p. 91.
3. *Ibid.*

John Bowlby

1. *International Journal of Psychoanalysis*, XLI (1960), 89–113.
2. "Discussion of John Bowlby's Work on Separation, Grief, and Mourning" (1958, 1969), first published in *Writings*, V, 167–86.
3. "The Nature of the Child's Tie to His Mother," *International Journal of Psychoanalysis*, XXXIX (1958), 350–73.
4. *Writings*, V, 174.

Anna Freud Speaks with Pediatricians

1. This was a discussion before the Study Group of the Society for Psychosomatic Research at the Royal College of Physicians, *Writings*, V, 379–406.
2. *Ibid.*, pp. 379–80.
3. *Ibid.*, pp. 380–82.
4. *Ibid.*, pp. 383–85.
5. *Ibid.*, pp. 387–89.
6. *Ibid.*, pp. 389–91.
7. "The Psychoanalytic Study of Infantile Feeding Disturbances," *Writings*, IV, 39–59; "The Establishment of Feeding Habits," *ibid.*, pp. 442–57.
8. *Writings*, V, 396–98.
9. *Ibid.*, p. 401.
10. *Ibid.*, pp. 405–6.

The Copenhagen and Edinburgh Congresses

1. Published under the title "The Theory of the Parent–Infant Relationship: Contribution to the Discussion," *Writings*, V, 187–93.

With the Menningers in Topeka

1. Karl Menninger, *The Vital Balance* (New York: Viking Press, 1963).
2. C. P. Oberndorf, *op. cit.*, p. 202.
3. Laura Fermi, *Illustrious Immigrants* (2d ed.; Chicago: University of Chicago Press, 1971), p. 151.
4. There is a detailed account in the *Bulletin of the Menninger Clinic*, XXVII, No. 3 (1963), 117–25.
5. "Regression as a Principle in Mental Development" appeared first in the *Bulletin of the Menninger Clinic*, XXVII, No. 3 (1963), 126–39, with references to the book "Normal and Abnormal Child Development," which appeared in 1965 under the revised title *Normality and Pathology in Childhood: Assessments of Development* (*Writings*, Vol. VI). "Diagnostic Skills and Their Growth in Psychoanalysis" was first published in the *International Journal of Psychoanalysis*, XLVI (1965), 31–38; it is not included verbatim in the book's final text, which gives only a synopsis of the thoughts expressed therein.

The lecture "Infantile Dependency as a Factor in Adult and Child Analysis" also appears in the book; it had not been previously published in any form.

6. Ramzy, *op. cit.*, pp. 123–24.

7. "A la mémoire de Marie Bonaparte," *Revue Française de Psychanalyse*, XXIX (1965), 1–2.

America, 1964

1. "Comments on Psychic Trauma," *Writings*, V, 221–41.

2. "An Appreciation of Herman Nunberg," *Writings*, V, 194–203.

3. Nunberg, *Memoirs, Recollections, Ideas, Reflections* (New York: The Psychoanalytic Research and Development Fund, 1969).

4. Nunberg and E. Federn, eds., *Minutes of the Vienna Psychoanalytic Society*, trans. M. Nunberg (4 vols.; New York: International Universities Press, 1962–75).

5. (New York: International Universities Press, 1955).

6. Published as "Psychoanalytic Knowledge and Its Application to Children's Services," *Writings*, V, 460–69.

7. Evidently the wife of the child psychoanalyst Samuel Arnold Guttmann.

8. "Anna Freud Doctoral Award Address," *Journal of the American Psychoanalytic Association*, XV (1967), 833–840, after-dinner speech by Floyd S. Cornelison.

9. Waelder in *ibid.*, p. 832.

10. *Writings*, V, 511–16.

11. *Ibid.*, p. 515.

12. Karl Emil Franzos, "Tote Seelen" ["Dead Souls"], *Neue Freie Presse*, March 31, 1875. Quoted from G. Büchmann, *Geflügelte Worte* ["Winged Words"] (Frankfurt: S. Fischer, 1957).

Cindy

1. The complete case history and comments on it were published in Joseph Goldstein and Jay Katz, *The Family and the Law: Problems for Decision in the Family Law Process* (New York: Free Press, 1965), pp. 1034–54. Anna Freud's comments and the Dobuce County Welfare Department's response appear in *Writings*, V, 450–59.

2. *Writings*, V, 450.

3. *Ibid.*, p. 451.

4. *Ibid.*, pp. 452–53.

5. *Ibid.*, pp. 453–54.

6. *Ibid.*, p. 454.

7. Goldstein and Katz, *op. cit.*

8. Joseph Goldstein, Anna Freud, and Albert J. Solnit, *Beyond the Best Interests of the Child* (New York: Free Press, 1973).

Anna Freud, CBE, LL.D., Sc.D.

1. "Obsessional Neurosis: A Summary of Psychoanalytic Views as Presented at the Congress," *Writings*, V, 242–61.

2. *Writings*, VI, 63–64.

3. *Ibid.*, p. 233.

4. *International Journal of Psychoanalysis*, XLVIII (1967), 97–101.

5. *Ibid.*, pp. 102–7. Mead alludes here to Anna Freud's first English publication, "The Psychoanalysis of the Child," in C. Murchison, ed., *op. cit.*

René Spitz

1. "Eine Diskussion mit René Spitz" ["A Discussion with René Spitz"], *Psyche*, XXI (1967), 4–15. In 1970, Anna Freud wrote an English version, which was first published in *Writings*, VII, 22–38.

2. See Spitz, "Anaclitic Depression: An Inquiry into the Genesis of Psychiatric Conditions in Early Childhood, II," *The Psychoanalytic Study of the Child*, II (1946); *No and Yes: On the Genesis of Human Communication* (New York: International Universities Press, 1957); Spitz and W. G. Cobliner, *The*

First Year of Life: A Psychoanalytic Study of Normal and Deviant Development of Object Relations (1965; 5th ed. New York: International Universities Press, 1975).

Anna Freud in American Intellectual Life

1. "Some Thoughts about the Place of Psychoanalytic Theory in the Training of Psychiatrists," *Bulletin of the Menninger Clinic*, XXX (1966), 225–34; *Writings*, VII, 59–72.
2. "A Short History of Child Analysis," *Writings*, VII, 48–58.
3. "Residential vs. Foster Care," in Helen L. Witmer, ed., *On Rearing Infants and Young Children in Institutions*, Children's Bureau Research Reports, No. 1 (Washington: U.S. Department of Health, Education and Welfare, 1967), pp. 47–55; *Writings*, VII, 223–39.
4. "Adolescence as a Developmental Disturbance," in S. Lebovici and G. Caplan, eds., *Adolescence: Psychosocial Perspectives* (New York: Basic Books, 1969); *Writings*, VII, 39–47.
5. *Writings*, VII, 73–93.
6. "Acting Out," *Writings*, VII, 94–109.
7. *International Journal of Psychoanalysis*, IL (1968), 124.
8. "Difficulties in the Path of Psychoanalysis: A Confrontation of Past with Present Viewpoints," in *Freud Anniversary Lecture Series* (New York: International Universities Press, 1969); *Writings*, VII, 124–56.
9. "Child Analysis as a Subspecialty of Psychoanalysis," *Writings*, VII, 204–19.
10. *Ibid.*, p. 145; cf. note 4 above.
11. *Ibid.*, p. 148.
12. "Painter v. Bannister: Postscript by a Psychoanalyst," *ibid.*, pp. 247–55.
13. "Address at the Commencement Services of the Yale Law School," *ibid.*, pp. 256–60. There is also a reference in the *International Journal of Psychoanalysis*, LI (1970), 126.
14. *Writings*, VII, 110–23.
15. "James Strachey," *ibid.*, pp. 277–79.
16. "The Symptomatology of Childhood: A Preliminary Attempt at Classification," *ibid.*, pp. 157–88.
17. "Child Analysis as a Subspecialty of Psychoanalysis."

Return to Vienna

1. Erica Jong, *Fear of Flying* (New York: Holt, Rinehart and Winston, 1973).
2. "Une visite à la Berggasse," in *Les mouvements de la libération mythique* (Montreal: Les Editions Quinze, 1978).
3. "Comments on Aggression," *International Journal of Psychoanalysis*, LIII (1972), 163–79; *Writings*, VIII, 151–75.
4. Transcript of an Austrian Broadcasting System program of December 2, 1975, directed by Dr. Eva Laible, "Anna Freud—von der Arbeit ihres Lebens" ["Anna Freud—From Her Life's Work"], on the occasion of Anna Freud's eightieth birthday. Quoted with the generous permission of Dr. Eva Laible.
5. Anna Freud quoted here from a manuscript by K. Eissler she had in front of her. It was published in *The Psychoanalytic Study of the Child*, XXVI (1971), 25–78. Cf. also Eissler, *The Psychiatrist and the Dying Patient* (New York: International Universities Press, 1955).
6. *The Notesbooks of Malte Laurids Brigge*, trans. Herter M. Norton (New York: W. W. Norton, 1949).
7. *The Book of Hours*, trans. A. L. Peck (London: Hogarth, 1961).
8. Communication to the author from Mrs. Gertrud Baderle Hollstein, February 7, 1979.
9. See note 4 above.
10. Verbal report to the author by a participant.

Conclusion

1. *Writings*, VII, 73–74.
2. "Die Bedeutung der Kinderanalyse, Sigmund Freud-Vorlesung in Wien" ["The Significance of Child Analysis: Sigmund Freud Lecture in Vienna"], May 8, 1978, in *Sigmund Freud House Bulletin*, II (1978), 8–13.

Index

"About Losing and Being Lost" (A. Freud), 197
Abraham, Karl, 34, 38, 66, 68–69, 70, 88, 89
    death of, 69, 105, 111
Abrahamsen, Karla, 186
"Acting Out" (A. Freud), 237
Action Committee for Hospitalized Children, 200
Adler, Alfred, 37
adolescence, 171, 179
    Anna Freud's views on, 140–142, 205, 237
    prolonged, 141
"Adolescence" (A. Freud), 205
Adorno, Theodor, 113
aggression, 59–60, 171, 175, 177, 218, 241–242
    "freedom for," 203
    identification with aggressor and, 133, 134–137
Aichhorn, August, 47, 102, 108, 111, 112, 123, 179–183, 189, 207, 243–244
    Anna Freud influenced by, 41, 45, 46, 57, 179, 182–183, 248
    death of, 179, 182, 183
    youth welfare and, 100, 101, 104, 180, 181
Alexander, Franz, 123, 124, 153, 222
All-German League, 5
altruistic surrender, 19–21, 133–134
American Association for Child Psychoanalysis, 236–237, 239, 240
American Imago, 8
American Psychoanalytic Association, 31, 64, 153–154, 176, 178, 185, 190
Amsterdam, psychoanalytic congresses in, 188–191, 232
Andreas-Salomé, Lou, 8, 41–47, 49, 50, 51, 68, 106, 111, 116
    Anna Freud's correspondence with, 47, 50, 53, 120
    death of, 145
    diary of, 44–46
    midwife role of, 42, 46

Sigmund Freud's correspondence with, 24–25, 33, 41–42, 46–47, 48, 49, 50, 53, 56, 70, 114, 115–116, 119, 130–131
Andrews, Mrs., 228, 229
anorexia nervosa, 216–217, 218
Anschluss, 146–151
anti-Semitism, 5–6, 117, 124–126, 132, 146
Anton, Gabriel, 30
anus:
    fantasies and, 75, 76
    use of suppositories and, 212–213
anxiety, 63, 171, 202–203. See also castration anxiety; separation reactions
"Application of Analytic Technique to the Study of Psychic Institutions, The" (A. Freud), 130
Argentina, psychoanalysis in, 172
arts, Freuds influenced by, 6–8, 9
asocial behavior:
    Anna Freud's views on, 183
    juvenile delinquency as, 104, 180, 181. See also aggression
"Assessment of Borderline Cases, The" (A. Freud), 203
Austria, Nazis in, 12, 117, 145, 146–151
Austria-Hungary:
    Jewish population of, 5–6
    World War I and, 21, 33
Autobiographical Study, An (S. Freud), 118

Baderle, Gertrud, 11, 17, 18
Bad Homburg, 68–69
Bahr, Hermann, 7
Balint, Alice, 57, 62–63, 179
Bartemeier, Leo H., 178, 190–191, 198, 221
Baumgarten Nursery, 61–62, 100, 165, 225
"Beating Fantasies and Daydreams" (A. Freud), 41, 43, 46, 47, 48–49, 137
Beers, Clifford, 221
behavior therapy, 39